# John A. Johnson
## THE PEOPLE'S GOVERNOR

Moffett, Chicago, 1909

*John A. Johnson*

# John A. Johnson

# THE PEOPLE'S GOVERNOR

## *A Political Biography*

by

WINIFRED G. HELMES

UNIVERSITY OF MINNESOTA PRESS, Minneapolis

LONDON · GEOFFREY CUMBERLEGE · OXFORD UNIVERSITY PRESS

PRINTED AT THE JONES PRESS, INC., MINNEAPOLIS

*To My Mother and Father*

# Acknowledgments

ONCE a piece of work is finished, the pleasure comes in thanking those who helped the most along the way. It was my good fortune to do the research for this study and to write it under the experienced and critical eye of Professor George Malcolm Stephenson, for whose scholarship and plain-spoken honesty I have the greatest admiration.

I am deeply grateful to Professor Alice Felt Tyler, who with patience, understanding, and humor safely guided me through most of my graduate work at the University of Minnesota. Her enthusiasm for her work is contagious, and her capacity for work is enviable.

Certainly I am indebted to the staff of the Minnesota Historical Society for much assistance, and I especially want to thank Miss Bertha L. Heilbron and Mrs. Mary Wheelhouse Berthel for their encouragement and friendliness. The constant and courteous attention I always received from Miss Helen M. Smith and Miss Elizabeth Henderson made my work at the University of Minnesota library easier and pleasanter.

I want also to pay my respects to the staff of the University of Minnesota Press for their professional assistance in turning my manuscript into a finished book.

Finally, the tedious work of proofreading and the making of the index were turned into a game and made fun through the devoted efforts of two of my friends, Dr. Harold A. Davis of Bradford Junior College and Miss Bertha Sheppard Adkins of Salisbury, Maryland. For their generosity I am forever grateful.

W. G. H.

*June 1949*
*Bradford, Massachusetts*

# Table of Contents

# John A. Johnson
## THE PEOPLE'S GOVERNOR

*Heritage and Youth*

THE years from 1850 to 1860 have been called the era of "The Great Migration," for in that decade about 2,600,000 Europeans crossed the Atlantic to settle in the United States. In those years the number of foreign born in the United States increased from 2,244,600 to more than 4,000,000. "This migration was great in comparison with the native American population, great in the trails of settlement it broke, great in the cultural foundations it laid. Subsequent decades were to see a larger volume of arrivals, but no migration paid richer dividends to American civilization." [1]

The number of Scandinavians who came to the United States in the 1850s increased from 18,000 to more than 72,500,[2] and an average of 1690 emigrants left Sweden for America each year. Most of these emigrants were "sons of the soil" [3] who came from the Swedish counties that had poor soil and climate for agriculture and were areas of small farms. Between 1845 and 1855 the largest emigration came from the neighboring counties of Jönköping and Östergötland in southern Sweden. Jönköping County and the southern part of Östergötland were hilly, rocky, wooded regions. From these counties came the parents of John Albert Johnson, first native-born governor of the State of Minnesota and the most beloved governor Minnesota had up to his time.

Little is known of the ancestry of John A. Johnson. Neither of his parents maintained connections with relatives and friends in Sweden, and his father never mentioned his family or his early life in his native land. Both parents were without family ties in the United States. John A. Johnson grew up never knowing grandparents, aunts, uncles, and cousins, and he heard only about his

[1] Marcus Lee Hansen, *Atlantic Migration, 1607–1860*, p. 280.
[2] *Ibid.*
[3] According to Hansen, the migration of the nineteenth century was predominantly a rural migration. See *Immigrant in American History*, p. 19.

3

mother's family.[4] Like most children of immigrants who settled in America, Johnson would have found it difficult to trace his lineage, but to him and to most first-generation Americans and their immigrant parents it was not your family tree or what you did in the "old country" that counted, but what you were and what you did in America.

Gustav Johnson, John's father, came from Jönköping County in the province of Småland, Sweden.[5] There until sometime shortly after he came to America he was known as Gustav Jönson, and then he changed his name to Johnson, which he considered the American equivalent of Jönson.[6] Gustav's father had been a small landholder and farmer, but Gustav did not follow in his father's footsteps. He became a blacksmith and a woodworker and was well trained and proficient in his trades. Although he was not well educated, he could read and write, and he was very fond of talking about politics.[7] In fact, he liked to talk about anything. He won a reputation as an entertaining storyteller and was listened to with interest and amusement. Gustav was a tall, slender, fair-haired, blue-eyed man, good-natured, kindly, generous, jovial, and very sociable, with a happy disposition, a keen sense of humor, and a vivid imagination.[8] But he was a failure in his community. He did not seem to have industry and ambition enough to work diligently at his trades, but instead spent much of his time sitting around with boon companions talking and drinking and idling away the days. When he did settle down to his work, he went

[4] What information there is about the early life of Johnson's parents was gathered by Frank A. Day and Theodore Knappen when they prepared their eulogistic biography of Johnson just after his death. Their account must, therefore, be heavily relied upon. Miss Hattie Johnson, sister of John A. Johnson, has kindly supplied the author with some additional material about her mother's early life.

[5] The date of Gustav Johnson's birth is unknown. Hattie Johnson was not able to supply any information. According to Elinor Johnson Smith, widow of John A. Johnson, members of the Johnson family in America did not know the date. When she ordered a tombstone to be placed upon Caroline Johnson's grave, she asked John if he would like to have his father buried in the family plot. He agreed, but efforts to find where Gustav Johnson was buried came to naught. Nevertheless, a tombstone was erected on the family plot to his memory. According to Day and Knappen, he was in his thirties when he was married in 1858. William Gresham, in his *History of Nicollet and Le Sueur Counties, Minnesota,* states that Gustav Johnson was thirty-three years old when he came to America. See vol. 2, p. 492.

[6] Day and Knappen, *Life of John Albert Johnson,* p. 43. Here Day and Knappen declare Johnson was known as Gustav Jensen in Sweden, but his name probably was Jönson. The American equivalent of Jönson is Johnson.

[7] *Ibid.,* pp. 39, 50.

Hattie Johnson and Elinor Johnson Smith to W. G. H.

about it happily and singing merrily, but he could not keep himself steadily at his tasks. His harder working neighbors in the parish regarded him as a likeable but shiftless, lazy individual.

Gustav Johnson realized he was not making a success of his life, and he was restless, insecure, and without responsibility for anyone save himself. He spent plenty of time dreaming about making a success of himself elsewhere, mostly in America. As early as 1846 news items about the United States appeared in the *Jönköpings Tidning,* and they interested and stirred the imaginations of many people in the province. Letters from such early settlers as Gustaf Unonius and Captain Polycarp von Schneidau of the Swedish Pine Lake Colony in Wisconsin had attracted emigrants from Småland and Östergötland to America, and these settlers had in turn attracted others by their letters.[9] It is quite likely, also, that Gustav Johnson saw and talked with parties of emigrants bound for America en route to Swedish ports. In Småland in the early 1850s "America fever" was in the air, and not a few succumbed to the disease. The more Gustav Johnson thought about going to America, the stronger became his conviction that this was what he needed and wanted. There he could begin life anew.[10]

When a group of his neighbors began to make plans and get ready to leave Sweden for the land across the sea, Gustav desperately wanted to go with them, but he was without funds to pay his own passage. In the party about to leave for America, however, were Mr. and Mrs. Carl A. Johnson, friends of Gustav, who thought that emigration to a new land might serve as a "moral tonic" for him. He thus would be removed from his old haunts and companions and could begin a new life in a wonderful new land, which they thought would be enough of a challenge to him to cause him to discard his bad habits and settle down. At least they thought he deserved a chance to try, and Carl Johnson paid Gustav's passage to America in return for the meager inheritance of about seven dollars a year which Gustav received

[9] George M. Stephenson, "Letters Relating to Gustaf Unonius and the Early Swedish Settlers in Wisconsin," *Augustana Historical Society Collections,* vol. 7, p. 11. The Pine Lake Colony is usually designated as the first Swedish settlement to be established in the United States in the nineteenth century. It was founded in 1841 and was soon well known in Sweden.

[10] Day and Knappen, p. 39.

from his father's estate — a small amount which Carl Johnson never collected.[11]

When he left Sweden Gustav Johnson was in his thirties. Certainly if he was going to begin a new life it was then or never for him. But it took courage to leave his native land to go to a strange country where everyone spoke a different language. One had to be sturdy even to make the journey. Gustav and his friends went by inland waterways to the Swedish port of Gothenburg, from there by boat to Hull, England, where they boarded a sailing ship for the voyage across the Atlantic.[12] The trip across the sea to Boston took something over six weeks, which was fairly good time. It could not have been a pleasant journey for the party of Swedes, since the ships carrying emigrants were small vessels at best, with scarcely enough room for the passengers they carried.[13] Passengers had to supply their own food and cooking and eating utensils, and the women, cooking for from three to four hundred people, struggled to get an opportunity to use the cookstove, which generally was out on the open deck. Food and water were anything but fresh as the voyage lengthened. So closely packed were the passengers that conditions were not only uncomfortable but unsanitary, and disease broke out and deaths were not unusual.[14] For example, in 1853 a ship from Sweden arrived in Boston with fifty-eight on board dead of cholera.[15] But Gustav did not seem to suffer from the sea voyage. He is reported to have spent most of the time resting easily in his bunk.[16]

The emigrants landed in Boston probably sometime in 1853.[17] There they evidently had no difficulties with interpreters and runners, "the beasts of prey in human form" who eagerly awaited the arrival of emigrants in order to take advantage of their ignorance

[11] *Ibid.*, p. 40. It might be surmised that Carl Johnson realized from the start that he never would be in a position to collect Gustav's inheritance once he came to America and that he paid Gustav's passage as a friend who could help one in need of it.
[12] *Ibid.*
[13] Hansen, *Immigrant in American History*, p. 32; Carl Wittke, *We Who Built America*, p. 114.
[14] *Ibid.*, pp. 114–18; Hansen, *Immigrant in American History*, pp. 35ff.
[15] Wittke, p. 116. A smallpox epidemic broke out on the ship which brought Swedish Hans Mattson to Boston. The ship had to be quarantined outside the harbor. Hans Mattson, *Reminiscences, The Story of an Emigrant*, p. 14.
[16] Day and Knappen, p. 40.
[17] Gustav Johnson worked for a year in Chicago before he went to Minnesota in the spring of 1855. Since it took several months to make the journey from Sweden to Chicago, he must have arrived in Boston in 1853 or early in 1854.

of the English language and of American conditions in general.[18] Gustav Johnson and his party went to Chicago, which was a distribution point for western immigration. One Chicago resident wrote, in 1853: "One fourth of the persons you meet in Chicago cannot speak a word of English, and a good part of the remainder cannot speak it well." [19] By 1854 the city had several Swedish churches, and their pastors and Captain von Schneidau, now the vice-consul for both Sweden and Norway in Chicago, gave aid, comfort, and advice to their countrymen. They secured work for both men and women, found shelter for and fed the destitute, and supplied information for those who wanted to move on elsewhere.

Gustav Johnson remained in Chicago a year, working as a blacksmith and accumulating some money.[20] The "moral tonic" had begun to take effect. During the year he heard much about the Territory of Minnesota, probably from Swedes living in the territory who were urging their countrymen to join them. In 1851 a Swedish settlement was founded at Chisago Lake, Minnesota, which attracted emigrants from Småland and other Swedish provinces. Two years later Hans Mattson led a group of Swedish emigrants from Moline, Illinois, to Minnesota, where they established a settlement at Vasa, and by 1855 quite a large community had developed there.[21] Johnson may have heard of Minnesota's climate, resources, and beauties even before he left Sweden. In Chicago he and his friends probably heard that the rich agricultural land in the southern part of the new territory was being surveyed and offered for sale. They decided to move to Minnesota, but not until someone had gone on ahead to see if the territory was attractive enough for the others to come to join them. Gustav and Hans Johnson, Carl's brother, made the journey.[22]

In the spring of 1855 a great many emigrants streamed into Minnesota, among them Gustav and Hans Johnson and Hans's wife. They went from Chicago by railroad to Galena, Illinois, and from there by steamboat to St. Paul. This was the most commonly used means of traveling from Chicago to St. Paul in the fifties.

[18] Wittke, p. 119.
[19] *Ibid.*, p. 123, quoted from the *New York Times*, June 21, 1853.
[20] Day and Knappen, pp. 40–41.
[21] Mattson, pp. 33ff.
[22] Carl Johnson and his family came to Minnesota sometime between 1855 and 1858.

Just a year before, the Chicago and Rock Island Railroad had completed laying tracks between Chicago and Rock Island, which opened up the route from Chicago to the Mississippi River. The railroad celebrated the important event by organizing a party of notables, including ex-President Fillmore and the well-known historian, George Bancroft, to make an excursion up the river to St. Paul. On the Great Excursion five steamboats carried the party slowly up the Mississippi, and their arrival in St. Paul was the occasion for a large banquet and many speeches.

The inauguration of this new route meant a great deal to Minnesota, for in the warm season Chicago was now only thirty hours away from St. Paul, and a shorter and easier journey was possible for the thousands of emigrants who wanted to come to the new territory. The height of steamboat traffic on the Mississippi came in 1857 and 1858, when about one thousand steamers a year arrived in St. Paul. St. Paul was then a flourishing frontier town of about four thousand people with the territorial capitol building, business houses, and a hotel. When or how long the Johnsons remained there is unknown.[23]

From St. Paul Hans and Gustav Johnson decided to go to Traverse des Sioux in southern Minnesota to take preemption claims on the rich prairie land. When they inquired about the cost of transportation, however, they found the trip by steamboat would take all the money they had. But they were undaunted. They set to work building a rowboat which carried them about a hundred and fifty miles up the Minnesota River to their destination.[24] In Traverse Township, Nicollet County, they found preemption land, and at a branch land office in nearby St. Peter each applied for eighty acres. They could not afford to buy more. Then each began to build a one-room cabin on the land. Gustav Johnson also built a smithy and began to practice his trade. Crops were planted, and a year later, in 1856, Gustav and Hans Johnson walked one hundred and forty miles to the government land office in Winona to pay for their land and receive their titles to it.[25]

That year, too, Gustav Johnson met the girl he married two

[23] W. W. Folwell, *History of Minnesota*, vol. 1, pp. 358–59; James H. Baker, "History of Transportation in Minnesota," *Minnesota Historical Society Collections*, vol. 9, pp. 16–17.
[24] Day and Knappen, p. 41.          [25] *Ibid.*, pp. 42–43.

years later. Her name was Caroline Christine Hedén. She was
born on March 5, 1838, the daughter of Lothrop and Brita Hedén
in Linköping, Östergötland, Sweden.[26] Lothrop was an ambitious
and hard-working farmer and a master cabinetmaker who earned
a good living for his wife and five children and had a fine reputation for his skill. He had an inventive and thoughtful mind and
a great curiosity about things, and he was a voracious reader.[27]
Exposed to the same influences which created the "America fever"
in Gustav Johnson and so many other Swedes in Östergötland and
Småland, Lothrop Hedén contracted a severe case of the "fever."
He was far more ambitious and energetic than Gustav Johnson,
and he had a strong desire to give his children greater opportunities than he himself had ever had.[28] Once he made up his mind to
move to America, he sold everything he owned save his household goods and his tools, and in May 1853 he and his wife and
children and his sister departed from Sweden for the Promised
Land. They were more than eleven weeks crossing the Atlantic.
They, too, landed in Boston and went directly to Chicago. And
there tragedy struck the Hedén family.[29]

First an "interpreter" fleeced Lothrop Hedén of all his money,
and then cholera spread through the family, causing the death
of Caroline's parents, her aunt, and one of her brothers. The young
emigrant girl, fifteen or sixteen years old, without money, unable
to speak English, and never having worked, was left in a strange
city, in a strange land, with three younger brothers and an infant
sister. The children were put into an orphans' home, where Caroline, too old to be admitted, was given work. Soon afterward she
became a domestic servant for first one family and then another.
Then her infant sister died, one brother was apprenticed to a tin-
smith, and the two others were adopted by families in Illinois.[30]

[26] Caroline Hedén's father must have changed his first name when he came to America, for *Lothrop* is not a Swedish name. In Day and Knappen the family name is
spelled *Hadden*, which is their spelling of the Swedish name *Hedén*.

[27] *Ibid.*, p. 43; Hattie Johnson to W. G. H. Miss Johnson's information about her
mother's life comes from notes her mother dictated to her. She recalls her mother's
often remarking that Lothrop Hedén seldom sat down to a meal without a book.

[28] Hattie Johnson to W. G. H. Caroline Johnson told her daughter that though he
had not lived to see it, she thought her father's dreams were fulfilled when his grandson became governor of Minnesota.

[29] Day and Knappen, pp. 44–46.

[30] *Ibid.*, pp. 46–47. Caroline never again saw her brothers and never knew what
became of them.

Caroline had been invited to come to St. Paul, Minnesota, by an uncle who lived there. Now she decided to go to live with him. When she arrived in St. Paul, however, she learned that her uncle had moved to Carver. She was all alone in another strange city, and she had to find work. For a year she worked as a domestic servant for the Dayton family, who were very kind to her.[31] In the fall of 1856 she went to visit a friend at Traverse des Sioux, but winter arrived early, the river froze over, and Caroline could not return to St. Paul.[32] She obtained work with a family in Traverse des Sioux, and Hans Johnson met her at gatherings in the Swedish Lutheran church there. He introduced her to Gustav Johnson, and on February 28, 1858, Gustav Johnson and Caroline Hedén were married.[33]

Caroline Johnson was a small young woman with blue eyes and dark brown hair. Serious minded, a hard worker, and without a sense of humor, she was a decided contrast to her husband. When she was married, she did not know about Gustav's early days in Sweden. She was alone and wanted a home; he was alone and needed a wife; and his friends thought it would be good for him to have the responsibilities of a wife and family.

Gustav Johnson had worked long and hard since he came to America. He had earned money to pay for his land, labored planting crops, and worked as a blacksmith. A busy, happy, and sober man, he seemed to flourish in the New World. Emigration had been what he needed. Caroline, who was considerably younger than Gustav — she was twenty years old when she was married, and he must have been some seventeen years older [34] — had shown she, too, was a hard worker, and both she and Gustav had shown they possessed courage and fortitude. They were not at all unlike hundreds of other emigrants in their joint experiences. They had a common Swedish background and spoke the same language. There was a good reason to think they could together create for themselves a happier and better life than they had experienced in Sweden.

Gustav and Caroline Johnson were only two in the flood of

[31] Hattie Johnson to W. G. H.
[32] Ibid.
[33] Ibid.; Day and Knappen, p. 48.
[34] If he was thirty-three years old when he came to America in 1853, he would have been thirty-eight in 1858.

emigrants who came into the Territory of Minnesota in the 1850s. Minnesota's population jumped from 6077 in 1850 to about 40,000 in 1855, 100,000 in 1856, 150,000 in 1857. During those years thousands of acres of land were surveyed and sold, farms developed in the wilderness, towns and villages sprang up, more townsites were laid out, roads were built, and railroad and steamboat connections were made between Chicago and St. Paul and between St. Paul and Minnesota towns.[35] As early as 1856 Minnesota inhabitants began to think they were ready for statehood, but it was not until May 11, 1858, that Minnesota became the thirty-second state of the Union.

Larger than all New England with Maryland added, the new state had an area of 84,287 square miles of fertile, rolling prairie land, forests providing plenty of timber and game, rich mineral lands, and thousands of beautiful lakes. At first to Americans living in the South and East this region was considered so far north as to be "scarcely habitable" and more like the frigid zone than anything else.[36] But as more intrepid souls ventured into the area and explored and settled down, more favorable reports of Minnesota came back to families and friends. To easterners it became the "New England of the West." In the spring of 1857 the *Buffalo Commercial Advertiser* stated:

Though it may be doubted whether a country can be very picturesque which lacks mountain scenery, all who have visited Minnesota concur in pronouncing it a region of great loveliness. . . . The air is cool, bracing, and invigorating; the water pure and excellent. Fever and ague . . . [are] entirely unknown. No languor, no debility is felt by the inhabitants of this charming region which is ample compensation for winters of considerable severity. . . . The rapid growth of Minnesota ceases to excite surprise, when we consider the advantages it offers to the emigrant.[37]

To Fredrika Bremer, the well-known Swedish novelist and traveler, Minnesota was "just the country for a New Scandinavia."[38] Enthusiastically she wrote: "What a glorious New Scandinavia might not Minnesota become. Here would the Swede find his

[35] Folwell, vol. 1, pp. 359–60; *Minnesota in Three Centuries*, vol. 2, p. 508.
[36] *Nicollet County, Minnesota, as an Agricultural and Dairying Section and St. Peter as a Manufacturing Center*, p. 3.
[37] Reprinted in the *St. Peter Free Press*, June 3, 1857.
[38] Fredrika Bremer, *Homes of the New World*, vol. 2, p. 55.

clear, romantic lakes, the plains of Scania rich in corn, and the valleys of Norrland; here would the Norwegian find his rapid rivers . . . and both nations their hunting fields and their fisheries." [39]

Most of the settlers who came to Minnesota in the fifties went to the southern part of the state, so that by 1857 most of the land in the Minnesota River valley and south to the Iowa line was pretty well settled. Nicollet County had been organized only two years when Gustav Johnson went there to live. The town nearest his farm was Traverse des Sioux, which for a long time had been a crossing place on the Minnesota River for the Sioux Indians and had become a trading post and mission. The town in the fifties was growing rapidly. About a mile or so away was the new settlement of St. Peter.

St. Peter was founded by a group of enterprising men who sought to make money selling land. They wanted to build up a new and vigorous community and make it the capital of the state. These men — among them Willis A. Gorman, territorial governor of Minnesota, and Henry A. Swift, soon to be one of the early governors of the new state — organized the St. Peter Company, a joint-stock company with a capital stock of about a hundred thousand dollars, laid out the town, and had 319 acres of land surveyed and platted into town lots to be sold to settlers. At first a town lot was offered free to any settler who would build a house on it, and by 1856 eight members of the company had built homes on free lots in St. Peter.[40] Charles Flandrau of Traverse des Sioux became the attorney for the company.

The town's first hotel, built by James M. Winslow, was opened in October 1855 by S. L. Wheeler. General stores were soon opened for business, a post office was established, a foundry and machine shop built, the first bank founded, and the *St. Peter Courier*, the *St. Peter Free Press*, and the *Minnesota Statesmen* came into being. From 1858 until 1870 the United States government maintained a land office in St. Peter.[41] Grist mills, a cigar store, and a jewelry store came into existence. Dr. H. W. Catlin came from Indiana to be the first physician in the town. Settlers bought town

[39] *Ibid.*, pp. 56–57.
[40] Gresham, vol. 1, pp. 191–96.
[41] *Ibid.*

lots, built their houses, and established themselves in their trades and professions. E. St. Julien Cox came in 1857 and established himself as an attorney; J. B. Sackett came the same year as county auditor and registrar of deeds. On May 19, 1858, the *St. Peter Free Press* announced that St. Peter, with a population of 960, was the largest town on the Minnesota River. By 1862 St. Peter had grown into a flourishing town of two thousand people.

The founders of St. Peter had been so sure their town would become the capital of Minnesota that when the town was laid out the main street was made a wide one befitting a capital city and lots were set aside for public buildings. It was understood that the company would furnish a new capitol building for the state. But by a peculiar and novel turn of affairs St. Peter never became the state capital.

On February 6, 1857, the speculators of the St. Peter Company introduced in the territorial legislature a bill to remove the seat of government from St. Paul to St. Peter. There was no real reason to shift the capital except for the material benefit of the members of the St. Peter Company, and St. Paul was vigorously opposing the attempt. The speculators had enough personal and political force, however, to get the bill passed by both houses of the legislature, and Governor Gorman, a shareholder of the company, was prepared to sign it.

The bill was sent to the enrolling committee of the upper house for final enrollment before going to the governor for his signature. A majority of the committee, including the chairman, Joe Rolette of Pembina, opposed the bill, and they held it for several days until a member of the council finally moved that it be reported. Then Joe Rolette disappeared with the bill in his possession. The bill could not be reported. It could not be found. An opponent of the bill asked for a roll call, and only Joe Rolette was missing from his seat. It was then moved to suspend the call, but the vote was nine to five, and the rules provided that a two-thirds vote was necessary to suspend a call of the council. The presiding officer refused to accept the nine votes as two thirds of fourteen, and no one changed his vote.

For one hundred and twenty-three hours the council remained in session, deadlocked. While meals and cots were brought into the chamber for weary members, Joe Rolette was comfortably settled in a rear room of a St. Paul hotel, and the bill was in the safe of a St. Paul banker. Rolette knew that no session of the legislature could exceed sixty days and that on midnight of March 7 the session would automatically come to an end. Just as the clock was striking midnight on that day Joe Rolette walked to his seat in the council chamber, but before he could say much the presiding officer declared the session adjourned. The bill never became a law. A copy of the original bill had been prepared in the lower house and was signed by the speaker, but the president of the council refused to sign a bill which had not been regularly passed. Governor Gorman signed the copy of the original bill, but the court declared it had not been properly passed.[42]

During the litigation involving the bill the St. Peter Company believed it would become law and went ahead with the building of a five-thousand-dollar capitol building. When it was learned that St. Peter never would be the capital of Minnesota, the building was given to Nicollet County to be used as a courthouse when the county seat was moved to St. Peter from Traverse des Sioux.[43] From then on Traverse des Sioux was a little village, almost a suburb of St. Peter, and St. Peter never developed into the important big city of which its founders had dreamed.

During this period of decision as to the fate of St. Peter, Caroline and Gustav Johnson lived happily on their farm near the town. Two children were born to them, the second child a son named John Albert Johnson, born on July 25, 1861. John was a little over a year old when the family's way of life was changed because of the terrible Sioux massacre.

The Sioux Outbreak was a general uprising of all the Sioux bands and one of the most serious Indian massacres in American history. All the settlers in the Minnesota Valley were terror-stricken by it, and many lost their lives in the war. Though the Sioux Outbreak came suddenly and was a distinct shock to the settlers, there had been warnings that the Indians were dissatisfied.[44] Since 1851, when they had made treaties surrendering their lands

[42] Folwell, vol. 1, pp. 382–87; Charles E. Flandrau, *History of Minnesota and Tales of the Frontier*, pp. 115–17; Henry L. Moss, "Biographic Notes of Old Settlers," *Minnesota Historical Society Collections*, vol. 9, pp. 155–56.
[43] Folwell, vol. 1, p. 386, note 48.
[44] *Minnesota in Three Centuries*, vol. 3, pp. 280–85.

to the United States government in return for annual cash payments and payments of goods and supplies, the Indians had been disgruntled with the treatment they received.[45] When, in the spring of 1862, they gathered at agencies to collect their annual payments, they were told that the money had not yet arrived and that until it came they would not get their allotments of food. The only reason food was not distributed was because the agent, Thomas J. Galbraith, refused to check the rolls then and once again when the money arrived. Badly in need of the food and knowing it was stored in the agency warehouse, the Indians reasonably could not understand why they could not have it.

All during the summer months the Indians were put off until on August 15 their spokesman, Chief Little Crow, served notice that the Indians would seize their due if it was not soon forthcoming. Two days later a few Indians killed five whites on a Meeker County farm, and the following day the Indians took to the warpath.[46]

An Indian band attacked the Redwood agency, killing everyone found there, while other bands pillaged farms and murdered settlers in the countryside near the reservation.[47] Fugitives fled to Fort Ridgely with the horrifying news, and word of the outbreak spread to New Ulm, St. Peter, Traverse des Sioux, Le Sueur, and on northward to St. Paul. Fort Ridgely and New Ulm were attacked, and there was panic throughout the Minnesota Valley. Refugees poured into St. Peter for protection. Gustav and Caroline Johnson with their two babies fled from their farm and joined the throng in St. Peter. Few had time to bring with them clothes and provisions, so that the people of St. Peter had not only to find shelter but also feed the refugees and clothe some of them. The Ewing House, a vacant hotel of some fifty rooms, was opened up to refugees. Every home in St. Peter received as many people as possible. Refugees found shelter in an uncompleted store, in

[45] *Ibid.*, p. 280. They received about thirty dollars in cash and supplies which amounted to about twice that sum.
[46] Wilson P. Shortridge, *Transition of a Typical Frontier*, pp. 148–49; Marion P. Satterlee, "Narratives of the Sioux War," *Minnesota Historical Society Collections*, vol. 15, pp. 349–55.
[47] Folwell, vol. 2, pp. 109ff; the story of the massacre is told in Chapter 5 (pp. 109–46). Also John Ames Humphrey, "Boyhood Remembrances of Life among the Dakotas and the Massacre of 1862," *Minnesota Historical Society Collections*, vol. 15, pp. 342–45.

barns, even in sheds.[48] The town was teeming with people, and everyone was afraid. People feared not only for their lives but for the farms they had left. All they possessed had been left to be pillaged or burned by the Indians.

Captain William B. Dodd of St. Peter and Judge Charles Flandrau of Traverse des Sioux soon raised[49] a force of about one hundred and forty men to march to help defend New Ulm, the most exposed to attack of all the frontier towns. Dr. Asa W. Daniels went with the group as surgeon. The St. Peter force was joined by a band of men from Le Sueur, among them Dr. W. W. Mayo, whose sons became the famous surgeons. A company of horsemen also went from St. Peter to New Ulm. With this company were Horace Austin and Henry A. Swift, future governors of Minnesota.[50] Groups of men from Nicollet, Mankato, and other towns hurried to New Ulm.

For two days preparations were made for New Ulm's defense, and Judge Flandrau and Captain Dodd were given command of the companies of men gathered there. On August 20th, a Saturday, the Indians attacked New Ulm. Women and children were sent for safety into the cellars of houses and stores; the Dacotah House and the Erd Building, a dry goods store across the street, served as hospitals where Doctors Mayo, Daniels, and Ayers cared for the wounded.[51] Severe fighting lasted all day Saturday and all through the night and part of the next day. Twenty-six men, including Captain Dodd, were killed, and many more were wounded.[52] Almost two hundred structures in the town were fired by the Indians or by orders of the commanding officer as a war measure. New Ulm, when the fighting ceased, was a town of ruins, and, though the Indians seemed to have retreated for good, there was the possibility that they might return. Provisions and am-

[48] Dr. Asa W. Daniels, "Reminiscences of the Little Crow Uprising," *Minnesota Historical Society Collections*, vol. 15, p. 324.

[49] William B. Dodd was one of the founders of St. Peter. He built the first home there and was one of the most prominent men of the town. Charles Flandrau was an associate justice of the Minnesota Supreme Court and one of the best known men in the state.

[50] Daniels, pp. 325–26.

[51] The Dacotah House was the hotel built and operated by Adolph Seiter, one of New Ulm's first settlers, and the Erd Building belonged to his brother-in-law, Frank Erd. Gustav Johnson's son Frederick was to marry one of Adolph Seiter's daughters, and Mr. and Mrs. Frederick Johnson succeeded Mr. and Mrs. Seiter as proprietors of the hotel.

[52] Folwell, vol. 2, pp. 142–43.

munition were running out, and it was decided to evacuate the town. Some two thousand men, women, and children — on foot, in wagons, and on horseback — left New Ulm for Mankato, St. Peter, and St. Paul to get away from the area of immediate danger.[53] The wounded were cared for in Mankato. The rest moved on to St. Peter and St. Paul.

During those terrible August days the frontier town of St. Peter was "a depot of supplies and a garrisoned fort" as well as a refuge for some ten thousand people.[54] Once the danger was over, however, settlers who had come to St. Peter for safety took their families and went back to their homes in the countryside.

All this was a terrifying experience for the Swedish emigrants, Caroline and Gustav Johnson. It also marked a turning point in their lives. With their two babies they went back to their farm, but Gustav Johnson was restless and dissatisfied. While he had stayed in St. Peter he had become convinced that he could do better in town operating a smithy than he could farming.[55] True, he had a smithy on his farm, but in the country there was not much business. Also, and equally important, life in St. Peter was more pleasant. It was more sociable. There one met and talked with people daily, and Gustav liked people. The country provided more isolation and loneliness than anything else to one who was by nature as convivial as Gustav Johnson. Evidently his wife did not object, for soon Gustav sold his farm and moved his family to St. Peter. There he built a house for them and a blacksmith shop where he began to work at his trade.[56]

The removal to St. Peter was a great mistake. On their farm the Johnsons had lived happily and well for four years. There Gustav was busy all day with neither time nor opportunity to fall back into his old habits of the earlier days in Sweden. For a while things went along well for them in St. Peter, but soon upon occasion Gustav began to yield to his weaknesses. Farmers in town for the day left their horses to be shod at Johnson's blacksmith shop. When they paid their bills for the work done, many of them would ask Gustav to join them in a drink at the nearest saloon.

[53] Adolph Seiter's wife and children walked and rode in wagons all the way to St. Paul.
[54] Gresham, vol. 1, p. 207.
[55] Day and Knappen, p. 49.
[56] Ibid.

As the men talked on, more drinks were consumed and Gustav remained longer away from his smithy. At first Gustav was merely being sociable and coming to know his customers; gradually, however, he was spending more time talking with idle companions and drinking more than was good for him. It became easier and easier for this companionable man to leave his work. At the same time his family was getting larger,[57] his responsibilities became correspondingly heavier, and he began to have difficulty making both ends meet. Talking and drinking, he forgot his troubles for the time being.

Gustav continued to work and struggled to support his family, however, until the death of his favorite child, a little girl named Katie. That tragedy broke him. Until then he had tried to master his weaknesses with some success. Now he gave up trying. He neglected his business more and more and escaped from his troubles by drinking steadily.[58] His neighbors in St. Peter came to regard him as a miserable failure, the town drunkard, a burden and a curse to his family.

Caroline Johnson was now obliged to help support the family. She did the only thing she could do, since she could not leave her small children. She took in washing. Poverty descended upon the household, for Caroline could not earn enough to feed and clothe her family adequately though she labored day and night. With resolution and courage she had met and survived tragedy before. Now, after only a few years of happiness, she accepted the fate of having a drunken husband who at least was never unkind, bore the grief he caused her, and suffered the loss of four children, two of whom died when the family was poorest.[59] She never forgot, however, the misery and disgrace Gustav Johnson brought upon his family, and as she bent over the washtub and the ironing board trying desperately to earn enough to support her children, she developed a deep resentment toward her husband which she retained until her dying day.

The boy, John Albert Johnson, could not have had a very

[57] Gustav and Caroline Johnson had eight children, five daughters and three sons. Four of the daughters died in childhood or infancy. Edward and John were born on the farm; the rest were born in St. Peter between 1863 and 1875, when the youngest — twin girls — were born.
[58] Hattie Johnson to W. G. H.
[59] Day and Knappen, p. 53.

happy childhood. Early he must have been aware of the troubles in his family. He never knew his father sober for long. He never saw his mother happy or at rest. There never was enough to eat for him and his brothers and sisters, nor were they adequately clothed. Fuel was too dear to be had in the necessary quantities, and all winter long the family suffered from cold. He knew what it was to receive charity from kindly neighbors. The Johnsons' house was small with few furnishings. "The furniture of the little house was meager almost beyond description. One pail served Mrs. Johnson as a milk pan, bread pan, dish pan, and water pail. She baked bread on a picked up piece of sheet iron or an old kettle cover. There was one table in the house, and two or three wooden benches. There was no such thing in the house as a bureau, box, or chest, and only one bedstead." But everything was very clean.

John and his older brother, Edward, early learned to help their mother. They collected and delivered washing for her, milked the one cow the family possessed, and did odd jobs that came their way. Both boys were sent to school by great effort on the part of their mother. At home they had learned to speak Swedish. At school they worked hard to learn to speak, read, and write English. One of John's teachers noticed the thin little boy, so poorly clothed, because he was always late for school in the morning. When she learned it was because he and his brother rose early each morning to help their mother wash, her heart went out to the lad. She spent considerable time with him after school hours teaching him to speak and write English. In those early years he impressed his teachers as a bright boy who did his work well and who, in spite of hardships, was a good-natured, fun-loving boy who was never to be soured by misfortunes.[60]

As a boy John showed none of the skill both his father and his grandfather Hedén had in the use of their hands. His brother Edward was trained to be a blacksmith like his father,[61] but John had no liking for the work. He did not have much time to think of what he would like to do, however, for one day in 1874 Gustav Johnson sold his blacksmith shop, took the money, and disappeared for a year. John was then only thirteen years old. At once he decided to quit school and go to work to help his mother sup-

[60] *Ibid.*, pp. 54–61, 193.
[61] Arthur Evenson to W. G. H.

port the family. His mother protested, for she put great stock in education. But John had made up his mind. He could not bear to watch his mother toiling over the washtub. A family friend, Matthias Evenson, obtained a job for John as a clerk in Charles Colin's general store in St. Peter. He was paid ten dollars a month, which he gave to his mother.[62]

For the next dozen years John held a variety of jobs, each paying him a little more and offering new experiences. When Mr. Colin went out of business, he found a position as clerk for John in Henry Jones's drugstore. From there John went to clerk in a general store run by Starke Brothers and Davis. His salary was soon large enough so that he took over the full support of his family, and his mother no longer had to be the village washerwoman. The day he told his mother she need never again take in washing was one of the happiest days of his life.[63] Then he went to Decorah, Iowa, as a drug clerk, and later became a supply clerk for the Larson, Peterson, and Erickson Company, a railroad construction firm.

The *St. Peter Herald* deplored John's leaving St. Peter. In an article announcing his going, it declared: "John has been one of our most prominent young men and took a leading part in all social enterprises, and when he leaves he is going to leave a host of friends who will miss him very much. We would much prefer to see him remain." [64] John did not remain away long, for the following year, 1887, through the efforts of his friends he was brought back to St. Peter to become the editor of the *St. Peter Herald*.

That year, too, the family was relieved of the worry and support of the drunken father. In 1875 Gustav Johnson had returned after a year's absence. For a while he tried to get hold of himself and change his ways, but he failed and disappeared once again. When he returned in 1887 he was a hopeless drunkard with his health shattered and his sanity threatened. Through the efforts of Dr. A. W. Daniels and Matthias Evenson, Gustav Johnson was committed to the Nicollet County poorhouse, where he died.[65]

[62] Day and Knappen, pp. 60–63.
[63] *Ibid.*, p. 64.
[64] *St. Peter Herald*, February 5, 1886.
[65] *Minneapolis Journal*, October 31, 1904. According to this account Gustav Johnson died on October 9, 1889.

John paid the funeral expenses for his father, but at their mother's request none of the family attended the funeral. To Caroline Johnson her husband had been dead for years.[66] In time John managed to pay off the mortgage on the family home and bought furnishings for it.

By the end of 1887 the Johnson family consisted of Caroline, her two older sons, Edward and John, and two younger children, Frederick and Hattie. The girl Hattie was the youngest, born in 1875. A year or two older than John, Edward, like his father, found it difficult to stick to his work.[67] It was John who took the place of a father in the household. He supervised Edward and saw to it that the older brother kept at his work. The younger children adored their brother John, who sang to them, told them stories, brought them gifts, and kept them in school. If John worried about his responsibilities he never allowed anyone to know it, but always appeared happy and optimistic, singing or whistling at his work and around the home.[68] John A. Johnson was first popular with his family.

John is still remembered with warm affection by his relatives and friends, from whose recollections the following descriptive data have been drawn. In 1887 John was twenty-six years old. In his boyhood and as a young man he made a favorable impression upon the people of the little town in which he lived. The townspeople had profound sympathy for the ill-clad, thin little lad who collected and delivered washing for his mother; they also marveled at his bright spirit and cheery smile and took an immediate liking to him. As he grew into a gangling, awkward youth, business and professional men in the town noticed him and gave him help in many ways. Some obtained work for him; others helped the family. One man directed his reading, and a few gave him sound advice.

At twenty-six John was a slender, loose-jointed, big-boned, long-armed, long-legged young man a little over six feet tall. He had a long, well-shaped head with large ears close to his head, straight, light brown hair, heavy brows over keen blue eyes, a long, rather large nose, a sensitive mouth and good teeth, a strong,

[66] Arthur Evenson to W. G. H.
[67] Ibid.
[68] Hattie Johnson to W. G. H.

firm chin which jutted out, and a clear pink and white complexion. Already there were tiny lines around his eyes, lines produced by smiling, for his face readily broke into a naturally attractive smile. When he was amused or telling a funny story, his eyes fairly danced. He carried one shoulder higher than the other, and when he walked he ambled with the awkward, curious gait peculiar to him. When he talked, using his fine hands gracefully in gestures, he moved restlessly, giving the impression of one full of nervous force. He was careless of his clothes to such a degree that he was known to appear in public with one brown and one blue sock on his feet. Whether or not his suits fitted him was of little interest to him. He never stood up to his full height, but developed a slight stoop. When standing he slouched, and he seldom sat in a chair; he lounged with his feet swung up on the nearest piece of furniture.

His warmth, his engaging and winsome manner, and his keen sense of humor impressed everyone who met him. Even tempered, John was never known to lose control of himself; if he did become angered he did his best not to show it. He was natural and easy in manner with people. Like his father, he liked people, and he came to know everyone in St. Peter. He called most people by their first names, chatted with everybody from the street cleaner and well digger up, remembered their little troubles, and never failed to ask about their families.

To John living was exciting. He was full of enthusiasm about many things and had a lively curiosity. Sorrows and troubles at home did not depress his spirit. He was interested in everything, but especially everybody. Other people's affairs always interested him, and he was a sympathetic listener. Fond as he was of talking, his own voice did not intoxicate him. He was too eager to hear what others had to contribute, and he had no illusions of his own importance. Always courteous, tolerant, gracious, and kindly, John won people to him quickly. He was inclined to be flattering. Sometimes he "laid it on too thick," but this was because he genuinely liked most people and always wanted them to feel happy. He could not bear to have anyone dislike him. He liked to tease, but never did he carry teasing to the point of hurting anyone. He could make a joke of anything. Buoyant in spirit, optimistic and naturally easygoing, John met each problem as it arose. He had no ambition for himself save that of earning enough to keep his family comfortably. From his mother he inherited a strong will and the determination to do what he thought best. He was a man of integrity.[69]

Young John A. Johnson had a keen sense of social responsibility and participated in all sorts of community activities. As a boy he had attended the Methodist church in St. Peter,[70] but when he became well acquainted with the Presbyterian minister he began to attend services in that church. He loved to sing, had a good tenor voice, and soon was singing in the church choir. Then he became librarian for the Sunday school and an usher at the Sunday evening services.[71] A newly organized debating society found him one of the charter members, and in it he first tested his ability to speak. In debates with other societies in surrounding towns John gathered experience. In 1883 he enlisted as a private in a newly organized company of the Minnesota National Guard, becoming a captain before he was honorably discharged five years later.[72] It was his duty for a time to call the roll of his company, and he made a great impression on the men by accurately calling the names from memory.[73]

John was one of the leading members of a gay and exclusive group, the Nineteen Eligible Young Bachelors, which did much to make the social life in St. Peter more exciting. The N.E.Y.B. provided the young women of the town with a series of dinners and dances during the year. John would rather dance than eat, and he never missed attending any dance in town if he could help it.[74] Thoughtfully and gallantly he danced with the older women and the wallflowers as well as the girls of his choice. He did not do it from a sense of duty or for effect, but because he wanted to do his share in seeing that everyone had a good time. He took it upon himself to see that anyone who was apparently neglected

[69] The above paragraphs on the characteristics of Johnson are based upon interviews with Elinor Johnson Smith, his wife; Hattie Johnson, his sister; Mrs. Fred W. Johnson, his sister-in-law; Mr. and Mrs. George Nutter, Adolph Holmstead, and Henry N. Benson, who knew him well in St. Peter; Mr. and Mrs. Arthur Evenson of St. Paul, long-time close friends; H. G. McCall, Julius Schmahl, and Mrs. C. H. Helmes, of St. Paul.

[70] Arthur Evenson to W. G. H.

[71] Day and Knappen, p. 99.

[72] *Ibid.*, p. 80.

[73] Mrs. Arthur Evenson to W. G. H.

[74] Arthur Evenson and Mr. and Mrs. George Nutter to W. G. H.

had some attention, and he had the gift of making everyone feel that he was their friend.[75] One reason the ladies liked to dance with him, too, was that he never had the smell of liquor on his breath. John was a ladies' man until he was married, and once he became interested in any girl, no one else could get near her or get in a word to her.[76]

With others in St. Peter John helped to organize picnics, amateur theatricals, and operas performed by local talent, and he took part in some of them himself. A good mimic, he was frequently called upon to amuse his friends. Most often he would "take off" the Swedish emigrant, and then "Yon Yonson" threw his audience into convulsed laughter.[77] He early developed a passion for baseball and was an excellent player as a youth; in fact, he was good enough to be asked to play professional baseball and thought seriously about it before he refused the offer.[78] As a young man, however, he played only on such occasions as picnics, when games were planned as part of the day's entertainment. Once he played in a game between the Leans and the Fats and donned a long suit of underwear and a sweater and stuffed wads of cotton in the legs of the underwear to show well-developed muscles. Burlesquing his playing, he was vastly amusing to his audience. To all appearances he could make a fool of himself, yet never lost his quiet dignity.[79] All his life he delighted in baseball games, and he became a fairly regular spectator at the ball park. He was one of the organizers of a ski club [80] and was interested in all sports and sporting events. Once he reached manhood, however, he did not participate in any sport.[81] Walking became his favorite form of exercise. His characteristic walk was well known in St. Peter.

John possessed two favorite indoor sports: reading and cardplaying. The taste for reading he developed in school remained with him always. As a lad he had been guided in his reading by J. C. Donahower, who once was his Sunday school teacher. Donahower not only chose the best literature for John to read, but also

[75] Arthur Evenson to W. G. H.
[76] *Ibid.*
[77] Mrs. Arthur Evenson to W. G. H.
[78] Day and Knappen, p. 190.
[79] George Nutter to W. G. H.
[80] *St. Peter Herald,* February 5, 1886.
[81] Mrs. Arthur Evenson to W. G. H.

gave the boy a six months' subscription to the public library.[82] From then on John greedily read fiction, drama, and history — everything he could get from private libraries and the public library. Later, when he was asked what books had influenced his career most, he wrote:

I presume the great dramatist exerted a greater influence than any other writer because of the delineation of so-many-sided characters. Out of him came the inspiration to read more. Historical dramas directed me to the history of England, and Hume and Macaulay naturally followed. Then I turned to France to study her romantic history; from there to Germany and then back to Rome and Greece, Egypt and the Aryan regions. The tendency of the above and kindred books interested me in the literature and history of my own country, and the growth of the appetite for this food for thought doubtless created a desire to know more about the institutions of government here and abroad. All my work in this direction must have from time to time fired me with ambition and exalted my spirit of patriotic duty. In other words my increased knowledge of the world and the men who made its history and affairs fitted me in some measure for the duties of life.[83]

And once when he was asked what his chief ambition in life was, he replied: "As a life work, I would rather be able to provide for the needs of a family, enjoy the fellowship of good books and good friends, and write one book that would be read one hundred years from now, than to be able to amass all the money in the world." [84]

As an editor John became an avid reader of newspapers. Gifted with a wonderfully retentive memory, he remembered much of what he read. He taught himself a great deal.[85] As soon as he could afford the luxury, he began to build a fairly large library, and he collected every volume in the English language he could find on Napoleon, whom he admired.[86] But there was never any danger that he would become a bookworm; his was not that kind of a temperament.

[82] Day and Knappen, pp. 75–76.
[83] *Ibid.*, pp. 76–77.
[84] "John A. Johnson, the 'Dark Horse,' " *Current Literature*, January 1908, vol. 44, p. 34.
[85] Elinor Johnson Smith and Henry N. Benson to W. G. H.
[86] Arthur Evenson to W. G. H.

Card games had a fascination for John. He enjoyed matching his skill against others in playing, but more than that, he liked the sociability of the card table. Poker was his favorite game, but he never played if the stakes were high. He could not afford it, and the occasion playing cards offered for talk and companionship was more important to him than the opportunity to gamble. In St. Peter he played with men who had little more money to risk than he had.[87]

In all his life Johnson was never a drinking man. From his earliest years he had before his eyes the specter of his father, and he knew that any drinking he might do would terrify his mother. He said himself that he never dared take the risk. He came to enjoy a glass of beer or a glass of wine occasionally, but his wife and his friends never saw him take two drinks in an evening. He did not object to others' drinking. Being at a stag dinner party, a poker game, or a political meeting where most of the men drank did not bother John at all, but he seldom offered anyone a drink and never encouraged anyone to take a drink.[88]

From these reminiscent statements of the friends of the young man, it is evident that John A. Johnson at twenty-seven was sober, hard-working, self-respecting, fun-loving, and well-liked. He was popular in his community.

In the latter part of 1886 Henry Essler, publisher of the *St. Peter Herald,* was looking for a new partner and editor. His associate, John Blackiston, was in ill health and wanted to sell out his share in the paper and move to California.[89] Mr. Essler after some thought decided that Johnson was the man he wanted and needed in Blackiston's place. He presented the proposition to an amazed young man. Surprised and pleased that Essler should have thought of him, John had nevertheless to consider seriously whether he could accept the offer. He had not been with the construction company long and did not have the money to buy Blackiston's interest in the paper, and he did not want to get into debt. But the idea of editing a paper appealed to him as no other kind of work ever had. When Henry Essler assured him that some of

[87] Elinor Johnson Smith, Henry N. Benson, Arthur Evenson, George Nutter, Mrs. Fred W. Johnson, and Mrs. C. H. Helmes to W. G. H. Mrs. C. H. Helmes and Mrs. Fred W. Johnson were sisters.

[88] *Ibid.*; also H. G. McCall and Julius Schmahl to W. G. H.

[89] Arthur Evenson to W. G. H.

his friends in St. Peter would lend him the necessary money and that it would not put him deeply in debt, John finally agreed.

Addison L. Sackett, a businessman who had been mayor of St. Peter and a state senator, Matthias Evenson, old family friend, son-in-law of Carl Johnson, and the man who had made arrangements to commit Gustav Johnson to the county poor farm, Dr. A. W. Daniels, the Johnson family physician who had never put their names in his account book, and three other men loaned John the money. Most of them agreed to take what he owed them in the form of advertising in the *Herald*.[90] So, on December 17, 1886, there appeared in the *Herald* the announcement that the firm of Essler and Johnson was formed and that John A. Johnson was to be the new editor of the paper as of February 1, 1887. John's family was wildly happy that he was to be at home with them once again, and they were very proud of him.[91]

In 1887 the son of the village drunkard and washerwoman began his career. The work suited him, and he liked it. Yet that first year was full of hard work, grief, and pain. Though newspaper editing was new and exciting, it must have been an arduous job for John to learn it and get adjusted to it. And in the fall there was more trouble at home. On November 4, under the heading of "Locals in Brief," there appeared in the *Herald* a simple announcement of the death of John's fourteen-year-old sister Mary from typhoid fever. His younger sister, Hattie, had the disease, too, but had only a slight case. Then about a month later, on Christmas night, John collapsed with a very serious attack.[92]

No one knew just how the Johnson children contracted the disease. Their mother thought they might have got it from contaminated dairy products sold to them regularly by a farmer. Two of his children had died of typhoid.[93] There was probably an epidemic of typhoid fever in the area around St. Peter, however, for in the *Herald* during the months of October, November, and December there were notices of cases in the neighborhood around the town.

John was so seriously ill that for a while his life was in danger.

[90] *Ibid.*; Day and Knappen, pp. 71–72.
[91] Hattie Johnson to W. G. H.
[92] *Ibid.*; *St. Peter Herald*, December 30, 1887.
[93] Hattie Johnson to W. G. H.

He slowly began to recover, then suffered a relapse on January 20. For several days again his life was despaired of, but he gradually improved and by February 10 was able to sit up a little each day. Almost another month passed before John was back in his office at work.[94] The long and severe illness did permanent damage. Johnson ever afterward suffered from an intestinal disorder which brought him long periods of physical pain and ultimately caused his death.

For the next few years John lived quietly with his family, performed his duties as editor of the *Herald*, and remained an eligible young bachelor active in St. Peter affairs. In the fall of 1893, however, John fell in love with Elinor Preston, who had come to St. Peter to teach art in the parochial school. Miss Preston's father, John Preston, had come to the United States from England for his health. He settled in Wisconsin, where he met and married Josephine Matteson of Wonewock. Their only child, Elinor, was born on January 13, 1874, and shortly afterward both her parents died. She was reared on her grandfather Matteson's Wisconsin farm. An aunt who lived in Rochester, Minnesota, arranged for Elinor's education in the Lady of Lourdes Academy, which she entered in 1889. Soon after that she became ill with typhoid fever and was one of the first patients in St. Mary's Hospital, where she remained for eleven weeks.

St. Mary's was a new hospital conducted by the Sisters of St. Francis.[95] The physician in charge was Dr. W. W. Mayo, pioneer Rochester doctor, and his two sons, Dr. Will and Dr. Charlie, made up the staff. The young patient became well acquainted with the Mayos — father and sons — during her long stay, and from that time on they were good friends. The old doctor made daily calls and frequently lingered to entertain the little girl with blood-curdling tales of the 1862 Indian massacre. The opal ring he wore entranced her with its changing colors. Well again and out of the hospital, she continued her education for the rest of the year, and for four years more. Then, at the age of sixteen, she went to St. Peter to teach.[96]

[94] *St. Peter Herald*, January 6, 13, 27, February 3, 10, March 9, 1888.
[95] Helen Clapesattle, *Doctors Mayo*, pp. 245ff, for an account of the founding of St. Mary's Hospital.
[96] All details of her life told above were related to W. G. H. by Elinor Preston Johnson Smith.

She soon met the young editor of the *Herald,* and all during the winter and spring he was her constant escort. Elinor was impressed by John's sunny disposition. "He seemed much more like an Irishman than a Swede. He was so warm and fun-loving, and liked to joke so well." After knowing each other for about seven months, and after an engagement of one week, Elinor Preston and John A. Johnson were married in a quiet ceremony on June 1, 1894.[97] John was thirty-three and Elinor seventeen. In the *Herald* for that day appeared this item: "It is a fact . . . that one chair in the council chamber of the N.E.Y.B. will be vacant after today. Boys, we feel for you and perhaps you feel for us."

The bride and groom did not go off on a honeymoon immediately, but went to live at the Nicollet Hotel. They planned to go to the Black Hills of South Dakota later, when it was more convenient for the editor. An apartment was added to the Johnson family home, and John and Nora, as he always called her, occupied this until they built a new home for themselves later. His young wife was as gay and sociable as John, and together they took an active part in the town's social life.

Aside from a natural interest in events in St. Peter, Johnson, as editor of the *Herald,* had to know about community affairs, be interested in them, and to a great degree take part in them. Yet he felt very keenly that the affairs of any community ought to be the interest of every citizen of that community, and that the development of the community should be the concern of all, not just of a few public-spirited souls.[98] He not only published in the *Herald* all notices of concerts, theatrical performances, dances, Fourth of July picnics, and other community functions, but he urged everyone to attend and with his wife went to most of them himself. Johnson was one of the boosters for the building of a new opera house in St. Peter, and he helped bring speakers to the town. He himself developed a reputation for his ability to make short, graceful speeches, and was called upon to speak on more and more occasions.

Johnson and his wife soon were popular with the younger people of the town and served as chaperons at many of their dances. As a member of the Knights of Pythias, John helped organize

[97] *Ibid.*
[98] *St. Peter Herald,* November 8, 1889.

their dances and was always one of the speakers at their banquets. Usually he delivered the toast to the ladies.[99] Frequently he spoke at Fourth of July picnics. For years he was active in the Nicollet County Agricultural Society, for a while as its secretary. The affairs of Gustavus Adolphus College in St. Peter were duly noted in the *Herald,* and upon occasion Johnson spoke at the college banquets. He knew the faculty and many of the students and developed a lively interest in the little college.

Johnson deplored the tendency of people in St. Peter to divide into social "sets," with one group assuming superiority over another. He urged the people of the town to meet together on one social level, join together in every enterprise affecting the town's development, and have a common interest in enjoying themselves and promoting St. Peter.[1] Johnson never believed that birth or wealth entitled anyone to a superior position in society. A true child of the frontier, he judged people by what they made of themselves. He never alluded to his own humble background, but he felt himself quite the equal of any free American citizen. He condemned snobbishness and social division and urged men to behave toward each other as brothers. He believed in the dignity of mankind. As a citizen of St. Peter he waged war on class consciousness, and he was just as much inclined to sit on the curb to chat with the street cleaner as to relax in more luxurious surroundings to talk with the wealthiest man in town. Johnson was a democrat in the large sense of the word.

[99] *Ibid.,* December 12, 1890, and January 2, 1891.
[1] *Ibid.,* January 30, 1891.

## CHAPTER II

*Country Editor*

WHEN John A. Johnson became editor of the *St. Peter Herald*
the paper was two years old. It had been founded by Henry Essler and John Blackiston on October 17, 1884, at the suggestion
of St. Peter Democrats who wanted a more lively paper to represent their party and who offered to finance its establishment.
The two men had planned to found a newspaper in Jordan, since
there were already two newspapers in St. Peter, but they were
persuaded to change their plans.

The *St. Peter Journal*, edited by Horace Greeley Perry as a
Democratic organ, was a dull, heavy, thoroughly uninteresting
newspaper. Founded in 1878 by T. M. Perry, Jr., as the *St. Peter
Times*,[1] it was sold to Will E. Cowles in 1897, and then became
a Republican newspaper.[2] The oldest newspaper in St. Peter was
the Republican *St. Peter Tribune*, founded in 1860 by J. K.
Moore. Moore was its editor until 1885, when he sold out to
Andrew Ryan McGill, who made his son editor. McGill became
governor of Minnesota in 1887 and sold his paper in 1888 to P. V.
Collins, who published it until 1890, when he sold it to Dan Fichthorn and B. F. Borge.[3] In 1894 the *St. Peter Free Press* was established by H. C. Miller. This became a Republican organ, too.

Four newspapers in St. Peter — three Republican and one
Democratic — offered a challenge to their editors to produce better written, more readable, and spirited newspapers. It also produced the opportunity for quarrels, bitterness, and name calling.

Up to the time he became editor of the *Herald*, Johnson's political affiliations were known to be Republican, but he was

---

[1] T. M. Perry, Sr., had founded the *St. Peter Advertiser* in 1865, and his son published it until 1875, when it went out of existence. See *St. Peter Herald Diamond Ju-
bilee Anniversary Number*, October 1, 1930.

[2] *St. Peter Journal*, December 4, 1897.

[3] *St. Peter Herald*, October 1, 1930. Fichthorn was editor of the *Tribune* until 1920,
when he retired and his newspaper came to an end.

young, opportunistic, and willing to conform when he learned that Henry Essler and his financial backers wanted to keep the *Herald* a Democratic paper. His political convictions were not set, and to Johnson then it was of greater importance to obtain an agreeable means of earning a living which might have a future for him than it was to remain a Republican.

As for training or education which would fit him especially for editorial work, Johnson had none. He had never practiced writing and knew nothing about newspaper management. He was a typical editor of a Minnesota country newspaper in that respect. The great majority of rural newspaper editors in Minnesota during Johnson's time had little more than grade or high school education. Many became newspaper editors because they had been apprenticed to printers and then worked up to become editors. Or some, like Johnson — without any such experience — simply had the opportunity to become editors and took it.[4]

Johnson's first years as the *Herald* editor were difficult. He had much to learn, and just after he became editor the old building where the *Herald* was printed burned down and all the equipment was destroyed. Essler and Johnson had to move into cramped quarters in the rear part of the second floor of a drugstore. They had to buy a hand press, which it took both men to operate, and Johnson wrote his editorials on the top of an old washstand. Before long, however, the firm could afford to enlarge its quarters, buy the office furniture it needed, and put in a new cylinder press.[5] As he got accustomed to his work, Johnson had

[4] Some Minnesota country newspaper editors who began as printers' apprentices were Henry Essler, Johnson's partner on the *Herald*, William B. Mitchell of the *St. Cloud Journal-Press*, John E. King of the *Red Lake Courier*, Robert C. Dunn of the *Princeton Union*, John C. Wise of the *Mankato Review*, H. C. Hotaling of the *Mapleton Enterprise*, J. C. Morris of the *Morris Tribune*, and G. S. Pease of the *Anoka Union*. Liberty Hall traveled for the D. Appleton publishing house before he became an editor. C. F. MacDonald of the *St. Cloud Times* gained experience in the offices of the *Belle Plaine Enquirer* and *Shakopee Argus*. H. C. Miller ran a cigar store and was active in the Republican party before he established the *St. Peter Free Press*, and Frank A. Day of the *Martin County Sentinel* entered the newspaper field through politics. Only a few rural editors were men of more formal education. Frank Day's brother, H. G. Day of the *Albert Lea Standard*, read law in the office of a Chicago law firm, and C. W. Stanton of the *Appleton Press* was a lawyer as well as an editor. Probably the best educated of all the rural editors was Charles S. Mitchell; he was a graduate of the University of Michigan, became the editor of the *Alexandria Post-News*, then editor of the *Duluth News-Tribune*, and finally left Minnesota to join the editorial staff of the *Washington Post*. (See H. C. Hotaling, *History of the Past Presidents of the Minnesota Editorial Association, 1867–1934*. This little booklet has unnumbered pages.)

[5] Day and Knappen, pp. 83–84.

time to play a few harmless jokes on his landlord, a man named Poetz who owned the drugstore and building. Once Johnson covered every door knob of the building — except those of the *Herald* office, of course — with printer's ink. That caused much merriment as well as some curses and work removing the ink.[6]

Henry Essler took care of all business affairs for the *Herald*, and Johnson did all the writing and, for a long time, all the gathering of news. In the days before the telephone, news gathering meant plenty of leg work and a great deal of talking. Johnson liked to sleep late, get to his office about noon, and work until late at night, a habit which brought criticism from some of his early-rising neighbors.[7] Usually whistling or singing, John arrived at the *Herald* office to see how things were going and talk to Henry Essler before he started out to find news. His arrival had a cheering effect upon Essler and anyone else who was in the office,[8] for he would tell an amusing story or tease a bit or maybe play a joke on someone.

Then the tall, lanky, rather stooped young man with his characteristic walk went from store to store and person to person, talking, asking questions, listening, and scribbling in his notebook. Once he wrote that being a good reporter meant being a "gilt-edge loafer." A good reporter, he explained, had to appear to loaf, to appear to have plenty of time on his hands, to be a good listener even if bored, and to be able to meet all kinds of people, high and low.[9] More than once Johnson sat on a curb while he listened to a street sweeper, who, leaning on his broom, expounded opinions on the way the town was run and on local and national politics. Johnson listened patiently while people told him a great deal more than the bits of news he could use. He talked about St. Peter's business conditions, business in general, and politics with the men in the town; he talked about crops, the weather, and politics with the visiting farmers; and he talked about families, babies, illnesses, and social events with the women. Sometimes he took his horse and buggy and drove around to see the farmers in the neighborhood. Soon he came to know everybody around St. Peter, and their wants and opinions.

[6] Adolph Holmstead to W. G. H.
[7] Elinor Johnson Smith and Adolph Holmstead to W. G. H.
[8] *Ibid.*
[9] Editorial in *St. Peter Herald*, January 1, 1892.

He visited the courthouse and went to other towns nearby when he needed additional news or when something special was going on. One time, for example, when Johnson was in Mankato waiting to report on a trial which was about to take place, he mingled with some of the jurors. As he chatted and joked with them, someone suggested he give a speech. With alacrity he agreed, but asked what they would like to hear about. Someone suggested he talk about the flag, and Johnson stood above the group and spontaneously delivered an interesting and amusing speech about the American flag.[10] This was just one of the occasions on which Johnson spoke extemporaneously, surprising and impressing his listeners with his knowledge and his ability to make an impromptu speech.

Johnson did not always have to go out of the *Herald* office for the news he gathered or to talk with "the boys." The *Herald* office soon became a popular place for men to come and talk. Sometimes they interrupted Johnson as he sat writing up the news items he had collected. Or they disturbed him as he sat reading newspaper exchanges, slouched in his desk chair with his feet on his desk or on the nearby window sill. Usually he smoked one of the corncob pipes which he bought by the dozen and threw away when they got too strong.[11] But Johnson liked such interruptions. He welcomed visitors warmly and enjoyed sitting, smoking, and talking with them. His friends called to talk a while, farmers in town for the day came, and the *Herald* office became a mecca for many of the traveling salesmen who regularly visited St. Peter. Johnson always came to know any new salesman, for he never failed to greet a stranger, and usually stopped to talk; within a few minutes the stranger felt he had made a friend in St. Peter.[12]

Most men who visited the *Herald* office talked politics and crops. Occasionally a few gathered in the evening to play poker, but usually there were too many at the poker sessions for the *Herald* office, and most of the time the games were played at the Nicollet Hotel. When a telephone was installed in the *Herald* office, Johnson announced the fact in the paper, and added: "The *Herald* telephone is No. 1. When you have a piece of news call us

[10] Denny Donohue of Mankato to W. G. H.
[11] Adolph Holmstead to W. G. H.
[12] Denny Donohue to W. G. H.

up. If you have friends here or are going away yourself let us know about it. You can also subscribe to this paper or order job work over the telephone. That is one of the things we got the machine for." [13]

The *Herald* under Editor Johnson was in tone as genial, optimistic, and lively as he. It was the most interesting and readable of the four St. Peter newspapers, and it was one of the best edited of the country newspapers of the state. Unlike some of his fellow editors, Johnson tended to be concise rather than verbose. The *Herald* was never filled with long editorials bitterly attacking anyone or anything, calling for radical and immediate reforms, or demanding the maintenance of the *status quo*. Johnson's editorials were brief, full of humorous and shrewd observations, and quietly philosophical. He was tolerant of political parties and people, he had no ax to grind, and he was not given to writing at length about anything. When he occasionally did write a long paper to be delivered at a meeting of the Minnesota Editors' and Publishers' Association, he was by no means as successful as when he wrote his brief editorials. He was not comfortable writing at length. In a speech before the editorial association he said: "I believe that every newspaper should have an editorial column. Personally, I like to make . . . [editorials] short and crisp, because I do not like to tax the gray matter of my brain getting down to the bottom of a matter that perhaps I do not understand when I have written it. That is the only kind I can write, anyway, so I write them short." [14]

Johnson got stirred up on occasion. Once when a member of one of Spain's noble families came to the United States and his visit created quite a furor, Johnson wrote an angry editorial condemning the American people for becoming a race of snobs. He objected to the fact that many Americans were impressed by any individual with a title or by those who were very wealthy through no effort of their own. He wrote:

We would like to see more independence, more manhood and less fawning and cringing. The man who is honest, upright, intelligent and manly, is the equal of any man and if he is a free citizen, ought to feel

[13] *St. Peter Herald*, June 3, 1898.
[14] *Proceedings of the Minnesota Editors' and Publishers' Association, 1867–1894*, 1893 meeting, pp. 19–20.

his oats to such an extent as to refuse to be a worshipper of such false gods as titled nobility or cod-fish aristocracy. A true aristocracy consists of true worth and this ought to command respect and reverence, but it is a sad fact that it does not. We are acquiring snobbery and far too rapidly.[15]

Most of his editorials, however, were written about local problems and politics.

Like most country newspapers, the *Herald* was about eight pages in length with items of local news, news of the state and nation, a digest of world affairs, reprints from prominent city newspapers, exchanges from other country papers, advertisements, and the editorial page. The local items Johnson enjoyed collecting and writing because he was interested in the people of the community. Their affairs were his affairs, and he knew they liked to read about their own activities and see their names in print. As he wrote these items, he put them in a drawer until he was ready to set up the paper.

On the editorial page he wrote a column called "It's a Fact," which was made up of the editor's pithy sayings. Johnson was not the only editor who offered such a column. For example, Robert Dunn in his *Princeton Union* wrote a similar column under a different heading. But Johnson won a reputation among the country editors for what he wrote in his column. "It's a Fact," wrote Johnson,

That Santa Claus may be a myth, but he is an expensive one at that.

That it is funny that it is always the other fellow who is suffering from the big head.

That a young man at LeSueur took his girl out riding. She fell out and he drove a mile without missing her. She probably fell out on purpose, for no girl would want to ride with that kind of fellow.

That life without hope is not life. There is no hope without faith, and little faith without confidence. If you would hope for faith in others, do that which would inspire them with confidence in you.

That flattery never goes unrecognized but it pleases just the same.

That money talks, and to most of us it is not vulgar talk at that.

That of the books that have held men in their life, the bank book is a pretty close candidate for first place.

[15] *St. Peter Herald*, May 12, 1893.

That that life contains fewest mistakes which is earnestly and sacredly devoted to doing good to those with whom it comes in contact. And that life which is most successful is that which often attracts the least notice or attraction.

That our distinctions do not lie in the places which we occupy, but in the grace and dignity with which we fill them.[16]

In this column Johnson often quoted from the works of great men of literature. He was especially fond of quoting Mark Twain and Shakespeare, and he showed he was familiar with Cicero, Cato, Swift, Samuel Johnson, Macaulay, Tennyson, Lowell, Emerson, and Oliver Wendell Holmes. The column contained much that was of interest only to the people of St. Peter and much that had reference to the political figures and battles of the moment. Johnson's subscribers read it with pleasure.

Probably Johnson most enjoyed reading the exchange newspapers he received, reprinting and commenting upon some of their editorials and answering others. He refused to become involved in quarrels with other editors on any issue, and he urged his fellow editors to be as courteous to each other and as pleasant in their journalistic utterances as they would be if they met daily on the street.[17] In the *Herald* he carefully avoided bitter invective and personal attacks of any kind. He tried to print only what he knew to be the truth. Gossip he could not bear. He wrote in the *Herald*:

What is the cure for gossip? Simply culture. There is a great deal of gossip that has no malignity in it. Good-natured people talk about their neighbors because, and only because, they have nothing else to talk about. Gossip is always a personal confession, either of malice or imbecility, and the young should not only shun it, but by the most thorough culture relieve themselves from all temptations to indulge in it. It is low, frivolous, and too often a dirty business. There are country neighborhoods in which it rages like a pest. Churches are split in pieces by it. In many persons it degenerates into a chronic disease which is practically incurable.[18]

In a speech to the editors of southwestern Minnesota Johnson urged that they be advocates of right against wrong and warned

[16] *Ibid.*, January 2, 23, February 6, March 6, 13, December 25, 1903; January 19, November 2, 1894.
[17] *Ibid.*, July 8, 1892.
[18] *Ibid.*, December 12, 1890.

them not to abuse the power they had in controlling the press but to "exercise it with mercy, kindness and fairness. Court truthfulness and avoid harshness. Rebuke error gently and kindly and remember that kindness and gentleness are stronger than force and brutality." [19]

Second to the local news, the accounts of and editorials on Minnesota politics appealed to the majority of readers of the country newspapers. Every local, county, and state political gathering, campaign, and election was discussed in full detail, and every editor of a country newspaper became involved according to his political stripe. Most of the editors were Republican, and not a few were active in the affairs of their party, with some holding or running for political office. Of the few country editors who were Democrats in the Republican state of Minnesota, the most influential were Frank Day of the *Martin County Sentinel*, his brother, H. G. Day of the *Albert Lea Standard*, J. C. Wise of the *Mankato Review*, Carlos Avery of the *Hutchinson Leader*, John E. King of the *Red Lake Courier*, C. F. MacDonald of the *St. Cloud Times*, and John A. Johnson of the *St. Peter Herald*. These men played an important part in the political life of the state, for they presented in their papers strong opposition to the usually dominant Republican party. They seldom managed to elect their own party ticket, but they remained a healthy opposition.

The country newspapers were highly individualistic. They reflected the personalities as well as the philosophies of their editors. For that reason many of them were interesting to read — some more interesting than the big city dailies, which were becoming more and more impersonal. While the *St. Peter Herald* showed the even temper of John A. Johnson and never called names or hurled accusations, the *Princeton Union* reflected the personality of its editor, the fiery, combative, aggressive, and profane Robert Dunn. The urbane Joel Heatwole became involved in quarrels and political strife in the *Northfield News*, and Alvah Eastman in the *St. Cloud Journal-Press* could bitterly attack a political opponent. The suave, cool editor of the *Martin County Sentinel* maintained an unruffled calm as he supported the Democratic party in every

[19] *Ibid.*, July 8, 1892. Upon other occasions before the Minnesota Editors' and Publishers' Association, Johnson repeated much of this speech.

campaign after 1896, when he left the Republican party. A few editors followed Johnson's example in positively stating principles and upholding issues, but too many of them at times lost their tempers and attacked personalities rather than principles and issues. No one could pick a fight with Johnson, however; with quiet good humor he always turned away any attempt.

Many of the editors of the Minnesota country press came to know one another very well. In addition to exchanging papers, they had opportunities to meet personally twice a year. The Minnesota Editors' and Publishers' Association met once a year, in February, for professional purposes, and each summer it sponsored a social excursion of some kind for its members. This organization was founded in St. Paul on February 18, 1867, by a group of twenty-five editors upon the call of the publishers of St. Paul newspapers. They met in the "very cozy hall" of the Minnehaha Engine Company.[20] The following night the citizens of St. Paul gave a banquet for the editors, which Governor Sibley attended. At this first meeting not only was the association organized, but it "secured the passage of the law providing for the publication of the laws passed by the legislature in all the state papers . . . and secured an increase in the rate allowed by law for the publication of delinquent tax lists." [21] In 1868 it was decided to hold annual meetings and sponsor the summer excursions. From then on the association had an attendance of about thirty editors each year and was very active until 1874, when interest seemed to wane.

Between 1875 and 1884 interest in the business sessions rose and fell, but the summer excursions became more and more popular. The business session in 1884 was held during the summer excursion, and it was at Ashland, Wisconsin, that President Benjamin Briggs Herbert suggested that the Minnesota association take the initiative in calling a national convention of editors to organize a national editorial association. E. R. Otis of the *St. Paul Globe* then introduced a resolution that such a convention be called by the Minnesota association to meet in New Orleans dur-

[20] Thomas F. Barnhart, "History of the Minnesota Editorial Association, 1867–1897," p. 8.
[21] H. P. Hall, *History of the Minnesota Editors' and Publishers' Association, 1867–1896*, p. 76.

ing the following winter or spring.[22] New Orleans was chosen because a World's Exposition was being held there. Delegates from Minnesota were selected, and in December 1884 a circular was issued to editors all over the country inviting them to attend a convention on February 12, 1885. More than a hundred editors attended, coming to see the exposition and the Mardi Gras as well. The National Editorial Association was organized, and B. B. Herbert of Minnesota was elected its first president. Thus the Minnesota association had the distinction of initiating the National Editorial Association. At the 1885 meeting of the Minnesota Editors' and Publishers' Association a record number of one hundred editors attended, probably to hear Mr. Herbert's report on the organization of the national association.

The next three years were uneventful, but in 1889 the state association adopted a new constitution and inaugurated a policy of collecting and preserving historical information concerning the press of Minnesota. The association seemed to take on new vitality and during the following years developed into a more active group. As the number of newspapers in Minnesota increased, so did the membership of the association, but probably at no time during Johnson's membership were more than half the editors of the state active in the association. The aims of the association were to discuss and adopt measures which would promote the interests of the profession and to cultivate friendly relations among the editors and publishers.[23]

Johnson became one of the active members of the association and never missed a meeting unless he was forced to. He had not been a member very long when he was asked to lead discussions and give papers on assigned topics. At the annual meeting in 1890 he presented a paper on the "Law of Libel," and at the 1891 meeting he led a discussion on the subject of legal advertising. The editors were angry because they were not paid the full fee allowed for publishing legal advertising; a discount of from 20 to 50 per cent went to the lawyers.[24] Johnson began the discussion by saying:

[22] B. B. Herbert, *First Decennium of the National Editorial Association of the United States*, vol. 1, p. 39.
[23] *Proceedings of the Minnesota Editors' and Publishers' Association*, 1889, p. 34.
[24] Such legal notices as those of sheriff's sales, foreclosures of mortgages, notices in probate, and the like had to be published in the country press.

It has been many years since I have seen any legal advertising in my paper. I have the utmost contempt for the attorney or man who walks into our sanctum and demands a rebate on legal advertisements . . . and I think that this convention ought to take some action at this session to stop this work of giving reductions for legal advertising. . . . I would like to see the legal rates doubled. . . . You can't make them too high for me.[25]

The editors who joined in the discussion fully agreed with him, and a resolution was passed demanding the full fee for the publication of legal notices. At the same meeting H. G. Day of the *Albert Lea Standard* read a paper on "The Regulation of Common Carriers," which called for political reforms to secure government regulation of railroads and telegraph and telephone lines. William B. Mitchell of the *St. Cloud Journal-Press* read a paper on "The Encouragement of Immigration by the State." He urged the newspapers of the state to put on a campaign to attract people from the East to Minnesota; he thought Minnesota already had enough foreigners to Americanize. The association endorsed a bill then before the legislature providing for the creation of a state board of immigration.

The veteran editor, H. P. Hall, was elected president of the association for the coming year, and the freshman member, John A. Johnson, was elected secretary. When the voting was over there were cries of "Johnson, Johnson," and he rose and modestly replied:

I am duly appreciative of the honor you have conferred upon me. . . . It seems to me that the distinguished honors ought to have fallen on worthier shoulders, but I shall certainly go into office with a whole soul, always working for the interests of the Association. If the members are disposed to have me do anything more than I promised to do here, they only need to tell me what it is. . . .[26]

Each meeting had its full agenda of papers to be read and discussed. Such topics as "The Relation of the Country Editor to Politics," "The Newspaper Editor," "Newspapers and Legislation," "Newspapers and the Public," "Newspaper Ethics," "How to Build Up a Circulation," "Country Correspondence of a Coun-

[25] *Proceedings of the Minnesota Editors' and Publishers' Association,* 1891, p. 15.
[26] *Ibid.,* p. 47.

try Newspaper," "The Business End of Country Newspapers," "Independence in Journalism," and other pertinent subjects were discussed. Johnson, always an attentive listener, learned much.

The annual meeting in 1893 was a memorable one because of the lengthy and heated discussion of the question, "What Constitutes a Newspaper?" Several members, including Johnson, had come prepared to speak on the subject, and others entered into the discussion spontaneously. This was the first time in the association's history that anyone had tried to define a newspaper. G. N. Lamphere of the *Moorhead News* was the first speaker. When he declared "that a newspaper is a paper printed regularly with an established place of business and real *bona fide* subscribers, men who pay their subscriptions in money or its equivalent; that it should contain news of various classes: local, telegraphic, and editorial, both local and 'of the heavy sort,' and that it should have local and foreign advertisements — it was then the excitement started." [27] One editor after another rose to make his contribution to the subject, and finally Ed Paradis of the *Midway News* suggested that the association "settle what a newspaper is and have the state define it for us for the purpose of printing legal and public notices." [28]

When Johnson took the floor, he chose to speak of the newspaper and its editor with sentiment and eloquence. He began by saying, "I scarcely know whether it is in my power to define what a newspaper is or to tell the members present what constitutes a newspaper, because so many of them have been in the business so much longer than I have, and so many of them edit and publish better papers than I do." [29] Then he went on to read his speech:

I think the proper definition of an editor would be "a sentinel upon the watchtower of human liberty." That is a quotation, by the way, and not original with me, as very little I say is. . . . He ought, with eyes and ears open, to be upon the lookout for that which would inure to the benefit of those with whom he comes in contact in a literary way. . . . His paper should be a central telephone exchange, through which the people of the community could talk with each other, and

[27] Barnhart, pp. 140–41.
[28] *Proceedings of the Minnesota Editors' and Publishers' Association*, 1893, p. 17.
[29] *Ibid.*, p. 18.

we ought to allow only such conversation to pass over that telephone line as would be music to the ears of the people who happened to catch on to the 'phone. (Applause)

An editor's function should also be to enter the homes where sorrow . . . has invaded and replace the tears of grief with the pearls of joy. He always ought to be actuated by a spirit of kindness and fairness, and in securing the news for his paper he ought not to be so vigilant that the spirit of fairness be crushed out of him by the undesirable ambition to conduct what might be sometimes termed in the slang of to-day, a hustling newspaper. I believe that too much news, if it is not good news, is just as bad as too little news. But I feel that every editor . . . should be an active man. I believe he should be so active that in his community he would secure all the news . . . and he ought to convert the news . . . into newsy matter so interesting that it would be read with pleasure and profit by all who take and read the papers. The newspaper man ought to edit a newspaper . . . that would be received at all times with delight; a paper that the girls would get up from the table and ask for, that the boys would cry for, and that father and mother would fight for . . . I believe that the editor should be as fair in politics as he is in love and war. I believe he should say no unkind things prompted by a spirit of maliciousness. I believe he should confine himself to a discussion of the issues in a campaign and avoid all personalities . . .

I am an optimist with regard to the American press because I believe it occupies the highest point of any of the professions. . . . I believe it should counsel a man in business, upon the farm and in the workshop. . . . I believe it should be a monitor by which the public official should be governed and I believe it should be the watchdog of the treasury standing guard over every public officer.

I believe, representing as it does a constituency, that it has a right at all times to look into the public and official acts of every official servant, but I do not believe it has any right to go into the history of personal relations of that man or into his family. . . . His public acts it always has a right to criticize, but it never has a right to criticize his personal conduct or personal relations. I believe that in preparing material for his paper the editor should chronicle every item of gossip or otherwise truthfully, and he should be scrupulously careful to see that every item that goes into his paper can be backed up by facts. There is too much fiction in modern newspaper business. I see an item and jot it down, and perhaps being tired or hurried, I print the item without looking it up. It may cause tears to flow from the eyes of someone, and in that case I have done that person wrong. I think a man had better omit publishing an item and be considered derelict in the performance of his duty rather than to publish that which he does not know to be true.

I believe that the word of an editor should be as good as the word of a bank cashier; that it should pass as current coin in the realm of truthfulness . . . I believe the editor of a paper should be fair to his contemporaries. I do not believe in calling a man across the street a "hell-hound" in the heat of a political campaign, and then coming down here at our meetings and calling him brother and saluting him with as much fervor as if we were all at a prayer meeting. I believe that temperance should characterize all our efforts . . .[30]

When Johnson concluded, H. G. Day continued the discussion, commenting further upon the bona fide and the fly-by-night newspapers. Both Day and David Ramaley urged legislation to drive out of existence the newspapers which did not deserve the name and which existed chiefly to obtain the fee the state gave for the publication of laws. Johnson then made a plea to the editors to urge more of their profession to join the association. Since only about a hundred and fifty of the four hundred editors of the state were members, Johnson suggested that the following year be devoted to increasing the membership. He also stated that for the good of the association its next secretary should be from the Twin Cities.

The editors then decided to visit the Chicago World's Fair as their excursion for the year. L. P. Hunt of the *Mankato Free Press* had been appointed superintendent of the State of Minnesota exhibit, and he had persuaded the editors to put pressure on the state legislature to appropriate a good sum for the exhibit. The editors, in fact, felt it was due to their efforts that Minnesota was to have a good exhibit, and they were anxious to see it.

When it came time to nominate officers for the coming year, T. E. Barnum, veteran editor from Sauk Center, arose and congratulated the retiring president, G. S. Pease of the *Anoka Union*, on his year's work for the association. Then he went on to make a nomination for the presidency for the coming year:

[30] *Ibid.*, pp. 18–19.

I have in mind a young man who, it seems to me, has the interest of the association at heart second to no member in it. I refer to Mr. John A. Johnson of St. Peter. . . . I think with him at the head of this association we would go down to Chicago in splendid shape. I think there is no member of this association who would infuse so much life into it and bring it before the country so well as Mr. J. A. Johnson of St. Peter, and I hope you will vote for him and elect him as your next president.[31]

Johnson thanked Mr. Barnum, declaring that he was yet a new member of the association and had plenty of time to become its president. Someone nominated G. S. Pease for re-election, and Ed Paradis, H. G. Day, and G. N. Lamphere were also nominated. After three ballotings Johnson was elected. The question of rotation of office was then thoroughly discussed, and, in order to give more men the opportunity to serve as president, the association passed a resolution that no member could thereafter hold office for more than two successive terms.

Johnson was almost thirty-two years old when he was elected the fourteenth president of the editorial association, and he put into his term all the sincerity, effort, and humor he possessed. He began to inject some new life into the association in May, when the editors made their annual excursion to Chicago to visit the World's Columbian Exposition and to attend the World's Press Congress which was to be held there at the same time.

The exposition opened on May 1 with a speech by President Grover Cleveland. Upon the conclusion of his address the president pressed a gold key and "started the mighty machinery and the rushing water and the revolving wheels in the World's Columbian Exposition." [32] Great fountains began to throw sprays of water; machines in the various buildings began to hum. People came from all over the country to visit the exposition.

The Minnesota editors planned to make their visit at the fair coincide with Governor Knute Nelson's dedication of the Minnesota Building, which they felt they had had a great part in bringing into being. The building was "plain but imposing" [33] and contained specimens of the flora and fauna of the state and Indian relics. There was the oil painting of the 1862 Indian massacre

[31] *Ibid.*, p. 47.          [32] *St. Paul Pioneer Press*, May 1, 1893.          [33] *Ibid.*

at New Ulm by Anton Gág, and Alexis Fournier's painting of Minnehaha Falls. Minnesota also had an exhibit in every building of the fair except those of the other states; for example, there was a Minnesota forestry exhibit in the Forestry Building and a Tom Lowry streetcar in the Transportation Building.

The dedication of the Minnesota Building was announced for May 18, and the editors had been especially invited by L. P. Hunt to attend the ceremony. On May 14 the editorial party gathered in St. Paul. About a hundred and sixty of them — editors and wives — were ready to depart when Governor Nelson announced that the dedication would be postponed until June 1. No reason for the postponement was given. The news was a blow to the editors, but en route to Chicago Johnson, H. P. Hall, C. C. Whitney, and a few others discussed a plan for the editors to have their own dedication of the building. As soon as possible President Johnson, H. P. Hall, and L. P. Hunt sought permission from the state commissioners for the use of the Minnesota Building on May 17. After much discussion permission was granted. By this time the editors had decided to make the dedication as formal and complete as possible so that no other dedicatory ceremony would be necessary. Everything was arranged. Only a brass band was missing — they had been unable to secure one for the occasion.

At eleven o'clock on the morning of May 17 the dedication ceremony began before a crowd of people in the Minnesota Building, which had been decorated with flowers and plants for the occasion. President Johnson formally opened the ceremony by asking the Reverend Brown of Mankato to give the invocation. Then Oscar Lienau of the *St. Paul Volkszeitung* sang a song, and a dedicatory ode was recited by F. W. Lee of the *St. Paul Daily News*. President Johnson delivered the dedication speech. He began by saying that the intellect of the State of Minnesota would never be better represented at the fair than at this particular time; he went on to state that it was in large part due to the efforts of the editors of Minnesota that there was a Minnesota Building, which made it only right that the editors should dedicate the building in their own way. When he finished speaking he formally presented the keys of the building to State Senator Henry

Keller who, on behalf of the state, accepted them and delivered a short speech. There followed a series of addresses by H. P. Hall, F. W. Lee, F. J. Mead of the *Minneapolis Times,* State Senator J. W. Craven of the *Norwood Times,* and State Representative S. A. Langum of the *Preston Times.* Henry A. Castle made the concluding address for the editors. Then Mrs. Lienau broke a bottle of wine on the broad stairway of the building, and the performance concluded with the singing of "America" by the assembled crowd.[34]

The editors from Minnesota were amused and pleased with their dedication ceremony. They had thought to take only a small part in the formal dedication planned around state officials and Governor Nelson, but now they had carried off their own complete ceremony. On May 19 there appeared in the *St. Paul Pioneer Press* a tiny announcement, so small and so placed in the paper as to go unnoticed, stating that Governor Nelson had decided to abandon all plans for any other dedication of the Minnesota Building at the Chicago Fair. The editors had put on such a thorough performance that Governor Nelson did not think any repetition was necessary.[35] Nelson had been annoyed by the editors' action but he accepted it, especially after one of the commissioners from the fair came to St. Paul to suggest to Nelson that no other ceremony take place. Some Minnesota newspapers called the editors' dedication "a farce" and "a burlesque," but it was soon explained that it had been undertaken seriously. The World's Fair commissioners and the Chicago newspapers were delighted.[36]

The twenty-seventh annual meeting of the association was opened by its president, who delivered the presidential address, "The Mission of the Press." Johnson was a happy speaker, and he always held his audience. His manner of speaking was informal and conversational and his voice unusually pleasing to hear. He began his address by saying:

The student of the classics will remember it was Cicero who said that eloquence was mistress of all the earth. That to this quality were

[34] The account of the dedication of the Minnesota Building is based upon information taken from H. P. Hall's *History of the Minnesota Editors' and Publishers' Association,* pp. 190–93, and the reports of it in the *St. Paul Pioneer Press,* May 16–19, 1893

[35] *Ibid.,* May 19, 21, 1893.

[36] *St. Peter Herald,* June 2, 1893.

his people indebted for the liberty they owned and their removal from all the ills of a savage and barbarous life. This ancient hero was an orator and lived in that age when men learned from the lips of another. A man not so great, perhaps, as Cicero, for few men are great now, has more truthfully said that "the newspaper is the school of the people." . . . In these days it is the newspaper that binds mankind by the community of privilege, of laws and of civil society. . . . In the days when the minds of the masses were uncultivated it was comparatively easy to sway a multitude with the shower of pearls which fell from . . . lips. Then prejudice and passion were easily appealed to, and men were ruled by wit and words. Centuries have rolled along and men have advanced until to-day the seat of power is not of physical force but intelligence. The people are learned, and dominion over men now is and only can be reached through conviction. Conviction can only be created through but one medium — the power that has wrought the beautiful civilization of the grand nineteenth century, the press. . . . The profession, while not divine, is coordinate with that of the church in that it teaches a code of morals and ethics to a class which cannot be reached by those who sound their ideas from the pulpit. Day by day I am more convinced that to complete the grand superstructure of our government, to raise man to his highest position in life, the realization of the theory of the brotherhood of man, to create a more perfect harmony and unity among all the people, is the unfulfilled but present mission of that profession. . . . [The press] is a guardian of our rights. It has created the true liberty. . . . It is the custodian of virtue and civil rights, and . . . [every editor] should be proud to be a sentinel upon its watch tower of human liberty.

As he continued his speech, he became grandiloquent and bombastic, looking with great optimism to the future:

We stand upon the threshold of a new century, and, as we look into the glass of the future, we intuitively glance at the past, and can only proclaim for the future a golden success. The progress of the past century has found an improvement that is both startling and wonderful. In every age the banner of progress has been borne aloft. It has been handed down from one generation to the next, until to-day it seems the end must have been reached, but not so, for the coming will be greater than the going. The next century will be brighter and better than this, and the progress of journalism will keep up its swift pace. . . . In that golden future [the newspaper] will become invincible in its advocacy of right, and will be well-nigh omnipotent as a force for the destruction of evil and correction of wrongs and abuses, and thereby maintain its sovereignty in maintaining dominion over the honest convictions of mankind, convictions upon which rest the right of free thought and free speech. When the founders of this government embodied in the bulwark of liberty the right of free speech they enthroned the press and made it sovereign, and that sovereignty has been maintained in its acts which have firmly established it in the hearts of the people and planted it highest upon the throne of public opinion.

Then Johnson came down to earth, and the Fourth of July oratory was discarded as he discussed the mission of the press and the ideal editor in more practical and understandable terms. The rest was a repetition of much that he had said in his previous speech on "What Constitutes a Newspaper?" Again he urged the editors to be fair, honest, truthful, kind, and generous:

All honor does not spring from the fountains of wealth, but no man is without honor who discovers his duty to his fellow men and carefully performs that duty. I would have the profession in love with the calling, and of such a nature should be that love that the ear would at all times be deaf to the stern voice of corrupting influence. The man who has conceived a financial view, and that alone, has reared aloft a false standard of success. There is a legitimate and practical business aim in the profession, which is equal, if not paramount, to that view which has wedded so many to it. Prosecute your business with energy and thrift, and elevate it to that dignity to which it is entitled. No man who loves the profession forgets his business, but always bears in mind that man was born to hustle, and that close attention to the details of business is the quality which ultimately wins. In this restless age of activity there is no place for laziness, and this kind of man has absolutely no place in the profession of journalism. In his display of thrift a man should not make his gold his god, but ought to be actuated in a great degree by his love for mankind and his love for his calling.

Gold without love is a plant which does not bud or blossom and lacks that sweet perfume which should permeate our hearts and fill our souls with human happiness. Perhaps I have already taxed your patience, but I hope I may be pardoned if I add: shun bitter invective, avoid personal attack, criticize fairly, but for the sake of the other worlds and other conditions of society, avoid gossip. This has a place in a sewing circle and in that field it is better taken care of than you could ever hope to. Be a student and remember that we are never too old or too wise to learn. He who is too wise to learn from others is too learned for the humble calling which we advocate. We should be impartial and fair in our political utterances, and bear in mind that as we are not infallible and therefore not always right, neither are our opponents always wrong.[37]

Johnson concluded by urging the editors to give careful consideration to the association's business organization. He suggested that a day of the meeting be set aside for a thorough discussion of reorganization for "a more perfect business union." The editors had been prone to enjoy the summer excursions but less inclined to attend the business sessions, and several members were anxious that more emphasis be placed upon the business aspects of the association's program. The idea of reorganizing had been suggested at each meeting since 1884; now H. G. Day brought the idea into focus. He presented a concrete plan of reorganization which would make the association a business organization — to furnish its members and others with "so-called patent insides, or ready-printed sheets, to print a newspaper or newspapers for itself, its members and others," to plate material for printing, to buy and sell paper and all kinds of printer's supplies and appliances, to solicit and supply advertising, and to "carry on a business in general relating to the publishing business and printing craft." [38] After much discussion, a committee was appointed to find out what the other editors of the state thought about such a reorganization and to draw up a plan.

H. G. Day was elected president of the association to succeed Johnson. Robert Dunn gave a short speech urging the editors to pay more careful attention to the kind of men they backed for election to the state legislature. He advised them to support a man who would support the newspapers and their bills, regardless of that man's political party.

It was the custom for the association meeting to include an annual banquet, usually an elaborate and lively affair. Sometimes it was given by the city of St. Paul or Minneapolis, where the association alternately held its meetings, or by the press clubs of

[37] *Proceedings of the Minnesota Editors' and Publishers' Association,* 1894, pp. 6–10.
[38] *Ibid.,* p. 27.

those cities. Occasionally some business organization gave the banquet. This year the editors were the guests of the city of Minneapolis, and Mayor Eustis of that city presided at the banquet and presented President Johnson with the keys to the city in his opening speech. Johnson replied, and then Governor Nelson responded to a toast, "To Our Commonwealth." Other toasts followed, but the high light of the evening was the appearance of Robert Ingersoll, who came to the banquet after making a speech that evening in Minneapolis. He spoke briefly to the gathering of about five hundred editors and others who were present as guests of the city.

Following the banquet the visiting editors and the Minneapolis and St. Paul press clubs, preceded by a brass band, marched to another hall where they enjoyed a "smoke social," another annual custom of the association. There speeches were delivered, stories told, and songs sung; specialty acts were performed by professional actors from theatrical companies playing in the Twin Cities.[39]

Johnson loved it all — the business sessions, the banquets to which the wives of the editors came, and the "smoke socials." He liked to come to the Twin Cities where, with his wife, he attended the theater, went on trips specially organized for the editors, and generally had a good time. It became customary for Johnson to be called upon to deliver the "Speech to the Ladies" at the annual banquets. After he had done this regularly for several years, his wife protested, "Why don't you tell them you are through being funny? Why don't you give a serious speech for a change?" [40] But it was not until Johnson became governor of the state that he could refuse.

At the next annual meeting of the association the plan for business reorganization was discussed again. Johnson declared himself in favor of the plan, but he thought the two organizations, the Minnesota Editors' and Publishers' Association and the new organization being discussed, should remain separate. Many others agreed with him, and it was voted to keep the new business organization separate. All members of the association seemed satisfied with this, and at a special meeting in June 1895 the new busi-

[39] Hall, *History of the Minnesota Editors' and Publishers' Association,* pp. 197–98.
[40] Elinor Johnson Smith to W. G. H.

ness organization was formed under the name of "Northwestern Publishers' Association."

Johnson was active in the state association meeting of 1896, and he attended the 1897 session even though he was just recovering from a serious surgical operation. At the banquet in 1898 Frank Day in a speech called the attention of the editors and their guests to Johnson by saying, "Here is my brilliant friend, John Johnson, a man I want to see on the next Democratic ticket as governor or lieutenant governor." [41] Johnson had not yet been elected to any political office in the state, but Frank Day and some of the other Democratic editors of the association were encouraging him toward a political career. James J. Hill delivered the speech of the evening, "Newspapers, Railroads, and Prosperity," and Johnson gave another "funny" talk entitled "Some People Who Ought to Be at St. Peter." He went on as many of the summer excursions as he could. In 1898 the Minnesota editors were invited to visit Milwaukee and Detroit by the press clubs of those cities, and Johnson, C. W. Stanton, president of the association for the year, and H. P. Hall made the speeches in response to toasts at the luncheon given by the Milwaukee club. Johnson also was called upon to make the presentation speech when President Stanton was given a gift by the Minnesota association.

At the 1903 meeting the question of going to Washington, D.C., or to the St. Louis Exposition for the annual excursion was discussed. H. P. Hall called upon Johnson for his opinion, since he knew something about the dedication of fair buildings. Johnson replied that he would go on the annual excursion, and "as to the dedication of buildings, why, we had something to do with that; and I think the State Editorial Association has established . . . a precedent that will stick. . . . Now I personally would prefer to go to Washington." [42] For the rest of the session Johnson was teased by some of the other members for wanting to go to Washington; the political implications were emphasized and exaggerated. But the association decided to go to Washington on its excursion, and Johnson and his wife were in the party.

A visit to Mount Vernon was planned for the editors, and be-

<hr />

[41] *Proceedings of the Minnesota Editors' and Publishers' Association*, 1898, p. 63.
[42] *Ibid.*, 1903, p. 72.

fore the mansion of the first president of the United States Johnson had been asked to present Frank Day with a gold watch, a
gift from the association to its president. Day was a great friend
of Johnson's, and with the connivance of others Johnson decided
to have some fun with him. Deadly serious, Johnson made an
elaborate speech full of appreciation of Frank Day's abilities and
performance as president of the association and ceremoniously
presented him with the gift. When Mr. Day investigated the gift,
however, he found he had received a huge cheap watch, easily
recognized by the audience for what it was. The editors laughed
heartily at the joke, and it took a few minutes for Mr. Day to
recover before he made his speech of grateful acceptance.[43]

Johnson remained an active member of the Minnesota Editors'
and Publishers' Association all his life. While he was governor of
the state he attended the meetings whenever he could, and he
was always friendly with the press. He learned much from association meetings. The papers he wrote and delivered, those to which
he listened, and the discussions of all of them covered many of the
phases of country and city journalism. He became thoroughly familiar with his profession; he also became thoroughly acquainted
with his fellow editors, and they talked about more than their professional problems. Minnesota and national politics were of major
interest to the editors, and they discussed political platforms, political records, and candidates.

Not a few of the country editors ran for political office, and
some were successful in their campaigns. Joel Heatwole, for example, was secretary of the Republican state central committee
from 1886 to 1888 and chairman of that committee from 1890 to
1892; from 1895 to 1903 he served in the United States House
of Representatives. Frank Day served in the lower house of the
Minnesota legislature for one term, and in the senate for three
terms. The election of 1894 will further illustrate the political activity of the editors. That year Heatwole was elected to Congress;
Robert Dunn became state auditor; Frank Day, H. J. Miller of
the *Luverne Herald*, S. A. Langum of the *Preston Times*, W. M.
Fuller of the *Little Falls Transcript*, and E. K. Roverud of the
*Caledonia Journal* were elected to the state senate; Jens Grondahl
of the *Red Wing Daily Republican* and L. J. Ahlstrom of the *Mis-*

[43] George Nutter to W. G. H.

*sions Bladet,* official organ of the Swedish Baptists, were elected to the lower house.

At the annual meetings of the editorial association Johnson met political figures in the state. The governors and some members of the legislature and of the supreme court were guests who addressed the editors at their annual banquets. Usually Johnson was one of the speakers at the banquet, and sitting at the head table with the guest speakers he came to know them better than if he had been but one of the audience. At association meetings, excursions, and banquets he gained a great deal of experience giving speeches. He amused his fellow editors, but he also impressed them with his serious speeches at the business meetings. The summer excursions gave him an opportunity to see some of the United States and meet members of the press in other states. He developed a love of travel and a keen desire to see all of his country and the rest of the world. He gained the reputation of being "a good fellow," but he also was recognized as a very able young man. His interest in and conscientious work for the association early impressed the veteran members; whatever he was asked to do, he did well, and he became one of the most dependable and loyal members. Just four years after he became an editor, the association made him its secretary and two years later its president. H. P. Hall, in his *History of the Minnesota Editors' and Publishers' Association,* published in 1896, gave an indication of what the editors thought of Johnson. Hall referred to him as the "Tom Sawyer of Minnesota Journalism" and an able editor, then wrote:

Mr. Johnson is an orator as well as an editor, and no editorial meeting or banquet at which he is present fails to find him "on the list" as one of the speakers. It can be added that no more enjoyable speech than his is made upon such an occasion. If he had been a member of the dominant political party he would long since have attained high political position. A credit to his profession, having gained a wide state prominence in the brief ten years of his newspaper life, he has the ability to win fame in a wider field, and it will always be a matter of congratulation on the part of the Editorial Association in future years to point to the fact that John A. Johnson has filled the position of president.[44]

In 1908 Johnson was asked to write an estimate of his own

[44] Hall, pp. 185–86.

newspaper career. He did not think it worth much comment, for he wrote: "My newspaper career was very ordinary in its character, and while it covered a great many years there was nothing in it which has not come to every country newspaper editor and publisher." [45] Johnson was a typical country editor and edited a typical good country newspaper. But he was more interested than most editors in the profession and its advancement.

As an editor Johnson had a reputation for his sense of fairness, his charity, his refusal to stoop to recriminations and name calling, his rejection of all that was petty, his devotion to high principles. He won the respect of his fellow editors for the way he conducted his newspaper. As a man Johnson was by no means regarded as ordinary by the editors who knew him so well. They recognized him as one of their leaders, as a man with unusual mental ability and irresistible personal charm. Some among them shared the opinion of H. P. Hall and Frank Day that Johnson was capable of becoming more than a country editor. But Johnson was a Democrat in the Republican state of Minnesota. For success in politics, a Democrat in Minnesota needed more than ability and personal charm. He needed an unusual opportunity.

[45] J. A. J. to John F. McCabe, February 5, 1908.

## CHAPTER III

*Debut in Politics*

As EDITOR of the *Herald* Johnson naturally turned his attention to national and local politics. Grover Cleveland, the first Democratic president since Buchanan, was serving his first term as president of the United States, and his administration did little to relieve the dullness and monotony which had characterized national politics since the Hayes administration. Yet Cleveland, unlike Hayes and Arthur, his predecessors, and Harrison, his successor, at least had some insight into the problems facing the country and made an attempt to deal with them.

The Civil War and Reconstruction had come to an end, but party politicians continued to exploit sectional differences and animosities instead of trying to weld the nation into a friendly whole. The Industrial Revolution was transforming the economy of the country, and large trusts and monopolies were forming, which meant the concentration of great power and much wealth in the hands of a few. The traditional American philosophy of laissez faire was becoming outmoded, yet politicians continued to espouse it. Most of the politicians of the day were content to let Big Business run politics, and the ethics of one were applied to the other. Big Business had its representatives in Congress; there sat such men as Nelson W. Aldrich of Rhode Island who thought in terms of the interests of sugar, iron, steel, and Eastern manufactures, rather than in terms of the interests of the people and the country as a whole. There were a few earnest and conscientious men of integrity who strove to serve the people of the nation, but they struggled against the majority. Big Business ran both parties, though its contributions to the Republican party were more generous.

Until Cleveland's administration both parties had refused to come to grips with the farm problem, the dangerous restlessness in the labor ranks, the need for civil service reform, the popular demand for tariff reform, and the serious division in the United States on the money question. Neither party appreciated the position and responsibilities of the United States as one of the important nations in the world. Cleveland by no means attempted to solve all these problems, but he had the courage to tackle some of them.

In spite of determined opposition within his own party, Cleveland succeeded in advancing civil service reform. He also won the eternal hatred of the Grand Army of the Republic by approving an order returning captured Confederate battle flags to their states; by appointing L. Q. C. Lamar, the Confederate general, as his Secretary of the Interior; and by his consistent opposition to pension legislation. He vetoed many private pension bills, which saved the government from having to pay thousands of dollars to men who never had suffered any disability during the Civil War; he signed only the private pension bills he thought were valid. In 1887 he vetoed the Dependent Pension Bill, which granted pensions to all veterans suffering from any disability no matter how contracted. In this way he alienated the G.A.R., one of the most powerful pressure groups in the country and an organization with a membership of about half a million during the middle eighties.

Railroad companies, lumber companies, and cattle ranchers who were defrauding the government and despoiling western forests and lands became the targets of Cleveland's investigation. The government forced them to restore to the United States about eighty million acres of public land.

The Democrats had committed themselves to a downward revision of the tariff when Cleveland was elected. Cleveland, however, was advised to avoid the tariff problem despite the party's obligation and the country's demand for reform. He disregarded this advice and in 1887 devoted his annual message to Congress to that problem, dramatically demanding a reduction of the tariff for the benefit of the nation. Immediately Roger Q. Mills introduced into the House of Representatives a bill providing for a downward revision of the tariff, and the Senate Republicans led by Nelson W. Aldrich drew up a bill of their own. Neither bill ever reached Cleveland, but the tariff question had been brought to the attention of the country and the Democratic party was forced to adopt tariff reform as its chief issue in the presidential election of 1888. Cleveland, of course, was renominated for the presidency.

Blunt, forthright, and stubborn, Cleveland had not the finesse or personal magnetism to draw people to him. His integrity, dignity, courage, and devotion to duty won him admiration, but his adherence to high principles alienated some Democrats who cared nothing for principles and did not like Cleveland's bluntness. Cleveland realized that there were plenty of Democrats who were lukewarm toward tariff reform, and he made the mistake of allowing two such Democrats to manage his campaign for re-election.[1]

The Republicans nominated Benjamin Harrison of Indiana, grandson of President William Henry Harrison, a Civil War veteran, able lawyer, and former United States senator. Harrison was honest, conscientious, and as stubborn, unimaginative, and aloof as Cleveland. Many of the Republican party leaders found Harrison so frigid in manner that they were uncomfortable in his presence.[2] Most important, however, were Harrison's unassailable political record and his devotion to a high protective tariff. He was the choice of the party bosses,[3] and the Republican campaign manager was Senator Matthew S. Quay of Pennsylvania, boss of the Republican machine in his state and a recognized representative of the alliance between politics and Big Business. Two of the country's leading capitalists, John Wanamaker of Philadelphia and Mark Hanna of Ohio, worked hard to raise a huge campaign fund for the Republicans. The unusual feature of this campaign to maintain the protective tariff was the "direct, open, and aggressive participation of the country's leading capitalists and the new techniques they brought to politics."[4]

Cleveland was defeated, although he had more popular votes than Harrison; the electoral majority went to the Republican. Cleveland's refusal to endorse David Hill, the Democratic candidate for governor of New York, split the party in that state, and

---

[1] Allan Nevins, *Grover Cleveland; A Study in Courage*, p. 415.

[2] *Ibid.*, p. 488; Matthew Josephson, *Politicos, 1865–1896*, p. 481.

[3] Senator Aldrich, Thomas Platt of New York, Stephen B. Elkins of West Virginia, Matthew Quay, the boss of the Pennsylvania Republican machine, and J. S. Clarkson, Republican boss in Iowa, met in secret on June 23, 1888, and agreed upon Harrison as the Republican candidate. Josephson, *Politicos*, p. 418.

[4] *Ibid.*, p. 423.

Hill was elected while Cleveland lost the state which would have won him the election.

Minnesota politics during the first Cleveland administration were in a state of flux. A revolution in politics was threatening. Farmers and laborers were banding together to exert pressure on their own behalf upon the two political parties. In September 1886 the Farmers' Alliance and the Knights of Labor held a joint convention in St. Paul. The convention did not nominate a state ticket but drew up a platform of demands to offer the Republicans and the Democrats; whichever party agreed to incorporate these demands in its platform would be supported by the Alliance-Labor voters. The platform was drafted by the gifted Minnesota radical, Ignatius Donnelly, who had been a Democrat, a Republican, and an Anti-Monopolist. Included in the platform were the following demands: reduced railroad rates; prohibiting the issue of watered stock by the railroad corporations; an amendment to the state constitution limiting the exemption from taxation of railroad property; the establishment of a local system of grain inspection; prohibiting railroad companies from issuing passes to federal, state, and local officials; an income tax law; the establishment of a state bureau of labor statistics; free textbooks in the public schools; aid to injured workers; equal pay for men and women doing the same work; and the prohibition of child labor in mines and factories.[5]

The convention then appointed a committee of thirty, led by Donnelly, to submit their platform to the Democratic and Republican state conventions. The Democrats would have nothing to do with the Alliance-Labor demands, but the Republicans incorporated almost all of them in their state platform. The Republican candidate for governor that year, 1886, was Andrew Ryan McGill of St. Peter, who ran against Dr. A. A. Ames of Minneapolis, the Democratic nominee. The election was not a true test of the strength of the Alliance-Labor-Republican coalition, however, because the liquor issue had been injected into the campaign. The Republicans advocated high license and local option, which Dr. Ames vigorously opposed, and so Ames was strongly backed by the liquor interests of the state. McGill won the election by a

[5] Folwell, vol. 3, pp. 169–70.

small plurality, and Donnelly was elected to the state house of representatives as an independent.[6]

Under McGill a law was passed setting high license fees for liquor dealers, a bureau of labor statistics was established, state farmers' institutes were provided for, and increased railroad regulation was imposed. The state railroad and warehouse commission was given the power to set "just and reasonable" freight rates, but that power was soon declared unconstitutional by the Minnesota Supreme Court.[7]

As the presidential election year rolled around, the Minnesota Republicans were anxious to carry the state for Harrison. They hesitated to nominate McGill again, for they were afraid he would be defeated if the liquor interests once more supported the Democratic candidate for governor. Taking no chances, they nominated William Rush Merriam, a young man from a wealthy family who was president of the Merchants' National Bank in St. Paul. He had served two terms in the legislature and was elected speaker of the house of representatives in 1886.

The Farmers' Alliance and the Knights of Labor decided this election year to organize a third party. At a conference of their leaders they organized the Farm and Labor party and nominated Ignatius Donnelly as their candidate for governor. Donnelly was willing to run but found he lacked support and so threw his influence to Merriam.[8]

This was the year that John A. Johnson of St. Peter made his debut in politics. Nicollet County was normally a stronghold of Republicanism, and there was little hope of political attainment for a Democrat. Johnson, however, took his responsibilities as editor of a Democratic paper seriously and became an active member of the Nicollet County Democratic party. He had plenty of encouragement from Henry Essler, A. L. Sackett, A. J. Lamberton, and others who were anxious to add to their slender ranks a young man of Johnson's ability and social gifts. In the spring of 1888 Johnson took the lead in organizing the Young Men's Democratic Club in St. Peter and became its first president. Essler was then chairman of the Nicollet County Democratic committee.

[6] *Ibid.*, pp. 171–73.
[7] *Ibid.*, p. 179.
[8] *Ibid.*, p. 183, note.

When in August 1888 the time came to elect delegates to the
Nicollet County Democratic convention, Essler and the "Young
Democrats" met and elected fourteen delegates, including Essler
and Johnson. In the columns of his *St. Peter Tribune* editor P. V.
Collins referred to this meeting as a gathering of the "Democratic
Kids." [9]

The "Kids," however, had opposition from some of the older
members of the party, led, strangely enough, by E. St. Julien Cox.
Cox was one of the pioneer settlers of St. Peter, where he had
practiced law. He was active in the Indian wars, served in the
Minnesota legislature, and in 1877 was elected judge of the ninth
judicial district. In 1881 Judge Cox was impeached and convicted
of misconduct in office. His reputation had suffered correspondingly, and his activity in Nicollet County politics in 1888 was a
last attempt to re-establish himself.[10] He called a meeting of some
of his Democratic followers, all "out of their teens," and they
elected a contesting delegation.[11]

The Nicollet County Democratic convention was held in the
courthouse at St. Peter, and both delegations appeared, each declaring itself the legally elected delegation. As chairman of the
party committee for the county, Essler called the meeting to
order, and then Johnson immediately sprang up to nominate E. J.
Boys as chairman of the convention. Judge Cox tried to nominate
Gus Rabe of Nicollet, but Essler refused to recognize Cox. Boys
was made chairman and appointed a credentials committee which
seated the Essler delegates. The convention then proceeded to
elect delegates to the state Democratic convention. John A. Johnson was one of the delegates chosen, who were pledged to support
Eugene M. Wilson for the nomination for governor. At the same
time a committee to guide the Democratic party in Nicollet
County for the next two years was appointed, and Johnson was
named a member of it. For a fledgling Johnson was in the thick
of Democratic politics in his county.[12]

His first experience at a state convention came in August, when
he attended the Democratic convention in St. Paul as a duly

[9] *St. Peter Tribune,* August 15, 1888.
[10] Folwell, vol. 3, pp. 408–18.
[11] *St. Peter Tribune,* August 15, 1888.
[12] *Ibid.*

elected delegate. The chief candidates for the nomination for governor were Eugene Wilson and Dr. A. A. Ames, both from Minneapolis. Wilson, an able lawyer who had served as a representative in Congress, was a man of high ideals and considerable personal popularity.[13] He was backed by the Minnesota Democratic political bosses, Michael Doran and P. H. Kelly. Dr. Ames had been the Democratic gubernatorial candidate in 1886, had served in the state legislature in 1867, and had been mayor of Minneapolis in 1876, 1882, and 1886.[14] He was the candidate of the group which was out to wrest control of the party from the Doran-Kelly machine. The anti-Doran-Kelly faction was no reform wing of the party but a group seeking power for their own interests. In fact, the *St. Paul Pioneer Press,* a Republican newspaper, declared the Doran-Kelly machine the lesser of two evils and referred to Ames as one "whose name alarms, disgusts and repels every decent Democrat." [15] At the convention there was a real fight for control, which could not have been lost on Johnson. The Doran-Kelly faction won. Wilson was nominated for governor and Daniel Buck of Mankato for lieutenant governor. The convention endorsed the Cleveland administration and the Mills tariff bill.

Satisfied with the nomination of Wilson, the Nicollet County delegation returned home to plan for the county convention to nominate candidates for the legislature and county offices. P. V. Collins noted in the *Tribune:* "The Democratic kids swear that there shall not be a delegate in the county convention over thirty-five years of age." [16] He jokingly warned such veterans as A. L. Sackett and A. J. Lamberton to be sure to attend with their birth certificates in their hands, and he pointed out that Editor Johnson expected the Democrats "to reward his flop from the Republican ranks by nominating him for the legislature." [17] Twitting Johnson, Collins declared:

The *Tribune* will be furnished free during the campaign to every delegate to the Democratic convention . . . who will vote for John A. Johnson's nomination for the offices of representative, county auditor, treasurer and probate judge. The *Tribune* will never be mean enough

---

[13] Folwell, vol. 3, p. 183.
[14] *Ibid.,* p. 172.
[15] *St. Paul Pioneer Press,* August 16, 1888.
[16] *St. Peter Tribune,* August 29, 1888.
[17] *Ibid.*

to recognize more than extraordinary ability, and this is a bona fide offer made in good faith as a reward of merit for his modesty in not aspiring to the Court House janitorship too.[18]

The men who had backed Johnson financially were anxious to see him active in the party, and since there were so few young men interested in the Democratic party in Nicollet County, it was perhaps inevitable that Johnson be earmarked for nomination to office. It was probably with a good deal of amusement that he declared he would run for all offices including the governorship.

When on September 11 the St. Peter Democrats met to elect delegates to the county convention, A. L. Sackett presided at the meeting and Johnson was its secretary. Lamberton moved that Judge Cox be barred from participation in Nicollet County Democratic politics, and the motion was carried. When Lamberton, Essler, Johnson, and their followers attended the county convention the next day, Cox and his friends were conspicuously absent. The convention nominated Johnson to run against the Republican candidate, Charles R. Davis, for the state house of representatives. Judge Cox threatened to run for the legislature as an independent if Johnson was nominated, but he did not get any encouragement to try it.[19]

Johnson proved to be an unusually good campaigner, good enough to frighten the Republicans of Nicollet County, who soon began to pay attention to this young Democrat. P. V. Collins urged that the Republicans wage a strong campaign against Johnson. Collins began his own attack fairly late for he admitted afterward he could not find much to criticize about Johnson, whom he considered an able and honest man.[20] But Collins did something he bitterly regretted and for which he apologized to Johnson. In his paper he printed an attack by Judge Cox charging Johnson with the responsibility for allowing his father to be committed to the Nicollet County poorhouse. Actually, although Johnson was a young man at this time, he did not know his father was being committed until the act had been accomplished. To have his father's unfortunate career brought up in his first political campaign hurt Johnson deeply. Never again would he run for

[18] *Ibid.*, September 12, 1888.
[19] *Ibid.*, and September 19, 1888.
[20] *St. Peter Herald*, September 14, 1888.

office without the dread that someone would revive the story of his father's life.

It was not until Johnson had aroused Collins to anger by an article in the *Herald* that Collins began to attack him. On October 17 there appeared in the *Herald* the following brief article:

The visit to St. Paul to see Merriam, by the editor of the *St. Peter Tribune,* previous to that paper endorsing the former's candidacy, recalls the following conversation which actually occurred upon the street a few days prior to the visit.

FARMER: Collins, they say Merriam is using considerable money to secure his election!
COLLINS: So I hear.
FARMER: Why don't you get some of it?
COLLINS: That is what I want and is what I shall have.
*Result of trip*: Editor converted.[21]

Collins was so angry he threatened to sue Johnson, but he declared this would be useless since he knew neither Johnson nor Essler had any money. He accused Johnson of being bought out of the Republican party for the five hundred dollars loaned him by leading Democrats to buy his interest in the *Herald.* Angrily he wrote:

A man who leaves one political party to become an editor for another political party, for revenue only, is not the sort of man to be trusted in places of temptation. Voters are fully justified in suspecting that a man who is a Democrat for revenue only, might become a legislator for revenue only. There will be money influences to tempt legislation this year, as there always is. Can Nicollet County voters whether Democrats or Republicans afford to trust their interests to a youth who within the last two years sold out one party for another for a paltry loan? [22]

Then Collins reprinted in the *Tribune* a letter in Johnson's handwriting in which Johnson had set forth a brief sketch of his past career for the people of Nicollet County:

John A. Johnson, of the firm Essler and Johnson, proprietors of the *St. Peter Herald,* began life in the city which now it is his province to boom. He is a young man of 26 years of age and professionally a

[21] *Freeborn County Standard,* November 2, 1904.
[22] *St. Peter Tribune,* October 24, 1888.

journalist but a year. For nine years he followed the vocation of making pills and potions. In 1886 he accepted the position as paymaster for a railway construction company which position he resigned at the end of the year to assume editorial charge of the *Herald*. While yet young in the profession he stands foremost among the country editors of Minnesota. He finds time for other duties and holds several society offices, among them the captaincy of the local militia company. Through his efforts the company has gained considerable renown and is considered second only to one company in the state, that being the famous Co. D of St. Paul. He is a young man of more than ordinary ability and will some day be heard from.[23]

Johnson must have had fun composing that letter. By no means an egotist, he simply expected others to have a sense of humor too. Collins, however, made the most of the letter by "this renegade Republican, this smart Aleck of 'more than ordinary' self conceit. . . . All men," he wrote, "respect a sincere Democrat. Neither Republicans nor Democrats respect a Benedict Arnold nor an ass." [24] Less bitterly, Collins wrote on October 3: "Johnny Johnson the young man who writes he has more than ordinary ability said last Saturday he did not expect to be elected because the voters of Nicollet County did not know how to vote. Thanks Johnny! But you are wrong again."

On election eve Johnson and his friends gathered in the *Herald* office to await returns from the Associated Press. When it was evident that their candidates had been defeated, they left the office and went home to bed. C. R. Davis defeated Johnson by only one hundred and ninety-six votes; a total of 1303 votes were cast for Davis and 1107 for Johnson.[25] In his first campaign for a political office, at a time when the Republicans carried the state, Johnson made a good showing. Merriam was elected governor by a good plurality, and Harrison carried the state. From the second congressional district, which included Nicollet County, a young Republican by the name of John Lind was re-elected to the national House of Representatives.

John Lind was born in Småland, Sweden, in 1854, seven years before Johnson's birth. His parents brought him to America in

[23] *Ibid.*
[24] *Ibid.*
[25] *Ibid.*, November 14, 1888.

1867, and the family settled on a farm in Goodhue County, Minnesota. At the age of sixteen Lind began his brief career as a school teacher. He read law in a lawyer's office, attended the University of Minnesota for a year, and was admitted to the bar in 1877. He began to practice law in New Ulm, and for two years he also was superintendent of schools for Brown County. Interested in politics, he first ran for Congress on the Republican ticket in 1886.[26] He and Johnson were to become political colleagues and the most widely known men of Swedish extraction in the state.

During the next six years Johnson sought no political office. He continued to comment on politics in the *Herald* and loyally supported the national and state Democratic candidates and policies. He was a member of the credentials committee of the Nicollet County Democratic convention in 1890 and made some political speeches in the campaign. John Lind was again running for re-election to Congress against General James Baker of Blue Earth, who had the support of the Democrats and the Farmers' Alliance.

Even during his brief experience as a Republican, Johnson had favored a low tariff. Now, of course, he supported Baker. Lind had voted for the unpopular tariff bill formulated by William McKinley, representative from Ohio, and Nelson W. Aldrich, senator from Rhode Island, providing for high tariffs to protect "infant industries." At a time when the country was demanding a downward revision of the tariff, this high protective tariff bill was the Republican's answer. When it became a law, a storm of protest broke out all over the nation. Of Lind's action Johnson wrote: "John Lind voted for the McKinley bill. This bill is a blow aimed at every farmer in the United States. Now will these farmers lick the hand that beats them? Will they honor the man who dishonored and defrauded them? Are we so lost to our own interests as to fawn while he bites? Let us say to him, we are done with you and your kind forever." [27]

Lind was the only Republican congressman re-elected from Minnesota. In the other four congressional districts, the Democrats elected three congressmen and the Farmers' Alliance one. This political "revolution" was true of the country at large, for a Democratic majority replaced the Republican majority in the

[26] George M. Stephenson, *John Lind of Minnesota*, chaps. 1–3.
[27] *St. Peter Herald*, October 17, 1890.

House of Representatives, and the Republican majority in the Senate was reduced to eight. McKinley himself failed of re-election. In the gubernatorial field, however, Minnesota remained solidly Republican and re-elected Governor Merriam over the Democratic nominee, Thomas Wilson, and the Farmers' Alliance candidate, Sidney M. Owen. In the state legislature, though, Democrats and Alliance candidates won more seats. Lind's election did not please Johnson, but he was glad that at least Lind was to be the only Republican congressman from the state.[28]

Never a reformer, and always one who believed in making changes slowly, Johnson was no admirer of Ignatius Donnelly, who in 1890 had wanted to be both president of the Minnesota Farmers' Alliance and its candidate for governor. He regarded Donnelly as "a theorist whose only ambition is ambition," [29] a man who for the last twenty-five years had been ready to unite with anybody to advance his political interests.[30] He watched with some impatience the organization of the Populist party in Minnesota and Donnelly's activities as one of its leaders.

The success won by the Farmers' Alliance all over the country in the 1890 elections stimulated agitation for the formation of a national third party.[31] Delegates from groups who were dissatisfied with the two major parties gathered in Omaha in July 1892 to draw up their platform and nominate a candidate for president of the United States. There were farmers, laborers, Greenbackers, Free-Silverites, and the followers of Henry George and Edward Bellamy. Their leaders, however, came chiefly from the ranks of the Farmers' Alliance and included such colorful men as "Pitchfork Ben" Tillman of South Carolina, Tom Watson of Georgia, David H. Waite of Colorado, and the less colorful but dignified and devoted James B. Weaver of Iowa. Donnelly attracted a great deal of attention. Recognized as the greatest orator of Populism, he had made the most of his talent at the convention and had

[28] *Ibid.*, December 5, 1890.
[29] *Ibid.*
[30] *Ibid.*, January 8, May 6, 20, 1892.
[31] John D. Hicks, *Populist Revolt*, pp. 178–81. The Alliance elected its candidates for governor in South Carolina, Tennessee, and Georgia, and elected enough members to the legislatures of those states and Texas, Alabama, Florida, Missouri, Mississippi, and North Carolina to control legislation. About forty-four Alliance men were elected to Congress. In Kansas the lower house of the state legislature was controlled by Alliance men, and in Minnesota and South Dakota the Alliance party held the balance of power in state politics.

written the famous preamble of the party platform. But Donnelly's past record with various reform groups put him out of the question as a presidential candidate. "Donnelly for president on any ticket would have been a joke, and the delegates knew it." [32] Most eligible and the man finally nominated for the presidency was James B. Weaver, who had run once before in 1880 for the Greenback party.

The Populist platform included the following demands: a graduated income tax, a sub-treasury system, free and unlimited coinage of silver, a flexible currency system controlled by the federal government and not by the banks, an increase in the circulating medium, postal savings banks, government ownership and operation of the railroads, telegraph and telephone lines, reclamation of railroad lands illegally held, prohibition of alien land ownership, restriction of immigration, an eight-hour day for labor, prohibition of the use of labor spies, direct election of senators, initiative and referendum, and the Australian ballot.[33] Most of the platform was not new to the Minnesota Farmers' Alliance, but it was regarded by conservatives all over the country as radical and "little short of communism." Johnson regarded Weaver as a man who had been "a rainbow chaser all his life" and the Populist platform as one which only such men as Weaver and Donnelly could advocate.[34]

The Democrats nominated Cleveland again, and the Republicans renominated Harrison. Democrats who wanted administrative honesty, tariff reform, and "unyielding conservatism in all that affected business and finance" [35] brought about Cleveland's nomination. Fearful of the Populists, and knowing the people of the country were disgusted with Harrison's approval of the McKinley tariff and the Sherman Silver Purchase Act, the Democrats were sure they could win with Cleveland. Harrison was easily renominated at the national convention held in Minneapolis, but many Republicans were not satisfied with him. He was not able to talk with a small group of men as easily as he could address a huge crowd. In "meeting a room full of men he froze them all

<hr />

[32] Ibid., p. 235.
[33] Ibid., pp. 210, 231.
[34] St. Peter Herald, July 8, 1892.
[35] Nevins, Grover Cleveland, p. 481.

into enmity." [36] And he had alienated some of the powerful party bosses, such as Quay and Platt, who detested him.

In Minnesota the Populists nominated the logical candidate for governor, Ignatius Donnelly. Since Governor Merriam did not attempt to run a third time, the Republicans by acclamation nominated Knute Nelson of Alexandria, who had proved himself one of the best campaigners and vote getters in the party.

Nelson was a native of Norway who was brought to America by his mother when he was six years old. During his boyhood he lived in Dane County, Wisconsin, and attended the public schools and Albion Academy. When the Civil War broke out Nelson enlisted, serving until 1864, when he was discharged after being seriously wounded and held captive by the Confederates. He then studied law and was admitted to the bar in 1867, and that year, too, he was elected to the Wisconsin house of representatives, where he served two terms. In 1871 he moved to Alexandria, Minnesota, to practice law. He was county attorney for two years and in 1874 was elected to the state senate. Then he served three terms as a representative in Congress, where he developed a reputation for sturdy independence. He had supported the Mills bill and was known to be strongly in favor of a downward revision of the tariff. An expert political strategist, Nelson was popular with his constituents and was to win the support of the whole state for many years to come.[37]

Again a delegate from Nicollet County, Johnson was made one of the secretaries of the Democratic convention and was one of a group of young party members who worked hard for the nomination of Daniel W. Lawler for governor. Lawler was a native of Prairie du Chien, Wisconsin, and a graduate of Georgetown University in Washington, D.C., and of the Columbia University law school. After establishing himself in a law practice in St. Paul, he became the city's corporation attorney.[38] Lawler was made the party nominee, and Johnson worked happily for his election and for Cleveland's.

In the *Herald* Johnson accused Nelson of belonging to "the Shylock firm of Merriam, Hill and Nelson," dictated to by the

[36] *Ibid.*, p. 488.
[37] Martin W. Odland, *Life of Knute Nelson,* pp. 1–158; Folwell, vol. 3, pp. 195–96.
[38] *St. Paul Pioneer Press,* August 4, 1892.

great empire railroad builder, James J. Hill. Lawler, he declared, was "not a railroad lawyer nor the henchman or paid servant of any private corporation and never had been. He would be no man's man and wear no man's collar. Can Knute Nelson say the same? We challenge him or any of his friends to say so." [39] Johnson constantly denounced the McKinley tariff, that "gigantic fraud," and called for the election of Cleveland, which would mean tariff reform. He accused Nelson of "waving the bloody shirt" and stirring up racial prejudice in the country.[40]

In spite of the fact that the election was a landslide for Cleveland, Minnesota remained Republican, cast its presidential electoral votes for Harrison, and elected Nelson. Then much to Johnson's disgust the legislature re-elected Cushman K. Davis to the United States Senate. Davis was a high tariff man for whom Johnson had no respect.[41] The Populists polled less than half the number of votes cast for Lawler, who received 94,600 votes. Too many Populists had opposed the leadership of Donnelly, and many of the disgruntled farmers found Nelson's views so close to those of the Alliance that they voted for him rather than take a chance with Donnelly.[42]

The 1880s and 1890s were years of many industrial strikes, but the *Herald* had little to say about them or about the demands of labor. Johnson, who had a deep aversion to any kind of violence, did deplore the pitched battle between the laborers and Pinkerton detectives during the industrial strife in the Carnegie Steel Company at Homestead, Pennsylvania. The steel company had cut wages and refused to negotiate with the Amalgamated Association of Iron and Steel Workers, who then went on strike. The strikers were locked out, and Pinkerton detectives were employed to protect the "scabs" hired to replace the workers. The clash between the strikers and detectives resulted in loss of life from both groups, and the state militia was called out to break the strike and establish peace. Johnson held that the strikers were wrong in battling with the detectives, since according to the law the company had the right to lock out the strikers and employ the detectives.

[39] *St. Peter Herald*, August 12, 1892.
[40] *Ibid.*, September 9, October 14, 1892.
[41] *Ibid.*, November 25, December 2, 1892, and January 20, 1893.
[42] Hicks, p. 258.

It was not that he believed the steel company was right and the laborers wrong; he thought the laws were wrong. He declared that the laws which allowed such a huge company to exist and act as a tyrant ought to be changed. The remedy was not in conflict between capital and labor but in legislative action against trusts and monopolies. Laws which would protect labor were needed.[43]

When in 1893 Governor John P. Altgeld of Illinois pardoned the three "anarchists" imprisoned as a result of the notorious Haymarket Riot of 1886, he became the focus of attack and criticism from all over the United States. He was charged with being an anarchist and aiding the forces of anarchy. Actually, Altgeld pardoned the men because he thought they were innocent and had been unfairly tried, convicted, and imprisoned. There was never any real evidence of the guilt of these men who had been charged with causing the bomb explosion at a mass meeting of strikers from the McCormick Harvester Company in Chicago. But Johnson was one of the editors who thought Altgeld had made a serious mistake.[44] Altgeld's action, in Johnson's opinion, showed abuse of the governor's power to pardon, and he suggested that the pardoning power be taken away from one man and placed in the hands of the state supreme court or a responsible body of men "less apt to err than one man whose kindness of heart is apt to warp his judgment too far to the side of mercy." [45]

Johnson's sympathy was all for the strikers in the great Pullman strike which occurred in 1894 when Mr. Pullman refused to discuss the grievances of his workers. When the strike paralyzed the transportation system of the United States, Cleveland called out federal troops to break it. Johnson believed the strikers to be right and their grievances just, and he hoped they would win.[46] He noted, however, that in the struggles between capital and labor, capital usually won. He thought strikes should be the last resort for the laborers, who often suffered more harm than good from them. The workers, he felt, should try to find some other means of gaining their demands, and that way should be by legislation.[47]

[43] *St. Peter Herald,* July 15, 1892.
[44] *Ibid.,* June 30, 1893.
[45] *Ibid.,* July 7, 1893.
[46] *Ibid.,* July 21, 1893.          [47] *Ibid.,* April 27, 1894, and September 13, 1895.

In the 1890s a revival of Know-Nothingism appeared in the form of the American Protective Association, which was made up of those Americans who hated and feared the Roman Catholic church. This organization worked to restrict the political rights and power of Catholics, to prevent states from aiding parochial schools and employing Catholics as public-school teachers, to limit immigration, and to make naturalization laws more stringent. Johnson strongly objected to the A.P.A., which he thought was neither Christian nor American in its aims. In the United States, he contended, a man's religion did not, and never should, debar him from political activity and officeholding, and he denounced making politics the basis of war against a religious denomination.[48] "The A.P.A. has got to go," he wrote. "Public sentiment and public policy are against it. It is intolerant and is contrary to the spirit of constitutional liberty. It has no place in the home of a free people." [49] Later in Johnson's career his attitude toward the A.P.A. won him many Catholic votes.

Johnson was a firm supporter of most of Cleveland's policies during the president's second administration. Soon after Cleveland's inauguration, business in the country was paralyzed by the panic of 1893. Railroads went into the hands of receivers, banks closed their doors, factories shut down, the government's gold reserve fell, and by the summer of 1894 there were about four million unemployed. There were a number of contributing factors,[50] but it was Cleveland's belief that the panic was brought about by the monetary uncertainty caused by the passage of the Sherman Silver Purchase Act during Harrison's administration.[51] A sound money man, he moved at once to have the Sherman law repealed. He called a special session of Congress, and in his message declared:

The people of the United States are entitled to a sound and stable currency and to money recognized as such on every exchange and in every market of the world. Their government has no right to injure them by financial experiments opposed to the policy and practice of other civilized states, nor is it justified in permitting an exaggerated

[48] *Ibid.*, November 10, 1893.
[49] *Ibid.*, November 17, 1893.
[50] Nevins, *Grover Cleveland*, pp. 523–25.
[51] Robert McElroy, *Grover Cleveland, The Man and the Statesman*, vol. 2, pp. 16–26.

and unreasonable reliance on our national strength and ability to jeopardize the soundness of the peoples' money. This matter rises above the plane of party politics . . . I earnestly recommend the prompt repeal of the act passed July 14, 1890, authorizing the purchases of silver bullion, and that other legislative action may put beyond all doubt or mistake the intention and ability of the Government to fulfill its pecuniary obligations in money universally recognized by all civilized countries.[52]

The Sherman Silver Purchase Act provided that the government purchase each month not more than 4,500,000 ounces of silver to be paid for in legal tender bills redeemable in gold or silver according to the discretion of the Secretary of the Treasury. The bill pleased no one. The southern and western farmers who wanted free and unlimited coinage of silver and the business interests of the East who favored a strictly gold standard were both disappointed. Foreign countries were on the gold standard, and when the United States appeared to adopt a bimetallic standard, business interests lost confidence. There was no hope that the countries of the world would agree to a bimetallic standard.[53]

A battle royal was staged in Congress over the repeal of the Sherman Act. During the debate in the House of Representatives, a freshman member, William Jennings Bryan of Nebraska, made the most stirring speech of the session. For three hours he spoke against repeal before an intent House and a full gallery. After a grim fight the act was repealed, however, and there was rejoicing among the businessmen and financiers. But the Silverites led by "Silver Dick" Bland of Missouri warned Cleveland that "we have come to the parting of the ways . . . I believe I speak for the great masses of the great Mississippi Valley when I say that we will not submit to the domination of any political party, however much we love it, that lays the sacrificing hand upon silver." [54] Cleveland may have won the battle for the moment, but from now on he had the bitter opposition of the Silverites within the Democratic party, and in 1896 the silver forces gained control of the party.

[52] James D. Richardson, *Messages and Papers of the Presidents*, vol. 9, pp. 404–5.
[53] Nevins, *Grover Cleveland*, p. 536.
[54] "The Parting of the Ways," in William Vincent Byars, *An American Commoner, The Life and Times of Richard Parks Bland*, p. 340.

Johnson heartily agreed with Cleveland on the money question and urged the repeal of the "iniquitous" Sherman Act. He was sure repeal would restore the confidence of businessmen in the government and bring prosperity to the country.[55] Never a convert to "Bryanism," he greatly regretted the division within the Democratic party on the silver issue. So it was easy for Johnson to become friendly with another "sound money" Democrat, Henry Watterson, the famous editor of the *Louisville Courier-Journal*, whom he met in 1894.

"Marse Henry," as Watterson was fondly called, was the writer of vigorous and belligerent editorials, a hotheaded political antagonist, a delightful conversationalist, and an unusual personality. He approved of Cleveland's money policy, but he had been critical of the president's efforts for civil service reform and of his appointments. He had not wanted Cleveland to be nominated in 1892, favoring instead the candidacy of John G. Carlisle of Kentucky. He watched Cleveland's second administration with irritation, for he believed the president by being less stubborn could have held the Democratic party together and with it behind him could have carried the country back to the gold standard once and for all. Instead, he watched Cleveland fight a losing battle with the silver leaders within the party.[56]

Johnson finally succeeded in getting Watterson to come to St. Peter to deliver one of his famous lectures, and on February 9, 1894, Watterson made his first appearance in St. Peter, speaking on "Money and Morals."

Attacking the materialism of Americans, Watterson pointed out that the "genius of the country is no longer engaged upon works of patriotic devotion, on works of imagination, on works of piety. It is engaged in business, in commerce, in constructive enterprises, in development in money-making." [57] Here in the United States, he declared, moral standards were low and money standards high, and it was the drive for accumulating wealth which was the danger of the whole country:

And this Money Devil is the lion right across the highway of your

[55] *St. Peter Herald*, October 30, November 3, 1893.
[56] Henry Watterson, *"Marse Henry," An Autobiography*, vol. 2, pp. 143–44.
[57] Henry Watterson, *Compromises of Life and Other Lectures and Addresses*, pp. 127–28.

future, standing just at the fork of the roads, one of which leads up the heights of national fame and glory, the other down into the depths of plutocracy, which yawns before us, opening its ponderous jaws and licking its bloody lips to swallow all that is great and noble in our national life. Already it costs a million of dollars to set a Presidential ticket in the field, already a hundred thousand dollars to sustain a contest for a seat in the Senate of the United States; how long shall it be before our public men become a race of Medician princes without the learning, or the arts of Florence, the Presidential chair itself a mere commodity to be auctioned off to the highest bidder? Beware of that Money Devil! Beware of the man who puts his party above his country, his pocket above his conscience.

He went on to warn and advise:

We must cast forth the devil of party spirit, and kill the Money Devil outright, if we are to reach the summit of our destiny. The statesmanship which is to lead us thither must address itself somewhat more to the moral nature of the people; it must seek, indeed, to unite tradition and progress, going forward at all times, but never forgetting the humble homespun source of our being as a nation and as a people.[58]

Much impressed by Watterson's speech, Johnson enthusiastically reviewed it in the *Herald*. If the moral danger to the country lay in the devotion of so many men to the money god, Johnson thought the American people should stir themselves to nominate and elect men to public office who would give their whole energy and intelligence to the service of the people.[59] In an editorial written a few weeks after Watterson delivered his speech, Johnson declared that the world of politics then did not offer much to a young man of ability:

To win now, one must be cunning, expert in device and learned in the art of deception. . . . To politize or play the politician one must sacrifice his honor, his integrity and his manhood and what is worse and more deplorable still, he must have lots of money and be willing to spend it. As Watterson says, the danger to this nation lies not in changes in the tariff schedules but in the losses of principle, a want of conscience and the selfish love of money and preferment.[60]

He went on to urge people to think through the issues of the day and not vote blindly for a political party as a matter of habit.

[58] *Ibid.*, pp. 132–34.  [59] *St. Peter Herald*, February 16, 1894.  [60] *Ibid.*, March 2, 1894.

Watterson's lecture was so well received in St. Peter that he was invited to return the following year to deliver his famous address on Abraham Lincoln. During these two visits Johnson and Watterson became friends. Johnson continued to follow Watterson's views as expressed in the *Courier-Journal,* and Watterson never forgot Johnson. Later in Johnson's career Henry Watterson was influential in bringing the Minnesota Democrat to the attention of the whole country.

The year Johnson first met Henry Watterson, 1894, was one of the darkest the country had experienced for a long time. The repeal of the Sherman Act did not halt the steady drain of gold from the treasury. Hurriedly the holders of silver certificates brought them to the treasury to be redeemed in gold, and the government, legally or otherwise, could not refuse to redeem them. In order to build up the gold reserve the government sponsored a series of sales of government bonds to be paid for in gold, but since the purchasers simply drew gold from the treasury to purchase the bonds, the gold supply was not augmented. Not until the Treasury Department floated the fourth and last loan did the gold crisis come to an end. By 1894, also, there was a deficit in the treasury as a result of the heavy national expenditures pledged by the "Billion Dollar" Congress under Harrison, and the McKinley tariff had brought a reduction of income from customs duties. The great Pullman strike was just one of several strikes that disturbed the country that year, and this was the year Cleveland did his best to get Congress to revise the tariff.[61]

In consultation with the president, William L. Wilson, chairman of the House Ways and Means Committee, had prepared a tariff bill which embodied Cleveland's ideas of admitting raw materials free of duty and imposing a moderate duty on manufactured goods. Here was an attempt to reduce tariff rates, and the House of Representatives passed the bill. The Senate, where the business interests were entrenched, gave formidable opposi-

[61] Cleveland and Henry Watterson had ceased speaking to each other over the tariff plank in the 1892 national platform. Watterson was a free trade advocate and demanded that a ringing condemnation of the McKinley tariff be put in the platform, as well as the declaration that a high protective tariff was unconstitutional. Cleveland, who saw the possibility of losing many votes by accepting Watterson's suggestions and who was more moderate on the subject of the tariff, had to be persuaded to accept the plank which Watterson and his friends put over.

tion. There were forty-four Democrats, thirty-eight Republicans, three Populists, and three vacancies in the Senate, and not even all the Democratic senators favored the Wilson bill.

For five months the Senate debated and modified the Wilson bill, and the result was called the Gorman bill. With over six hundred amendments which completely changed the character of the original bill and removed coal, sugar, and iron ore from the free list, the Senate bill went to the House and thence to a conference committee. The bill that finally emerged became law without Cleveland's signature because, although he was dissatisfied with the bill, he considered it an improvement on the McKinley tariff.

The Wilson-Gorman tariff was a defeat for Cleveland and the tariff reformers; it was a high tariff measure in spite of a few reductions here and there. To counterbalance any reduction in customs duties, one provision of the bill placed a two per cent tax on incomes over four thousand dollars, but the Supreme Court in 1895 declared this provision unconstitutional.[62]

The elections of 1894 once more brought about a complete reversal in Congress. This time the Republicans won a large majority in the House and a plurality in the Senate, and Populists took many votes from the Democratic party in the South and West. Johnson took an active part in the election in Minnesota. A delegate to the state Democratic nominating convention, he mingled with the party leaders and was offered the nomination for secretary of state.[63] There seemed to be little hope for a Democratic victory in Minnesota in 1894, and Johnson refused what he regarded a barren honor. The Democrats nominated a veteran leader of the party, George L. Becker, for governor. The Republicans renominated the popular Knute Nelson, and the Populists, turning away from Donnelly, nominated Sidney M. Owen.

In their platform the Republicans declared themselves in favor of bimetallism, a protective tariff, the suppression of trusts, arbitration of labor disputes, exclusion of undesirable immigrants, generous pensions for veterans, a single six-year term for the president and vice-president, reasonable charges for the transportation of agricultural products, and taxation of land granted by the gov-

[62] McElroy, vol. 2, pp. 107–19; Nevins, *Grover Cleveland*, pp. 563–88.
[63] *St. Peter Herald*, August 31, 1894; *St. Peter Tribune*, August 29, 1894.

ernment to the railroads but not used for railroad purposes.[64] The Democrats endorsed the Cleveland administration and the national platform of 1892 and favored direct election of senators by the people. The Populists stood upon their 1892 national platform, advocating also the prohibition of trusts and other unlawful combinations, the enforcement of all laws governing all corporations, initiative and referendum, woman suffrage, nationalization of the sale of liquor to be manufactured by the state on a nonprofit basis, and the prohibition of the use of public money for sectarian purposes.[65]

Pledged to support the Democratic state ticket, Johnson returned to Nicollet County to attend the county nominating convention on September 15. At this time he seemed to have no real political ambition. He could write: "There is truly a fascination about politics, but there is also a fascination about a happy hearthstone before which the other dwindles into insignificance." [66] Johnson had just married and was evidently enjoying life in his home. Just before he went to the state Democratic convention, he wrote in the *Herald*, under the heading "The Philosopher":

I ran for office but once. This was some years ago, and at the earnest solicitation of my friends, in an unguarded moment, I allowed my name to be used as a candidate for the office as representative of the people. How was I to represent them if elected never occurred to me; I was willing to represent them and that was enough. If I live to celebrate my hundredth anniversary I shall never forget the scene of wild excitement which was occasioned by my nomination, at least it seemed so to me. Those tender words of encouragement and congratulation, those visions of future distinction and greatness. No one could pass through such a moment and forget it. I accepted the endorsement of my character and fitness and sailed out to win, expecting to carry every town by storm. Prior to this move I had been considered a decent kind of man, but when the organ of the opposition appeared, revelations were made which not only froze myself and friends but would have chilled the blood of a Sioux Indian. A susceptible public was gravely informed that I was not fit for office, that I was foolish, besides that, I had existed under very suspicious circumstances. It would have said that I starved my deaf old grandmother to death

[64] Folwell, vol. 3, p. 198.
[65] *Ibid.*, pp. 198–200.
[66] *St. Peter Herald*, September 28, 1894.

. . . that I had stolen my grandfather's clothes and sold them. It would have said these things in addition to what it did say had it not been for the fact that everybody knew that I never had anything to do with a grandparent of either persuasion. What was true in my case is equally true of almost everybody that tinctures his soul with politics. I was lucky in being beaten; it was not a blessing to the other man that he was victorious . . . I agree . . . that "business is business" but politics is something else.[67]

Yet Johnson believed it was his duty, at least in his county, to run for office if he was asked to do so. When he was nominated by acclamation by the county convention he accepted, and this time he felt he had some chance of being elected.[68] Reporting on the convention, he wrote:

For the position of senator, the choice fell upon the writer. He was born and raised in Nicollet County and has resided there continuously. Eight years ago he became a part owner of this paper and is known to the voters of the county with whom he is perfectly satisfied to leave the matter of election. All we wish to say is: so far as he is concerned, the campaign shall be void of personalities and conducted solely upon its merits. If elected he shall endeavor to honestly do his duty, favoring none and serving all.[69]

The Republicans of Nicollet County split over the nominee for state senator. Their county convention had regularly nominated John Peterson, a native of Sweden who came to the United States in 1869. He became a railroad contractor, served on the St. Peter city council from 1881 to 1895, and was a member of the board of trustees of Gustavus Adolphus College and a director of the State Hospital for the Insane. No Republican had any objection to Peterson, but his nomination was disappointing to C. R. Davis, who wanted the office himself. Davis had defeated Johnson for the state house of representatives in 1888 and had been elected to the senate in 1890. He wanted to be re-elected, and, ignoring the action of the Republican county convention, he announced himself as an independent candidate for the state senate.[70]

The split among the Republicans brought into existence a new

[67] *Ibid.*, August 3, 1894.
[68] *Ibid.*, September 21, 1894; *St. Peter Tribune*, September 19, 1894.
[69] *St. Peter Herald*, September 21, 1894.
[70] *St. Peter Tribune*, August 29, 1894.

Republican newspaper, the *St. Peter Free Press*, edited by H. C. Miller, who strongly supported Davis. The *St. Peter Tribune* had backed Davis in the past, but disgusted with him now, it took the lead in opposing him and supporting Peterson. Davis had angered many Republicans in Nicollet County because, contrary to his campaign pledge, he had voted against Cushman K. Davis when the latter was a candidate for re-election to the United States Senate. Johnson thought this situation in the Republican party would elect him, and he called upon all the Democrats to support their ticket. If elected, wrote Editor Johnson of candidate Johnson:

. . . he will fulfill every promise he makes and will do exactly as he agrees. If elected he will represent the people to the extent of his ability and will stand between the people and the greedy corporations. He will vote for any measure which will promote the public good and will vote for any measure in the interests of the farmer, laborer and the mechanic. He promises this and he will do it. He has been schooled in poverty, and believes that capital can take care of itself and that laws should be enacted in the interest of the great mass of the people. He believes in taxing Pullman car property. He believes in taxing mining lands. He believes in regulating express and other rates of transportation upon an equitable and just basis.[71]

The St. Peter Democrats organized to elect Johnson,[72] and he made many campaign speeches. During the last week in October and the first week in November, Johnson spoke in Belgrade, Courtland, Norseland, New Sweden, Granby, Traverse, West Newton, and North Mankato. He did his best but the Republicans carried the whole state including Nicollet County. Peterson was elected with a vote of 1075. Johnson received 942 votes, and Davis polled 716 votes.[73] The Democrats had anticipated defeat, but they had not expected to be "wiped off the earth." Nelson was swept into the governor's office with a vote of 147,943, a plurality of 60,053 over Owen, who received more votes than Becker. Minnesota, as usual, was satisfied with the Republican administration.

On November 9 there appeared in the *Herald* a "Card of Thanks" signed John A. Johnson:

[71] *St. Peter Herald*, October 19, 1894.
[72] *Ibid.*, October 26, 1894.
[73] *Legislative Manual of the State of Minnesota*, 1895, p. 473.

When a member of one's family passed to that bourn from which few
if any strangers ever return, it is usually customary for certain relatives of the deceased to publish a card of thanks to those who have
kindly rendered assistance during the period of bereavement. It is
rarely if ever the case that the one who dies feels called upon to thank
those who buried him or even those who attempted to keep him alive.
In political death this condition can be reversed and the man who
suffers political decease is permitted to perform this duty for himself.
It is a privilege of the undersigned to say to the many kind friends
who so firmly stood by him in the late campaign that he not only returns his warmest and most sincere thanks, but is also filled with a
kindness which will never permit him to forget their friendship. . . .
To these he desires also to say that he will look for an opportunity
to repay them with acts of equal kindness. For those who honestly
and openly opposed him upon grounds of principle, he has only respect
and admiration. For those who pretended to be his friends but con-
nived to defeat him, by the use of a political stiletto he can only say
that while he does not approve of their conduct he hopes he can forget and forgive. A political campaign always engenders bitterness and
feeling. This is unfortunate and no one deplores this more than the
writer. At the outset he determined to conduct a campaign free from
venom and personal abuse and he is proud to say he maintained that
course throughout. Time will wear away the few rough edges and political enemies will again be friends. In the election as such he finds
little occasion for thanksgiving; at the same time he thanks fortune
for living through it and being again in a position to edit a newspaper.
For our friends we have only thanks and for our conquerors we have
an olive branch which we trust will be accepted.

Four years passed before Johnson again ran for political office,
and during those years much happened to change the course of
the Democratic party. Disgusted with the repeal of the Sherman
Silver Purchase Act and disappointed in the Wilson-Gorman tariff,
the agrarian interests of the South and West became more dis-
contented. Many felt that Cleveland had failed the laborers when
he allowed federal forces to be called out against the Pullman
strikers. The growing strength of the Populists alarmed the eastern conservative business and financial interests. Bryan came close
to victory in running for the Senate in the Republican state of
Nebraska on a free silver, pro-labor, and anti-railroad platform.
The Republicans, too, had trouble with the free silver element.

During 1895 and 1896 the "silver craze" spread across the West "like a prairie fire." In western and southern states "Silver Democrats" gained control of the state organizations, and Senator Teller of Colorado, a "Silver Republican," prepared "to lead his Western followers into the new crusade" for silver with the Silver Democrats.[74] Among the people, too, a strong cry against monopolies and trusts was heard.

With the Democratic party split into factions for and against Cleveland, Mark Hanna, the Republican boss of Ohio, took advantage of the discord and began to build up his candidate for the presidency, William McKinley, who was governor of Ohio. When the Republican National Convention met in St. Louis in 1896, the nomination of Hanna's candidate was a foregone conclusion. But the attempt of McKinley and Hanna to make the tariff the chief issue of the campaign failed. The eastern capitalists had made it clear they would not assist the party unless it stood firm for "sound money," [75] and a gold plank was included in the party platform. Whereupon the Silver Republicans, led by Senator Teller, bolted the convention.

Soon after the Republican convention a group of Minnesota's Silver Republicans also bolted the party. Sixteen of them, including John Lind, Frank Day, Charles A. Towne, Frank Nye, and J. B. Sanborn, issued a declaration that the Republican party had repudiated a fundamental doctrine of the party in rejecting bimetallism, which the party had advocated since 1888, and the signers pledged themselves to the bimetallic standard.[76] Both Lind and Day had promising futures as Republicans. They had everything to lose and little to gain by their action. Johnson had great respect for these men for their adherence to their beliefs and their independence of action. He did not agree with their views, but he deplored the way the Republican newspapers criticized and attacked them.[77]

The Democratic National Convention met in Chicago in July. Both "Silver Dick" Bland and William Jennings Bryan had been at work organizing the Silver Democrats. Both had done everything they could, too, to get the Silver Republicans to unite with

[74] Josephson, *Politicos*, p. 619.    [75] *Ibid.*, pp. 655–58.
[76] *Martin County Sentinel*, July 10, 1896.
[77] *St. Peter Herald*, July 3, August 14, 1896.

them. Bland had a strong lobby at the Republican convention, and Bryan had attended. They had issued an "Appeal to the Silver Democrats," urging them to unite and gain control of the party organization. The Silver Democrats took heed, and by the time the convention met they had control of the party. They were ready to write a silver platform and nominate a silver candidate for the presidency. The "sound money" Democrats thought Cleveland was the safest man to lead the party, but they lost control to those who had vigorously repudiated Cleveland. The president himself was determined not to run for a third term,[78] but he lent his moral support to the "Gold Democrats."

The conservative Gold Democrats had control of the national committee and sought to make David B. Hill of New York temporary chairman of the convention. The Free-Silverites, however, rejected Hill and elected John W. Daniel. They also overruled the national committee and seated contesting silver delegations, including the Bryan delegation from Nebraska. Senator White of California was chosen permanent chairman. Then came the debate on the platform. Hill and Governor William E. Russell of Massachusetts spoke for the gold plank, then "Pitchfork Ben" Tillman so fiercely denounced Cleveland and so vehemently demanded the silver plank that at times he was incoherent. Disappointed in Tillman, the crowd of about twenty thousand people waited with intense excitement as William Jennings Bryan made his way to the platform.

Bryan, the "silver-tongued orator of the Platte," was only thirty-six years of age in 1896. A country-town lawyer who never had made much money, he had a brief political career behind him. He had served in the national House of Representatives for two terms and had been defeated in his campaign for the Senate. In 1892 he won national attention by his speech on the tariff and in 1893 for his opposition to the repeal of the Sherman Silver Purchase Act. From 1894 to the convention in 1896 Bryan had worked to organize the silver forces and also to prepare the way for his own nomination for the presidency. He had attended the Republican convention in St. Louis ostensibly as a reporter for the *Omaha World-Herald*. Actually he was there to give all the

[78] McElroy, vol. 2, pp. 214–15.

encouragement he could to the Silver Republicans. Later Bryan wrote: "The convention turned out as I expected and the looked for bolt took place. I felt that the action of this convention would have a large influence at Chicago." [79] When Charles A. Towne, a Silver Republican from Minnesota, "exultant over the developments at St. Louis, said to Bryan, 'We are going to Chicago to nominate Senator Teller! You had better come along and help us!' Bryan replied curtly, 'I can't do it. I am going to be nominated myself.' " [80]

A single-minded fanatic, an evangelist, and an orator with power to sway huge crowds, Bryan saw himself leading a great crusade for free silver. Far from modest about his political ambitions, Bryan and his wife had written thousands of letters to state organizations and leaders of the party enlisting their support, and at the convention he spoke seriously to delegates, asking for their votes. "Carefully the young man wheeled himself into position to be struck by presidential lightning. He was delighted when he contrived to appear in the momentous debate over the silver plank, serving as one of the 'keynoters' of the Western silver uprising within the party. It was a further stroke of luck that he was the last speaker for the silver faction and was given additional time in return for augmented speaking time asked by the opposing Gold Democrats — Hill, Vilas, and Russell." [81]

Bryan's speech had been carefully prepared and rehearsed, and he knew it expressed the feelings of most of the convention. It was a great speech — dignified, impassioned, and ringing — and Bryan, handsome and confident, delivered it with such fervor and eloquence that he completely won his audience and made his nomination a certainty. Later he said:

From the first sentence the audience was with me. My voice reached to the uttermost parts of the hall. . . . I shall never forget the scene upon which I looked. I believe it unrivaled in any convention ever held in our country. The audience seemed to rise and sit down as one man. At the close of a sentence it would rise and shout, and when I began upon another sentence, the room was still as a church. There was inspiration in the faces of the delegates.[82]

[79] *Memoirs of William Jennings Bryan*, p. 100.
[80] Paxton Hibben, *Peerless Leader, William Jennings Bryan*, pp. 180–81.
[81] Josephson, *Politicos*, p. 671.
[82] *Memoirs of William Jennings Bryan*, p. 115.

Pandemonium broke loose in the convention hall when Bryan concluded his speech.[83] The demonstration lasted for almost an hour, and some of the Nebraska delegation carried Bryan on their shoulders as they marched around the hall. The silver forces had found their "Moses." Bryan left the convention hall, and Mrs. Bryan kept him informed of the balloting for presidential nominees by telephone from the stage of the convention.[84] The balloting took place the day after Bryan's speech. The most prominent candidates for the nomination had been Senator Richard Bland of Missouri, Horace Boies, ex-governor of Iowa, and Senator Henry M. Teller of Colorado. J. K. Jones of Arkansas and "Pitchfork Ben" Tillman of South Carolina had also looked longingly at the prospects of nomination. Bland was the strongest candidate, and until Bryan's speech it was believed he would be nominated. But Bland was handicapped, it was thought, in that he was a southerner and had a Roman Catholic wife. Also, he was an old man. On the first three ballots Bryan ran second to Bland, on the fourth ballot he took the lead, and on the fifth ballot he was nominated.[85]

Cleveland had been repudiated, a silver plank adopted, and the Populist planks incorporated into the Democratic platform. Hating "Bryanism," Cleveland gave as much support as he could to the Gold Democrats, who met in convention in Indianapolis in September and nominated John M. Palmer of Illinois for the presidency.[86] The Silver Republicans met in St. Louis and by acclamation nominated Bryan as their candidate. Minnesota's congressman, Charles A. Towne, was permanent vice-chairman of this convention.[87] At the same time the Populists also met in St. Louis, and they, too, accepted Bryan as their nominee. The "Great Commoner" found himself supported by Democrats, Silver Republicans, and Populists, and the leader of a great popular cause — not just the cause of free silver, but a struggle by the agrarian interests of the South and West to take control of the government from the business and financial interests of the East.

[83] For the complete text of this famous address see *Speeches of William Jennings Bryan*, vol. 1, pp. 238–49.
[84] Hibben, p. 186.
[85] Josephson, *Politicos*, pp. 667–68, 678–79.
[86] McElroy, vol. 2, pp. 223–37.
[87] William Jennings Bryan, *First Battle: A Story of the Campaign of 1896*, pp. 238–58.

As a Cleveland Democrat, John A. Johnson was not happy over the action of the Democratic convention. He believed Bryan to be an able man as well as a brilliant speaker, but he was no free silver advocate. In the *Herald* he stated his reaction to the platform:

The platform is not a desirable one. It does not meet with democratic approval and aside from the plank on the free coinage of silver, is a platform which will not stand the test of the coming campaign of sober judgment. This paper has been for so-called sound money. It is not for an absolute gold standard nor is it for an absolute silver standard which it seems would follow upon the adoption of the free and unlimited coinage of silver.[88]

When the Minnesota Silver Republicans nominated John Lind for governor, Johnson was not enthusiastic, although he considered Lind a more worthy candidate than the regular Republican nominee, Governor David Clough, for whom he had little respect.[89] The Silver Democrats, led by Leonard A. Rosing of Cannon Falls, T. D. O'Brien of St. Paul, and Charles d'Autremont of Duluth, controlled the Minnesota Democratic party, and they wrote a silver plank for the platform and by acclamation nominated Lind as their gubernatorial candidate. Daniel Lawler had been deposed as national committeeman and replaced by T. D. O'Brien. Lawler and others who agreed with him came together and nominated Dr. A. A. Ames for governor on a gold plank platform. The Minnesota Populists also accepted Lind as their candidate, so Lind ran as the candidate of the Fusion ticket. When he accepted the Populist nomination, Lind declared that he accepted "not as a Democrat, not as a Populist, nor a Republican, but as a citizen of our great state in hearty sympathy with the aims and endeavors of the united reform forces." [90]

Johnson looked at the matter from a narrower viewpoint. He regarded the nomination of Lind by all three groups as a spontaneous rebellion against the Hill-Clough-Merriam machine which had run the state so long.[91] This year of party bolting did not affect him. He believed anyone had the privilege to change his party

[88] *St. Peter Herald*, July 17, 1896.
[89] *Ibid.*, July 24, 1896.
[90] Stephenson, *John Lind*, p. 110.
[91] *St. Peter Herald*, August 21, 1896.

affiliation and should be admired for his independence in doing it.[92] But Johnson himself, once he had joined the Democrats, was always a party regular. By no means satisfied with Bryan and the national platform, Johnson nonetheless accepted both as the will of the majority of the party and as a loyal party member supported Bryan and Lind. It was not difficult for him to support Lind, for he believed Lind, if elected, would have nothing to do with the money question. He would be concerned with the administration of the affairs of Minnesota, and Johnson thought John Lind could be trusted with that.[93] What Johnson did not like was the alignment of class against class and section against section which Bryan had so clearly called for in his "Cross of Gold" speech.[94]

Lind made a hard campaign, traveling around the state speaking for free silver. Bryan came to Minnesota in October and spoke in several places, including St. Paul, Duluth, St. Cloud, and Anoka. But Senators Knute Nelson and C. K. Davis both stumped for Clough and "hard money." J. J. Hill assisted Mark Hanna in raising a huge amount of money to defeat Bryan. Even with the support of the silver and copper barons of the West, the Democrats could never hope to raise the money that Hanna got for McKinley's campaign. Against the financial and business interests of the country Bryan fought a losing battle. Many voters were stirred to support the "Great Commoner" in his crusade for the people, but many others were frightened into voting for McKinley by the Republican warnings against that "radical" and "anarchist" candidate Bryan, who was threatening the security of the whole country.

After an intensely exciting campaign, McKinley was elected by an overwhelming vote. In Minnesota his plurality over Bryan was 62,768, but Governor Clough's plurality over Lind was only 3552. Dr. Ames received 2890 votes. James T. McCleary, who had succeeded Lind in Congress, was re-elected over his free silver opponent, Frank A. Day.[95] Ignatius Donnelly, who had gone to the Populist National Convention hoping to become the Populist can-

[92] *Ibid.*
[93] *Ibid.*, September 4, 1896.
[94] *Ibid.*
[95] *Legislative Manual*, 1897, pp. 417, 487, 490.

didate for president, was elected representative to the state legislature. During the campaign he had supported Bryan and Lind.[96]

Free silver had been beaten at the polls. Business and finance had won over the agrarian interests of the South and West. Nevertheless, Minnesota, while standing firmly for McKinley, came fairly close to electing the Fusion candidate in 1896. And in 1898 Lind, as the Fusion candidate for governor, was to win. According to Lind's biographer, who has made a careful study of the election, Bryan and Lind were defeated in Minnesota in 1896 by the "conservative German, Swedish, and Norwegian voters, to whom Bryan's free silver remedy for the ills that beset the state was so radical that they believed it bordered on dishonesty." [97]

[96] Folwell, vol. 3, pp. 222–23.
[97] Stephenson, *John Lind*, p. 122.

## CHAPTER IV

*Victory and Defeat*

THE poverty of Johnson's early years and the nearly fatal attack of typhoid fever had left their effect upon the constitution of the tall, thin man. During the year 1896 Johnson suffered from attacks of severe abdominal pain. At first he ignored them, but as they increased in number he was forced to be concerned. He had an attack once when Dr. William J. Mayo of Rochester was making a visit to the St. Peter Hospital for the Insane. Mrs. Johnson called Dr. Mayo, who examined Johnson and advised him to come to Rochester for a thorough physical examination. Johnson put it off as long as he could, but his wife finally persuaded him to make the trip.

It was natural that the Johnsons should turn to the Mayo brothers when they needed medical attention. Nora Johnson had known the old doctor and his sons since her childhood. John had met Dr. Will and Dr. Charlie when they came on regular visits to the St. Peter Hospital for the Insane. Dr. H. A. Tomlinson, the superintendent of the hospital, frequently invited Johnson to his home when the Doctors Mayo were there. Dr. Will was the same age as Johnson, and they became good friends. It was Dr. Will who came to be Johnson's physician.[1]

On January 4, 1897, the Johnsons went to Rochester, and when Dr. Mayo operated he found an abscessed appendix and intestinal adhesions. Because of Johnson's condition, his appendix could not be removed and drains were put in the wound. The operation had proved a very serious one, and Johnson remained in Rochester for a month. For some reason he was not told at the time that his appendix had not been removed,[2] and from his hospital bed he wrote a letter to his readers about the operation:

[1] Elinor Johnson Smith and Henry N. Benson to W. G. H.
[2] Elinor Johnson Smith to W. G. H.

The little thing is gone. That small but sensitive being has been removed. No plow or wheel scraper was necessary. A man whom we could lick in thirty minutes if he dared enter our sanctum to "find the editor," simply spent a few minutes with a scalpel and the dear appendix which has given me so many evidences of its attachment, was put to rest in a pail. . . . Just how it was done is not perfectly clear to me at this moment, and any treatise upon the object of so much of my affection would be, of necessity, ambiguous or incoherent.[3]

He went on to express great admiration for Dr. Will's surgical skill. "Of the Drs. Mayo . . . it is not necessary to speak. Their renown would not be enhanced by aught I might say. The wonderful things reported of them are not exaggerations." [4]

Johnson returned from Rochester on February 2,[5] but for a while he was most uncomfortable. His wound finally healed, however, and by August he was well enough to join the Minnesota editors on their summer excursion to Milwaukee and Detroit.[6] This was a vacation for both Nora and John, and they enjoyed the trip even though it could not have been very restful, for the editors were royally entertained by their fellow editors of Detroit and Milwaukee.[7] Returning home, Johnson settled down to his editorial duties. He felt well and had no anticipation of a return of his ailment.

But during the following spring — a little over a year after his first operation — Johnson suffered more of the abdominal attacks. At times the pain became so agonizing that his doctor in St. Peter was obliged to give him morphine to help him bear it.[8] In April 1898 the Johnsons went again to Rochester, and John underwent a second operation by Dr. Will Mayo.[9] This time his appendix was removed,[10] and for a while Johnson felt well, but not for long. Until his death he suffered from recurrent intestinal abscesses, and for the rest of his life he experienced almost constant pain. Mrs. Johnson anxiously watched his face each day to see how he was feeling. Only a few of his close friends knew he suffered as he did.

[3] *St. Peter Herald,* January 29, 1897.
[4] *Ibid.*
[5] *Ibid.*, February 5, 1897.
[6] *St. Peter Free Press,* August 31, 1897.
[7] Day and Knappen, pp. 106–8.
[8] Elinor Johnson Smith to W. G. H.
[9] *St. Peter Tribune,* April 20, 1898.
[10] Elinor Johnson Smith to W. G. H.

To questions about his health he always replied that he was feeling fine. But his suffering showed in his eyes and in the deepening lines in his face. With infinite patience he bore the pain and never made any mention of it except to his wife when he needed help.[11]

Hardly recovered from his second operation, Johnson plunged into the political campaign of 1898.[12] On June 6 he was again elected a delegate from Nicollet County to the Democratic state convention, which was scheduled to meet in Minneapolis on June 15.[13] Earlier it had been agreed upon by party leaders that the Fusion parties would all hold their conventions in Minneapolis on the same day, and that John Lind would again be the nominee to head the Fusion ticket.[14] In April, however, Lind had enlisted in the Twelfth Minnesota Regiment of the United States Army, for the United States was involved in the war with Spain. The three parties — Democratic, Silver Republican, and Populist — met separately according to plan, and each nominated Lind for the governorship. Johnson still regarded Lind as a Silver Republican, not as a Democrat, and Lind himself in his first important speech of the campaign said he did not know that he belonged to any political party. "Perhaps it might be said of me that I am a political orphan," [15] he told his audience. Johnson supported Lind and the Fusion ticket, and wrote, "It's a fact that when Johnnie comes marching home it will be to accept the office of governor. He is going to be elected as sure as shooting." [16]

The Republicans experienced a bitter fight over their nominee for the governorship. Governor Clough and his political followers made a great effort to nominate Samuel R. Van Sant, a Winona businessman and Civil War veteran who had served in the state legislatures of 1893 and 1895. Judge Loren W. Collins, associate justice of the Minnesota Supreme Court and also a Civil War veteran, had supporters at the convention who were anxious to see him nominated.

[11] Elinor Johnson Smith, Henry N. Benson, and Mr. and Mrs. George Nutter to W. G. H.

[12] St. Peter Tribune, May 11, 1898. He returned to St. Peter on May 9 from Rochester.

[13] St. Peter Herald, June 10, 1898.

[14] Stephenson, John Lind, pp. 132–33. The decision to run Lind again as a Fusion candidate was made at the Jackson Day banquet held by the Democrats in Minneapolis, January 11, 1898. Lind was believed by many to be one of the most able men of the state.

[15] Ibid., p. 150.      [16] St. Peter Herald, July 1, 1898.

The third aspirant for the nomination was William Henry Eustis, a Minneapolis lawyer of exceptional ability and high character. A native of New York state, a graduate of Columbia University law school, and a man of professional experience, Eustis migrated to Minneapolis to practice law in 1881. He took an active part in the business and political affairs of the city and state. In 1892 he was elected mayor of Minneapolis, and it was partly due to his efforts that the Republican National Convention was held in the city that year.[17] The Republicans who supported Eustis were out to overthrow the Clough machine and to nominate for governor a man who was known to be free from the control of machine politicians. After a long struggle and three ballots, Eustis won the nomination.

There were some disgruntled Populists — or Mid-Roaders, as they were called — who had had enough of fusion and wanted to put a ticket of their own in the field. Led by Ignatius Donnelly, they bolted the Populist convention, met by themselves, and nominated Lionel C. Long, an editor and publisher, for governor with Ignatius Donnelly for the United States Senate.

In September, down in Nicollet County, Johnson was nominated by acclamation for the state senate on the Democratic ticket to run against the Republican nominee, J. S. Carlson, a professor at Gustavus Adolphus College in St. Peter.[18] Johnson announced his nomination in the *Herald* and stated that the editor "leaves his candidacy in the hands of the people. If elected he will serve the public with the best efforts he can give and if defeated will take his defeat philosophically, knowing that someone has got to be beaten." [19] The *St. Peter Tribune* and the *Free Press* took similar positions: ". . . the *Free Press* has nothing but the kindest regard for Mr. Johnson, but it cannot support him for state senator as against Prof. J. S. Carlson." [20] No one seemed to have any real reason for opposing Johnson except that he was

---

[17] "William Henry Eustis — An Autobiography," *Minneapolis Journal*, December 22, 1929, to January 28, 1930. Also see Stephenson, *John Lind*, pp. 142–43; and Folwell, vol. 3, p. 244. It is of interest that both Lind and Eustis had successfully overcome physical handicaps. Lind at the age of fourteen had lost his left hand as a result of an accident; Eustis had been permanently lamed by an illness when he was fifteen years old.

[18] *St. Peter Herald*, September 16, 1898; *St. Peter Tribune*, September 14, 1898.

[19] *St. Peter Herald*, September 16, 1898.

[20] *St. Peter Free Press*, September 17, 1898.

not a Republican. Over in Brown County Johnson's brother Fred, a Silver Republican and an ardent supporter of John Lind, warned the Republicans of Nicollet County that "if Johnson retains his health, he will make an active campaign, stumping every township in the county, and the Republicans all admit that on the stump they have no one who can equal him." [21]

Fred Johnson was right. Johnson made a strenuous campaign and spoke in every town in the county, coming into close contact with the voters through his informal, easy manner of meeting people and speaking to them and with them. Carlson did not do nearly so much speaking, and soon the Republicans began to worry about his chances for election.[22] Before long the *Free Press* and the *Tribune* were urging the Republicans of Nicollet County to vote for Carlson because a vote for him meant a vote for Knute Nelson and Cushman K. Davis. Davis was to be a candidate for re-election to the United States Senate when the next legislature met, and Johnson had stated that he would not vote against Davis if the senator needed his vote to be re-elected. Johnson advocated the election of Lind, of course, but he also declared Eustis to be an honorable and honest opponent.

The state campaign was a dull one. Van Sant did what he could for Eustis, but powerful Republicans, including Governor Clough, worked against him. John Lind was elected governor with a total of 131,980 votes to Eustis' 111,796. For the first time since before the Civil War the people of Minnesota had defeated the Republican candidate for governor.

Lind carried Nicollet County, and Johnson was elected by a vote of 1256 to Carlson's 1151.[23] Happily Johnson journeyed to New Ulm on November 15 to take part in a celebration of Lind's victory. There was a "glorious" torchlight procession. In the Opera House and in the Turner Hall speeches were delivered by Lind, Leonard A. Rosing, his campaign manager, T. D. O'Brien, and John A. Johnson. Johnson made "one of the happiest speeches of the evening." He asked all the people in New Ulm, regardless of party, to support Lind and thus give New Ulm the governorship for four instead of two years. St. Peter, he joked, would not

[21] *New Ulm Review*, September 14, 1898.
[22] *St. Peter Free Press*, October 15, 1898.
[23] *Legislative Manual*, 1899, pp. 458, 501, 511.

be jealous of New Ulm, for in the past forty years St. Peter had produced several governors for the state.[24]

A few weeks after the election there appeared in the *Herald* a notice that the paper was looking for a reporter to help Mr. Essler while the editor was in St. Paul serving in the legislature. "He must be a hustler in every sense of the word and be able to get up a good local paper." [25]

Johnson was especially pleased with two of Lind's appointments. He highly approved of Lind's naming Leonard A. Rosing to be his private secretary. Rosing was a native of Sweden who was brought to Minnesota by his parents in 1868 when he was seven years old. He had engaged in the mercantile business in Cannon Falls. Just two years later than Johnson, Rosing had left the Republican party and gone over to the Democrats. A genial man and a hard worker who soon had a wide acquaintance all over the state, Rosing was made chairman of the state Democratic central committee in 1896 and then chairman of the state Fusion committee. He managed both of Lind's campaigns and was to manage the third.[26] Rosing was a Democratic party leader of high principles and a man Johnson greatly respected.

The second appointment that brought joy to Johnson was the naming of his brother Fred to the post of state librarian. Fred had followed the example of his older brother and become the editor of the *New Ulm Review*.

As the year drew to a close, life must have looked good to Johnson. He was a happily married man in a home of his own, with his mother and sister living close by in St. Peter. His brother Edward was working in St. Peter, and Fred, in New Ulm, was not far away. Johnson had supported the family until his brothers and sister could take care of themselves. He had achieved notice as a successful editor, and now he had won his first victory in the political field. His was a busy life, and it suited him. If he had any real disappointment, it was that he had no children of his own. He was very fond of children and wanted a family. The children he knew in St. Peter liked him, and all called him "John." [27]

[24] *St. Peter Herald,* November 18, 1898.
[25] *New Ulm Review,* November 23, 1898.
[26] Charles E. Flandrau, *Encyclopedia of Biography of Minnesota,* pp. 443–44; *St. Paul Globe,* June 26, 1902.
[27] Elinor Johnson Smith to W. G. H.

The only real threat to Johnson's happiness and career was his frail health. He had too much nervous energy for his physical stamina and made greater demands upon himself than he could stand physically. When he was working hard under pressure in the *Herald* office, or when he was campaigning for office, he forgot about food and rest. He seemed to speak easily and without effort, yet, like many good speakers, when he was due to make a speech he got nervously keyed up, and it took a long time before he could relax, gain his normal composure, and eat anything. In the thick of a campaign he moved nervously and smoked much. His mind was so busy that he did not notice physical pain until it became so severe he was forced to stop his work and stay at home to rest.[28]

Shortly after Christmas Johnson and his wife went to St. Paul to attend the inauguration of Governor Lind and to be present at the opening of the legislature. Old friends Johnson saw around the state capital were Robert C. Dunn, who was serving his third term as state auditor; the veteran Democrat, Daniel Buck of Mankato, an associate justice of the Minnesota Supreme Court; and C. C. Whitney, editor of the *Marshall News-Messenger*, who was state printing expert. Johnson met and formed a lasting friendship with Senator Albert Schaller of Hastings, and in the senate he was to meet such able men as Bert Miller of Luverne, Fred B. Snyder of Minneapolis, and Edward T. Young of Appleton. This was probably Johnson's first opportunity to meet Jacob F. Jacobson, the colorful representative from Lac qui Parle County. Jacobson was beginning his fifth term in the lower house, and he and C. F. Staples of Dakota County were regarded as the leaders of the house of representatives.[29] A crude, bluff, unpolished individual, Jacobson was said to be the only member of the house "who talked almost all the time without talking himself to death." [30] Johnson developed an admiration for "Old Jake" and watched his career with interest. Unlike the lower house, the senate had suffered from a lack of leadership,[31] so there was a real opportunity for a new man to make himself known.

[28] Elinor Johnson Smith and Henry N. Benson to W. G. H.
[29] *St. Peter Herald*, March 10, 1899.
[30] Stephenson, *John Lind*, p. 162.
[31] *St. Peter Herald*, March 10, 1899.

At once Johnson was put on eight committees: education, the university and its lands, printing, enrollment, legislative expenses, hospitals for the insane, municipal corporations, and immigration, of which he was chairman. In most of these committees he must have felt fairly comfortable. He had the keen interest in education that one who is deprived of the opportunity for much education often has, and he was conversant with the problems of public education. Certainly he was well equipped to serve on the printing committee and also on that for legislative expenses. And the hours he had spent with Dr. Tomlinson at the St. Peter Hospital for the Insane must have given him much knowledge of the St. Peter hospital and some general knowledge of such hospitals.

His first impression of the legislature was of the brevity of its daily sessions and the frequency of adjournments. The most difficult job of the legislator, he mourned, was to kill time.[32] He reported to his *Herald* readers in a weekly "Capitol Letter," and it was not until February 10 that he could tell them the legislature was getting down to work in all-day sessions. He deplored a "whole week of banquets" given for Lind and Bryan and for the Minnesota editors. All the banquets, he observed, "were conducted along the lines of magnificent extravagance and probably cost in the aggregate $5000. This was paid out for things to eat and drink which really did no one any good and the only excuse for it all was good fellowship. That amount of money could have been placed to greater advantage in the direction of alleviating human suffering and distress and I imagine that all of it could have been properly disbursed in the Twin Cities to most excellent advantage." [33]

With the legislature consisting of a majority of Republicans in both houses, the governor and Fusion members could not hope to accomplish much, but Johnson was a worthy and alert opposition member and a legislator of independence. At the beginning of the session he was noticed by the astute and capable political writer for the *Minneapolis Journal*, W. W. Jermane, or "Jerry J," as he signed himself, who stated that of all the Fusion senators "John A. Johnson of St. Peter will probably end the session with

[32] *Ibid.*, January 20, February 3, 1899.
[33] *Ibid.*, February 17, 1899.

the most friends and the strongest influence. And it doesn't take much of a prophet to predict this, either." [34]

In his inaugural message Governor Lind asked for legislation to amend the gross earnings tax so that railway property would bear a fairer burden of taxation. He pointed out that the railroads in Minnesota were not taxed as much as in neighboring states and that they should be taxed more. J. F. Jacobson agreed with Lind and introduced a bill providing for an increase of from three to four per cent on the gross earnings of railways. Johnson voted for the bill, which passed the house but was defeated in the senate. He felt strongly that the bill ought to be made an issue in the election of 1900.[35] But H. C. Miller, editor of the *St. Peter Free Press*, declared the bill fit only for the wastebasket.[36] Lind was of the opinion that the railroad companies had bribed members of the legislature to vote against the bill, and there was popular indignation at its defeat.[37]

Johnson was one of the leaders in opposing the Anoka-Hastings hospital bill, which was passed by the legislature, vetoed by Lind, and repassed over the governor's veto.[38] The bill provided for the establishment of state insane asylums at Anoka and Hastings, cities that felt they had not received their share of state institutions. Lind and the State Board of Corrections and Charities favored the Wisconsin plan of caring for the insane, and the governor had recommended its adoption for Minnesota. According to the Wisconsin plan, insane persons were committed to a state hospital for treatment. Those who did not recover were sent to county asylums, where the ones who were able worked at what suited them and were happier at work than not. The patients were closer to their families and friends, and at times they might go to their homes for visits. The state paid the county $1.50 a week for the support of each patient, the county and the state thus sharing the cost of caring for these people. The commercial interests of the Twin Cities and the northern section of the state, however, supported Anoka and Hastings, and the governor's recommendation was defeated.[39]

[34] *Minneapolis Journal*, January 11, 1899.
[35] *St. Peter Herald*, March 3, June 2, 1899.
[36] *St. Peter Free Press*, March 25, 1899.      [37] Stephenson, *John Lind*, p. 164.
[38] *St. Peter Herald*, February 24, April 14, 21, 1899.
[39] *Ibid.*, March 31, April 14, 21, 1899; *St. Peter Free Press*, April 15, 1899; Stephenson, *John Lind*, p. 167; Folwell, vol. 3, pp. 247–48.

In the interests of the St. Peter asylum Johnson introduced two bills, one giving the superintendent rather than the hospital board the power to dismiss patients, and the other appropriating $5000 to enlarge the hospital. Both bills became laws.[40]

In 1897 a law was passed providing for the payment of a bounty of one cent a pound on sugar manufactured in the state. A sugar factory, therefore, was established in Minneapolis, and its officials soon applied to the state for a bounty of almost $20,000. The state treasurer declared he could not pay the claim until the legislature had passed an appropriation for it. This was done in the session of 1899, but Lind vetoed the bill, only to have it passed over his veto. Johnson voted for the bill. He agreed with Lind on the viciousness of a bounty law to help along an industry which otherwise would not have been self-supporting or profitable. But Johnson felt that since such a law had been passed, the state government was obligated to pay the factory's claim. Lind did not question the government's obligation, but he hoped by his veto to call the attention of the legislature to the evils of a bounty bill. Actually, Johnson and Lind did not differ on the subject, but the *St. Paul Globe* criticized Johnson for not following Lind's leadership. Johnson replied that Lind had not asked him to vote for or against the bill, and he had voted as he thought best. The bounty law was finally repealed, but the bounty claim was paid.[41]

Johnson also voted for a bill providing for the election by the people of three railroad commissioners. The bill became a law. Johnson always felt strongly that the people should elect "their own servants." [42] He voted against a drainage bill to improve farm lands in the northern part of the state. The Nicollet County farmers had paid for the drainage of their lands, and Johnson thought the northern counties could also "foot their own bills." [43] His attitude on this issue was to be used against him later. Johnson favored the Somerville Corporation bill which provided that all "foreign corporations" in Minnesota must pay fees equal to those paid by the domestic corporations.[44]

[40] *Minneapolis Journal*, January 12, 1899; *St. Paul Pioneer Press*, April 18, 1899.
[41] *St. Paul Globe*, February 22, 1899; *St. Peter Free Press*, April 1, 1899; *St. Peter Herald*, March 3, 1899; Stephenson, *John Lind*, p. 168.
[42] *St. Peter Herald*, March 3, 1899.
[43] *Ibid.*, March 24, 1899.
[44] *Ibid.*, April 21, 1899.

Toward the end of the first session of the legislature Johnson attracted considerable attention by standing alone among the Fusion senators against Governor Lind on an issue that brought Lind much criticism. The issue was the return of the Thirteenth Minnesota Regiment from the Philippine Islands. There was in Minnesota, as in the country at large, much opposition to the establishment of a colonial empire by the United States. A resolution opposing the annexation of the Philippines was introduced in the legislature but was defeated by a large majority in each house. Lind, however, favored the resolution and objected to the imperialistic policy of the McKinley administration. He opposed all large appropriations for the army and navy.

The Filipino insurrection added fuel to the flame of anti-imperialism, and in Minnesota it produced a demand for the return from the Philippines of the Thirteenth Minnesota Regiment. Lind received a cablegram from some of the officers of the regiment asking to have it ordered home, and he finally received assurance from McKinley and the War Department that the regiment would be recalled not later than June 1. Both the officers and Lind were severely criticized for their efforts. Lind was accused of being a "spineless governor" and the officers of being "weaklings." [45] Johnson heartily disagreed with Lind and all others who were so eager to bring the regiment home. In his "Capitol Letter" he wrote:

Many people who complained so bitterly because Governor Lind wanted the Thirteenth Regiment returned from Manila are now making themselves and the regiment ridiculous by a zeal far greater than any manifested by the governor. There are a whole lot of people who still believe that the regiment should not have been hurried home but maintained in Manila so long as their services were needed. If it was patriotic and proper to go there originally, it was not especially patriotic to come home before the war was over.[46]

At the time when Governor Lind favored the introduction into the legislature of a resolution demanding the recall of the regiment, the resolution was opposed by all the Republicans and supported by all the Fusion members except Senator Johnson of St. Peter. Johnson rose and made a brief speech in opposition to the resolution:

[45] Stephenson, *John Lind*, pp. 172–76; Day and Knappen, pp. 110–12.
[46] *St. Peter Herald*, August 11, 1899.

I hope that this will not be construed as a party matter. The administration at Washington is confronted by conditions that we way out here in the West cannot well understand. Deplorable as I believe this war to be, I, for one, believe that we should join together to uphold the hands of the government, regardless of the political color that may be lent to the situation. I believe the regiment should remain in the Philippines as long as the Stars and Stripes are liable to insult. If that be political treason make the most of it. I believe that the president is doing the best he can in this matter, and give him credit in the belief that his object is the perpetuity of the government. Let us say to him, the East and the West, the North and the South will stand by you, shoulder to shoulder, until the flag of our country can be brought home unsullied and unstained.[47]

Later in the *Herald* he reiterated his opposition to the withdrawal of the regiment until the Philippines were peaceful and settled.[48] But by that time the regiment was back in Minnesota.

Johnson's support of the sugar bounty bill and his speech against the return of the regiment moved the *St. Peter Free Press* to comment that Johnson did not seem to be on very friendly terms with Governor Lind. It added: "It must be exceedingly aggravating to Lind to think of being turned down by one in whose election he took such an active part." [49] The newspapers of the day were probably right when they said that Lind resented Johnson's opposition; he had enough opposition from the Republicans. He never really got over his resentment, and later Lind was not one of the warmest admirers of Governor Johnson.

For a long time Johnson had been interested in the building and improvement of roads. He had urged this cause in the *Herald*, and he was active with a group of other men who worked to improve the roads in Nicollet County. During his first legislative session he introduced a bill, which was passed, authorizing the councils of any city having a population of ten thousand or less to appropriate and expend money in assisting in the improvement and maintenance of roads leading into them.[50]

Johnson was not favorably impressed by his first experience in the legislature. Even before it was over he noted that most of the

[47] *St. Paul Pioneer Press*, April 19, 1899.
[48] *St. Peter Herald*, January 26, 1900.
[49] *St. Peter Free Press*, April 22, 1899.
[50] *St. Paul Pioneer Press*, April 18, 1899.

members were glad to see the end of the session in sight, and he commented:

As a matter of fact I cannot see what there is in being a member of the legislature that is so alluring to the average person. To a man who makes even the slightest pretense to honesty and whose official conduct is the result of the effort born of conscience, the due is not altogether pleasant. Financially, to such a man, there can be no inducement, for it requires the most rigid economy to make both ends meet.[51]

The session had not been a very exciting one, and the *Minneapolis Journal*, while lamenting that the session had produced no gubernatorial material, declared Johnson to be the one senator who drew attention because of his excellence as a speaker and suggested that he would be a worthy nominee for Congress from the second district.[52]

Back at his desk in the *Herald* office, Johnson turned with pleasure to his editorial duties. During the early months of 1900 he urged the renomination of Lind by the Democratic party, saying he was sure the governor would run again if renominated.[53] In June he was once again elected as a delegate to the state Democratic convention.[54] Since his political debut in 1888 Johnson had been a delegate to almost every state Democratic convention, and he had come to know the party leaders very well. The older men of the party were dying off, and Johnson's part in the policies of the Democracy of the state became of increasing importance as the leadership changed. In two years he was to be talked of as a possible nominee for the governorship, but in 1900 the Democrats did not seriously consider any other candidate for governor except John Lind. During the summer months Johnson watched with interest the actions of the Republican and Democratic national conventions. In a presidential year it would be more difficult to elect anyone but a Republican to the governorship in Minnesota if the state behaved as it usually did.

The Republicans renominated William McKinley for the presidency, and young Theodore Roosevelt, governor of New York, felt it best to accept the nomination for vice-president, although

[51] *St. Peter Herald*, March 24, 1899.
[52] *Minneapolis Journal*, April 18, 1899.
[53] *St. Peter Herald*, January 12, July 6, 1900.
[54] *Ibid.*, June 15, 1900.

the office seemed to him to be the "tomb of all his hopes." [55]
Neither Mark Hanna nor McKinley wanted Roosevelt to be nominated, but Republican party bosses Tom Platt of New York and Matt Quay of Pennsylvania were anxious to "shelve" him, since he had not behaved as they liked when he was governor of New York. Hanna was won over to the idea only at the last minute. He expressed his fear of "that damned cowboy" when he said to McKinley: "Don't you know that there is only one life between the Presidency and the Vice Presidency . . . ?" [56]

Roosevelt, the hero of the Philippine war, the "Rough Rider" who could speak as passionately and espouse a cause as fervently as Bryan, became for the Republicans a counterattraction to Bryan. McKinley stayed at home during the campaign, for Mark Hanna declared the Republican party would defeat the Democrats by "standing pat." But "Teddy" stumped the country in opposition to Bryan and the anti-imperialists.

In Minnesota this was the year for Samuel Van Sant. He had the support of all the "regular" Republicans, and he was a man to attract votes. Always a loyal party member and possessed of a pleasing personality, Van Sant was popular with the G.A.R., had taken his defeat by Eustis in 1898 in the best party spirit, and had never done anything to provoke the enmity of any Republican leader. Van Sant was unanimously nominated by the state convention. His candidacy was linked with the national ticket, and national issues were stressed over state issues by the Republicans.[57]

Once again the Democrats, the Silver Republicans, and the Populists nominated William Jennings Bryan for president, with Adlai E. Stevenson of Illinois, a bimetallist who had run with Cleveland in 1892, for vice-president. The Populists objected to Stevenson, so they ignored his nomination and named a candidate of their own, Charles Towne, the Silver Republican from Minnesota. For a while Bryan appeared to have two running mates, but after much negotiation and persuasion Towne decided he would not accept the Populist nomination. He announced that decision on the seventh of August! [58]

[55] Matthew Josephson, *President Makers*, p. 108.
[56] *Ibid.*; Mark Sullivan, *Our Times*, vol. 2, pp. 378–80.
[57] Stephenson, *John Lind*, p. 177; Folwell, vol. 3, pp. 256–57.
[58] *St. Paul Pioneer Press*, July 2, 6, 12, August 8, 1900; Hicks, pp. 365–75. A similar

Bryan dictated the party platform. Into it again went the plank for free and unlimited coinage of silver, but Bryan determined to make the chief issues of this campaign anti-imperialism and a fight against the trusts. The platform denounced McKinley's Philippine policy, opposed territorial expansion and militarism, and called for the complete freedom of Cuba. The Democrats pledged themselves to "unceasing warfare against private monopolies in every form" and condemned the Dingley tariff as a "trust breeding measure." They demanded increased powers for the Interstate Commerce Commission, the establishment of a department of labor, direct election of senators, statehood for Arizona, New Mexico, and Oklahoma, and the settlement of labor disputes by arbitration. They also expressed their sympathy with the Boers.[59]

The Gold Democrats met in New York in September and nominated Donelson Caffery of Louisiana for president and Archibald M. Howe of Massachusetts for vice-president. To Grover Cleveland, in retirement, Bryan's nomination was such an overwhelming disappointment that "for several months he ceased to discuss public questions, even with his intimate friends. During these dark days, the darkest of all his life, fishing and his family were his consolation." [60] According to one of his biographers, he gave no help or moral support to the Gold Democrats, and he declared he did not vote for McKinley. His biographer concludes that in 1900 Cleveland did not cast his vote.[61] Bryan certainly did not have a united Democracy behind him.

Johnson accepted Bryan and the Democratic platform with one reservation — the free silver plank. Aside from that he thought the platform one every Democrat could support, and he was grateful that the money question was not a major issue in this campaign.[62]

The state Democratic convention was scheduled to meet on September 6 in St. Paul, and to Johnson fell the privilege of delivering the nominating speech for John Lind. Certainly here was an opportunity for him to distinguish himself. Yet he delivered an unusually brief speech, and by no means a remarkable one. The

situation had existed in 1896, when the Populists, not liking Arthur Sewall of Maine as Bryan's running mate, named Thomas Watson as their vice-presidential candidate.
[59] *St. Paul Pioneer Press*, July 6, 1900.
[60] McElroy, vol. 2, p. 287.
[61] *Ibid.*, pp. 287–300.
[62] *St. Peter Herald*, July 13, 1900.

newspaper reporters were not impressed with it, and it is doubtful if members of the audience ever remembered what Johnson said.[63] It does not read as if it had been prepared beforehand. As he faced an audience that had just put on a demonstration of its enthusiasm for John Lind, Johnson said:

It would be useless, indeed, for me, gentlemen, to extol the man whose name I am going to present to you as candidate for governor of Minnesota. His work, his record is too well known to every one of you. But yet I feel that it would be ungrateful to you, to him, to myself, if I did not tell you why the Democracy of Minnesota and the fusion forces of this state look to him as their state leader. He is the only man who has stood on the threshold of the governor's office of this state, like Horatius on the bridge, with the people on one side and the greedy corporations on the other, and protected with all his strength the people from the corporations' greed. Gentlemen, no enthusiasm like that which you have displayed here today has ever been seen at a convention before. We are not only going to elect John Lind governor of Minnesota, but we are going to fill the state house, from governor down to railroad commissioners, with Democrats. "Honest John" Lind is the only man who has forced the railroads to come to him, and to make their schedules of rates in favor of the people and not in favor of the trusts. Gentlemen, of this convention, I take the deepest pleasure in presenting to you the name of John Lind for governor of Minnesota.[64]

After another demonstration, Lind was unanimously nominated. The Silver Republicans and Populists also nominated him, and he once again ran as a Fusion candidate, although at the Jackson Day dinner on January 10 he had declared himself a Democrat. In his acceptance speech Lind emphasized the antitrust issue and declared that taxation reform was of paramount importance to Minnesota. He regretted that the legislature had not seen fit to pass a law taxing the Standard Oil Company and the United States Steel Company, and he again urged the passage of an adequate gross earnings tax on railroad property.[65]

During the campaign Johnson made speeches for Lind all through Nicollet County. Bryan came to Minnesota to campaign, Lind joined his party, and they spoke from the same platforms

[63] *St. Paul Globe*, September 7, 1900; *St. Paul Pioneer Press*, September 7, 1900.
[64] *St. Paul Globe*, September 7, 1900.
[65] Stephenson, *John Lind*, p. 181.

on national and state issues. When they came to St. Peter on October 2, Johnson presided at a large outdoor meeting and introduced Lind, who spoke briefly and then introduced Bryan. Except for printing Bryan's praise of Lind and the usual political appeal to support the Democratic ticket, Johnson had little to say about Bryan in the *Herald* during the entire campaign.

The Minnesota Democrats fully expected Lind to be re-elected, and they were surprised when he lost to Van Sant — even though it was by only 2254 votes, when the victorious McKinley carried the state with almost 65,000 more votes than Bryan received. The Democrats believed Lind should have won, for some fifteen to twenty thousand ballots intended for Lind had been invalidated. On the ballot also was the name of Tom Lucas as the Social Democratic candidate for governor. Many voters, careless in reading the ballot, simply placed a mark opposite every candidate designated as a Democrat, so that many who voted for Lind for governor also voted for Lucas, and these ballots were thrown out in the count.[66]

"Talk about a landslide!" wrote Johnson. "It was an upheaval, a tidal wave, simoon, cyclone, and a wrecking of all hopes." But, he added, "The shock has been sustained and we comfort ourselves with the hope that in future years it can't be worse." [67] He suggested that Lind be the Democrat's candidate for 1902. As for Bryan, Johnson thought there was some sadness in the second defeat of a magnetic personality and an utterly sincere crusader devoted to the interests of the people, but he believed that Bryan's losing removed him forever from the list of Democratic candidates for the presidency. He declared that Bryan had dug his political grave by again insisting upon the inclusion of the free silver plank when the people had rejected free silver so completely in 1896. Johnson considered Bryan a one-idea man who refused to heed anyone's advice on the money question. Johnson was delighted to see Bryan turn to editing the *Commoner*, and at that work he hoped Bryan would remain. To his subscribers Johnson offered subscriptions to the *Commoner* at reduced rates.[68]

In January 1901 Johnson returned to St. Paul to attend the

[66] *Ibid.*, p. 183; *Minnesota in Three Centuries*, vol. 4, p. 265.
[67] *St. Peter Herald*, November 9, 1900.
[68] *Ibid.*, November 17, December 21, 28, 1900.

second session of the legislature and to begin "the usual grind of making laws and killing them." [69] He had been impressed with the host of office seekers who had almost overwhelmed Lind,[70] and now he saw a swarm enveloping Van Sant. In his "Capitol Letter" on February 8 he expressed pity for the politician who had spent most of his career in office, but who had saved nothing for his declining years and had to beg for any petty government position to maintain himself.

During this session Johnson once more supported Jacobson's gross earnings tax bill, and it finally passed both houses and was signed by Van Sant. He voted for a primary election bill which became a law. Representing his constituents who opposed the board of control bill, Johnson voted against it, as did all the senators from counties in which there were state institutions. He thought he could kill the bill by introducing an amendment placing the university and the state normal schools under the jurisdiction of the board of control. Everyone understood Johnson's reason for offering the amendment, and he had made it known previously that he was opposed to any outside interference with the University of Minnesota. To the surprise of many, however, the bill passed with the amendment, and a single, salaried board was created to manage and control the charitable, penal, reformatory, and educational institutions of the state. Later Johnson's stand on this bill was used against him.

Johnson gained some attention by his stout opposition to the motion granting $150 each to representatives of the newspapers reporting senate news; the motion was defeated largely because of his efforts. Passed by the legislature were Johnson's bills relating to the St. Peter Hospital for the Insane and his bill concerning public libraries.[71] Senator Knute Nelson was re-elected without much opposition in the legislature, but there was quite a struggle before Moses E. Clapp was finally elected to fill the vacancy caused by the death of C. K. Davis. After witnessing the contest and hearing the usual insinuations that bribes had been used and that J. J. Hill was back of Clapp, Johnson felt more

[69] *Ibid.*, January 11, 1901.
[70] *Ibid.*, February 3, 1899.
[71] *Minneapolis Journal*, February 27, March 20, 23, April 1, 3, 4, 12, 1901; *St. Peter Herald*, April 5, 12, 1901.

than ever that senators should be elected to Congress directly by the people.[72]

Van Sant in his inaugural message had urged the legislature to create a special commission to make a thorough study of tax reform. The legislature complied and created a commission whose members were to be appointed by the governor, attorney general, and auditor. The legislature adjourned earlier than was customary, expecting to be called in special session to consider the report of the tax commission.[73] In summarizing the work of the session and commenting upon the legislators, the *Minneapolis Journal* declared that Johnson "was heard from frequently and with credit." [74]

Late in 1901 Van Sant undertook a fight with the newly formed Northern Securities Company, an organization which consolidated the Great Northern, Northern Pacific, and Chicago, Burlington and Quincy railroads. The company was incorporated on November 13, 1901, under the laws of New Jersey. James J. Hill and J. P. Morgan controlled the Great Northern and the Chicago, Burlington and Quincy systems, and after a fierce struggle with the railroad baron, E. H. Harriman, they had gained control of enough stock in the Northern Pacific Railroad to help direct its operations. In June 1901 Hill and Harriman ceased their fight for control of the Northern Pacific, and it was announced "that an understanding has been reached between the Northern Pacific and the Union Pacific interests under which the composition of the Northern Pacific Board will be left in the hands of J. P. Morgan." [75] Harriman was made a director of the Burlington, and Union Pacific interests were represented on the Northern Pacific board of directors. Then Morgan, Hill, and Harriman pooled their interests in the Northern Securities Company. The Union Pacific, for example, surrendered its holdings in the Northern Pacific to the newly organized company and received in exchange $82,500,000 worth of Northern Securities stock. The board of directors of the new four hundred million dollar holding company included six men representing the Northern Pacific, four men from the Great Northern, two from the Union Pacific, and two di-

[72] *Ibid.*, January 4, 25, 1901.          [73] Folwell, vol. 3, pp. 257–58.
[74] *Minneapolis Journal*, April 12, 1901.
[75] Joseph Gilpin Pyle, *Life of James J. Hill*, vol. 2, p. 154.

rectors "at large." J. J. Hill was regarded as the head of the company.[76]

The organization of the Northern Securities Company startled and alarmed even conservative men in the country. "A few more such moves on the chess-board of finance capitalism and, as Professor W. Z. Ripley commented at the time, the industries of the nation might be contained within one great holding company, controlled from one banking office" such as that of J. P. Morgan.[77] Even Mark Hanna did not approve. Both President Roosevelt and Governor Van Sant were spurred to action. Roosevelt asked his attorney general, Philander C. Knox, for an opinion as to the legality of the Northern Securities Company, and when Knox replied that it violated the Sherman Anti-Trust Act of 1890, Roosevelt told him to bring suit against the company. The government's suit was introduced in the United States Circuit Court in St. Paul in March 1902, and the case was sent on to the United States Supreme Court, which in 1904 declared the formation of the Northern Securities Company a violation of the Sherman Anti-Trust Act and ordered the company dissolved.[78]

Governor Van Sant also had taken steps against the Northern Securities Company. Immediately after its charter was granted, he issued a protest against the merger of the three railroad systems and declared it violated a Minnesota law that forbade the consolidation of parallel or competing lines within the state. He then invited the governors and the attorneys general of states having anti-consolidation laws similar to Minnesota's to a conference to discuss possible action against the new company. Officials of North Dakota, South Dakota, Oregon, Washington, Montana, and Minnesota met at Helena, Montana, to consider the problem. They adopted a resolution condemning the organization of the Northern Securities, declared the consolidation of the three railway systems to be a violation of laws of the states, endorsed any court action which might be taken against the company by any state to test the validity of such a consolidation, and unanimously protested against any consolidation restricting free competition in trade or commerce of the United States.[79]

[76] *Ibid.*, p. 168; Balthasar H. Meyer, "A History of the Northern Securities Case," *Bulletin of the University of Wisconsin*, vol. 1, 1904–6, pp. 229–41.
[77] Josephson, *President Makers*, pp. 126–27.
[78] Meyer, p. 242.          [79] *Ibid.*, p. 243.

Van Sant then directed Minnesota's attorney general to get permission from the United States Supreme Court to file a bill of complaint against the Northern Securities Company of New Jersey. On the grounds that the court could not proceed as a court of equity without the presence of the two railroad companies involved and that "if the companies were made defendant, the constitutional jurisdiction of the court would not extend to the case," the motion for leave to file the bill was denied.[80] The state's suit against the company was then taken to the Ramsay County District Court and from there to the United States Circuit Court, where it was tried in June 1903 before Judge William Lochren. Judge Lochren's decision maintained that the Northern Securities Company was not a railroad company and so was not violating any Minnesota law. The state then appealed the case to the United States Supreme Court, which decided that no federal question was involved.[81] Van Sant was preparing to bring new action against the company, but this proved to be unnecessary when the federal government got the decision it wanted from the United States Supreme Court, ordering the dissolution of the Northern Securities Company. This merger question served as good political capital for Van Sant, and he ran for re-election on the issue in 1902. The people of Minnesota heartily supported the governor in his fight against the merger, and Johnson expressed his approval of Van Sant's action in the *Herald*. Johnson's strong stand in opposition to the merger was later to be of importance to him politically.

The special session was duly called by Van Sant, and for about a month in 1902 the legislature considered the work of the tax commission. Many of the legislators did not like the tax code which the commission had drawn up. Changes were made and amendments added, and finally a revised code was passed. But when this was submitted to the voters in the general election of 1902, they rejected it. During the session the legislators talked much politics, and it was generally recognized that Van Sant was eager to succeed himself. His closest competitors for the nomination would be Judge Loren Collins and a younger Republican, Robert Dunn, but the legislators thought Van Sant would be re-

[80] *Ibid.*, pp. 243–44; Folwell, vol. 3, p. 260; Pyle, *Life of James J. Hill*, vol. 2, p. 169.
[81] *Ibid.*, pp. 172–73; Folwell, vol. 2, p. 260.

nominated.[82] Johnson felt that too many legislators frittered away valuable time in talk and that the extra session was an expensive mistake for the state. He consoled himself with the thought that at least the legislature had done nothing drastic during the special session. He believed in making changes slowly.[83]

Back in the *Herald* office, Johnson continued to urge the nomination of John Lind for governor in 1902. Lind, who had opened a law office in Minneapolis after his defeat in 1900, did not want the nomination, but without him at the head of their ticket the Democrats had little hope of winning the governorship in 1902. As they gathered in Minneapolis for their state convention on June 25, some of the party leaders believed Lind would consent to his nomination because of the party enthusiasm for him. The *St. Paul Globe* on June 24 predicted his nomination, declaring he could not refuse. But Lind held firmly to his decision, and the party leaders were forced to consider other candidates. Some of the possibilities discussed were Leonard Rosing, Daniel Lawler, W. H. Harries of Winona, O. C. Baldwin of Duluth, and John A. Johnson of St. Peter.

There was much sentiment in favor of Johnson. Many delegates considered him the strongest candidate next to Lind.[84] His victory in the Republican stronghold of Nicollet County led some to believe he could poll many votes among Republicans in southern Minnesota. So, when the convention recessed at noon, party leaders offered Johnson the nomination. After carefully listening to them, Johnson quietly turned down the offer. "He told them frankly that he did not believe he could win, and that he felt that he was too young a man to take the responsibility of heading the ticket." [85] The leaders next turned to Leonard Rosing, who agreed to accept the nomination, which he then received by acclamation.

Johnson was also among the candidates put up for lieutenant governor, but he withdrew his name and Robert A. Smith of St. Paul was nominated. Smith was a Gold Democrat chosen by the party leaders to offset the Bryanism taint of Rosing.

The convention was a dull one with the delegates accepting the

[82] *St. Peter Herald*, February 21, 1902.
[83] *Ibid.*, March 14, 1902.
[84] *St. Paul Pioneer Press*, June 25, 1902.
[85] *Ibid.*

dictates of the party leaders. In general there was a feeling of apathy, for few really believed the Democrats had much of a chance without Lind as their standard-bearer.[86] The platform endorsed the national platform of 1900 and William Jennings Bryan. Lind's policies as governor were praised, and the Democrats declared their opposition to the Northern Securities merger and urged the direct election of United States senators and an eight-hour day for labor. Regretting that Lind refused to accept the nomination, Johnson wrote of Rosing as "a splendid representative of the Young Democracy of the country, strong in his beliefs and vigorous in his enunciation of those beliefs." [87]

On July 1 Van Sant was nominated for governor by the Republicans, who endorsed the administration of Theodore Roosevelt, the protective tariff, the Republican Philippine policy, and Van Sant's fight against the merger.[88]

Lind became the Democratic candidate for Congress in the fifth congressional district. He did not think he could be elected governor, but thought he had a better chance for election to Congress. Johnson filed for renomination for state senator. This was the first time Minnesota used the primary election system, and Johnson won the nomination.[89] He had no competition! To oppose him in the November election the Republicans chose Charles A. Johnson of St. Peter.

Charles A. Johnson, a native of Sweden who was taken to Minnesota when he was a boy, had little more education than John A. Johnson. He had taught school for a brief time and then established himself in the mercantile business in St. Peter.[90] Both the *St. Peter Tribune* and the *Free Press* supported his candidacy. The *Free Press* confined itself pretty much to booming C. R. Davis for congressman from the second district. The *Tribune,* which had opposed Davis violently, now ignored him and devoted itself to urging Republicans to support Charles A. Johnson. Nicollet County had to choose between two Johnsons, both of Swedish extraction. John A. Johnson ran on the slogan, "one good term deserves another," and again made a strenuous campaign, speaking

[86] *Ibid.*          [87] *St. Peter Herald,* July 4, 1902.
[88] *Ibid.*; *St. Paul Pioneer Press,* July 2, 1902.
[89] *St. Peter Herald,* September 19, 1902; *St. Peter Free Press,* September 20, 1902.
[90] *St. Peter Tribune,* August 13, 1902.

throughout Nicollet County.[91] Both Senator Moses Clapp and Governor Van Sant came to St. Peter to speak for the Republican ticket.[92]

Toward the end of the campaign there occurred an incident which probably lost Johnson some votes. He was one of a delegation sent to a special meeting of the Lutheran Minnesota Conference of the Augustana Synod at New London to discuss the question of moving Gustavus Adolphus College to the Twin Cities. The college, moved to St. Peter in 1876, had grown and was in need of new buildings. At a mass meeting held in St. Peter on March 26 a committee had been appointed to raise money for a new auditorium, and out of the meeting came a discussion of whether the growing college should remain in the small town of St. Peter or be moved to the Twin Cities. St. Peter, of course, wanted to keep the college.

On October 24 the New London Conference convened. Johnson, naturally, was there to speak for St. Peter, and so was his opponent, Charles A. Johnson. On October 29 Johnson addressed the conference, urging that the college remain in St. Peter. Then, feeling that he had done all he could once he had delivered his speech, he left to meet a speaking engagement elsewhere. The conference voted to remove the college from St. Peter to Minneapolis after hearing John Lind's promise that he would see to it that about $250,000 was raised for the college before the next conference meeting. Johnson declared that the conference had been carried away by Lind's promise before he left and that there was no reason for him to stay.

Charles A. Johnson stayed until the conference was over. There is no evidence that he did as much at the meeting as John A. Johnson, but he stayed through it. That was enough. "John A.," as he was called, was severely criticized because he had not waited for the outcome. Stunned by the decision of the conference, St. Peter seemed to need a scapegoat, and Johnson was it. Both the *Free Press* and the *Tribune* made the most of the matter.[93] But

---

[91] *St. Peter Herald*, October 10, 1902.

[92] *St. Peter Tribune*, October 15, 1902. Clapp came to St. Peter on October 13 and Van Sant on October 22.

[93] *St. Peter Herald*, October 31, 1902; *St. Peter Free Press*, November 1, 1902; *St. Peter Tribune*, October 29, 1902; Conrad Peterson, *Gustavus Adolphus College, A History of Eighty Years*, pp. 70–72.

Johnson had support, some of it from Republicans, in his contention that he left the conference only after he realized there was nothing else he could do. On October 29 the following letter appeared in the *St. Peter Tribune,* signed by Henry N. Benson, H. L. Stark, A. H. Freeman, F. A. Blomgren, and William Mueller:

Whereas some criticism has been made of John A. Johnson for having returned to St. Peter before the end of the New London Conference, we the members of the committee, who were in attendance, voluntarily make this statement of facts:

Mr. Johnson attended the Conference, labored earnestly with the committee, addressed the delegates and did all in his power while there to keep the college at St. Peter. The Conference was simply stampeded by the promise of John Lind, for the Twin Cities, to raise $250,000. This statement is voluntarily made to correct any false impression or false rumor.

Johnson publicly declared that he never would have left the conference to meet a speaking engagement if he had thought he might have succeeded in doing more. He announced that he would gladly sacrifice the senatorship if that would keep the college in St. Peter.[94] He had always been a friend of the college. He knew the faculty members and the students and had frequently spoken at college banquets. In fact, he had addressed the alumni at their banquet a few months earlier, when Governor Van Sant had also been a guest speaker.[95] As a booster for St. Peter, he had always been a booster for Gustavus Adolphus College as well.

Actually the whole thing turned out to be a tempest in a teapot. Lind and his friends, who had promised to raise $250,000 before the next conference meeting in 1903, by 1904 had secured only $150,000 in pledges. St. Peter then offered the college $15,000 for the construction of a new auditorium, which the conference accepted by a vote of 141 to 105. The college remained in St. Peter.[96]

Just how much effect the whole issue of the college had on the election results is hard to estimate, but it probably had some influence in favor of Charles A. Johnson. The contest was exceedingly close and exciting. John A. Johnson was defeated by only eighty-eight votes. His total vote was 1138 to Charles A. John-

[94] *St. Peter Herald,* October 31, 1902.
[95] *Ibid.,* May 30, 1902.
[96] Peterson, pp. 72–76.

son's 1226. Van Sant carried the state, polling 155,849 votes to Rosing's 99,362. Considering Rosing's poor showing, Johnson did amazingly well. Nicollet County itself remained Republican.[97] "Charles A. won and John A. lost," wrote Johnson, who added that John A. submitted to the verdict not because he wanted to but because he had to.[98]

In losing the senatorship Johnson was to gain the governorship, but that was something he could not foresee. On November 24 his friends gave him a surprise party, a testimonial supper in his own home, to which over seventy-five people came. H. P. Hall, the veteran editor and a great friend of Johnson's, attended, and in a speech he assured everyone that Johnson would have been nominated for governor if he had not absolutely refused to run. No one at the party had any thought that Johnson's political career was finished because of his defeat.[99]

[97] *Legislative Manual*, 1903, pp. 460, 516, 522.
[98] *St. Peter Herald*, November 7, 1902.
[99] *Ibid.*, November 28, 1902.

THE strenuous campaign for re-election to the state senate in 1902 left Johnson in poor physical condition. Since his second operation in 1898 he had made two hard campaigns that would have taxed the strength of a man in excellent health. It was not surprising, then, that in the early months of 1903 he suffered more and more frequent attacks of severe abdominal pain. In the summer he became so ill he realized he would have to consult Dr. Will Mayo, and near the end of August he and Mrs. Johnson went to Rochester. There Johnson learned he must submit to a third operation for intestinal adhesions. On August 29 Dr. Mayo performed the operation, which proved to be a very serious one, and for a week Johnson was dangerously ill. By mid-September he was slowly gaining strength, and he was back at the *Herald* office the first week in October after an absence of more than a month.[1]

Johnson's illness never caused him to lose his enthusiasm for living or his optimistic outlook, and he seldom curtailed his activities because of his pain. During the next few months, however, he was obliged to be more careful of himself than he usually was.

As an editor and a Democrat Johnson watched with keen eyes and great interest the political events of 1903 and the early months of 1904. Leonard Rosing's crushing defeat in 1902 had taken the life out of the Democratic party. The Republican party seemed to be firmly in control without any apparent threat to its hold upon the state administration. But conditions developed which brought internal strife in both political parties in the state. Because of the shrewdness of its leaders the Democratic party managed to maintain its unity, but the Republican party was so split that it took several years to heal the rift and reunite the party.

[1] *St. Peter Free Press*, August 29, September 5, 12, 19, October 3, 1903.

Van Sant had scarcely been inaugurated when two eager aspirants for his office began to prepare the way for their nominations. They were Judge Loren W. Collins and Robert C. Dunn. Between them developed the most bitter fight for the Republican nomination for governor that Minnesota had yet witnessed. Both Collins and Dunn were self-made men and loyal party members, but in personality they were radically different, and the fight between them became one of personalities rather than of issues.

Judge Collins was the older of the two. He was born in Lowell, Massachusetts, on August 7, 1838, the son of Charles Collins, an overseer in one of the Lowell cotton mills. A restless man, Charles Collins went to California during the gold rush of '49 and returned to Massachusetts a year later with little more money than he had when he left. In 1854 he moved his family to the Territory of Minnesota, and during the next six years he failed at every enterprise he attempted. His son, Loren, tried farming with his father, but found he had no taste for it. Having a high school education, he taught country school for a year for the sum of sixty dollars and room and board. Then he began to read law in a firm at Hastings, Minnesota, and saved some money he earned copying briefs and records for the court.

In 1862 Loren Collins, as one of the "Hastings Rangers," enlisted in the United States army and was immediately commissioned a second lieutenant in the Seventh Minnesota Infantry. Honorably discharged in 1865, he settled in St. Cloud, Minnesota, where he formed a law partnership with Seagrave Smith. Soon he became county attorney of Stearns County, a position he held for almost ten years. Then he was city attorney of St. Cloud for four years and mayor for five years. In 1880 he was elected to the lower house of the state legislature and was re-elected in 1882. The following year he was appointed judge of the seventh judicial district, and in 1887 he became an associate justice of the Minnesota Supreme Court.[2]

The "little judge," as Collins was called because of his short stature, was active in the Republican party all during his career as a lawyer. He had been for several years a contender for the governorship, and in 1904 he and his friends felt that the time for

[2] Loren W. Collins, *Story of a Minnesotan*, pp. 1–84.

his nomination had come.[3] Collins was an able and dignified man with an unassailable record. It was widely understood that he was Van Sant's choice and that the administration machine was ready to support him. The only criticism made of him was that he was too old, for in 1903 he was sixty-five years of age.

A group of vigorous, young Republicans were eager to take over the control of the Republican party from such older leaders as Van Sant and Collins, men who could always depend upon the support of the G.A.R. These young Republicans wanted a governor who was too young to have any affiliation with the G.A.R., and their candidate in 1904 was Robert C. Dunn of Princeton.

Robert Campbell Dunn was born on February 14, 1855, in County Tyrone, Ireland. In 1876 he migrated to Minnesota — with no money but with plenty of energy and ambition — and became editor of the *Princeton Union*. Two years after his arrival he was elected town clerk, an office he held until 1889, when he was elected to the Minnesota house of representatives. He was renominated in 1890 but lost after an election dispute. In 1892, however, he was again elected to the lower house of the legislature, and from 1894 to 1902 he was state auditor. While he served in the legislature he was greatly interested in the preservation of pine timberlands in northern Minnesota and their protection from timber thieves. His record as state auditor was regarded as creditable, and he won high praise from Governor John Lind for his work.[4]

Dunn's political ambition was to be governor of the state, but he "was so coy that he scarcely admitted it to himself unless he was alone." [5] He was talked of as a candidate in 1902, but he did not think it wise to oppose Van Sant. H. P. Hall recorded the rumor that Dunn stepped aside for Van Sant in 1902 in return for Van Sant's promise to return the favor in 1904. There is no evidence to support this rumor, and it is highly improbable that Van Sant would have made such an agreement, for he was then very popular and was renominated without much opposition.

[3] *Ibid.*, p. 85; Charles B. Cheney, *Story of Minnesota Politics*, p. 20.
[4] Warren Upham and Rose Dunlap, *Minnesota Biographies, 1655–1912*, in *Minnesota Historical Society Collections*, vol. 14, p. 191; *Legislative Manual*, 1895, p. 555; Folwell, vol. 3, p. 273; *St. Paul Dispatch*, July 2, 1904; *St. Paul Pioneer Press*, August 22, 1904.
[5] H. P. Hall, *Observations*, p. 320.

The self-educated "Bob" Dunn was popular with the people of Princeton, and as an active member of the Minnesota Editors' and Publishers' Association, he had a wide acquaintance among the editors of the state. As state auditor he had won the distinction of being called "Honest Bob." An alert, genial, and colorful man without any pretense, Dunn considered himself one of the common folk. There had been no refining influences in his life; his habits and manners were crude, and his speech was peppered with profanity. Once when Dunn denied he was a candidate for governor, his fellow editor, John A. Johnson, replied good-humoredly: "Bob Dunn swears that he is not a candidate. One thing is certain. Bob swears whether he is a candidate or not." [6]

Dunn paid little attention to his appearance and in dress, manner, and speech gave the impression of being a "roughneck." Tactless, impulsive, and quick to anger, he often did himself more harm than good. He was more at home talking with men in the streets, in hotel rooms, and in his office than in a drawing room. He was quite a contrast to the aloof "little judge." But his friends accepted him as he was and dwelt on his accomplishments. [7]

Governor Van Sant hesitated about supporting the candidacy of either Collins or Dunn. As a matter of fact, Van Sant had become reluctant to retire from public life and longed for a third term to continue his fight against the Northern Securities Company. In an interview on November 5, 1903, he stated that the Republican nominee for governor should be one who was in sympathy with his fight against the merger. [8] He hoped the public would interpret his statement to mean that he was the best man to continue the fight. But when no party or public demand that he run a third time developed, he let it be known that he would support Judge Collins.

Once Collins was assured that Van Sant would not run, he announced his candidacy. In a frank statement to the newspapers on November 10 he declared: "It has been well known that for several years I have aspired to the position of governor

[6] St. Peter Herald, August 23, 1903.

[7] This sketch of Dunn is based upon interviews with Henry N. Benson, Julius Schmahl, and Dr. George Osborne Orr of St. Paul, all Republicans who knew Robert Dunn, and upon the impression received of Dunn from reading many of the Minnesota newspapers of the time.

[8] Hall, Observations, pp. 317–18.

of this state. . . . My friends say that the time to announce
an open and active candidacy has arrived." [9] He went on to say
that he would stand upon the Republican state platform of 1902.
No one was surprised at the announcement, and few were very
excited about it. Robert Dunn commented: "The expected has
happened. . . . We are in a position to say that Judge Collins
will not be nominated by acclamation." [10] The general reaction
of Republican newspapers was favorable, and most editors noted
that Collins would have behind him the Van Sant machine and
the G.A.R. Even Joel Heatwole, an ardent supporter of Robert
Dunn, wrote: "Judge Collins is a gentleman of high character
and is undoubtedly well qualified to fill the position of chief executive. He is a man whose integrity is unquestioned and whose
public record is an enviable one. In short, the Judge is a hightoned gentleman." [11]

Heatwole added that Collins, of course, would now resign his
seat on the Minnesota Supreme Court bench, since he certainly
would not continue to hold the seat and run for a political office
at the same time. But Collins had no intention of resigning; in
fact, when he decided to run for governor, he did so with the express understanding among his friends that he would not resign
the judgeship.[12]

The Dunn Republicans started their campaign at once, and they
immediately began to hammer away at the point that Judge Collins had not resigned from his office. During the rest of November
and all of December the Dunn newspapers kept the issue alive.
They stirred up so much public opinion on the point that on January 1, 1904, Collins sent his letter of resignation to Van Sant, to
take effect on March 31, the end of the court term. But that was
not enough — the Dunn press then criticized him for not making
his resignation effective at once.[13]

Collins' resignation gave Governor Van Sant the opportunity to
appoint Wallace B. Douglas of Moorhead to the court vacancy,

[9] *St. Peter Herald,* November 13, 1904; *Northfield News,* November 14, 1904; *St. Peter Free Press,* November 14, 1904.
[10] *Ibid.*
[11] *Northfield News,* November 14, 1904.
[12] Collins, p. 85.
[13] *St. Paul Pioneer Press,* January 1, 1904. This newspaper took the lead for all the Dunn newspapers. Also *St. Paul Globe,* January 7, 1904; *Bemidji Pioneer,* January 7, 1904; *Duluth News Tribune,* January 1, 1904.

and William J. Donahower of St. Peter to Douglas' position as attorney general of Minnesota. These appointments caused considerable disappointment among the Republicans of Hennepin County, for they had wanted a Republican from their county to replace Collins in the Supreme Court. There were other aspirants for Collins' position who were also disappointed. None of them liked Collins any the better for Van Sant's appointments.[14]

James A. Martin of St. Cloud resigned his position as chairman of the State Board of Control to become Collins' campaign manager. Sam Fullerton of Duluth, executive agent of the Game and Fish Commission, Samuel Johnson, public examiner of Minnesota, and Judge Robert Jamison, private secretary to Van Sant, all prominent Republicans, joined Martin in his efforts for Collins. They were all Van Sant "Old Guard" Republicans who were determined to retain the political power and patronage they had, and, to do it, they knew they had to fight the Dunn "crowd." This struggle for control was almost ruinous to the party.[15]

When, on January 1, William H. Eustis declared that he would accept the nomination for governor if it were offered him, there was little interest in the announcement.[16] But there was great interest, if no surprise, in Robert Dunn's declaration of his candidacy. First he made the announcement at a public reception given in his honor by the town of Princeton. A few days later, on January 7, his formal announcement appeared on the editorial page of the *Princeton Union*. It was a long and elaborate statement, very different from Collins' brief declaration, but essentially Dunn too took his stand on the Republican platform of 1902.

With Dunn's announcement the struggle between Dunn and Collins, which had been going on behind the scenes with only slight repercussions in the newspapers, broke out into the open. The astute Frank Day made two prophecies in his *Martin County Sentinel*: "It will be a battle royal between Bob Dunn and Judge Collins with indications that so much bitterness will be engendered that the Democrats will be able to elect John A. Johnson to suc-

[14] *Northfield News*, January 16, 1904, and *St. Paul Globe*, January 1, 1904. The *Globe*, a Democratic newspaper, charged that Donahower got his position after agreeing to support Collins and to contribute to his campaign.

[15] *Ibid.*; *Faribault Pilot*, January 5, 1904; *Crookston Times*, January 2, 1904; *St. Paul Pioneer Press*, January 2, 1904.

[16] *Ibid.*, January 1, 1904.

ceed Van Sant." [17] And he prophesied that Collins would be defeated at the Republican state nominating convention or at the polls.[18]

Dunn's pre-convention campaign was carried on by Joel Heatwole, editor of the *Northfield News*, W. E. Verity, editor of the *Wadena Tribune*, Conde Hamlin, manager of the *St. Paul Pioneer Press*, C. S. Mitchell, editor of the *Alexandria Post-News*, George Flinn, who had been in the state auditor's department with Dunn, James A. Peterson of Minneapolis, and Eli Warner of St. Paul. It was known that Heatwole did not like Senator Moses Clapp, and some suggested that Heatwole wanted Clapp's office. Peterson had his eyes on Knute Nelson's senatorial post. There is little doubt that Dunn and his friends were out for more than the governorship.[19]

When Dunn announced that he approved the Republican state platform of 1902, he said in effect that he agreed with Van Sant in his fight against the Northern Securities Company. But the Collins men examined Dunn's stand on the merger in 1902 and found that he had publicly condemned Van Sant's fight against it and had refused to speak for Van Sant in the campaign because he differed with him on the "merger issue." Before he declared his candidacy, Dunn had said more than once that the merger was a dead issue.

John A. Johnson took exception to this statement: "The *Herald* confesses a fondness for rough and ready Bob Dunn, who wants to be governor of the state, but it can't agree with some of his newspaper friends that the 'merger is dead.' " [20] It was Johnson's opinion that Dunn would be defeated if he ran for governor on a platform which did not include the continuation of the fight against Hill and his newly formed holding company.

When the Collins forces accused Dunn of an alliance with J. J. Hill, Dunn replied that he had favored the organization of the Northern Securities Company because it meant success to James J. Hill in his struggle with Harriman and that he would always support a Minnesota man in such a struggle. Especially would he

[17] *Martin County Sentinel*, January 8, 1904.
[18] *Ibid.*
[19] *Minneapolis Journal*, February 6, May 25, 1904; *St. Peter Herald*, January 9, February 6, April 29, 1904; *Faribault Pilot*, May 17, 1904.
[20] *St. Peter Herald*, December 4, 1904.

support a man like Hill who had been so active in building up the railroads in the state. Hill, Dunn admitted, was a friend of his, but he insisted that he was under no obligations to Hill and would not give him favors at any time. He said he never had approved of the violation of a Minnesota law by an individual or corporation. Thoroughly confused in his argument, Dunn concluded by repeating that he stood upon the 1902 Republican state platform, which could only mean that he did not approve of the merger. The Collins faction had got what they wanted: Dunn's answer was contradictory, and his position on Hill and the merger was left in doubt.[21]

Just at this time the Minnesota Editors' and Publishers' Association met in Minneapolis. The annual banquet was held at the Nicollet Hotel on February 19, and Judge Collins and Robert Dunn both were present, along with the man most talked of as the Democratic nominee for the governorship, John A. Johnson. All three of them were on the program for speeches, and the other speakers of the evening jokingly referred to the political situation. Frank Day, for one, playfully suggested that if he were running for governor he would cultivate the country editors and entertain them at a banquet each week during the whole campaign. "My friend John A. Johnson . . . is going to do it and you want to look out for him," said Day.[22]

In concluding his address, Judge Collins paid tribute to James J. Hill and Archbishop Ireland, whom he called "great men of Minnesota." He made no reference to the pre-convention political struggle that was going on among the Republicans.

Robert Dunn, however, devoted his informal remarks primarily to the current political situation. Making a plea for the editors' support, he told them he realized that he owed much to the country press for the success of his political career. After agreeing with Collins that J. J. Hill was one of the great men of the state, Dunn remarked that if he had made such a statement first he would have been called a "mergerite." Then he made a plea for fair treatment of each other by the candidates in the coming state campaign. "It won't make any difference, ladies and gentlemen, a hundred years from now who is governor of Minnesota in the year of

---

[21] *St. Paul Pioneer Press*, February 11, 1904; *Princeton Union*, February 18, 1904.
[22] *Proceedings of the Minnesota Editors' and Publishers' Association*, 1904, pp. 70–72.

our Lord 1904. He will be forgotten. Life is too short to go into any bickerings and quarrels among friends and say unkind things. . . . " [23] If he was nominated, said Dunn, he would treat his opponent with fairness whoever the man might be. "It might be my friend Johnson — he's a good fellow; if he happened to be elected governor he would be a good governor, just as good as I would be." [24]

Some of the country editors considered Dunn's speech in bad taste, and others were so antagonized by it that from then on they refused to support his candidacy. Judge Collins had won some friends.[25]

Johnson was scheduled to give a humorous speech on "What to Do with Our Past Presidents," so it was easy for him to avoid any reference to state politics. He suggested in jest that all past presidents be made honorary members of the state legislature.

For the first time in several years, Joel Heatwole was present at the annual meeting. He was one of Dunn's close political friends and did much talking for him among the editors. He and W. E. Verity of the *Wadena Tribune* made every effort to have W. C. Whiteman, editor of the *Ortonville Herald*, elected president of the association in order to give the impression that the Minnesota Editors' and Publishers' Association stood solidly behind Dunn, but they failed in their attempt. C. F. MacDonald, a Democrat and the editor of the *St. Cloud Times*, supported by John A. Johnson, was elected president.[26] The country editors did not like the tactics of the Dunn men. At the time of their meeting, the *Minneapolis Journal*, the most vigorous Collins organ, stated that the three hundred and fifty Republican country newspapers were evenly divided between Dunn and Collins.

When in March the United States Supreme Court declared the Northern Securities Company to be illegal and ordered it dissolved, the Dunn men breathed easier and thankfully declared the merger no longer an issue. The Dunn headquarters in Minneapolis and in St. Paul were busy places. Heatwole, Verity, C. S. Mitchell,

[23] *Ibid.*, p. 88.
[24] *Ibid.*
[25] *Midway News*, March 12, 1904. Ed Paradis, editor of the *News*, also quoted the *Hinckley Enterprise*, which agreed with him that Dunn's speech was in bad taste. Paradis was an active member of the editorial association and knew Robert Dunn well.
[26] *Minneapolis Journal*, February 19, 1904; *St. Cloud Daily Journal-Press*, February 20, 1904.

and others worked to produce literature on Dunn's life and political career. They published his record as state auditor in pamphlet form and circulated it throughout the state.

The mud-slinging indulged in by both Dunn and Collins intensified as time passed. Most of the newspapers refused to print what Dunn and Collins called each other and what Dunn called Van Sant. In the *Princeton Union,* however, there is some indication of how Dunn performed. On March 17 he lashed out against the deputy state auditor, A. W. Thompson, in the *Union:* "The 'dirty campaign' prediction made by James A. Martin, Collins' manager, is being materially helped along by the *Preston Republican,* a small but abusive sheet of which Deputy State Auditor A. W. Thompson is part owner and financial backer." He accused "the dignified and immaculate Collins" of offering a bribe of three hundred dollars to R. E. Chase, editor of the *Anoka Herald,* for his support.[27] All through the campaign he attacked "that fiction fiend," Charles B. Cheney, political writer for the *Minneapolis Journal,* which he called a "yellow sheet." As to the Collins followers, Dunn wrote: "Some of the backers of Judge Collins seem to be past masters in the art of mud-slinging and villification. Mud balls are usually made by the crawling and creeping things of earth, and it begins to look as if some two-legged animals have drifted back to their first state." [28]

In an anonymous letter sent around the state by the Collins faction, Dunn was criticized for his profanity, quick temper, and careless way of dressing, and it was charged that he was frequently under the influence of liquor.[29] People began to ask themselves if they would want Bob Dunn in the governor's chair. The circulation of the letter was deplored by Republicans who on principle objected to the use of such political methods, but the damage was done. A public protest against the criticism of Dunn's personal qualities was drawn up and signed by some of his friends, including Dr. George Bridgeman of Hamline University.[30] The *Minneapolis Journal's* Charles Cheney, however, kept up a running attack on Dunn with frequent references to his "reckless

[27] *Princeton Union,* March 17, 1904.
[28] *Ibid.,* March 24, 1904.
[29] *Rochester Post and Record,* March 16, 1904.
[30] *Princeton Union,* March 31, 1904.

speech," "fiery temper," and his tendency to call his opponents
names.

With the merger no longer a live issue, the Collins men infuri-
ated Dunn by persuading Governor Van Sant to order Public Examiner Samuel Johnson to investigate Dunn's record as state auditor. Dunn was proudly using his record as state auditor as
good campaign material, and such an investigation would imply
to the public that there was something wrong. Sam Johnson, who
employed an expert accountant to do the investigating, was reported to have remarked: "Unless something is found, Mr. Dunn
will be the next governor." [31]

Dunn and his followers maintained that the investigation could
reveal nothing to reflect upon the integrity of "Honest Bob" Dunn,
because every legislature had investigated the auditor's books
while he had been in office and all reports had been commendatory.
Why, asked Dunn, should another investigation take place two
years after he had left the office unless it was an attempt to smear
him? He declared the method of investigation to be "foul, sneak-
ing, indecent politics." [32]

The first week in May the public examiner reported that although the investigation was by no means finished, it had already
revealed that Dunn had been much too lenient with the big lum-
bermen in settling with them for trespassing on state timberlands.[33] But this charge was answered effectively by the *St. Paul
Pioneer Press* in an editorial on May 6 and in a letter on May 17
from C. H. Warner of Aitkin, who had been in the auditor's office
when Dunn was auditor. It was shown clearly that with such a
vast extent of timberland in the northern part of the state, it was
impossible for the state auditor's office with its limited crew and
meager budget to check adequately upon every acre of timberland
in a year's time. Whereas the state needed at least fifty cruisers
to do the job efficiently, there were no more than six, because the
auditor's budget provided for no more. Timber stealing was the result. During his three terms as auditor Dunn had collected from
trespassers about ten times the amount of money that had been
collected by all the auditors who preceded him. He had found it

[31] *St. Paul Pioneer Press,* March 12, 1904.
[32] *Ibid.; Princeton Union,* May 6, June 9, 1904.
[33] *St. Paul Pioneer Press,* May 6, 1904; *Minneapolis Journal,* June 1, 1904.

difficult to obtain enough evidence to prove willful trespass in some cases and so had made certain settlements on the best terms he could. But he had brought order and efficiency into the auditor's office and was the best auditor the state had had for many years. Nonetheless the Collins faction made the most of their charge against Dunn's record.

Collins was continually making references to the close connection between Dunn and J. J. Hill, insinuating that Dunn "wore Hill's collar." In fact, W. W. Jermane, Washington correspondent for the *Minneapolis Journal,* declared that J. J. Hill, determined to defeat Van Sant and all his friends for their attack on the Northern Securities merger, wanted to put Dunn in the governor's chair and Joel Heatwole in the United States Senate.[34] During the pre-convention campaign the *Journal* frequently referred to the "Hill-Dunn-Heatwole" combination. Dunn, in a speech in Minneapolis on May 6, said he had met J. J. Hill on the street and that Hill was very angry at Collins for his determined stand against the merger. Then Dunn went on to make a countercharge against Collins:

I have it upon the authority of James J. Hill that when Judge Collins was running against Judge Willis for the supreme bench, the Great Northern Railway contributed between $30,000 and $40,000 to his campaign fund; and I have it on the same authority that E. A. Nelson, state librarian, went to the Great Northern Railway to get $25,000 for Judge Collins in the present campaign. I will withdraw from the gubernatorial campaign right now if it can be proved that the Great Northern has been asked or that money has been given by the road for me in this campaign.[35]

Judge Collins wasted no time in replying. He immediately sent the following letter to Robert Dunn:

Did you use this language, or any other of like import? If you are correctly reported you accuse Mr. Hill, as well as myself, of very serious offenses. You placed him in the attitude of furnishing funds to corrupt the voters of this state, a common boodler, and I am accused of soliciting a large sum of money from Mr. Hill for the purpose of corrupting and boodling the voters. I simply want to know if you used this or similar language. An early and direct reply is earnestly solicited.[36]

[34] Quoted in the *St. Peter Herald,* February 6, 1903.
[35] Hall, *Observations,* p. 322; *Mankato Free Press,* May 10, 1904.
[36] Hall, *Observations,* p. 322.

Dunn ignored the request for a reply but indicated to the newspapers that he had been quoted correctly. Whereupon, on May 13 Collins issued a long statement to the newspapers. It began:

During my residence of fifty years in Minnesota, never before have I been called upon to publicly resent an attack upon my personal character. I cannot allow the recent attack of Mr. Dunn to go unnoticed. He has a right to his own views upon public questions, and he may choose his political associates, but he has no right to defame others who differ with him and his friends upon those questions. I judge him from his own language and acts.[37]

Then Collins attacked Dunn's stand on the merger issue. He quoted a statement that Dunn gave to the *St. Paul Pioneer Press* on January 3, 1902, in which Dunn said: "I believe that the fight against Mr. Hill was inspired by rival railway companies, and I am heartily out of sympathy with it because of this belief."

Collins went on to explain that he had written to Mr. Hill and asked him the following questions: "Did you contribute any sum whatsoever to my campaign fund when I was a candidate against the Hon. John Willis, or have you ever contributed to that fund in any other campaign? If so, when, where, how much, and to whom was the money paid?" and "Did I ever solicit or receive from you, or from anyone connected with you in business or otherwise, any money whatsoever for campaign purposes? If so, when, where, how much, and to whom was the money paid?" Hill replied that Collins' letter was somewhat ambiguous, and he asked just how detailed an answer Collins wanted. Collins clearly restated the charge made against him by Dunn and repeated his questions. Hill's second reply read:

I am in receipt of your letter of the 10th inst., and if you desire a personal interview on the subject of the letter I will be at home all of this week and will see you at my office any time you desire. No contribution was personally solicited by you or made to you by me. By whom contributions were solicited and to whom made is a proper subject for a personal interview rather than of correspondence.

Collins felt that this letter cleared him of Dunn's charge, and he stated unequivocally that he never had requested or received any campaign contribution from J. J. Hill nor had he ever asked

[37] *Ibid.*, p. 323.

anyone else to do so for him.[38] E. A. Nelson also issued a statement denying that he had solicited money from Hill for the Collins-Willis campaign in 1894.[39]

Johnson came close to judging the situation correctly when he commented upon Dunn's charge: "Bob Dunn must be pretty close to Jim Hill to get him to make a statement like that. Jim wouldn't tell that to a stranger or an enemy." [40] Later, Johnson wrote that he had no doubts that Hill was backing Dunn in his campaign against Collins.[41]

With Collins insisting that Dunn was spreading lies about him and Dunn calling the first report of the investigation of his record as state auditor a "mess of lies," [42] the state of the campaign worried such a long-time Republican as William H. Grimshaw, United States marshal and loyal party member. He wrote to Senator Knute Nelson about the situation:

I earnestly hope that neither Dunn nor Collins will procure the nomination, if we can dead-lock the Convention, there may be a show for Eustis or Eddy, but the whole thing is dependent upon Hennepin County, Dunn already has Duluth and St. Paul, if he carries Minneapolis he will be nominated. I think that Dunn is more objectionable than Collins, every slap we have had has come from the Dunn forces, all of the Dunn men opposed Clapp as temporary Chairman of the Convention, and to my way of thinking it is absolute folly to conciliate the enemy. What the Hill, Heatwole, Dunn combination really need is a damned good licking. Do not listen to any emissaries that the Dunn people will send to Alexandria. Jim Peterson and many others will soon be making pilgrimages to your town, they are all . . . in a combination secretly working . . . against Clapp and some of them against you, therefore remain perfectly neutral and do not give the Dunn forces any encouragement. Frank Eddy has more good hard sense than Dunn and Collins combined. Eustis is a good fellow but he is afraid he cannot win. Old Van Sant is still a candidate and this of course is hurting Collins. . . . Of one thing I am sure, Bob Dunn is spending Jim Hill's money at the present time . . . [43]

Soren Listoe, a good friend of Senator Nelson's, wrote that he

[38] Ibid., pp. 323–26; Minneapolis Journal, May 13, 1904.
[39] Hall, Observations, p. 326.
[40] St. Peter Herald, May 13, 1904.	[41] Ibid., May 27, 1904.
[42] Minneapolis Journal, June 1, 1904.
[43] Knute Nelson Papers, in Minnesota Historical Society, Grimshaw to Nelson, May 13, 1904.

thought Bob Dunn was too much of a "rough diamond" to be
governor of Minnesota and that Collins was not much of a candidate either. He suggested the time had come for a "*first* class
third man to step in." [44]

Then on June 4 a group of men including Dunn and his arch-
enemy, Charles Cheney of the *Minneapolis Journal,* stood talking
on the corner of Sixth and Wabasha streets in St. Paul. In the
course of the conversation someone teased Dunn about the *Journal*'s opposition to him. Dunn's temper flared, and he replied that
he was lucky to have that "dirty sheet" against him. Then he
turned to Cheney and sneeringly said: "I can buy that old paper
for ten cents. I can buy you for ten cents. That's how cheap you
are, Cheney." Cheney colored and asked Dunn just what he
meant, and Dunn swore at him in reply. Cheney was angered
and suggested that Dunn retract his words, whereupon Dunn hit
Cheney over the head with his umbrella, crushing Cheney's derby
hat. Cheney hit back at Dunn before other men in the group realized what was happening and separated them. [45]

The Collins faction was jubilant! Dunn had given them more
campaign ammunition, and they made the most of it. Few newspapers agreed with the editor of the *Bemidji Sentinel,* who declared that Cheney had got what was coming to him. The *Mankato Free Press* was sure that Dunn was unfit to be governor, and
the pro-Collins *Minneapolis Tribune* pointed out that the governor's chair was no place for a man who could not control his
temper and whose speech was so profane. [46]

Cheney's *Minneapolis Journal* devoted a long editorial to a discussion of the subject, "The Office of Governor of Minnesota."
It said that for a long time the *Journal* had been aware of the personal defects which would make Dunn's elevation to the governorship a "public misfortune" but that the paper had tried to keep
its opposition to the political issues of the campaign. Dunn, however, by his brutal attack upon Cheney and the language he used
to Cheney, language so foul "as not to be printable," had turned
the attention of the people of the state to the question of what

[44] *Ibid.,* Listoe to Nelson, May 10, 1904.
[45] *Mankato Free Press,* June 6, 1904.
[46] *Ibid.,* June 8, 1904; *Bemidji Sentinel,* June 8, 1904; *Minneapolis Tribune,* June 6,
1904.

qualifications a man should possess to fill the position of chief executive of Minnesota. According to the *Journal*, the governor of the state should be one who had the respect of all his fellow citizens, who was of high character and gentlemanly demeanor, who was recognized as clean in thought and speech, and who conducted himself upon all occasions so that the people would never be ashamed of him or fearful of what he might say.[47]

Johnson voiced the sentiments of many people of the state in an editorial in the *Herald*:

Few states have had the misfortune to witness so disgraceful a gubernatorial campaign as that now in progress between rival Republican candidates in this state. Charges of dishonesty are made every day, and strange to relate, unproved except by a denial that leaves the public poisoned with distrust. . . . Honest men desirous of good government can find little excuse for supporting either [candidate]. . . . Think of it — when the statements of leaders are branded lies; when public men are all accused of unworthy motives; when the statements of men in high places are all discredited, the situation is not only hopeless but disgraceful and deplorable. About all that either side has successfully demonstrated up to date is the unfitness of both.[48]

Such was the state of affairs on the eve of the Republican National Convention and the state nominating convention.

The Republicans held their national convention in Chicago, and on June 23 Theodore Roosevelt was unanimously nominated for president of the United States. His nomination had been a foregone conclusion, and the convention was a dull one. Under Roosevelt's orders, Henry Cabot Lodge of Massachusetts had drafted the uninspiring party platform, which endorsed the gold standard, a protective tariff, Roosevelt's record on government restraint of trusts, and the Republican Philippine policy.

Minnesota Republicans were solidly for Roosevelt. They were sure he would carry the state — but they were not sure Robert Dunn would do the same. On the eve of the Republican state nominating convention the Dunn and Collins factions seemed about evenly matched, and they had agreed finally upon Senator Moses Clapp as temporary convention chairman. Clapp had not openly expressed himself for either Dunn or Collins, but it was

[47] *Minneapolis Journal*, June 6, 1904.
[48] *St. Peter Herald*, June 10, 1904.

believed he preferred Collins. Certainly the Dunn men had to be persuaded to accept him as temporary chairman.

The night before the convention opened, the Republican state central committee, consisting of seventeen Collins men and twelve Dunn men, met at the Windsor Hotel in St. Paul to issue badges of admission to the regular delegates and tickets to the gallery to delegates whose credentials were contested. That took until about midnight, and then word came to Judge Jamison, chairman of the committee, that a large crowd had gathered at the governor's office and was clamoring to see Van Sant and Jamison. Van Sant was in the hotel, too, so the two men walked to the capitol together to meet about a hundred anxious and excited men.

In substance, the group wanted the state central committee to make up a final roll of official delegates to the convention. Their plan was that, immediately upon Judge Jamison's calling the convention to order, someone would rise and offer a resolution to the effect that the roll of delegates drawn up by the committee be accepted; then Judge Jamison would declare the resolution adopted no matter what might be the reaction of the convention. Since there was a majority of Collins men on the state central committee, the recognition of the contesting Collins delegates from Hennepin and Ramsey counties would be assured.

But Judge Jamison, a Collins man, stoutly refused to entertain the suggestion. He patiently explained that he could not do more than call the convention to order — that to do more would be a discourtesy to Senator Clapp, the chosen presiding officer. The incident indicated that the Collins men were worried.[49]

The next morning, on June 30, the delegates assembled in St. Paul. Judge Jamison called the convention to order, and Senator Clapp took his place as temporary chairman. The general feeling was that Clapp would be fair in his rulings, and both factions were relieved that there was not to be a struggle over the temporary chairmanship.[50]

The first problem to be settled was that of contesting delegations, particularly the large delegations from Ramsey and Hennepin counties. The local party organizations in those two counties

[49] Hall, *Observations*, pp. 327–30.
[50] *Ibid.*, p. 330; *St. Paul Dispatch*, July 1, 1904.

were controlled by Collins men, and the Dunn faction charged that in the primary elections for delegates to the county conventions the voters had had difficulty in finding Dunn ballots. Also it was charged that nonresidents came into the counties to vote for Collins and that in the county conventions held to choose delegates to the state convention the chairmen had refused to recognize Dunn delegates. The Dunn forces thereupon bolted both county conventions, held conventions of their own, and elected delegates to the state convention.[51]

The Collins men, of course, claimed the Dunn delegations from Ramsey and Hennepin counties were illegal. A credentials committee agreed upon by both factions was then appointed by Senator Clapp. It consisted of fifteen members, seven Dunn men and seven Collins men and one man representing Frank Eddy, who had offered himself as a candidate for governor in case of a deadlock between Dunn and Collins. Eddy's representative was State Senator Ward of Alexandria, who was thought to be a Collins follower. When the personnel of the committee was announced to the convention, the "Collins men were accordingly jubilant, and the Dunn men grew a little belligerent, talking about taking matters in their own hands if they were likely to be defeated by an eight to seven decision." [52]

The convention recessed, and the credentials committee began to hear the evidence from the contesting delegations. Although the committee remained in session far into the night, it was not ready to report until four o'clock the next afternoon. Then Senator Ward presented a majority report which, by a vote of eight to seven, seated the Collins delegations from both Ramsey and Hennepin counties. A minority report recommended that the Collins delegation from Ramsey County and the Dunn delegation from Hennepin County be seated. This meant that one hundred and thirteen votes from Hennepin County would go to Dunn, and the Dunn faction was sure its candidate needed those votes to be nominated. After about two hours of discussion, the convention, by a vote of 622½ to 450½, accepted the minority report.[53]

[51] St. Paul Pioneer Press, June 28, 29, 1904; Minneapolis Journal, June 29, 1904.
[52] Hall, Observations, p. 332.
[53] Ibid., pp. 337–38; Princeton Union, July 7, 1904; St. Paul Pioneer Press, July 1, 2, 1904; Minneapolis Journal, July 1, 2, 1904; Folwell, vol. 3, pp. 274–75.

The Dunn men were exultant! As the Dunn Hennepin County delegates took their seats on the floor of the convention amid much cheering, the Collins delegates dejectedly went into the gallery or out into the halls and the street. W. H. Grimshaw, United States marshal and a member of the ousted Hennepin County delegation, had to ask one of the members of the committee on permanent organization to make his report for him. He had been chairman of that committee, but now he was not even a member of the convention. During one of the recesses that day he had written Senator Knute Nelson:

The battle is on and . . . I am of the opinion that Robert Dunn will be nominated Governor, they have corrupted many of our delegates and thrown others out by fake contests, were it not a presidential year I should say that Mr. Dunn could not be elected, but I think the presidential majority will pull him through. . . . [54]

Once the convention had accepted the minority report, the nomination of Dunn was only a matter of form. James A. Peterson of Minneapolis delivered the nominating speech for Dunn, and then James A. Martin, Collins' campaign manager, moved that the nomination be accepted by acclamation. His motion was adopted.[55]

Actually Dunn would have been nominated without the votes from Hennepin County. A canvass of votes showed that Collins had only 563½ votes even with those from Hennepin County, and 588 votes were needed to nominate him. The bolting by the Dunn forces in Ramsey and Hennepin counties had been unnecessary, and it had left among the Collins men a deep resentment which led some of them to begin at once to plan for Dunn's defeat.[56]

The convention adopted a platform which reaffirmed the Republican national platform and endorsed the nomination of Theodore Roosevelt for president. Tribute was paid to Van Sant, and all the Republican representatives to Congress were endorsed. Confidence in Senators Nelson and Clapp was expressed and the support of Clapp for re-election by the new legislature was pledged. The platform demanded a system of good roads for Min-

[54] Nelson Papers, Grimshaw to Nelson, July 1, 1904.
[55] *St. Paul Dispatch*, July 2, 1904; Hall, *Observations*, p. 341.
[56] Folwell, vol. 3, p. 275.

nesota, an eight-hour working day for labor, legislation regulating trusts, and equal taxation for all classes of citizens.[57]

Most of the Republican newspapers of the state accepted Dunn's nomination, and whether or not they had been for Collins before the convention, most of them began to urge the election of Dunn. Conde Hamlin's *St. Paul Pioneer Press* took the lead in an editorial on July 3:

Robert C. Dunn is not a great statesman, a learned jurist or an accomplished scholar. But he is nevertheless one of the most deserving and popular candidates for governor ever presented to the people of the state. He is strong with the plain people of the state for the same reason that he was strong with the Convention which represented them. For he is one of them himself — a plain man of the plain people, whose sturdy, native common sense and rugged honesty and firmness of character and purpose united with a large and intelligent public spirit and a keen and comprehensive capacity for public affairs made his administration of the office of state auditor a memorable epoch of progress and reform in the history of the state, and . . . lifted him . . . high above any other candidate in public favor for the highest office of the state.

Two days later, in answer to some criticism of Dunn's personal qualities, the *Pioneer Press* replied that Dunn was no Chesterfield in dress and manners but had an intelligent grasp of public issues and devotion to duty which eminently fitted him for the governor's chair. The *Minnesota Union Advocate,* the official organ of the Minnesota Federation of Labor and the Trades and Labor Assembly of St. Paul, hailed Dunn's nomination with the statement:

Robert C. Dunn's nomination for governor has struck a popular cord with the working people of Minnesota, and especially with members of labor organizations. Never before has a man possessing a union card been nominated for chief executive of this state, and the common people are looking hopefully forward with the expectation of having a staunch friend in the governor's chair with the beginning of next year.[58]

Johnson commented that Dunn's victory was "a Jim Hill victory, the most sweeping of any that a state political manipulator

[57] *St. Paul Dispatch,* July 1, 1904; *Minneapolis Journal,* July 2, 1904.
[58] Quoted in the *Princeton Union,* July 14, 1904.

has ever won." But, he added, "all good loyal Republicans will go to work in a solid phalanx to elect the ticket. But, oh, how it will grind some of them." [59] According to the Democratic *Faribault Pilot*, the Democrats of Minnesota could rejoice over Dunn's nomination, for "they believe he is the weakest candidate that the Republicans could have nominated. Shrewd Democrats figure that there are enough independent, incorruptible voters yet in Minnesota to elect a governor." [60]

It remained for the *Minneapolis Journal* to state the reaction of the resentful Collins group. In an editorial entitled "Nomination of Dunn," the *Journal* declared war upon him:

R. C. Dunn has been nominated by the republicans for the office of governor of Minnesota. The *Journal* has opposed this choice because it is thoroughly convinced that Mr. Dunn is not a fit man for this office, either from the standpoint of private character or public record. The fact that he has been able to receive the nomination does not alter our judgment in any particular. He may be elected, but if he is, nothing will ever happen in connection with that election which will give the *Journal* as much satisfaction as the reflection that it has not been party to this unfortunate result at any stage in the proceedings.[61]

During July and August there was an increasing feeling of dissatisfaction with Dunn's nomination. On July 20 the *Minneapolis Tribune* warned: "It is well that a respectable number of personally respectable Republicans in Minnesota desire to defeat the Republican candidate for governor." The *Bemidji Sentinel*, trying to keep up its courage, replied on August 3: "Pshaw! The Collins men in this state are just about the same kind of fellows as the Dunn crowd and when anyone tells us that even a respectable number of Republicans are going to keep mad simply because they got a licking in a convention we choose not to believe them." The paper then made a plea to the Collins men to give up their grievances and join with the rest of the Republicans to elect a Republican governor.

Nonetheless, the disaffected Republicans waited with unusual interest to see who would be the Democratic nominee. If he was acceptable to them, they were ready to help elect him governor of Minnesota.

[59] *St. Peter Herald*, July 8, 1904, and quoted in the *St. Paul Globe*, July 19, 1904.
[60] *Faribault Pilot*, July 7, 1904.　　　[61] *Minneapolis Journal*, July 2, 1904.

## CHAPTER VI

*The Election of 1904*

THE Democrats had watched with great interest the strife in the Republican party, but they could take little hope from it unless they put their own house in order. The Minnesota Democrats split upon candidates, too, but upon the candidates for the presidency — Judge Alton B. Parker and William Randolph Hearst.

The leaders of the national Democratic party were determined not to run Bryan again. Twice he had been defeated; that was enough. The party leaders resolved to choose a candidate who would appeal to the conservative East, and they settled upon Judge Alton B. Parker of New York, a man of intelligence and substance, but "placid, colorless, mediocre, and conservative." [1]

Some of the Bryanites, however, flocked to the standard of William Randolph Hearst, owner of the *New York Journal* and a man who had done his best to cause war with Spain in 1898. Ambitious, colorful, and full of vitality, Hearst wanted political power and recognition. He gained the support of some former Populists and many industrial workers, and when the Democratic National Convention met at St. Louis, Hearst was there with a hundred and four delegates instructed for him. A few of those delegates came from Minnesota.

The Minnesota Democrats had met in convention on June 22 to elect delegates to the national convention, and at this state convention a bitter struggle developed between the Parker and the Hearst Democrats. Johnson was one of the Nicollet County delegation, which was pledged to Parker. The "Big Four" of the Democratic party — John Lind, Leonard Rosing, T. D. O'Brien, and Frank Day — were Parker men, but some of the other party leaders were for Hearst.

In a great battle of words "in which nearly every recognized

[1] Hibben, p. 250.

136

leader in the state was called a traitor and no better than a Republican," [2] the Democrats turned their convention into pandemonium until C. D. O'Brien of St. Paul, in great disgust, mounted the platform and shouted for order. Then followed a short speech by John Lind which was the most dramatic incident of the convention. After urging the delegates to cease attacking one another, Lind shocked his listeners by announcing his retirement from politics. Many Democrats had counted on Lind to oppose Robert Dunn.

Sobered by this unexpected development, the convention elected a delegation to the national convention that was uninstructed and divided, half for Parker and half for Hearst.[3]

When Minnesota Democrats received the news that Alton B. Parker had been nominated to oppose Theodore Roosevelt, they knew that Parker would lose the Republican state of Minnesota, where Roosevelt was highly popular. The Parker men, however, retained control of the party, and their next job was to plan for the state nominating convention to be held in August.

The party leaders regretted Lind's decision to quit politics. In a letter to Lind, Leonard Rosing discussed the situation:

I regret very much indeed that your resolution is "irrevocable," because I believe your candidacy this year would mean more for Democracy than it ever has before. I believe that with you as a candidate for Governor, we could also elect a Lieutenant-Governor and an Attorney-General . . .

If you absolutely refuse to become a candidate, I believe that the politics of the situation demands the nomination of some strong hightoned American who will particularly appeal to the high grade native American voter. Dunn has shocked the sentiment of those people by his uncouth ways, profane language and the coarseness of the campaign. The situation demands that in case a new man should be chosen to represent the Democracy as its nominee this fall we should at once begin lining up for the man decided upon.

The Convention coming on August 30th. makes it too late to present a new man to the voters; but if we could through conferences agree upon the nominee within the next 10 days or two weeks and then begin to advertise him through our country papers and through

[2] *Duluth News Tribune,* June 23, 1904.

[3] *Ibid.,* June 23, 24, 1904; *Duluth Evening Herald,* June 23, 1904; *Minneapolis Tribune,* June 22, 23, 1904; *St. Paul Globe,* June 22, 1904.

the medium of the daily papers that are opposed to Dunn, then much can be accomplished. If we let the matter run until August 30th. without the selection of a man around whom we can rally, then it will discourage the anti-Dunn Republicans and they will gradually pull in their horns or crawl into their holes and the advantage that we hoped to derive from the soreness existing in the Rep. party will be lost.[4]

In his reply Lind suggested L. L. Brown of Winona as a possible candidate, but Rosing rejected him and proposed W. H. Harries. There seemed to be no enthusiasm for either of these men on the part of other party leaders.

All during the year there had been much talk of Johnson as the Democratic candidate for governor. He had drawn attention when he delivered the nominating speech for Lind in 1900, and in 1902 there had been a definite movement to draft him to run for governor. No sooner had Dunn announced his candidacy than some of the country newspapers as well as the Twin Cities' newspapers suggested that John A. Johnson of St. Peter would probably be Dunn's opponent. As early as February 27, 1904, the *Minneapolis Journal* stated that Johnson was the favorite of the political speculators as the best possible Democratic candidate, "but has turned it down positively."

As the Dunn-Collins fight developed, letters from Republicans as well as Democrats flooded the *Herald* office, urging Johnson to become a candidate for the nomination.[5] Among those who pressed Johnson to run were H. J. Miller of Luverne, R. E. Thompson of Preston, and A. O. Eberhart of Mankato, all Republican leaders. Among the Democratic leaders Frank A. Day of Fairmont was an untiring advocate of Johnson. In his *Martin County Sentinel*, Day had been urging Johnson's candidacy for many years. Now he was utterly convinced that Johnson was the candidate the party needed, and he zealously talked of Johnson's qualifications to the other party leaders.[6]

After Dunn was nominated, the *Minneapolis Journal*'s political writer, Charles B. Cheney, suggested that the Democrats nominate Johnson for governor. "The St. Peter editor is one of the strong men in the Democratic party of the state, with a good

[4] John Lind Papers, in Minnesota Historical Society, Rosing to Lind, July 18, 1904.
[5] Charles B. Cheney, "Johnson of Minnesota," *Outlook*, January 25, 1908, vol. 88.
[6] Day and Knappen, p. 120.

legislative record, and known to be conservative and clear headed. He's a good debater, and his only disqualification is that he is not a man of wealth to contribute to the campaign which is likely to be a fundless one." [7] The *Preston Times* declared that all indications pointed to Johnson as the Democratic candidate and noted that almost all the Republican newspapers of the state had stopped in the midst of the Republican fight to say kind words about Johnson when he was mentioned as the Democratic nominee.[8] Not a Republican editor spoke unkindly of Johnson.

On August 8 there gathered in the offices of C. D. and T. D. O'Brien a group of Democratic leaders which included Rosing, Day, Lind, Pierce Butler, Judge C. M. Pond of Minneapolis, Carlos Avery of Hutchinson, William Gausewitz of Owatonna, W. H. Harries, L. L. Brown, and a few others.[9] All these men were Parker Democrats, and they were meeting to discuss possible candidates for governor. Most of the discussion centered around Johnson. Those present seemed to agree that he was the logical candidate, but there was some opposition from John Lind. It was reported later that Lind would not "swallow" Johnson because Johnson had not supported him on all measures while he was governor and Johnson was in the legislature.[10] Apparently others of the group also had reservations about Johnson, for two days after the meeting William Gausewitz wrote the following to Lind:

In order for us to win, we must nominate a man for the head of the ticket, the very opposite of Dunn. This, I do not think, Johnson is. Judging from the remarks you made, Judge Pond would come closer to it, and I hope that someone will turn up before the 30th. who will be better suited for the office of Governor than the Editor.[11]

Nor was Rosing enthusiastic about Johnson, although he had no strong objections to "the editor." [12] Several factors had to be considered. In the first place, the Parker men had to have the approval of their candidate by the Hearst faction, for they could

[7] *Minneapolis Journal*, July 4, 1904.
[8] *Preston Times*, April 20, 1904.
[9] *St. Paul Globe*, August 8, 1904; *St. Paul Dispatch*, August 9, 1904; *Minneapolis Journal*, August 9, 1904; *Duluth News Tribune*, August 10, 1904.
[10] Elinor Johnson Smith and Henry N. Benson to W. G. H.; *St. Paul Pioneer Press*, August 10, 1904; *Duluth News Tribune*, August 10, 1904; *St. Paul Dispatch*, August 10, 1904. Also, see above, pp. 99–100.
[11] Lind Papers, Gausewitz to Lind, August 10, 1904.
[12] *St. Paul Dispatch*, August 10, 1904.

never elect a Democrat governor of the state without the cooperation of all Democrats. Secondly, they hoped to choose a candidate who would be acceptable to the Collins-Van Sant Republicans, and third, the Democrats knew they would need as much money as they could scrape together to pay for a campaign. Finally, they had no assurance that Johnson would consent to become the Democratic nominee. He had been in touch with some of them and had indicated that he was not interested in the nomination. On August 19 in the *St. Peter Herald* he made public his attitude:

Some ten days ago at a conference of a number of democrats held in St. Paul, John A. Johnson of this paper was selected as an available candidate for the democratic nomination for governor this year. The papers of the state took the matter up and many kind and complimentary things have been said. Letters from republicans and democrats of many parts of the state have been received all in the same vein. That this has been very gratifying and pleasing to Mr. Johnson is only natural, and it is all the more so in that it has all been done without solicitation and free from any suggestion whatsoever from him. It is a great compliment and will be a source of pleasure so long as the recipient shall live. But Mr. Johnson has not been a candidate for that nomination and is not now, and is not likely to be when the Convention assembles. Appreciating the great honor of that nomination, whether it brought success or defeat, Mr. Johnson has not yet seen his way clear to yield to the importunities of his friends. He is nevertheless grateful to his friends at home and abroad and to his newspaper friends thruout the state for their generous and almost lavish expressions of good will. These he will never forget.

Johnson was not being coy. He really did not feel that he could seriously entertain the idea of being a nominee for several reasons. He was a man of modest means and had just finished paying for a new home. He had no money to contribute to a campaign. More important, his health was delicate, and the leaders of the Democratic party knew it.[13] No one could be sure just how well he would endure a strenuous state campaign. Also, Johnson was not at all convinced that the Democratic nominee stood a chance to win. Some of the newspapers expressed the opinion that he was too good a man to be sacrificed for the party.[14]

[13] Dr. George Orr to W. G. H.
[14] *Minneapolis Journal*, August 13, 1904.

Most of the state's newspapers had only favorable reactions to the possibility of Johnson's candidacy. The *Mankato Review* expressed the opinion of most of the Republican papers when it commented: "Mr. Johnson is one of the bright and prominent newspapermen of this state. While he cannot expect the support of every brother editor in Minnesota, yet one thing is certain, none can help but speak or refer to him in the most friendly and kindly manner, and way down in the corner of their hearts they will wish him success." [15] The Republican editors would not relish working for Johnson's defeat, and the worst they could say of him was that he voted the wrong ticket.[16]

Johnson's friend, Frank Day, was certain Johnson would be the ideal candidate for the Democrats. He expressed his opinion of Johnson in the *Martin County Sentinel* on August 12:

[He] is a man of acknowledged ability and fitness for office. He is an accomplished orator and would conduct a whirlwind campaign. He is a good mixer, a man whom everybody enjoys meeting and greeting. He is popular among the newspaper boys and would receive the support of several influential republican journals. He has a large experience in public life, and is thoroughly familiar with the different branches of government. And best of all, he is a man whose character, in the language of President Roosevelt, is "as clean as a hound's tooth!"

Not long after the meeting of August 8 another conference was held, including about twenty party leaders representing both the Parker and the Hearst factions. The Democratic state convention was scheduled to meet on August 30, so the party leaders had to come to an agreement upon a candidate for governor. Johnson had been informed of the conference, and while it was going on, he sent Frank Day a telegram explaining that he had just written a statement for the *St. Paul Globe* which "would make it impossible for him to be considered for the nomination." [17] Day called him on the telephone and persuaded him not to send the statement until he had talked personally with Day. Then the question was brought to a vote in the conference, and every man except one, who refrained from voting, cast his ballot in favor of Johnson.

---

[15] Quoted in the *St. Paul Globe*, August 20, 1904.
[16] *Fairmont News*, quoted in the *St. Paul Globe*, August 20, 1904; *Rochester Post-Record*, August 25, 1904.
[17] Day and Knappen, p. 121.

When the meeting was over Frank Day had just enough time to catch the train for St. Peter to see Johnson. "It was a hot summer day, a storm was impending, Mr. Day was tired, and the gloom of the weather seemed to combine with the apathy of the meeting and his own physical condition to discourage him from his errand. At St. Peter, Johnson, by prearrangement, met Day at the rear of the train, unnoticed, and the two hastened to the Johnson home. The storm had just broken with a cyclonic fury, Johnson was indifferent, Day was dejected, and altogether it did not seem as if the time were propitious for the birth of an enterprise." [18]

All evening and into the next morning Johnson, his wife, and Frank Day sat on the Johnsons' front porch discussing the situation. They considered the disaffection in the Republican party and reviewed the state by counties, and finally Day convinced Johnson that the Democrats had an unusual opportunity to win. Johnson decided he would accept the nomination if it came to him without any effort on his part, if he did not have to make any financial contribution to the campaign, and if Frank Day would consent to become his campaign manager. Mrs. Johnson had hoped her husband would run and was happy with his decision. [19]

Frank Day returned to St. Paul, and on August 25 Johnson went there to confer with the party leaders, who then accepted him on his own terms. [20] The next day Johnson made the following announcement in the *Herald*:

Mr. Johnson did not believe it possible for him to yield to the importunities of his friends, but the pressure has been so great, the offers of friendship so cordial that Mr. Johnson has come to the conclusion that duty is stronger than personal wishes. He therefore has concluded that if the nomination is tendered him by a united party and by the unanimous action of the convention he will accept the nomination. He appreciates the fact that it has not yet been offered, but in case it is and it comes without the bitterness of contest, he will accept it.

The *Duluth Labor World*, whose editor, William McEwen, was an ardent Bryan follower, was not at all pleased with the plan of

[18] *Ibid.*, pp. 121–22.
[19] *Ibid.*, pp. 122–23; Elinor Johnson Smith to W. G. H.
[20] *Minneapolis Journal*, August 25, 1904; *St. Paul Pioneer Press*, August 26, 1904.

the Democratic leaders. The nomination of Johnson, a Gold Democrat and the only party member to oppose Lind in the legislature, "would be a reward for treachery and party disruption," declared the *Labor World*.[21] The paper suggested that if the Collins Republicans supported Johnson, the Hearst Democrats should agree to support Dunn. But the leaders of the Hearst faction had already agreed to back Johnson, and all that remained was for the Democratic state convention to nominate formally the full ticket drawn up by the party leaders.

The state convention opened at noon on August 30 in Exposition Hall in Minneapolis. The Parker Democrats were in control, and the Hearst faction made no attempt to challenge their power. Nothing occurred which had not been planned by the party leaders. Winfield S. Hammond of St. James delivered the speech nominating Johnson for governor. One after the other, the counties seconded the nomination, and Johnson was nominated by acclamation. The whole convention then rose to its feet and "howled itself hoarse." [22]

In the midst of this enthusiastic demonstration, Johnson came to the platform to accept the nomination. Smiling, he told the convention that the nomination was not unexpected but that it was unsought and unsolicited by him. Declaring that he was grateful for the honor bestowed upon him by the Democratic party, he promised to go into the campaign with all the energy and enthusiasm he possessed. Then he put himself on record as being opposed to the merger of the Northern Pacific and Great Northern railroad companies, which he condemned as "unholy" and as a crime against the laws of the state. He stated his opposition to all combinations "made for the restraint of trade and the restriction of competition" and to all private monopoly. Finally, he urged reciprocity with Canada. In conclusion he declared:

If I win I have only this promise to make: I shall give to the state my best service, and an administration of affairs which shall be dictated by an honest conscience. Should I lose, I trust I may say as that matchless leader said recently at St. Louis: "You may deny that I made a gallant fight, but you cannot deny that I have kept the faith!" [23]

[21] *Duluth Labor World*, August 27, 1904.
[22] *St. Paul Dispatch*, August 31, 1904.          [23] *Ibid.*

Johnson showed himself to be a winner of men at the convention. Cordial, frank, natural in speech and in manner, he impressed the delegates with his ability, sincerity, wide acquaintance, and enthusiasm.

The rest of the party ticket was then nominated: Fendall G. Winston of Minneapolis for lieutenant governor, John E. King, editor of the *Red Lake Falls Courier*, for secretary of state, T. J. McDermott for attorney general, and Byron J. Mosier of Stillwater for treasurer. The party platform included the following demands: support of the national platform, revision of the tariff and a tariff convention with Canada, increased power for the Interstate Commerce Commission, the end of private monopoly, increased power for the State Railroad and Warehouse Commission to enable it to set just rates, prohibition of the merging of competing railroad lines, readjustment of distributing rates that would do away with discrimination against Minnesota shippers in favor of those from outside the state, condemnation of the practice of corporations contributing to political campaigns, a constitutional amendment providing for the increase of the gross earnings tax from 3 to 4 per cent, the right of labor to organize, the selection of judges without regard to political party, and the direct election of United States senators.[24]

After reading the Democratic platform, the *St. Paul Dispatch* commented that there were few issues about which the Democrats and Republicans could quarrel and that the campaign would certainly be one of personalities rather than issues.[25] The rabid Dunn paper, the *Pioneer Press*, admitted that the Democratic ticket was "a fairly good one" and that "John A. Johnson and F. G. Winston are both men who have the respect of the people of the state and who are probably entirely fit for office, so far as their personal character is concerned. Neither, however, possesses any conspicuous qualities either of native ability or of experience to make him a strong competitor of his Republican opponent." [26]

Joel Heatwole, who was beginning to have difficulties with Robert Dunn, complained that the Democratic and Republican platforms were so much alike that all the Republicans who did not like

[24] *Ibid.*
[25] *Ibid.*
[26] *St. Paul Pioneer Press*, September 1, 1904.

Dunn could vote for Johnson with clear consciences. Heatwole considered Johnson a man whose personal life was above criticism and one whose record showed him to be an independent, all of which would appeal to the disaffected Republicans.[27] A good many citizens of Minnesota agreed with the *St. Cloud Times,* which declared that if Johnson was elected governor of Minnesota the state would never have occasion to be ashamed of him.[28] And Robert Dunn himself said: "John A. Johnson is a clean, upright man, and if elected, would make an excellent governor." [29] The *Duluth Evening Herald* noted that there was so much good will toward Johnson reflected in the newspapers all over the state that he must be a man of merit and worth.[30]

The Democrats were encouraged by the favorable press comments and began to organize for the campaign. On September 1 Frank Day was elected chairman of the Democratic state central committee, which included H. L. Buck, Leonard A. Rosing, William Gausewitz, M. F. Kain of St. Paul, and Albert Fessler of Duluth. Rosing agreed to assist Frank Day with the management of the campaign.

Both Johnson and Dunn were country editors, and each had newspapermen as campaign managers. (Conde Hamlin and W. E. Verity were directing Dunn's campaign.) In addition to Johnson, there were three newspapermen on the Democratic ticket — John E. King, editor of the *Red Lake Falls Courier,* who was running for secretary of state, H. E. Hoard, editor of the *Montevideo Leader,* who was a candidate for railroad and warehouse commissioner, and Swan Turnblad, editor of the Swedish newspaper, *Svenska Amerikanska Posten,* who was a candidate for presidential elector. The editors were to be more prominent and more active in this campaign than ever before in the history of the state.

Fortunately for Johnson, Frank Day, although a Parker Democrat himself, was friendly also with the Hearst men. Aggressive, suave, shrewd, energetic, and optimistic, he was an adroit handler of men and proved to be an excellent organizer. And he had the help of the experienced Rosing and of Richard T. O'Connor, the boss of the Democratic machine in St. Paul. Day had a passionate

---

[27] *Northfield News,* September 3, 1904.
[28] *St. Cloud Times,* September 7, 1904.      [29] *Ibid.,* October 26, 1904.
[30] *Duluth Evening Herald,* September 9, 1904.

belief in Johnson and was certain, as few others were, that Johnson would prove himself a winner. Day had watched Johnson captivate individuals and groups, and he knew the people of the state, once they saw and heard the Democratic candidate, would lose their hearts to him.

In contrast, not all the Republicans who supported Robert Dunn were satisfied with Conde Hamlin, his campaign manager. Senator Clapp thought Hamlin too cold and aloof to handle a campaign. He urged Dunn to choose someone who was able to meet and convince people. In fact, Clapp considered this matter so important that he tried to get Senator Knute Nelson to dissuade Dunn from insisting upon Hamlin.[31] Nor did Clapp and his friends have any love for Joel Heatwole or W. E. Verity, both of whom were Clapp's political enemies. As for the Collins Republicans, they liked Johnson as a candidate and were organizing to defeat Dunn. Judge Ell Torrance of Minneapolis wrote to Van Sant on September 5 concerning Dunn:

It is only a question of time when there will be a public protest against his election on the part of many well known and influential republicans, and it seems to me it would be much better for you to lead than to follow in that matter. There is no possible way of remaining neutral. We will have to be either for him or against him and I am not prepared to sacrifice my self respect nor am I willing to remain indifferent and see the administration of the State's affairs placed in incompetent and dangerous hands.

The reasons for opposing Dunn should be framed with the greatest care — clearly and concisely stated — serving as a platform upon which every good citizen, regardless of party, can conscientiously and honestly approve. I think the report of Johnson [Public Examiner Johnson] should be given to the public soon. I am glad it was not public prior to the nominating convention . . .

As soon as the primaries have been held I think the "campaign of reform" should open and that in the meantime the pledges of leading republicans, who are not going to support the head of the ticket, should be procured. I will stand by you through thick and thin and would prefer to sink alone than rise as part of the tail to the political kite that will float from the new state Capitol in case of Dunn's election.[32]

[31] Nelson Papers, Fred von Baumbach to Nelson, undated letter.
[32] Ell Torrance Papers, in Minnesota Historical Society, Torrance to Van Sant, September 5, 1904.

Judge Collins devoted all his time to planning Dunn's defeat and was in close communication with Van Sant and Torrance in this effort.[33] Another who was working with the Collins Republicans was Alvah Eastman, editor of the *St. Cloud Journal-Press*. Eastman felt that the defeat of Dunn would purify the Republican party and produce better political leaders and methods, and he predicted Johnson's victory if "honest and fearless Republicans in Minnesota . . . do their duty." [34]

Thus with the Dunn forces split into pro-Clapp and anti-Clapp factions, and with the Collins men out to defeat Dunn, the Democrats were hopeful of success.

One of the first things Frank Day did was to see that Johnson made a good appearance on the platform. He did not have to worry about Johnson's manners, and he knew Johnson was not given to rash talk and profanity, but he was well aware of the fact that Johnson gave little thought to his clothes. The editor of the *Herald* was inclined to wear a suit until it looked worn or until the coat sleeves were too short and the trousers too tight. Johnson seemed to be utterly oblivious to colors and materials. So Day enlisted the cooperation of Mrs. Johnson, and together they saw to it that Johnson purchased some well-tailored suits which fitted him properly. It was Mrs. Johnson's duty to see that he appeared correctly dressed on each occasion.[35]

Dunn had been widely criticized for the way he dressed before the campaign started, and once the campaign got underway he was laughed at still more because he insisted on wearing a small dark skullcap which he left on his head when he removed his hat. He explained that he wore it to protect his bald head from the cold.[36] As late as October 29 the *Duluth Labor World* was still trying to excuse Dunn's appearance. In an editorial entitled "Bob Dunn's Clothes," the newspaper defended Dunn as a man of the plain people, a man of Jeffersonian simplicity with Lincoln's disregard for appearance. The paper boasted that "Minnesota is going to show them all this year how a thorough union man, whose clothes don't fit, will look in the governor's chair." But some Re-

[33] *Ibid.*, Torrance to his daughter, Alice Fiske, September 15, 1904.
[34] *Ibid.*, Eastman to Torrance, September 15, 1904.
[35] Elinor Johnson Smith and Arthur Evenson to W. G. H.
[36] *St. Paul Dispatch*, October 19, 1904.

publicans were offended at the very thought of a man of Dunn's appearance in the governor's chair.

The Republicans soon discovered that Dunn was a poor campaigner. They knew he had never been a good speaker, but they learned that in public he was irascible and frequently lost his temper. His campaign managers realized that nothing could keep him from making rash statements when someone or something stirred him to anger.

Johnson, on the other hand, was a happy campaigner to whom the game itself appealed. He warmed up to the campaign as it progressed, and he had the gift of talking to his audience in an informal, personal way. There never was any doubt of his sincerity, and his speeches were full of humorous stories. He could always keep his audience in a good humor.[37]

Frank Day planned a whirlwind campaign, and Johnson traveled up and down the state delivering a hundred and three speeches in seventy-four of the eighty-four counties — all in forty-two days! He traveled by train and automobile, giving little heed to food and rest. He caught a heavy cold, but he continued speaking. An account of one day's campaigning went like this:

Having spoken at Canby the evening before . . . he arose at 4 A.M., and drove breakfastless twenty-nine miles to Clarkfield, where he talked an hour and a half. Then he caught a freight train and rode thirteen miles to Dawson, where in the afternoon he spoke for an hour and a half. Still taking no food, for which the cold had given him a distaste, he drove thirteen miles to Madison, where he finished a foodless day by speaking for two hours and a half in the evening. Total travel, fifty-five miles; total speaking, five and a half hours.[38]

Only those who had known Johnson in southern Minnesota, in the editorial association, and in the state legislature, knew what an excellent speaker he was. The state as a whole was unprepared for a candidate of such personal magnetism and charm. On September 27 he was scheduled to speak in Duluth, and an apathetic audience, skeptical of a man it had never seen or heard, gathered in the Armory to hear him. When he had finished speaking, the

[37] Henry N. Benson and Julius Schmahl to W. G. H.; and newspaper accounts in general.
[38] Winthrop B. Chamberlain, "A Great Democratic Governor," *World's Work*, April 1908, vol. 15, p. 10135.

audience, impressed by the fine flow of language and captivated by the man, was wildly enthusiastic. Listeners realized that they had heard one of the most effective speakers Minnesota had ever had.[39]

A story is told of a group of traveling salesmen who met after listening to Johnson speak. One of them remarked that Johnson had made a wonderful speech, and a Republican standing nearby broke into the conversation to say he did not think Johnson had said anything very startling. The traveling salesman replied fervently that he did not care what Johnson had said; it was the way he had said it that appealed to him.[40]

Johnson attracted so much attention that the Republicans became uneasy and frightened. To combat him, they put into the field an impressive array of speakers. They brought into the state Senator Charles Fairbanks, who was running for vice-president on the ticket with Theodore Roosevelt, Speaker of the House of Representatives Joseph Cannon, and Senator Jonathan Dolliver of Iowa. Senators Nelson and Clapp and six Minnesota congressmen spoke throughout the state for Dunn, as did William H. Eustis. But Governor Van Sant refused to do anything for the Republican candidate. Neither Senator Nelson nor even James A. Martin could persuade Van Sant to speak for Dunn. He flatly refused, stating that his self-respect kept him from speaking for a man who had called him vile names.[41] Dunn promptly retorted that Van Sant was the most ungrateful man in the world and had "no more backbone than an eel." [42]

The Democrats and the disaffected Republicans organized Roosevelt-Johnson clubs all over the state; Democrats who felt that Parker had no chance in Minnesota agreed to support Roosevelt if the Republicans would support Johnson.[43] A Swedish Republican club was organized to elect all the Swedes on the Republican ticket, but Dunn was no Swede. The Democratic publicity bureau sent out literature about their candidate, and as Johnson's life and career became known to the people of the state, it took on a romantic tinge — the early poverty, the rise of the washer-

[39] *Duluth Evening Herald,* September 27, 28, 1904.
[40] Henry N. Benson to W. G. H.
[41] *St. Paul Dispatch,* October 18, 1904.
[42] *Ibid.,* October 21, 1904.
[43] *Ibid.,* October 17, 1904.

woman's son, and the fact that Johnson, if elected, would be Minnesota's youngest and first native-born governor. In view of what happened later, it was perhaps unfortunate that the *facts* about Johnson's father were not included in this publicity material.

The campaign opened with Dunn attacking Johnson's legislative record on the State Board of Control. Johnson had opposed the creation of the board originally, and, in the endeavor to kill the bill providing for it, had offered an amendment which placed the University of Minnesota and the state normal schools under its control.[44] Johnson never expected such an amendment to pass, but it did, with the bill. Everyone in the state senate understood his reason for this action, but Dunn now charged him with responsibility for putting the educational institutions under the control of the board. Dunn reminded the people that he had been the first to recommend the creation of such a board for correctional and charitable institutions.[45]

In reply Johnson patiently explained his reasons for opposing the board of control bill and for offering the amendment to it. He declared that he had never approved of having the university and the state normal schools under its jurisdiction and that he favored action to remove them from the board's control. He reiterated this as he spoke all over the state.[46]

On September 15 the Collins-Van Sant forces gave the Democrats plenty of ammunition when Van Sant released to the press copies of the public examiner's report on Dunn's record as state auditor. The report was so technical that many people did not try to understand it, but the Dunn leaders and the Democrats studied it carefully and the latter had it printed in full and circulated it throughout the state. It repeated the charge that Dunn had been too lenient in settling with trespassers and had not stopped others from stealing state timberlands.

More serious was the charge that Dunn had leased state mineral lands to the relative of a clerk in his office who had special knowledge of these lands and who later came into possession of the leases. The leases were made out to Mabel Evans of Princeton,

[44] All of the state senators who represented counties with state institutions had opposed the bill.
[45] *St. Paul Pioneer Press,* September 10, 1904.
[46] *Ibid.,* September 12, 1904; *Faribault Pilot,* September 15, 1904.

and Dunn must have known she was the sister of a clerk in his office; in fact, Dunn admitted he knew Mabel Evans but declared he had not noticed her name when he signed the leases. The admission that he had not looked at the name of the person to whom he was leasing valuable mineral lands made him seem guilty of gross negligence. Also, Dunn had refused to give leases on the same land to one Pearl H. Smith a few days before he allowed Mabel Evans to lease them.

Most of Dunn's reply was devoted to abuse of Van Sant and Public Examiner Johnson.[47] He charged that Public Examiner Johnson was his bitter personal and political enemy and that the report was full of deliberately false statements. He asked S. G. Iverson, who had been his deputy auditor and was now state auditor, to examine the report, and Iverson in an interview with the press stated that the charges against Dunn were false, misleading, and inspired by malice.[48]

To combat the effect of the report, the Republicans called upon Senator Knute Nelson to speak for Dunn. Nelson was popular with the people of Minnesota, and they usually listened when he spoke. Accordingly, Nelson had been asked to inaugurate the speaking campaign on September 23 with an address at Madison in Lac qui Parle County, an area in which there was much feeling against Dunn.[49] After an introduction dealing with general issues, Nelson turned to the question of "our candidate for governor and the state ticket." He said he understood that the Democrats hoped to win in the coming election because there were some Republicans who would not support Dunn. He reviewed the preconvention Dunn-Collins fight and stated that one of that closely matched pair had to be defeated. In a plea for all good Republicans to think of the welfare of the party in the state and the nation, he urged his listeners to vote the Republican ticket and to remember there was "no valid ground on which any good, sound Republican can vote against Mr. Dunn."

[47] St. Cloud Journal-Press, September 19, 1904.
[48] Minneapolis Tribune, September 19, 20, 1904; Princeton Union, September 22, 1904.
[49] Nelson Papers, W. E. Verity to Nelson, September 7, 14, 1904; C. M. Reese to Nelson, September 19, 1904. Both Verity and Reese were concerned with the opposition to Dunn in Lac qui Parle County, and Verity wanted Nelson to make a strong speech for Dunn. He asked for advance copies of the speech, which was translated into Swedish and Norwegian and circulated throughout the state.

Then Nelson launched into a defense of Dunn's record as state auditor. Clearly and convincingly he explained the great difficulty in tracking down state timber trespassers, securing proof against those who were suspected, and arranging a settlement with those who were caught. He stressed the fact that the state auditor never had enough funds to employ a sufficient number of men to check on trespassing. Proof of Dunn's efforts in collecting damages from trespassers, said Nelson, was the deadly enmity the trespassers now bore Dunn. He showed that the Minnesota Supreme Court, in the case of Minnesota versus Shevlin and Carpenter Company, had aided the trespassers by practically nullifying the Act of 1895, which provided that willful trespassers pay double or triple damages. During Dunn's administrations the number of trespassers who escaped was fewer than ever before, said Nelson, and Dunn had collected ten times as much money from trespassers as had all his predecessors together.

Nelson was less successful in trying to answer the attacks made upon Dunn's personal qualities. He admitted that Dunn was not refined and that he did swear upon occasion. He said:

It is true that Mr. Dunn is not a Chesterfield in his ways. In the strenuousness of our modern life the Chesterfields have become obsolete and mere academic quantities. A dignified mummy in the executive chair would no doubt be fine to look upon, but not of much practical use. A man of energy and action, of vigilance and alertness is required in the executive chair. He must keep a vigilant eye on all the varied interests of the state. He must be in touch with the legislature and know how to secure the necessary legislation. He must be able to meet, contend with, and not be overreached by, all kinds of spoilsmen. He must possess an encyclopedia of knowledge of state affairs and public men. Sometimes, for the good of the state, he must be mild mannered, argue, and implore, and at other times he must almost assume the attitude of a pugilist, to fend off unconscionable and over-persistent spoilsmen. And such a man, in his texture and make-up, and by training, is Mr. Dunn.[50]

Nelson's speech helped Dunn, but there was increasing criticism of Ray Jones, who was running for lieutenant governor on the Republican ticket. "Holy" Ray Jones, "the timber expert" and partner of Thomas Shevlin, the lumberman, had at one time

[50] *Ibid.*, manuscript of Nelson's Madison speech, September 23, 1904.

been fined heavily for stealing pine timber from the state.[51] His record was being examined, too. The *Faribault Pilot* suggested that the party emblem for Dunn and Jones should be "a pine tree with Bob Dunn in the foreground presenting the tree to 'Holy' Ray Jones." [52] They were, of course, accused of being the candidates of the railroad and lumber interests.

When Dunn joined Senators Fairbanks, Dolliver, and Clapp on their speaking tour in Minnesota, the Republican leaders believed he was in safe hands and could make only a good impression. In Albert Lea, however, Dunn did not speak with the others, and the *Albert Lea Tribune*, a Republican paper, accused him of being drunk and unable to deliver a speech.

This accusation spread all over the state. The *St. Paul Pioneer Press* explained that Dunn had been perfectly sober, that there had not been time for him to speak, that he had spoken in towns before he arrived in Albert Lea and after he left, that on the same night he had delivered an address in the Peoples Church in St. Paul, and that, in fact, he had not had one drink on the whole trip.[53] Senator Nelson was obliged to discuss the incident in his speech in Mankato on October 15, explaining further that Dunn had not been a drinking man for the past two or three years and that he had been with Fairbanks, who was a temperance advocate, all during the speaking trip. Nelson again tried to make a point of Dunn's abilities and qualifications for office, though he admitted that Dunn would never look well in a drawing room.[54]

More important than all this was Dunn's reluctance to come out publicly in favor of Senator Clapp's re-election. Some Republican leaders were waiting for him to express himself on this point before they made up their minds to support him.[55] Clapp was speaking for the Republican national and state tickets and was doing all he could to elect Dunn. Senator Nelson knew that Joel Heatwole was violently opposed to Clapp, for Heatwole had written to Nelson explaining his stand and pledging his support to Nelson even though he worked against Clapp.[56] But despite

[51] *Freeborn County Standard*, October 5, 1904.
[52] *Faribault Pilot*, September 8, 1904.
[53] *St. Paul Pioneer Press*, September 28, 1904.
[54] *Ibid.*, October 16, 1904; *Mankato Free Press*, October 17, 1904.
[55] Nelson Papers, L. M. Willcuts of Duluth to Nelson, September 14, 1904.
[56] *Ibid.*, Heatwole to Nelson, September 17, 1904.

the close relationship between Heatwole and Dunn, Nelson finally exerted enough pressure upon Dunn so that he publicly announced his support of Clapp.

Nelson did more than that. On September 28 the Republican state central committee met, and in a desperate attempt to unite the Republican party W. E. Verity, secretary of the committee and good friend of Heatwole, was forced to resign. Nelson persuaded James A. Martin, who had managed Judge Collins' preconvention campaign, to take on the same job for Dunn, and C. H. Warner of Aitkin replaced Verity. Under the leadership of Nelson and Martin the Republicans now linked the three chief candidates for office — Roosevelt, Clapp, and Dunn — in an effort to detract the voters' attention from Dunn and to persuade them to vote a straight ticket. Dunn's campaign had been badly managed, and it was hoped Martin would be more expert than Conde Hamlin and Verity had been.[57] The day after the shift was made, C. S. Mitchell wrote to Nelson: "The outlook is bright. You can see a change everywhere . . . The *Journal* however still is nasty. It is the one exceedingly bad spot now." [58]

There certainly was a change — a change in the relations between Dunn and his old friends, W. E. Verity and Joel Heatwole. Once Dunn had announced his support of Clapp, he repudiated Heatwole; and when he allowed Nelson to force out Verity he indicated his complete abandonment of his friends as well as his complete submission to the Nelson and Clapp Republicans. Heatwole was furious. He had worked hard to get Dunn nominated, and now he saw Dunn, frightened by the signs of defeat, submitting to Nelson's dictates in order to be elected. Heatwole's friends felt that Dunn had double-crossed both Heatwole and Verity, and most of them repudiated Dunn and began to work for Johnson.[59] Heatwole blamed Clapp for this new dissension among the Republicans, for he insisted that the issue of Clapp's re-election need not have come up until after the November election.[60]

Both Heatwole and Verity insisted that Dunn had promised solemnly that if he was elected he would throw the entire state

[57] *St. Paul Dispatch*, September 29, 1904; *St. Cloud Times*, October 5, 1904; *Bemidji Sentinel*, October 5, 1904.
[58] Nelson Papers, C. S. Mitchell to Nelson, September 29, 1904.
[59] Dr. George Orr to W. G. H.
[60] *Northfield News*, October 15, 29, 1904; *St. Paul Dispatch*, September 29, 1904.

administration behind Heatwole to elect him senator in place of
Clapp. Dunn denied this, and Heatwole let him deny it right up to
election eve, although Nelson was warned that Heatwole claimed
to have some documents which would "fix Dunn." [61] Then Heatwole released to the press letters Dunn had written to him in the
fall of 1903. They revealed that Dunn had made an agreement
with Heatwole to oppose Clapp in return for Heatwole's support.
In one letter Dunn wrote: ". . . Understand Clapp's friends are
all for Collins. They are afraid of you. I don't give one d——n.
Now if he were to declare for me publicly I would not declare for
him. We may have to fight Clapp openly before long. If Nelson
keeps his hands off we do not care for him . . ." [62]

Dunn had to admit he wrote the letters, but he pointed out
that they were written before he was nominated, that the Republican platform had endorsed Clapp's re-election, and that he
had accepted the platform. Then he turned upon Heatwole and
charged him with being no gentleman for allowing his personal
correspondence to be published.[63] The whole episode lost Dunn
friends and votes.

Dunn made another error which proved to be costly. Many of
the traveling salesmen whose territory was southern Minnesota
knew John A. Johnson well and liked him. They became traveling
missionaries in his behalf, talking about him to their customers
as well as to their fellow salesmen. Consequently the Republicans
maintained that the jobbing houses were working to defeat Dunn
because at a meeting of the State Board of Equalization, as an ex
officio member, he had said that the jobbing houses were not taxed
one tenth as much as they should be and had urged that their as-
sessment be increased. Therefore their salesmen had been told to
talk against Dunn.

Whether or not this was true made little difference, for Dunn
himself soon antagonized the salesmen. In a speech at Jackson
he referred to them as a group of "calico peddlers and herring peddlers," and at another time he declared that "there are a lot of
men traveling throughout the state — traveling men — who are
villifying and lying about me, who are unfit to shine my shoes."

[61] Nelson Papers, Fred von Baumbach to Nelson, October 21, 1904.
[62] *Minneapolis Journal*, November 3, 1904 (letter dated November 29, 1903).
[63] *Ibid.*, November 4, 1904; *St. Cloud Journal-Press*, November 3, 1904.

Then on November 2, after an address in Mankato, Dunn returned to his hotel to be accosted by some salesmen who demanded that he retract these uncomplimentary remarks about them. He told them to present their grievances, and if they really had any he would apologize. But as questions and accusations were hurled at him, he lost his temper and stomped off to his room, declaring he "didn't give a damn for the traveling men anyhow." Thereafter there was much truth in the remark that the salesmen spent more time selling Johnson than they did selling their goods.[64]

The tenor of the Republican campaign against Johnson can be illustrated by the question they asked: "What has Johnson ever done?" Dunn charged that Johnson was not experienced enough to be governor of Minnesota. He pointed out that during Johnson's term in the legislature he was not responsible for one major piece of legislation. Again and again Dunn attacked Johnson's record on the State Board of Control, and he showed that Johnson had voted against bills to provide the state with a drainage commission and to drain swamps in northern Minnesota.

Then, because there was little left to accuse Johnson of, Dunn criticized him severely for having voted against a bill to appropriate funds for the writing of a history of the Minnesota troops in the Spanish-American War! And it seems that Johnson was the only senator who voted against a bill which provided that no sports be played within half a mile of any place where a memorial service was being conducted on Decoration Day. He felt that it was an interference with the personal liberty of the individual.[65]

Walter Wellman, political writer for the *Chicago Record-Herald* sent to observe Dunn's campaign, noted that the Republican candidate's speeches were very poor and that his grammar was "picturesque," to say the least.[66]

It was easy for Johnson to combat a man like Dunn. From the first he refused to indulge in personal attacks, and not once during the campaign did he make a remark that cast any reflection upon Dunn's personal characteristics. In his opening cam-

---

[64] *St. Paul Dispatch,* November 3, 1904; *Glenwood Gopher,* quoted in the *Princeton Union,* October 20, 1904; *Bemidji Pioneer,* October 20, 1904; *Mankato Free Press,* November 3, 1904; *St. Peter Free Press,* October 29, 1904; *Duluth Evening Herald,* November 1, 1904.
[65] *Princeton Union,* October 13, 1904.
[66] *Chicago Record-Herald,* quoted in the *St. Paul Dispatch,* October 20, 1904.

paign speech in Minneapolis on September 24, he made it clear
that the campaign was not a personal quarrel between himself and
Dunn. Answering the Republican charges, he explained why he
had opposed the creation of the State Board of Control, but since
it existed he proposed that its membership be nonpartisan and
chosen for special ability to handle the management of the state
institutions. He made the point that in the legislature he had been
an enthusiastic supporter of a bill to increase the gross earnings
tax, which Dunn had just now begun to advocate.

Johnson favored the primary election law, but suggested that
it be perfected before being applied to state officers. On the subjects of drainage, good roads, and the treatment of Civil War
veterans, he declared that he and Dunn did not differ. He warned
that Dunn's stand on the merger ought to be remembered, for he
felt that no one who had favored the merger should be elected
governor of the state. He asserted that labor had a right to organize and defend its rights, and he recommended the appointment of a nonpartisan judiciary.

Johnson did denounce Dunn for having settled claims against
trespassers for a small per cent of what was actually due the state.
He explained that if Dunn had done such a thing there was nothing to prevent other public officials from doing the same. With
force he declared: "The state has a right to expect absolute honesty in all of its public officials, and discretionary power, not conferred by law but assumed by the officers of the law, can be so
abused as to border on dishonest service and invite criticism." [67]

In a speech at Lake City on October 8 Johnson answered
Dunn's attack apropos of the Spanish-American War history.
The Minnesota veterans, he said, had never asked for such a book;
it was the McGill-Warner publishing house that wanted it written so they could publish it. To Johnson this had seemed a bit of
petty graft.[68]

His attitude toward trusts Johnson set forth in a speech at Duluth on September 27: "Aggregations of capital are sometimes
necessary, and so long as they are within the law, are legitimate
and not to be attacked." If, however, corporations go beyond the

[67] *Minneapolis Journal*, September 26, 1904; *St. Peter Herald*, September 30, 1904;
*Faribault Pilot*, September 29, 1904.
[68] *Minneapolis Journal*, October 8, 1904.

law, then they must be restrained. He praised James J. Hill for his part in the development of the Northwest, but, he reminded his listeners, James J. Hill did not make the region or its prosperity. The Northwest would have prospered without Hill, but Hill would not have prospered without the Northwest.[69] Later in Mankato Johnson condemned the Republican party for being subservient to the Great Northern Railroad and stated that the time had come to reform the party — a fact that some influential Republicans themselves recognized. Then he reproached Dunn for sacrificing his political friends, Heatwole and Verity, for political gains, and solemnly announced that this was one thing he would never do.[70]

F. G. Winston, candidate for lieutenant governor on the Democratic ticket, traveled all over the state with Johnson. The president of Winston Brothers, a firm of contractors, and a director of the Security Bank of Minneapolis, the Minnesota Loan and Trust Company, and the Minneapolis Plow Works, Winston was a man of high reputation among the businessmen of the Northwest. He was quite a contrast to "Holy" Ray Jones, who stood accused of stealing timber. There was nothing about Winston's personal or business life that the Republicans could attack. While not so effective a speaker as Johnson, he nevertheless bore his share of the burden of the campaign.[71]

John Lind was the only recognized political leader in Minnesota who spoke for Johnson. He had not wanted to aid in the campaign, but was persuaded to do so for the sake of the party.

On October 17 in a speech in St. Paul Lind made public a new charge against Dunn's record as state auditor. He accused Dunn of "recklessness and carelessness" in allowing some 43,000 acres of state land to be included in a land grant which was declared by the court to be the property of the Duluth and Iron Range Railroad. When Dunn discovered the error, attorneys quietly arranged to have the land returned to the state, but just as the negotiations were almost finished, Dunn delivered a tirade against the railroad company which delayed the settlement for a year. Lind maintained that since the railroad company had secured the

[69] *Duluth Evening Herald*, September 28, 1904.
[70] *Mankato Free Press*, November 1, 1904.
[71] *St. Cloud Times*, November 2, 1904; *St. Paul Globe*, September 25, 1904.

list of lands from the state auditor's office, the inclusion of state land was Dunn's error.

Dunn's reply to this charge was weak. He said he had not prepared the list of lands decreed to the railroad by the court and had not known the grant included state land.[72]

James A. Peterson offered to meet Lind in a public debate on Dunn's record, and the two men met on October 31 in Minneapolis before a large audience noticeably hostile to Peterson. Lind, in fact, had to keep order so that Peterson could be heard. And Lind's criticism of Dunn's record as state auditor was much more effective than was Peterson's defense of it.[73]

Lind wound up the campaign with a speech in Duluth, when he noted that the Republican candidate for lieutenant governor, Ray Jones, was being kept out of the state until the election was over.[74] Dunn in turn assailed Lind as a liar, a poor governor, and one of the "trickiest" politicians in the state, a chameleon of politics.[75] About his enemies Dunn wrote: "The dirty, contemptible, low, sewer-scraping persons who are engaged in passing along the slanderous stories about the nominee of the Republicans for governor would disgrace a seat on a scavenger wagon." [76]

Observing the campaign, Judge Torrance wrote to Van Sant: "'Nothing in heaven above or on the earth beneath or in hades under the earth' can save Dunn. His managers are offering *everything* to *everybody* in the hope of stemming the tide. Your attitude is good — dignified silence and the noble heart. We will, I trust, render the State of Minnesota a real service this fall." [77]

Letters came to Senator Nelson complaining about Dunn and urging Nelson to do what he could to save the ticket.[78] James A. Martin mourned that he had not enough funds to conduct the campaign properly, although he admitted that Conde Hamlin was doing all he could to raise money.[79] In desperation George Flinn suggested that the Republicans make a concerted attack on John-

[72] *St. Paul Dispatch*, October 19, 1904; *Princeton Union*, October 20, 1904; *Minneapolis Journal*, October 22, 1904.

[73] *Ibid.*, November 1, 1904; *St. Paul Dispatch*, November 1, 1904.

[74] *Duluth Evening Herald*, November 8, 1904.

[75] In a speech in St. Paul on October 26, reported in the *St. Paul Dispatch*, October 27, 1904.

[76] *Princeton Union*, October 20, 1904.

[77] Torrance Papers, Torrance to Van Sant, October 17, 1904.

[78] Nelson Papers.

[79] *Ibid.*, Martin to Nelson, October 20, 1904.

son's stand in favor of Canadian reciprocity, but Martin and Hamlin would not agree to this.[80]

. Meanwhile the Democrats were suffering some disaffection within their own ranks. J. M. Bowler of Minneapolis, one of the leaders of the Hearst Democrats, announced on October 20 that he would support Dunn and advised all progressive Democrats to do the same. According to Bowler, Johnson stood for nothing that entitled him to a position of trust. Bowler did not like the fact that Johnson was a Gold Democrat, and he objected to Johnson's refusal to support Lind on every measure.[81]

The Republican leaders welcomed Bowler's announcement, and they warned all Republicans that a Democratic victory would mean the loss of patronage to the Republicans. Once in office the Democrats would organize to win the 1906 election.[82] The *St. Paul Pioneer Press* informed the public that the Democrats were telling lies about Dunn — that they told the Scandinavians Dunn was a Catholic, that they told the Irish Dunn was an Orangeman, that they told the temperance people Dunn was drunk at Albert Lea, and that they told everyone Dunn swore all the time! In an editorial entitled "No 'Tailor's Dummy' for the New Capitol," the paper warned the voters not to be swayed by matters which did not have any real importance.[83]

As a last resort, the Republicans made an effort to smear Johnson. According to one of Johnson's oldest friends, Arthur Evenson, the Republican state central committee was divided on the question of circulating a pamphlet containing slanderous statements about Johnson, but finally it was agreed that Edward D. Claggett of Princeton, ex-sheriff of Mille Lacs County and a friend of Robert Dunn's, should prepare and circulate such a pamphlet. James A. Martin threatened to resign if the slander was given to the newspapers, so it did not appear in that form.

The Democratic committee had been warned that the Republicans were getting ready to release a "roorback" and could only wait and wonder when it would appear.

The pamphlet was circulated near the end of October. It con-

[80] *Ibid.*, Flinn to Nelson, October 8, 1904.
[81] *Princeton Union*, October 20, 1904.
[82] *Ibid.; Minneapolis Tribune*, November 1, 1904.
[83] *St. Paul Pioneer Press*, November 1, 4, 1904.

tained the charge that Johnson had been an unnatural son — that he had allowed his father to die in the county poorhouse and had put his mother out of the house when he married. The charge was in the form of affidavits sworn to by one Tip Witty and by G. A. Blomberg, clerk of the district court in Nicollet County.

Arthur Evenson got busy at once. He took W. W. Jermane, the best political writer of the *Minneapolis Journal,* to St. Peter, where Jermane talked to people who had known the Johnson family for a long time. He saw Johnson's mother, old Dr. A. W. Daniels, F. A. Donahower, and many others. Armed with the facts and angry straight through, Jermane returned to Minneapolis and wrote the truth in a story published in the *Minneapolis Journal.* He explained, besides, that it was very painful to Johnson to have the story of his father's life told, and he pointed out that Johnson's own life and career might well serve as an inspiration to all.

Johnson was in St. Peter when Evenson told him about the slander that was being circulated. With the example of the Republican pre-convention mudslinging before him, he had feared from the start of the campaign that the Republicans would resort to reviving the story of his father's career, but it had never occurred to him that they would falsify the facts. His immediate reaction was to offer to withdraw from the campaign, but after thinking it over, he decided to let others present the truth and to go on with the campaign.

One of those who was greatly aroused by the whole episode was P. V. Collins, who had been the editor of the *St. Peter Tribune* and was now editor of the *Northwestern Agriculturalist.* It was Collins who had printed in his paper the slanderous remarks Judge E. St. Julien Cox had made about Johnson's family in the 1888 campaign, when Johnson ran for state representative. At that time Collins had learned the truth, and now he came forward to do all he could to present the facts to the people of the state. Collins announced that he had known Johnson for many years and had never found anything about him that he did not respect.

Dunn also repudiated the slanderous story and declared that he had had nothing to do with its circulation. Those in charge of his campaign, of course, denied any connection with it. The *St. Paul Pioneer Press* agreed that the attack upon Johnson was unfair and deplorable, but it noted that Johnson was no hero for helping his mother since other boys had done the same thing. The Republican attempt to smear Johnson proved to be a boomerang, for when the truth was told, Johnson gained the respect of the people of Minnesota, and many deplored the campaign methods of the Republicans.[84]

Johnson doggedly continued his campaign, speaking several times every day, but the strain began to tell on him. On November 2, after addressing two meetings in Stillwater, he collapsed. The newspapers reported that he suffered from acute indigestion. Actually he had endured excruciating abdominal pain until he could stand it no longer. Mrs. Johnson came from St. Peter to be with him, but he refused to rest longer than two days. John Lind took his place on the platform those two days, speaking at New Ulm and Winthrop. During the evening of November 4, against the advice of his physician, Johnson addressed ten rallies in Minneapolis. No one could restrain him from finishing a campaign he had started.[85]

The campaign was over. Johnson was exhausted and ill, and Robert Dunn had felt the effects on his own physical well-being. Moses Clapp declared: "It has been the hardest campaign I ever went through." [86] On November 8 the people of Minnesota went to the polls, and Johnson spent the evening with his friends at the Democratic headquarters waiting for the election returns. Even though he firmly believed he would be elected, he had been defeated often enough in his political career to be prepared for that possibility.

When all the votes were counted, Johnson received 147,992 to Dunn's 140,130, and Minnesota had its first native-born governor. But the Republicans elected the rest of their state ticket, so that the lieutenant governor under Johnson was "Holy" Ray

[84] Arthur Evenson to W. G. H.; Executive Letters of Governor Johnson, in Minnesota Historical Society, Frank Day to C. P. Peterson of Glenwood, January 24, 1905; *Minneapolis Journal*, October 21, 29, 31, 1904; *Duluth Evening Herald*, October 31, 1904; *St. Paul Dispatch*, November 11, 1904; *St. Paul Pioneer Press*, November 2, 1904; *St. Paul Globe*, October 28, 1904; *Martin County Sentinel*, April 28, 1905; Day and Knappen, pp. 127-92. When Judge Torrance publicly repudiated Dunn, some of the Dunn men were so angry they endeavored to prepare a smear campaign against him, but James Martin stopped that.

[85] *St. Paul Dispatch*, November 2, 1904; *Minneapolis Journal*, November 5, 1904; *Mankato Free Press*, November 4, 1904.

[86] Nelson Papers, Clapp to Nelson, November 9, 1904.

Jones. Theodore Roosevelt, who won an overwhelming victory throughout the entire country, carried Minnesota by 163,000 votes. All nine Republican congressmen were elected. A solidly Republican state had a Democratic governor! [87]

The Democrats rejoiced. Johnson was very happy, though he admitted he never could have been elected if there had not been a Bob Dunn. Writing to his son, Ell Torrance voiced the sentiments of the Collins Republicans when he said: "The election went my way and I feel not only satisfied but greatly relieved." [88] In the *Princeton Union* of November 17 Robert Dunn published a letter of thanks to his friends, stating that he had made the best fight he could but that the odds against him were too great:

Never before in the history of the State was such an outrageously unfair and unjust warfare waged against any candidate for office as was waged against me — from start to finish it was a campaign of villification and misrepresentation on the part of my opponents. Personally I conducted a clean, manly fight, spoke no word in public or private derogatory to the character of my opponent or any member of his family and have no regrets on that score. If the traitorous ingrates of my own party who, under the leadership of S. R. Van Sant and L. W. Collins, so brutally and unjustly assailed my public and private character, can derive any comfort or consolation from my defeat they are welcome to it.

Even with the election over, Dunn had not finished attacking Van Sant. During the next year he referred to him as a "bombastic political traitor," all "gas and abdomen." The Collins Republicans he assailed scornfully as "yellow" and as "mongrel" Republicans.[89]

Governor-elect Johnson also used the columns of his paper to thank his friends, especially those in southern Minnesota, who had voted for him. He wrote: "It will be impossible to see all the people to thank them in person at this time, but I hope and trust my official life will be such that they will never regret their action . . ." [90]

[87] *Legislative Manual*, 1905, pp. 506–7, 527, 532. Johnson carried thirty-eight of eighty-three counties in Minnesota, including the heavily populated Hennepin and Ramsey counties.
[88] Torrance Papers, Torrance to Ell Torrance, Jr., November 12, 1904.
[89] *Princeton Union*, January 19, 26, February 9, 1905.
[90] *St. Peter Herald*, November 11, 1904.

Johnson's victory was not so much a Democratic triumph as a sharp rebuke to the Republican party for nominating a candidate for governor who was regarded by so many people as unfit for the office. Newspaper editors throughout the state advised the Republicans to give more thought to their choice of candidates in the future and to reorganize their badly split party. The *Preston Times* voiced a general sentiment among the editors when it said that Johnson "is a good man and there is a measure of satisfaction in knowing that at no time during the heat of the campaign has the *Times* said anything against his good name. We predict he will make a very acceptable executive and that the Republicans will have to get together if they have any idea of retiring him in 1906." [91]

The Democratic victory, however, cannot be explained simply in terms of Robert Dunn's unpopularity. Johnson's political experience was recognized by the Democrats, and his legislative record proved him to be an honest and conscientious legislator with a strong spirit of independence. His lack of experience as an administrator was the only criticism made of him, and many people were willing to take a chance on that. He proved to be an amazingly fine campaigner, who showed himself familiar with state problems and who urged progressive but not radical legislation. There is little doubt that his personality won him votes, and that the story of his life had a dramatic appeal which was emphasized when the Republicans tried to twist the facts in an effort to defeat him.

Certainly Johnson's Swedish extraction helped him to win, for the *Svenska Amerikanska Posten,* the *Minnesota Stats Tidning,* and the *Svenska Folkets Tidning,* all Swedish newspapers, supported him.[92] Still, the *Minnesota Stats Tidning* declared that Johnson did not win because the Swedes of Minnesota voted for him but because he deserved to win, and the paper had printed a letter written by a friend of Johnson's urging people to vote for him but reminding the readers that a Swede never votes for a

[91] *Preston Times,* November 16, 1904; *Bemidji Sentinel,* November 17, 1904; *St. Peter Tribune,* November 16, 1904; *Duluth Labor World,* November 12, 1904; *St. Cloud Times,* November 9, 1904; *Mankato Free Press,* November 9, 1904; *Minneapolis Tribune,* November 10, 1904; *Bemidji Pioneer,* November 10, 1904.

[92] *Minnesota Stats Tidning,* October 5, 12, 1904; *Svenska Amerikanska Posten,* October 11, 18, 25, November 1, 8, 1904; *Svenska Folkets Tidning,* October 5, November 2, 9, 1904.

person because he is Swedish but because he is capable and a man of character.[93]

It was a factor for victory, too, that Johnson's activities in the editorial association had won him the respect and affection of his fellow editors, and though some of them remained loyal Republicans, few if any could bring themselves to attack him. Nor can one ignore the aggressive, powerful force of the traveling salesmen who talked "Johnson" in stores, on trains, on the streets, and in hotels from the beginning of the campaign to its finish — because they believed he would give the state an honest and clean administration.

The support of the Collins Republicans was by no means insignificant. The tactics of the Dunn campaign managers disgusted Republicans who wanted the politics of the state carried on in a more dignified and ethical fashion. They preferred to vote for Johnson who, they believed, exemplified their ideals. And, finally, one cannot ignore the abilities and experience of such men as Frank Day, T. D. O'Brien, Leonard Rosing, and Richard T. O'Connor, who expertly managed Johnson's campaign.

Johnson's remarkable victory in Minnesota attracted nationwide attention. The story of his life, his career, and his election was told in newspapers all over the country. Especially were the Democratic papers interested, for the Democrats were searching for new men as possible presidential timber. Bryan had twice been defeated, and Judge Parker had aroused little enthusiasm even among the Democrats.

The *Baltimore News* rejoiced over the election of Johnson in Minnesota, W. L. Douglas as Democratic governor of Massachusetts, and Folk as Democratic governor of Missouri. The *News* hoped the nation would use these men as leaders in the Democratic party.[94] The *Boston Evening Transcript* drew a parallel between the election of Douglas and that of Johnson.[95] The *Chicago Record-Herald* published a long account of the election of the son of a pauper and a washerwoman and reported that Johnson was already being talked of as a possible Democratic candidate for the presidency.[96] A page-long column entitled "Elected Gov-

[93] *Minnesota Stats Tidning*, November 2, 16, 1904.
[94] *Baltimore News*, November 10, 11, 1904.
[95] *Boston Evening Transcript*, November 10, 1904.
[96] *Chicago Record-Herald*, November 11, 1904.

ernor by His Enemies" appeared in the *New York Herald,* and
the *New York Tribune* carried the story of Johnson's election.[97]
Henry Watterson's *Louisville Courier-Journal* simply noted that
Johnson was elected in spite of the fact that Roosevelt carried
Minnesota.[98]

But in spite of all this national attention, no one, including
Johnson himself, had any idea how rapidly he would rise to
prominence.[99]

[97] *New York Herald,* November 11, 1904; *New York Tribune,* November 7, 10, 1904.
[98] *Louisville Courier-Journal,* November 10, 1904.
[99] There is a story which illustrates how amazed some of Johnson's friends were when
he was elected governor. Early in 1904 Johnson and his wife and a group of friends
were driving from Minneapolis to St. Paul. They had been to the theater and were
in a festive mood. As they drove by the new state capitol which was still under construction, Johnson, in high spirits, jokingly exclaimed: "I will invite you girls to come
in for another holiday when I dedicate this building." The individual in the group who
later told this said that they thought Johnson had about as much chance of dedicating
the new capitol as any of them did to christen the next heir to the throne of Morocco.
"The girls mocked him and asked if he expected them to sit on the grass while he did
the dedicating." That year Johnson was nominated for governor and elected. He dedi-
cated the building, and his friends were there, but they did not sit on the grass (*St.
Paul Dispatch,* September 21, 1909).

ILL and exhausted, Governor-elect Johnson returned to St. Peter as soon as he learned the results of the election. He had no opportunity to rest, however, for the town gave a huge reception in honor of his victory. Special trains from the Twin Cities brought about ten thousand people from all over the state to St. Peter for the occasion.[1] Although in constant pain, Johnson happily took part in the celebration. Speaking in the open air, he addressed the assembled crowd and thanked them for their loyal support.

Among the listeners was his mother, for whom this was a great moment. It was for this that her father had brought his family to America. Her own life had been hard and filled with sorrow, but she had the satisfaction of knowing that all her children enjoyed more comforts and more social and political privilege than she or her father had ever had. Her son's election as chief executive of Minnesota was proof that America was indeed a land of opportunity.[2]

Johnson himself was not amazed by what had happened to him. He believed that any person with ability who worked hard and took advantage of his opportunities could make a success of his life. What that success would be depended upon the individual. So Johnson took his election in his stride, but also with a large measure of humility and a high sense of responsibility and duty.

Before he could assume his new office, however, he had to rest and recover his strength. Immediately after the St. Peter reception, he and Mrs. Johnson, accompanied by Mr. and Mrs. Frank Day and two other couples, went to New Orleans and other places in the South. For about two weeks Johnson rested, and when he returned he was feeling fit and ready for work. He went to St. Paul to confer with Frank Day, John Lind, Leonard Rosing, Rich-

[1] *St. Paul Dispatch*, November 14, 15, 1904.
[2] Hattie Johnson to W. G. H.

ard T. O'Connor, and others regarding appointments to offices.
Then he set up headquarters in the Nicollet Hotel in St. Peter
to receive office seekers, visitors, and a flood of mail.[3] There for
two days Leonard Rosing watched Johnson meet the people who
came to see him, and Rosing wrote to Lind: "I came away impressed that he was a bigger man than I had supposed."[4] Rosing
was only the first to be so impressed; later many of the Democratic
and Republican leaders were to marvel at the way Johnson grew
as he assumed increased responsibilities and as more demands
were made upon him.

In addition to his duties as governor-elect, he had to put his
personal affairs in order. Someone had to be hired to take his place
as editor of the *Herald*, and he persuaded his mother and sister to
live in the new home into which he and Mrs. Johnson had just
moved. When he left St. Peter for the capital city, he bade farewell to Henry Essler with these words: "I'll be back in two years.
Try to keep the subscribers in line, and don't let the ads get away
from you. Keep the job work going. So long!"[5]

Johnson's inauguration was scheduled for January 4, and he
was busy for several days writing his inaugural message. When
the day arrived, Johnson was nervous. He had bought a new suit
for the occasion, and he took considerable pains getting dressed.
Unable to tie his tie properly, he had to call for assistance from
an old friend, Henry N. Benson, whom he had invited to attend
the inauguration, and Benson and Mrs. Johnson finally pronounced him ready for the ceremony.[6]

Johnson was the first governor to be inaugurated in the new
capitol, where both houses of the legislature met together in the
chambers of the house of representatives to witness the ceremony.
Before members of the legislature, guests, and a crowded gallery
Governor Van Sant delivered his farewell address. Then Chief
Justice Start administered the oath of office to John A. Johnson.

. . . tall and erect and becomingly attired in a Prince Albert coat,
[Johnson] made a commanding figure, as he stood in front of the chief
justice, his hand raised and carefully following the oath as it was ut-

[3] *St. Paul Dispatch*, November 15, December 1, 1904; Day and Knappen, p. 132.
[4] Leonard A. Rosing Papers, in Minnesota Historical Society, Rosing to Lind, December 22, 1904.
[5] Day and Knappen, pp. 132–33.
[6] Henry N. Benson to W. G. H.

tered by the judge. His answer . . . was clear and sharp, and he had hardly uttered it and stepped forward to grasp the extended hand of Governor Van Sant before the galleries began applauding, and the house and senate members followed with vigorous hand clapping.[7]

The applause died away only when the speaker of the house raised his hand for silence. Johnson, deeply touched, seemed unable to speak for a few minutes. But when he began to read his message, his voice was strong and clear.[8] Solemnly and earnestly, he spoke to the legislature:

I wish to assure you that in the administration of state affairs, I shall be guided by one and only one purpose: that of serving the state as a whole and to that end I ask the co-operation of the legislature with the executive arm of the government. It should be your purpose and mine to place the state above party or personal interests, and as chosen servants of all the people, we should strive to serve the state without regard to any interest save the interest of the whole state, and to this end I pledge you all the support which the Executive can give.

Already impressed with the amount of time his many duties required, Johnson recommended that the tenure of office for the governor be changed from two years to four years by a constitutional amendment, that the change be put into effect at the end of his term, and that he be made ineligible for re-election. The longer term, he suggested, would give the chief executive more time to acquaint himself with his duties, the condition of the state institutions, and the problems of the state in general.

Declaring that "the primary education of the youth is the real basis of our citizenship and every opportunity for the encouragement of the early training of our youth should be employed," Johnson urged the legislature to consider plans for the construction of better equipped rural schools which would be manned by trained teachers paid higher salaries. County superintendents, he said, should be chosen for their educational qualifications rather than their politics.

He recommended that the legislature appropriate funds for hiring a special counsel to aid the attorney general in prosecuting suits against the railroads for the collection of back taxes, and for

[7] *St. Paul Dispatch*, January 4, 1905.
[8] *Ibid.*

the executive to begin a thorough investigation of timber trespassing. The public examiner had reported some mineral leases
which had been issued contrary to the law, and Johnson recommended that the legislature provide for the sale of mineral lands
to the highest bidder at a public auction after the lands had been
examined by the state mineralogists. He also recommended the
passage of a law providing for an inheritance tax.

On the subject of railroad rates Johnson was clear. Pointing
out that rates in Minnesota were higher than those in Iowa and
Canada, he condemned the practice of discrimination in rates. He
urged the establishment of a fair maximum freight rate by the
Railroad and Warehouse Commission and criticized his predeces-
sor for not having exerted pressure upon the commission to accomplish this earlier. He suggested the creation of a joint legislative committee to make a thorough investigation of rates and
urged the legislature to endorse the Cooper bill then being considered by Congress, which provided that the Interstate Commerce Commission be given increased authority to set rates for
interstate traffic. Citing telephone and telegraph companies as
well as railroads, he said: "Every public service corporation
which gets its authority from the state and its protection by the
state, should be forced to submit to public control."

For several years there had been increasing feeling in Minnesota against the granting of passes to public officials by the railroad companies. Johnson emphatically urged the adoption of a
law abolishing the pass system, but he did so tactfully. He said:
"I am not among those who believe that the giving or accepting
of a free railroad pass or frank is intended in any way as a bribe,
and yet the mere acceptance of the courtesy necessarily places
the recipient under some slight measure of obligation to the
corporation."

During the campaign Johnson had been attacked for opposing
appropriations for the drainage of swamplands in northern Minnesota; now he recommended that the legislature appropriate
money for that purpose. He suggested that the insurance laws of
Minnesota be completely revised to afford more adequate protection for the policyholders, and he recommended that the state insurance commissioner be paid a sufficient salary rather than al-

lowed to retain the fees he collected. All fees, he declared, should go into the state treasury.

There was little in the governor's message regarding labor, but he did recommend that a law be passed making the employer liable for any injuries to employees at work. He recommended also that a permanent bureau of immigration be created, that the activities of the State Board of Control be examined by the public examiner or some other state official, that a law providing for a review of election returns be passed, that the whole system for the care of the insane be reorganized on the basis of curing the disease rather than merely caring for the person, and that a more efficient system be set up for the conservation of state forest lands. In conclusion, Johnson again reminded the members of the legislature that they and he were servants of the state who must disregard political considerations in order to serve the people of Minnesota conscientiously.[9]

Johnson's message was well received generally. The *St. Paul Dispatch* commented that it was not a strong state paper and contained nothing to indicate it had been delivered by a Democrat rather than a Republican, but that there was much good in it.[10] The *Duluth Labor World,* on the other hand, declared the message to be "a masterpiece in logic, eloquence and common sense." [11]

During the next few months Johnson was besieged by hundreds of people every day, some of whom wanted to see and congratulate him, but most of whom sought positions. The Democrats were hungry for offices, and the Collins Republicans had to be rewarded. Letters from applicants poured in, and for every office Johnson had to fill, there were more than twenty applicants. He saw everyone who came to his office, chatted with them, soothed some, and graciously promised to do the best he could for others, but he felt the strain.[12] To a friend who had written congratulating him upon his election, he replied:

Referring to your wish that the office may be a pleasure to me, I de-

[9] *Inaugural Message of Governor John A. Johnson to the Legislature of Minnesota,* 1905.

[10] *St. Paul Dispatch,* January 5, 1905.

[11] *Duluth Labor World,* January 7, 1905.

[12] *Martin County Sentinel,* February 10, 1905; *St. Paul Pioneer Press,* January 5, 7, 15, 1905; Executive Letters, Johnson to John H. Reid of Hawley, January 13, 1905.

sire to say that I am passing through a siege with office seekers which is not especially delightful, but this will all be over in due time and I have no doubt that I shall enjoy the position which the people have so generously bestowed upon me.[13]

Almost immediately after his election Johnson had appointed Frank A. Day as his private secretary, and soon after his inauguration he appointed T. D. O'Brien as insurance commissioner, Leonard A. Rosing as a member of the State Board of Control, F. G. Winston as surveyor general of logs and lumber for the second lumber district, Judge Robert Jamison as attorney for the State Livestock and Sanitary Board, and Alvah Eastman to succeed himself on the board of directors of the state normal schools.[14] He had the pleasure of reappointing his old friend, Dr. Charles Mayo, to the State Board of Health, but Dr. Mayo refused another term of service and suggested his father-in-law, Dr. Christopher Graham, for the position. In reply Johnson wrote: "The appointment of Dr. Graham, while giving me great pleasure is purely the result of your request, because if there was any appointment which I desired to make, it was in some measure to show yourself and your brother Will some appreciation of past services for me." In accepting the appointment, Dr. Graham expressed the high regard he and the Mayo brothers felt for Johnson.[15]

In December Johnson had written to Judge Torrance: "As governor of the state, I will need the counsel and advice of men like yourself, and I shall be glad to come to you very, very often to ask for your opinion." [16] He suggested that Torrance make recommendations for appointments, and Torrance did suggest some individuals who were appointed by the governor.[17] Torrance himself refused an appointment, but he was happy that the new governor had remembered his friends.[18]

The fourth estate was, naturally, well represented in the new administration. Johnson appointed John E. King of the *Red Lake*

[13] *Ibid.*, Johnson to Charles R. Boostrom of Austin, January 21, 1905.

[14] *Ibid.*, Johnson to Ray Jones, president of the senate, January 5, 1905; *Princeton Union*, January 26, 1905; *St. Peter Herald*, January 6, 20, 1905.

[15] Executive Letters, C. H. Mayo to Johnson, January 11, 1905; Johnson to C. H. Mayo, January 14, 1905; Christopher Graham to Johnson, January 16, 1905.

[16] Torrance Papers, Johnson to Torrance, December 10, 1904.

[17] *Ibid.*, Torrance to Johnson, December 22, 1904; Johnson to Torrance, December 24, 1904; J. F. Gibbons to Torrance, April 29, 1905.

[18] *Ibid.*, Torrance to Johnson, January 21, 1905; Mrs. Torrance to Torrance, January 15, 1905.

*Falls Courier* to be state librarian, and for a while this appointment was held up in the senate, where some Republicans remembered the criticisms King had made of Ray Jones during the campaign.[19] John C. Wise of the *Mankato Review* was appointed, along with editor Alvah Eastman, to the board of directors of the state normal schools. E. J. Lynch of the *St. James Journal* became deputy labor commissioner, C. F. MacDonald of the *St. Cloud Times* was appointed to the board of trustees of the soldiers' home, and John King of the *Jackson Pilot* became oil inspector for his county. Cleve Van Dyke resigned as the governor's executive clerk and was replaced by Harvey Grimmer, a political writer for the *St. Paul Globe*.

Johnson's appointment of W. H. Williams as commissioner of labor appealed to the labor element of the state. As dairy and food commissioner, the governor appointed E. K. Slater, who had been recommended by the University of Minnesota College of Agriculture and who was so competent that the federal government tried to get him to come to Washington. Slater's efficient administration of his department strengthened Johnson's reputation all over the state. Van Sant appointees were left in charge of the Department of Public Instruction and told to manage the department without regard to politics.

Johnson had made a real effort to appoint men who were qualified for the positions they were to fill, and his appointments were regarded as excellent ones. The new governor soon made it a point to become acquainted with all government departments, and he broke precedent by attending all meetings of all the boards on which he was an ex officio member.[20]

Governor Johnson's relations with the Republican legislature were harmonious and pleasant. He realized that unless he wanted to cause a deadlock between the legislative and executive branches of the government, all he could do was to make recommendations to the legislature. He was content to recommend, but he expected the legislature to consider his recommendations seriously. The Re-

[19] Executive Letters, King to Frank Day, January 11, 1905; *Martin County Sentinel*, January 20, 1905. In a letter to Frank Day on December 28, 1904, Leonard Rosing warned Day that he and King had better stop attacking Jones, who was popular with the senators; he wrote the same advice to King (see Rosing Papers).

[20] William Hard, "John Johnson of Minnesota," *American Magazine*, October 1907, pp. 573–74; Chamberlain, pp. 10136–37; *St. Peter Herald*, January 6, 20, October 20, 1905.

publican legislature was not hostile to Johnson and was keenly aware of the political effect of its actions. Most of Johnson's inaugural recommendations were progressive and had so much popular appeal that the legislators decided it would not be wise to refuse to act upon them.[21]

The legislature proved unfriendly only when it extended the term of the State Capitol Commission which supervised the care of the new building. Since this action took some patronage away from the governor, Johnson objected to the bill, but it was passed over his veto. And he was hurt personally when a legislative committee appointed Edward D. Claggett of Princeton to be superintendent of the commission. Johnson was well aware that Claggett was the man chiefly responsible for the circulation of the slanderous pamphlet during the 1904 campaign. So he sent a vigorous protest to the commission, and Claggett was forced to resign; he was replaced by a man approved by the governor.[22]

One of the first actions of the legislature was to re-elect Moses E. Clapp to the United States Senate. Much of the time of the session was occupied with the completion of a codification of Minnesota laws which was begun in 1901,[23] but the legislature dealt with other problems as well.

One of these was Johnson's recommendation concerning free railroad passes for state officials. The railroad companies were believed to be playing a powerful role in state politics, not only influencing legislators and judges but also dictating the selection of nominees for the governorship. So many public officials had received free passes for so long that it was an accepted custom. Although the receivers were under no stated obligations for the passes, they tended to be grateful to the railroads. It was claimed that on critical legislation affecting the railroads the balance of votes was swung in favor of the railroads by the pass holders.[24] And all public officials collected traveling expenses from the state even though they rode on free passes!

[21] Folwell, vol. 3, p. 279; Day and Knappen, pp. 152–53.
[22] *St. Paul Dispatch*, March 27, 29, 30, 31, April 20, 1905; Executive Letters, Johnson to W. P. Dunnington, April 10, 1905, and Johnson to O. B. Clark, April 4, 1905; *St. Paul Globe*, January 11, April 20, 21, 1905.
[23] *Ibid.*, March 2, 6, 10, 13, 1905.
[24] Roy W. Oppegard, "Governor John Albert Johnson and the Reform Era in Minnesota State Government," master's thesis, University of Wisconsin, 1937, on microfilm in Minnesota Historical Society, p. 54; *Minneapolis Journal*, August 1, September 17, 1904.

Johnson, in recommending the abolition of the pass system, was asking the legislature to do what Wisconsin had done in 1899 and what Governor Joseph Folk of Missouri was then asking of the Missouri legislature. The first antipass bill introduced into the Minnesota legislature, in 1905, was similar to the La Follette antipass bill of Wisconsin; it prohibited the giving of free passes to candidates for and incumbents of public offices. The bill was defeated, and the free pass system remained to become an issue in the 1906 gubernatorial campaign.[25]

There was in Minnesota a good deal of sentiment in favor of the reduction of railroad passenger rates, and a bill providing for a maximum passenger rate of two cents a mile was introduced in the legislature. Railroad attorneys appeared before the senate committee on railroads to argue against both the antipass bill and the two-cent passenger rate bill. They were, of course, much more concerned about the two-cent passenger rate bill. The railroads' practice of charging higher rates for short distances was condemned by the governor. It was not in harmony with his idea that all citizens deserved the same treatment. But the bill did not pass the legislature, and it likewise became an issue in the 1906 campaign.[26]

The legislature, following Johnson's recommendation, appointed a joint committee to investigate freight rates, since the Railroad and Warehouse Commission had not shown any disposition to do it.[27] Shippers in the state wanted reduced freight rates and strongly objected to the railroad practice of discriminatory rates. George S. Loftus, secretary of the St. Paul Shippers' Association, testified before the committee on behalf of the shippers, and A. B. Stickney, president of the Chicago, Great Western Railroad, appeared to plead for government regulation of rates. He declared that there should be a uniform rate schedule to replace the many different schedules then in effect, and he asked that the Railroad and Warehouse Commission and the Interstate Commerce Commission be given more authority to regulate rates.

[25] *St. Paul Dispatch*, January 10, 24, 26, February 6, 7, 17, 18, March 10, 15, 21, 24, April 12, 15, 25, 1905.
[26] *Minneapolis Journal*, January 14, 24, February 7, 17, April 18, 1905; Oppegard, pp. 59–61.
[27] The committee included Senators A. O. Eberhart, E. B. Hawkins, and H. W. Stone, and Representatives W. A. Nolan, P. A. Gonred, J. H. Dorsey, and R. T. Lewis.

The legislature passed laws increasing the power of the Railroad and Warehouse Commission and directed the commission to reduce freight rates. A law was passed, too, prohibiting the railroads from granting rebates and special concessions to shippers, and a memorial was sent to Congress asking for the early enactment of a law giving the Interstate Commerce Commission enlarged powers to regulate railroad rates.[28]

Another bill that created considerable discussion but did not pass the legislature was the reciprocal demurrage bill. Demurrage was the payment a shipper made to the railroad companies for detaining a freight car beyond the time allowed for loading or unloading. Complaining of financial loss because the railroad companies were frequently slow in sending freight cars for loading and unloading, the shippers wanted reciprocal demurrage so that the railroad companies could also be fined for delay. The responsibility for keeping the rolling stock of the railroads moving would then rest upon both parties. The railroads strongly opposed the bill, which provided that the railroad companies furnish a sufficient number of cars to shippers within a specified time, that the loaded freight cars be moved at least fifty miles a day, and that the railroad companies be fined if the cars were not moving twenty-four hours after they were loaded.[29]

A "wide-open" tax amendment, giving the legislature more power in the matter of taxation, was passed for submission to the voters in 1906. A tax commission was created, and an inheritance tax bill was passed. Laws were enacted providing for the removal of the University of Minnesota and the state normal schools from the jurisdiction of the State Board of Control; a more comprehensive system of drainage of the state swamplands; the creation of a state drainage commission; the sale of timber from state forest lands, the defining of trespass, and the setting of penalties for trespassers; the prohibition of corporations from making contributions to political candidates and committees for political purposes; the creation of a state highway commission; and a state tax for the building of state roads.[30]

[28] *Minneapolis Journal*, January 14, February 3, 4, 16, 1905; *General Laws of the State of Minnesota*, 1905, pp. 228, 629–33; Oppegard, pp. 41–45; *St. Paul Dispatch*, February 7, 9, 17, 19, 1905.

[29] *Ibid.*, February 17, March 10, 15, 21, April 6, 15, 1905; Oppegard, pp. 48–51.

[30] *General Laws*, 1905, pp. 148–52, 193–95, 258–73, 303–41, 427–36.

The joint committee on public accounts investigated the charges made against Robert Dunn during the campaign of 1904, and a majority report exonerated him. Public Examiner Johnson, however, was charged with neglect of duty, and it was recommended that the position of public examiner be put on a civil service basis.[31]

What came to be one of the most important contributions of Johnson's career as governor was begun by the legislature of 1905, when, upon his recommendation, it passed a series of laws that provided for the reorganization of the State Insurance Department and for a thorough revision of the code of insurance laws. The Insurance Department was operating under the Law of 1895, which set an inadequate salary for the insurance commissioner and permitted him to supplement it by retaining the fees paid for his services. For example, all insurance companies in the state had to be examined by the commissioner each year, and during the examination the companies paid a fee of ten dollars a day. The insurance commissioner, if he chose, could arrange to collect increased fees from unscrupulous companies and allow them to go unexamined. These and other fees for similar services could amount to a considerable sum. Just before Johnson's election, an insurance commissioner had collected some $70,000 in fees, and an attempt was made to sue him for recovery of the money. But the attorney general had ruled that the commissioner was acting under the state law in collecting the fees, and the state could not recover the money he had taken for himself.

Johnson appointed as insurance commissioner one of the ablest men he knew, T. D. O'Brien of St. Paul. O'Brien immediately drew up suggestions for the reorganization of his department, and Senator Cole introduced a bill incorporating these suggestions. It provided that the insurance commissioner's salary be increased from $2500 to $5000 a year and that he be put under a $25,000 bond. The position of insurance actuary was created, and the salaries of the deputy insurance commissioner and clerks in the department were increased.

Once the Insurance Department was reorganized, O'Brien set to work to see that the insurance companies in Minnesota were on

[31] *St. Paul Dispatch*, March 16, 24, April 5, 18, 1905; *St. Paul Pioneer Press*, April 5, 15, 1905; *Princeton Union*, April 13, September 28, 1905.

a sound basis and that the policyholders were protected. In March he ordered an investigation of the Northwestern National Life Insurance Company of Minneapolis on the grounds that company officials were receiving excessively high salaries and that the management of the company had been severely criticized by a number of Minneapolis insurance men. The company had been investigated in 1904 by S. H. Wolfe of New York, who acted for the Insurance Department, and at that time the company was found to be in sound financial condition.

O'Brien obtained the services of S. H. Wolfe again, and the second investigation revealed that the company was in a deplorable financial state. It was decided, however, that with honest and economical management the company could be salvaged with little if any loss to its policyholders. On March 29 O'Brien made his report to Governor Johnson, who promptly announced that the officers of the company "may offer their resignations before six o'clock this evening or a receivership will be arranged for by that hour." The officers resigned. O'Brien then appointed a committee of Minneapolis citizens to suggest men to replace them. The committee included ex-Governor Lind, Mayor David Jones, Lucien Swift, and B. F. Nelson, and it selected Judge Loren Collins to act as president of the company. Collins was empowered to choose new directors for the company, and he named a group of Minneapolis bankers.

The Northwestern National Life Insurance Company was reorganized and put on a sound financial basis — all without alarming the policyholders. The grand jury of Hennepin County indicted the officers of the company as well as Elmer Dearth, insurance commissioner under Van Sant, a man Frank Day referred to as "the king of all Minnesota grafters." All but one, however, escaped conviction.[32]

About this time the entire country was aroused by the exposures of the Armstrong committee of the New York legislature concerning the low standard of honesty and morality of the big insurance companies in New York. The committee's investigations

[32] Executive Letters, Johnson to H. N. Nelson, December 7, 1905; Johnson to D. B. Avery, December 4, 1905; Frank Day to W. C. E. Ross, November 7, 1905. Also *St. Paul Globe*, March 30, April 1, 1905; *St. Paul Dispatch*, May 11, 12, 1906; *St. Paul Pioneer Press*, March 14, 1905; "Pollock's Clippings, a Memorial to John A. Johnson." vol. 1 (*New York City Post*, September 21, 1909) ; Oppegard, pp. 68–71.

had disclosed that the three big life insurance companies in New York — the New York Life Insurance Company, the Equitable Life Assurance Company, and the Mutual Life Insurance Company — all had engaged in questionable and fraudulent practices. These companies had secret funds which they kept in subsidiary banks or trust companies and used for illicit purposes. They contributed liberally to political campaigns, local and national, and bribed legislators; their officers were paid excessive salaries; they were using policyholders' money for questionable or speculative purposes; their policyholders paid too much for insurance; and they were tied up with the great banking houses of the country. Since the companies had policyholders scattered all over the United States, public indignation was widespread. The scandal aroused popular distrust not only of the officers who managed the three companies but also of the bankers and railroad promoters who sat on their boards of directors.[33]

T. D. O'Brien followed the Armstrong investigations with great interest. Talking with Governor Johnson he suggested that it would be a good thing to have a national insurance conference to discuss the abuses by insurance companies and to propose uniform state insurance laws designed to prevent such abuses. Impressed with this suggestion, Johnson sent O'Brien to Washington to present it to President Roosevelt.[34] He also wrote a long letter to the president, recommending that a national insurance conference such as O'Brien proposed be held as soon as possible, since state legislatures would be considering insurance legislation as the result of the current popular agitation.[35]

O'Brien's ideas appealed to the president, who agreed to call such a conference. When O'Brien returned to Minnesota, however, he discovered that Governor Johnson and Frank Day were making so much of his "mission and its success that President Roosevelt became annoyed and very nearly called the whole plan off!" The president was placated, and with other state insurance

---

[33] See series of articles on life insurance and the New York insurance scandal in *World's Work*, November, December, 1905, and January, February, March, April, 1906; *St. Paul Globe*, April 1, 7, 8, 22, 1905; *St. Paul Pioneer Press*, June 3, 6, 10, 20, 21, 22, 23, July 18, 21, 1905; Thomas Dillon O'Brien, *There Were Four of Us, or Was It Five*, pp. 49–50.

[34] *Ibid.*

[35] Executive Letters, Johnson to Theodore Roosevelt, November 24, 1905.

commissioners O'Brien began to plan for the national conference to be held on February 1 in Chicago.[36]

In the meantime O'Brien attended conferences in Chicago and New York regarding the investigation of the New York Life Insurance Company and took part in a conference on federal supervision of insurance companies.[37] Governor Johnson was invited to serve on the committee to select directors for the New York Life Insurance Company, and he accepted.[38] In a speech before the Ramsey County Bar Association on January 4, 1906, O'Brien urged the states to pass laws regulating insurance companies within their boundaries and declared that the insurance scandal in New York showed that the federal government should control all large corporations.[39] A few days later, before the Minnesota Municipal and Commercial League, he made a plea for legislation which would protect policyholders in Minnesota.[40] On January 30 Governor Johnson attended an insurance conference in Chicago, where he stated that the people of Minnesota wanted remedial insurance legislation which would restore their confidence in life insurance companies.[41]

The opening session of the national insurance conference took place on February 1 with Thomas E. Drake, insurance commissioner of Washington, D.C., presiding. More than a hundred state officials, including six governors and representing thirty-two states, were present.[42] Governor Johnson was unanimously elected permanent chairman, and in his speech to the conference he declared himself in favor of uniform state insurance laws rather than federal laws to regulate insurance companies. He suggested that plenty of publicity would help to eliminate some of the insurance evils.

[36] O'Brien, *There Were Four of Us, or Was It Five,* p. 50; *St. Paul Pioneer Press,* November 22, December 15, 1905. In his annual message on December 5, 1905, President Roosevelt asked Congress to consider the question of uniform laws and more strict regulation of insurance companies (see Richardson, *Messages and Papers of the Presidents,* vol. 11).

[37] *St. Paul Dispatch,* August 2, 1905; *St. Paul Pioneer Press,* August 4, 15, 17, November 21, 1905.

[38] *Ibid.,* October 8, 1905.

[39] *Ibid.,* January 5, 1906.

[40] *St. Paul Dispatch,* January 9, 1906.

[41] *St. Paul Pioneer Press,* January 31, 1906.

[42] The governors attending the conference were Johnson of Minnesota, Davidson of Wisconsin, Cummins of Iowa, Elrod of South Dakota, Sarles of North Dakota, and Beckham of Kentucky.

It was Drake's suggestion that an insurance code be drawn up for the District of Columbia which could then be used as a model for all the states in revising old insurance laws and drawing up new ones. T. D. O'Brien was made chairman of a committee of fifteen members to draw up such a code. O'Brien's committee held four meetings during 1906: in March it met in Chicago, in August in St. Paul, in October in Washington, D.C., and in November in Chicago. The committee was guided in its work by the recommendations made in the Armstrong committee report. By 1907 twenty-two states had revised their insurance codes along the lines suggested by O'Brien's committee.[43]

In his second inaugural address Governor Johnson urged the Minnesota legislature to study both the Armstrong report and the recommendations of O'Brien's committee and to pass laws which would give the people of the state more effective insurance protection.[44] Johnson and O'Brien worked hard to have the insurance reform movement well organized in the legislature, and as a result, Minnesota soon had a new code of laws regulating life, fire, and marine insurance.[45]

Johnson's insurance activities had brought him into contact with Thomas W. Lawson, the Boston multimillionaire who had become a muckraker in order to expose the crimes of some of his enemies in the business world. A colorful personality with a "powerful and original gift of language" [46] and an inordinate amount of energy, Lawson thoroughly enjoyed writing "Frenzied Finance," his exposé of the Amalgamated Copper Company, which he had organized with the aid of H. H. Rogers and William Rockefeller of the Standard Oil Company, James Stillman of the National City Bank of New York, and F. Augustus Heinze of Montana.

[43] St. Paul Dispatch, February 1, 2, 1906; St. Paul Pioneer Press, February 2, 3, 1906; O'Brien, There Were Four of Us, or Was It Five, p. 50. In reply to Roosevelt's insurance message, Congress decided to leave insurance legislation to the states.

[44] Inaugural Message, 1907, pp. 25-28.

[45] General Laws, 1907, pp. 47-50, 372-73, 469-83; Oppegard, pp. 80-81. Laws were passed providing that all insurance companies have standard policy forms, all policy forms be submitted to the insurance commissioner for approval before used, deferred dividend policies were to be abolished, contributions by insurance companies to political parties were forbidden, investments of the companies were to be regulated by law, life insurance contracts must contain the complete contract, individuals selling life insurance policies must be recognized as agents of the companies they represent, standardized annual reports must be made to the state insurance department, and the disbursements of the insurance companies were to be regulated.

[46] Louis Filler, Crusaders for American Liberalism, p. 179.

The story of how these men double-crossed him and fleeced the stockholders of the company was told in installments in *Everybody's Magazine*.

Only incidentally, to illustrate how some of the big financiers made their money, Lawson explained that these financiers considered the assets of the three big New York insurance companies as reserve funds to be used in their speculations. The public reaction to this was immediate. Lawson received so many letters asking to know more about the financial practices of the life insurance companies that he decided to show the people just how the companies were "tools of the great financiers." [47]

The Armstrong committee investigations followed, and Lawson became involved in the reorganization of the New York Life Insurance Company and the Mutual Life Insurance Company. On February 7, 1905, he went to St. Paul to ask Governor Johnson to serve as chairman of a committee to reorganize these two companies. Johnson agreed to serve on the committee but refused to act as its chairman, for he felt he could not leave Minnesota as often as would be necessary. Lawson had already spent about $300,000 collecting proxies from a majority of the policyholders of both companies, and he was determined to have directors elected who would represent the policyholders. He also wanted the men responsible for the life insurance evils prosecuted for their crimes. [48]

Lawson's committee soon merged with the International Policyholders' Committee, a group of nationally prominent men who were to represent the policyholders of the New York Life Insurance and Mutual Life Insurance companies, to nominate full boards of directors for the companies, and also to organize a permanent policyholders' association to supervise the companies. [49] At a meeting on July 9 the committee nominated candidates for the two boards of directors and asked the policyholders to vote on them by September 18. Governor Johnson and T. D. O'Brien both issued statements urging the twenty-seven thousand Min-

[47] *Ibid.*, p. 190.

[48] *St. Paul Pioneer Press*, February 8, 11, 27, 1906; Executive Letters, Lawson to Johnson, February 27, 1906, and Johnson to Lawson, March 2, 1906.

[49] *Ibid.*, Lawson to Johnson, March 6, 1906; Seymour Eaton to Johnson, June 12, 1906; Samuel Untermeyer to Johnson, June 20, 1906; Johnson to Untermeyer, July 26, 1906; Untermeyer to Johnson, July 2, 1906. Also *St. Paul Dispatch*, July 9, 10, 1906; *St. Paul Pioneer Press*, July 12, 1906.

nesota policyholders of the companies to cooperate with the International Policyholders' Committee.[50] Johnson was unable to attend the final meeting of the committee in September because it conflicted with the Democratic state nominating convention, but he had taken an active part in the committee's activities and had supported it to the limit.[51]

The popular election of directors of the New York and Mutual life insurance companies brought about by Lawson's International Policyholders' Committee "was the first and last serious effort to introduce democracy into insurance. After that, high finance assumed full and undisputed sway." [52] Nevertheless, insurance companies were made more efficient in their management, evils were wiped out, many states passed laws regulating insurance companies within their borders, and state insurance laws were standardized.

The movement begun by O'Brien to bring about standardization in insurance laws led to a meeting of representatives from fifteen states to discuss the possibility of securing more uniform laws on divorce, railroad regulation, pure food and meat inspection, and naturalization.[53]

Taking the lead in the insurance reform movement was for Johnson a happy and broadening experience. He mastered the intricacies of insurance problems so thoroughly that he was able to impress others with his command of the subject. Working with the recognized national leaders on the International Policyholders' Committee, he began to gain a reputation outside of Minnesota. Thomas Lawson was so impressed by Johnson that he talked about Minnesota's governor as he traveled around the country speaking for insurance reform. Time and again he was asked, "Who is John A. Johnson?" [54] Back in Boston in July 1905 after a speaking tour in the West, Lawson expressed his opinion of Johnson in an interview with the press:

It is impossible for me in any limited space to give my opinion of my journey, but I want to make one point: I am convinced there is but one man in the West that I bumped elbows with whose selection to fill the great Roosevelt's shoes would be anything other than sacrilege.

[50] Ibid., November 11, 1906.
[51] Executive Letters, Johnson to Untermeyer, September 7, 1906.
[52] Filler, p. 201.      [53] St. Paul Pioneer Press, August 26, 1906.
[54] St. Paul Dispatch, July 20, 24, 1905.

I found in the West one of the sturdiest Americans I have ever run across — an able, honest, fearless citizen of the republic, a personality to whom the great body of American citizens would warm and quickly make a hero of — Governor Johnson of Minnesota.

It just did my heart good to shake hands with him and to stand off and analyze him, and I do not hesitate a second in saying that, barring accidents, if the Democratic party nominates him three years from now, and the American people get a peek at him, nothing will stop him from landing in the White House with a majority well up with Roosevelt's. I am no politician, and as the American people know, I am not hired out to boom any man for anything, but I simply cannot hold this expression back.[55]

The St. Paul Pioneer Press was skeptical in reporting this praise of Johnson. It gave Lawson exclusive credit for "discovering" Johnson and declared that no one in Minnesota yet suspected there was anything notable about him or his career. Minnesota, said the Pioneer Press, "wants more proof of Johnson's great abilities than Lawson's opinion after a brief acquaintance." [56]

Johnson took Lawson's pronouncement as a "huge joke," and he wrote to a friend that he was complimented by Lawson's "kind expressions" but that Lawson "has not convinced me that I am presidential timber. As a matter of fact I have no ambitions in that direction . . ." [57] To a well-wisher from Maryland Johnson wrote: "I am not a candidate for President of the United States and do not expect to be." [58] While in Washington on business the following spring, Johnson declared that Bryan was the logical presidential candidate for the Democrats in 1908 and that he probably would be nominated.[59] Lawson, nevertheless, continued to talk about Johnson as presidential timber, and more and more people heard about Minnesota's governor.

But in Minnesota Johnson was doing his own talking. There were many demands made upon him to speak, and he conscientiously performed his duty. Soon after he was inaugurated he had the peculiar pleasure of welcoming the editors of the state gathered

[55] Martin County Sentinel, July 28, 1905; St. Paul Pioneer Press, July 24, 1905.
[56] Ibid., July 24, 1905.
[57] Executive Letters, Johnson to Reverend Alfred Bergin of Lindsborg, Kan., July 25, 1905.
[58] Ibid., Johnson to Francis B. Livesey of Sykesville, Md., July 25, 1905.
[59] St. Paul Pioneer Press, May 11, 1906.

in Minneapolis for their annual meeting.[60] He pleased them by stating: "We leave the State of Minnesota in its official capacity, and I return to you now in the humble capacity of a country editor of this great State." He refused to allow the editors to hold a reception for him and Mrs. Johnson, preferring simply to be one of them as he had been for so many years. The association endorsed Johnson's recommendations for railroad legislation and for the extension of the primary election law to state officials.

During the summer of 1905 Governor Johnson and his wife accompanied the editors on their annual excursion, which was a boat trip on the Great Lakes. At a banquet at Sarnia, the governor, responding to a welcoming toast, made a speech in which he urged the United States and Canada to establish reciprocal trade relations.[61] Johnson was also present at the editors' annual meeting in 1906 and delivered an address calling for the enactment of laws providing for the abolition of the free pass system and for the two-cent maximum passenger fare.[62]

Governor Johnson's first speech away from home was made before the Chicago Merchants' Club on February 18, 1905. Present to hear him were representatives of almost every railroad company whose trains entered the Chicago terminal, and representatives of the financial world as well. His speech, "Commercial and Political Integrity," was a strong condemnation of current commercial and political ethics and a plea for people to free the government from the grasp of Big Business. Naturally optimistic, Johnson opened his speech with the following words: "I am not among those who believe the nation is tottering, but among those who behold grave danger and have faith that this danger will be averted." That danger, according to Johnson, was the "surrender of government functions to private corporations under [the] guise of protecting the national welfare." He went on to say:

Lawson tells us an appalling story of financial chicanery and ruin; good men at the head of vast industries appropriate the money of the people to their own uses. Steffens tells us of municipal corruption that makes the story of Nero and Rome seem cheap. And all this time the

[60] *Proceedings of the Minnesota Editors' and Publishers' Association*, 1905, pp. 5, 6, 7.
[61] *St. Paul Pioneer Press*, August 21, 28, 1905; *St. Paul Dispatch*, August 26, 1905.
[62] *Proceedings of the Minnesota Editors' and Publishers' Association*, 1906, p. 56.

man of affairs will allow "business interests" to corrupt men in places of authority, while he shudders and stands aghast at the wrong doing of an ordinary criminal.

We boast to-day of a commercial reign unequalled in the world's history. . . . In this city are scores of multi-millionaires. In it are one hundred thousand who cloy the hungry edge of appetite by the bare imagination of a feast. . . . Our political system and our commercial system are out of tune. The tendency of the great to crush the small, with the indifference of the elephant to the worm, is too common.

Continuing, he pointed out such specific corporate evils as railroad rate discrimination, the exploitation of natural resources by a few who grew wealthy at the expense of the people, fictitious capitalization, special tariff bounties, and transportation rebates. Such evils, he warned, ought to be wiped out. But, he said:

As long as government is the fountain of special privileges, powerful interests will dominate legislation, law will be dictated by the corrupt lobby, corporations will control legislators and even judges, and executives will betray their trusts. As long as the law of the land is made the source of corporate dividends, the campaign contributions of corporate interests will control political conventions and party machines for the nomination and election of its candidates, and our so-called "public servants" will be private agents for the public undoing. There is just one remedy for official bribery and corruption, and that is, to remove the motive by cutting off all government grants of special privilege. The enforced guaranty of equal rights to all will free the party organization from corporate grasp and restore it to the common people. . . .

Forsaking the old ideas, we are confronted with a centralized commercialism more than feudal in power. The principles of Washington, Jefferson and Lincoln are supplanted by the influences of Harriman, Armour and Rockefeller. . . . The price of good government is good citizenship, even at the sacrifice of party affiliation. Will you do your share, and will I do mine?

Let us demand leadership consecrated to the public weal by the strong and simple ties of common honesty, equality and manhood. Let us consecrate our efforts to uphold the majesty of the law by enforcing its observance upon the most powerful as upon the humble.

Johnson called for public leaders who would have faith in the development of the United States, who would have the optimism to guide the country through troubled times, who would have the ability to study calmly the conditions needing change, and who would have a "fearless determination to arrive at what is best for all the people." And he concluded: "The true grandeur of the nation will assert itself; if not to-day, then to-morrow. An enlightened and quickened conscience has issued the American doctrine — Equal rights to all; special privileges to none." [63]

Johnson caused considerable national comment when he declined an invitation to deliver a Fourth of July address before Tammany Hall in New York because he had already accepted the invitation to make the Fourth of July speech in Luverne, Minnesota. The people of Minnesota were delighted, and editor H. J. Miller of the *Rock County Herald* facetiously invited Tammany Hall to come to the celebration in Luverne.[64]

Invited to be one of the speakers at a banquet in honor of Dr. William J. Mayo, who had just been elected president of the American Medical Association, Johnson desperately wanted to attend but at first had to decline because of a previous engagement. In a letter regretting he could not be present, he wrote the following appreciation of his physician and friend:

To me Dr. Mayo is at the head of his profession, not only in our state but in the nation. His position in the medical fraternity of our country is manifested by his election to this high and responsible office, a confidence shown to him by the members of his own profession. . . .

I owe my life to Dr. Mayo and I cannot put words on paper which will in any measure express my confidence, my affection and my esteem for this quiet gentleman who has won so high a place in the affectionate regard of all who know him.[65]

Later finding himself able to attend the banquet, Johnson offered a toast to "My Doctor." [66]

After speaking at the Minnesota Education Association's annual meeting in St. Paul on December 27, Johnson received an unexpected tribute from Cyrus Northrop, president of the Uni-

[63] "Commercial and Political Integrity," a speech by the Hon. John A. Johnson, 1905. The speech was well received (*St. Paul Globe*, February 20, 1905; *Martin County Sentinel*, February 24, 1905).

[64] Executive Letters, Frank Day to H. J. Miller, June 29, 1905.

[65] *Ibid.*, Johnson to A. T. Stebbins of Rochester, July 20, 1905.

[66] *St. Paul Pioneer Press*, July 25, 1905; Clapesattle, pp. 436–38; *Rochester Post-Record*, July 25, 1905.

versity of Minnesota. Addressing himself to Johnson as well as
to the teachers of the state, Northrop said:

I want to say to you, sir, that I wish to impress these teachers that
they may properly point to you, to your personality and conduct in
the office of governor of this state . . . as a worthy example for them
to follow. I would say this with just as much freedom of conviction
whether you were present or not. There is no campaign in progress
and I have no object in saying this except to emphasize the propriety
of giving you proper credit for the honest and independent manner
in which you have discharged the duties of your high and responsible
position.[67]

At the annual meeting of the Minnesota Municipal and Commercial League in January 1906, Governor Johnson, T. D. O'Brien,
and Leonard Rosing delivered the principal addresses. Rosing
called for legislation which would empower the State Railroad and
Warehouse Commission and the Interstate Commerce Commission to regulate railroad rates, and O'Brien asked for additional
legislative action to bring about more reforms in the insurance
field.[68] Johnson's speech was fairly long and chiefly concerned with
his plea for government regulation of railroads. Replying to the
claim "that the vested and chartered right of the corporation cannot be assailed, curtailed or abridged," he said: "I believe in the
obligation of contract. I believe that it should not be impaired.
But I believe that when the chartered corporation, going beyond
its chartered rights, refuses to abide by the laws under which it
has its existence and has its being, [it] can be regulated."

Johnson went on to state that there were a great many people
who thought the government should own and operate the railroads but that he did not believe the time to be ripe for government ownership. But, he warned, government ownership will
come rapidly if there is too much resistance to the right of the
government to regulate the railroads for the benefit of the people.
Answering the boast of the railroad owners that they had done so
much to build up the country, he said: "No great center of population can flourish and thrive except it flourishes and thrives upon
the smaller municipalities and upon the agricultural communities. The railroads of our state and of the Northwest have not

[67] *Martin County Sentinel*, January 12, 1906.
[68] *St. Paul Dispatch*, January 9, 1906.

shown the consideration to the rural communities of this state
to which they have been justly entitled." And he concluded:

In a village in Southern Minnesota last autumn, a great railway genius
advised the farmer to elect men to legislative positions who would be
true to the agricultural interests. Is not the advice on that occasion
pertinent to this? The remedy for many evils is the ballot, properly
and effectively used — not with blindness of party spirit or to promote the interests of individuals, but used with the broader idea of
promoting the general welfare and securing a more perfect civilization,
based, as it must be, on the principles of justice, equality and fairness.[69]

His speech was greeted with enthusiasm, and the Municipal
and Commercial League endorsed his demands for railroad
legislation.[70]

Johnson did a great deal of speaking during his first administration, most of it within Minnesota. His amazing ability to enter a
town he had never before visited and immediately see and understand its problems and interests drew people to him. And he liked
to meet the citizens of the state — those he met sensed that.

The people of Minnesota were satisfied with the appointments
Johnson had made; they liked his close attention to the activities
of the legislature; they approved the content of his speeches; they
were impressed by the way he mastered the questions put before
him before he made a decision; and they were proud of his participation in the insurance reform movement, which gave him a
national reputation. But most of all they liked his emphasis upon
the fact that he was governor of all the people and his insistence
upon the careful enforcement of the laws. A writer who was sent
to interview Johnson for the *American Magazine* made this ex-
planation for the governor's steadily increasing popularity:

It isn't his mind alone that has taken him forward. The quality that
makes the little girls in St. Peter call him "John" is largely responsible
for John Johnson's advance. It is a sort of universal human interest
and kindliness. . . . He has a good mind, a very good mind, an expanding mind. But if he has genius, it is a genius, not of mind, but of
temperament.[71]

[69] "Minnesota and the Railroads," a speech by Governor John A. Johnson, January
10, 1906.
[70] *St. Paul Dispatch*, January 11, 1906.
[71] Hard, p. 576.

## CHAPTER VIII

*A Second Term*

As EARLY as May 1905 there was much speculation as to who would be the Republican nominee for governor in 1906. Mentioned then as possible candidates were Secretary of State Peter E. Hanson, State Treasurer Julius H. Block, J. F. Jacobson, who had just been replaced by Leonard Rosing on the State Board of Control, and C. F. Staples, a member of the State Railroad and Warehouse Commission. By September State Senator Ripley Brower of St. Cloud and State Representative Albert L. Cole of Walker were added to the list.

As the new year dawned, Jacobson, Cole, and Block seemed to be the most frequently mentioned Republican candidates,[1] but Senator Knute Nelson judged the situation correctly when he wrote to his friend Soren Listoe: "They seem still to be at sea in Minnesota as to the Governorship. It will be no easy matter to find a man who can beat Governor Johnson. The campaign of two years ago left us in bad shape." [2] No one considered Robert Dunn as a candidate, but the support of Dunn and his friends was essential to any Republican nominee. Dunn never forgave the Republicans who had opposed him, and he was not likely to support anyone in 1906 who had not supported him in 1904. For that reason, he did not favor the candidacy of J. F. Jacobson.[3]

During February the Republican leaders held "harmony" meetings in the Twin Cities in an effort to heal the rift in the party,[4] and the Twin Cities' newspapers made much of the fact that the Republicans were now one happy family. But such was not the case. Sitting back and calmly observing the Republican attempts to unite, Frank Day wrote to a friend: "Our friends of the oppo-

[1] *St. Paul Dispatch,* May 13, 26, June 10, 21, September 6, 21, 22, 1905, January 19, 20, 26, 1906.
[2] Nelson Papers, Nelson to Listoe, January 2, 1906.
[3] *St. Paul Dispatch,* February 10, 1906.
[4] *St. Peter Herald,* February 16, 1906.

sition are still at sea as to whom they will nominate. Jacobson
seems to have the inside track at present, but the Governor thinks
he is anything but a strong man and is willing to cross swords
with him in the coming campaign." [5]

All was not perfectly serene for the Democrats, however, and
soon Frank Day was writing to a political friend in Duluth urging
him to attempt to win over to Johnson both the strong labor and
the Hearst elements in St. Louis County.[6] The Democratic leaders
decided to hold a late convention, to be followed by a brief, whirlwind campaign. This would permit Johnson to fill a great number
of the speaking engagements he had scheduled for the summer
months.[7]

Johnson's numerous speeches annoyed many Republicans. Robert Dunn, who kept up a constant sniping at Johnson and his
advisers, wrote:

Rumor sayeth that Frank O'Day is passing his Sundays in writing
speeches for Governor John to deliver at picnics and baseball meets
the coming summer. The governor will not, however, neglect his proposed sermons in churches, exhortations at camp meetings, and little
talks to mothers' associations and Sunday school classes in conse-
quence of his additional work. A remarkable man is Governor John.[8]

The *St. Paul Dispatch* noted with amusement that P. T. Barnum
never booked as many talks as Governor John and commented
that in the booking such factors as location, voting strength, and
nationality were considered. "His excellency is long on talks; he
does them beautifully," stated the *Dispatch*.[9] Earlier, the *War-
road Republican* had scornfully declared:

Talk about Johnson being hard to defeat! We should like to know
why? All he has done since he was elected is to run from place to place
making a good fellow of himself by agreeing with the popular local
sentiment on the various state issues. If that is all the governor of
Minnesota has to do, better abolish the office.[10]

In April, Julius Block, J. F. Jacobson, and A. L. Cole formally

[5] Executive Letters, Day to Cleve Van Dyke, February 21, 1906.
[6] *Ibid.*, Day to Fred L. Ryan, March 15, 1906.
[7] *Ibid.*, Day to A. P. Yngve, April 14, 1906, and Day to J. B. Galarneault, April 16,
1906; *St. Paul Pioneer Press*, May 5, 1906.
[8] *Princeton Union*, April 12, 1906.
[9] *St. Paul Dispatch*, April 14, 1906.
[10] Quoted in the *St. Paul Dispatch*, September 13, 1905.

announced their candidacies for the Republican nomination for governor.[11] Cole and J. F. Jacobson soon became the leading contenders for the Republican nomination.

An active, well-organized group of men were already working for Cole and had established headquarters at the Ryan Hotel in St. Paul.[12] Albert L. Cole of Walker was a merchant with a string of stores supplying food to the northern counties of Minnesota. Born in St. Lawrence County, New York, and educated in the New York public schools and at St. Lawrence University, Cole served as school commissioner for New York for seven years before he moved to Minnesota in 1882. Early in his career he had been a Democrat, but it was as a Republican that he was elected in 1902 to the Minnesota house of representatives, where he gained some attention for his interest in state drainage. Cole's record was not long; he was in his late fifties, and his health was poor; he was reserved and shy and personally not capable of arousing much enthusiasm. The Republican leaders could find no vulnerable spot in his personal life or career, but few people knew anything about him. His brother, Dr. A. B. Cole of Fergus Falls, who had been active in the Republican party in Minnesota for years, assumed the direction of his campaign.[13]

Jacob F. Jacobson of Madison was a native of Norway who settled in Minnesota in 1871. From 1873 to 1879 he was county auditor of Lac qui Parle County. He was a member of the lower house of the Minnesota legislature from 1889 to 1902 and was appointed to serve as a member of the State Board of Control, where he made an excellent record. With his long career as a Republican and his fine record as a legislator, Jacobson was entitled to consideration, but his bluntness, his forthright way of speaking, and his lack of polish and refinement reminded some Republicans of Robert Dunn. A colorful personality, utterly fearless and honest, Jacobson was well known throughout the state, and he had a considerable popular following. Certainly he was the strongest candidate the Republicans had for 1906, and right up to the eve of the convention it looked as though he would be nomi-

[11] *Ibid.*, April 7, 18, 26, 1906.
[12] *Ibid.*, April 28, 1906; *Princeton Union*, April 26, 1906.
[13] *St. Paul Dispatch*, May 25, 1906; *Legislative Manual*, 1905, p. 679.

nated.[14] His campaign managers were James A. Martin and Alvah Eastman.[15]

But the opposition to Jacobson was very strong if not widespread. Both the Robert Dunn and the Joel Heatwole forces preferred Cole, and some Republicans thought Jacobson was too radical. It was said that the corporations of the state were against him because of his legislative record — because, among other things, he had advocated an increased tax on the gross earnings of the railroad companies.[16] Alvah Eastman delivered a warning and an appeal to the Republican voters:

Republican voters of Minnesota remember this: The only way in which J. F. Jacobson can be prevented from receiving the nomination of governor at Duluth on June 13 is by the use of corporation money. If the corporations and the politicians keep their hands off he will be nominated by acclamation. He is the choice of the people. He is the only candidate who will receive votes from every section of the state. . . . He has a record for doing things. If the republicans of Minnesota really want a republican governor elected, the way is clear. Heed the voice of the people.[17]

At the Republican convention held in the Armory in Duluth, A. L. Cole was nominated for governor on the third ballot. The nomination was unexpected except by those Republican leaders who had determined beforehand that Jacobson was not to have it.[18] The *St. Paul Dispatch,* which had been a vigorous advocate of Jacobson's nomination, made a great point of explaining that the Republican convention was harmonious and that Cole's nomination, unexpected as it was, left no soreness or injured feelings and was accepted by all the party. The *Dispatch,* however, did admit that the majority of the delegates had favored Jacobson and said the "interests" were back of his defeat.[19] Frank Day's paper announced that the "interests" had got "Jake" at Duluth and were preparing to defeat Johnson in November.[20]

[14] *Ibid.,* p. 636; *St. Paul Dispatch,* June 5, 1906.

[15] *Ibid.,* June 1, 8, 9, 11, 12, 1906.

[16] Dr. George Orr to W. G. H.; *Martin County Sentinel,* June 22, 1906.

[17] Quoted from the *St. Cloud Journal-Press* in the *Martin County Sentinel,* June 1, 1906.

[18] Dr. George Orr to W. G. H.; *St. Peter Herald,* June 15, 1906; *St. Paul Pioneer Press,* June 14, 1906; *St. Paul Dispatch,* June 13, 1906.

[19] *Ibid.,* June 14, 1906.

[20] *Martin County Sentinel,* June 22, 1906.

The *St. Paul Pioneer Press* hailed Cole's nomination, saying that although he had less personality than Johnson, he would bring about more results. The paper also noted that Jacobson had made a good fight.[21] But it was generally agreed that Cole was a weak candidate, and most of the Republican newspapers gave him only halfhearted support. His campaign managers and the Twin Cities' newspapers, which backed him vigorously, were not equal to the task of selling him to the people of Minnesota, and he never gained popularity.

Also, there was some hearty opposition to Cole. Alvah Eastman, angry at the convention's action, announced in his newspaper: "Mr. Jacobson's defeat was accomplished by the efforts of the railroad and lumber interests. The people are entitled to the truth, and that is the exact truth." [22] Joel Heatwole warned that the old wounds of 1904 were not healed and that a complete reorganization of the party was necessary to unite it. Defeating Johnson would require the united effort of the party with all Republicans supporting the state ticket, he insisted.[23] And Robert Dunn bitterly predicted, "The traitors will put forth every means at their command to scuttle Cole." [24] In short, the Republican leaders supporting Cole knew that some party members would prefer to vote for Johnson rather than help elect the candidate of the men who had achieved Jacobson's defeat.

Nominated on the Republican ticket with Cole were A. O. Eberhart of Mankato for lieutenant governor, Julius Schmahl of Redwood Falls for secretary of state, Clarence Dinehart of Slayton for state treasurer, S. G. Iverson of Rushford for state auditor, and E. T. Young of Appleton for attorney general. The Republican platform endorsed all of President Roosevelt's policies; pledged support to Knute Nelson for re-election to the United States Senate; urged the passage of bills providing for the abolition of the free pass system, a two-cent maximum passenger rate, and the abolition of discrimination in freight rates; and supported all "just measures tending to the advancement of the causes of temperance, morality and good government." [25]

[21] *St. Paul Pioneer Press,* June 14, 1906.
[22] Quoted in the *Martin County Sentinel,* June 29, 1906.
[23] *Ibid.*
[24] *Princeton Union,* July 19, 1906.
[25] *St. Paul Dispatch,* June 14, 1906.

There was nothing in the platform which Johnson had not advocated for the past two years. In fact, the Republicans virtually declared the only issue of the coming campaign to be the election of a Republican governor rather than Johnson, who, they were certain, would be the Democratic candidate.

Johnson's reaction to Cole's nomination was expressed in a letter to a political friend:

I agree with you that we are fortunate in the outcome of the Republican convention. . . . If the election were held to-day, I am certain the result would be an overwhelming victory for us. What the effects will be of a lapse of four and a half months time, no one can say with certainty, but our reports indicate a condition at present that we could not ask to have improved. Our friend, the enemy, is comparatively unknown outside of an area in Northern Minnesota, and I believe it is going to be pretty hard for him to make any substantial impression on the independent vote of the state. The Republican whips will do everything in their power to get the voters in line for the ticket, but I agree with a good many of the Republican leaders that no weaker ticket was ever nominated by that party in the state than that put before the people at Duluth. I do not believe that Eberhart will strengthen the ticket with the Scandinavians, for he is by no means a strong character.[26]

Frank Day, too, expressed his pleasure with the Republican nominee in a letter:

The situation . . . certainly looks very encouraging for Governor Johnson. Hundreds of Republicans have visited the office and assured us of their support, and among them are a great many delegates who attended the Duluth Convention and were disgusted with the outcome. It is not denied that the lumber interests and other combines practically dictated the nomination of Cole and there is little doubt that the people will resent it.[27]

There was never any question as to who would be the Democratic candidate for the governorship. Johnson had behind him the great majority of Democrats in the state, as well as some independent voters and not a few officeholders who were nominally Republican but owed their positions to him. He had become acquainted with more and more people in the state and had won

[26] Executive Letters, Johnson to A. C. Weiss of Duluth, June 19, 1906.
[27] *Ibid.*, Day to H. T. Moland of Buffalo, June 26, 1906.

their affection. In March 1906 his mother had died, and the story of her struggles and his early years was revived, producing again a warm popular feeling toward him.[28] Also, his growing reputation outside the state made Minnesotans proud. In May, Johnson visited Washington, D.C., on business, and the excellent impression he made there moved Charles A. Towne, the veteran Silver Republican, to write to Frank Day: "If Mr. Bryan were not so supremely on deck, your Governor, in the event of his reelection, would certainly cut a very great figure in the national convention of 1908." [29]

The Democratic state convention, the largest the party had ever assembled, met on September 4 in the Bijou Theatre in Minneapolis. All the delegates were pledged to Johnson, so that his nomination was only a matter of form. Once again Winfield S. Hammond of St. James made the nomination. At his first mention of Johnson's name, there was wild cheering which halted his speech for some time, and when he finished speaking, there was an enthusiastic demonstration for the man he had named. Voices seconding the nomination came from all over the hall, and Johnson was renominated by unanimous vote of the convention.[30] He was summoned before a wildly excited audience and, very pleased and happy, made a brief and informal acceptance speech. He reminded the convention that two years ago he had received the nomination unsought and undesired and had promised to do his best if elected. He continued:

What my administration has been I leave to the people who made me governor to say. I have tried to do my duty.

We, and I speak of the democratic party, have made the theft of state timber an unprofitable calling.

I claim we are entitled to the victory that this state has gained in forcing a reduction on grain and merchandise rates.

We stand for state development, I tell you, that helps the people, not a few.

Then, with a quick change of mood, he brought smiles to the faces of those in the audience when he said: "My only regret, friends,

[28] *Ibid.*, Frank Day to J. S. Hughes, March 16, 1906; Harvey Grimmer to F. Day, March 20, 1906; Johnson to M. J. Donnelly, March 23, 1906.
[29] *Ibid.*, Towne to Day, May 21, 1906.
[30] *St. Paul Pioneer Press*, September 5, 1906; *Minneapolis Journal*, September 4, 1906; *St. Paul Dispatch*, September 4, 1906.

is that I have been unable to give you all offices. Had I enough
to go around you would all be provided for. But I have tried to
do better than that, [to] give you and the voters of the state who
elected me a fair and square deal. I believe we are going to win
again; at least I hope so." [31]

Another demonstration for Johnson followed, and then the convention settled down to finish its business. L. G. Pendergast of
Bemidji was nominated for lieutenant governor, P. M. Magnus-
son of St. Cloud for secretary of state, and A. E. Aarnes of Montevideo for state auditor. Led by two Hearst Democratic leaders,
T. T. Hudson of Duluth and James Bennett of St. Cloud, there
was some strong opposition to the election of Frank Day as chairman of the state central committee, but Johnson emphatically
announced that he would not run for governor if Day was not
chosen for the position. Day was chosen. No one could accuse
Johnson of deserting his friends.[32]

The platform adopted by the Democrats endorsed the administration of Governor Johnson and commended both T. D. O'Brien
for his leadership in the field of insurance reform and E. K. Slater
for his efficient and modern reorganization of the Dairy and Foods
Department. The platform recommended a fair system of taxation with the burden of taxpaying placed upon all the property
in the state; favored initiative and referendum; advocated an
eight-hour day for labor; approved of the extension of the direct
primary to all state offices; urged legislation to provide for the direct election of United States senators; demanded a law to allow
municipalities to own public utilities; asked Congress to revise the
Dingley tariff and enact drastic antitrust laws; congratulated
Bryan upon his leadership of the Democrats of the nation; and
demanded legislation giving Minnesota reduced railroad freight
rates, a two-cent maximum passenger rate, additional railroad
regulation by the state, and an end to the free pass system.[33] There
could be no doubt that the Democrats stood for more progressive
legislation than the Republicans, and Johnson stood on the Democratic platform.

During his first campaign for governor Johnson had been sup-

[31] *Ibid.*
[32] *Ibid.*; *Martin County Sentinel*, September 14, 1906.
[33] *Minneapolis Journal*, September 5, 1906.

ported by the *Minneapolis Journal,* the *Minneapolis Times,* and the *St. Paul Globe,* but not one of the Twin Cities' newspapers supported him in his second campaign. The *Times* and the *Globe* had gone out of existence, and the *Journal* was back in the Republican fold earnestly supporting Cole. Declaring that Johnson's strongest qualifications were his agreeable personality and irreproachable character, the *Journal* warned that he would have a stiff fight for the governorship, because Cole was a man of excellent record, the Republicans were united behind him, and Johnson would be judged upon his record without any benefit of sympathy because of assault upon his family.[34]

The *St. Paul Dispatch* and the *Pioneer Press* both called upon all Republicans to support Cole and stated that Johnson was elected in 1904 only because the Republicans were split into factions; Johnson's prominence outside Minnesota was explained simply by the fact that he was a Democratic governor in a strong Republican state. But even while urging the election of Cole, the *Dispatch* had to admit that there was nothing about Johnson's administration to be seriously criticized, that he had been astute in meeting all situations as they arose, and that most of his appointments were good, and some excellent. The *Pioneer Press* repeatedly warned that a vote for Johnson was an endorsement of William Jennings Bryan.[35]

The *Duluth Labor World* and the *Duluth Evening Herald,* however, both came out for the election of Johnson. About a month before he was nominated, the *Labor World* observed that the people of the state were well satisfied with Johnson's administration and believed he had been as capable a governor as anyone who had ever held the position.[36] Johnson, the paper declared, had added dignity and honesty to the govenorship; he had won the confidence and respect of the president of the United States and officials in other states; he had demonstrated great moral courage in administering the law; and he had not tried to build up a state political machine to perpetuate himself in office, which could not be said of his Republican predecessors.[37] The *Evening Herald*

---

[34] *Ibid.,* and June 16, 1906.
[35] *St. Paul Dispatch,* September 5, 1906; *St. Paul Pioneer Press,* September 5, 1906.
[36] *Duluth Labor World,* August 4, 1906.
[37] *Ibid.,* September 15, 1906.

stated that the only issue in the campaign was whether A. L. Cole would be a better governor than John A. Johnson, and after examining the record and listening to Cole, that paper decided in favor of Johnson.[38]

The campaign, which proved to be a dull one, opened on August 27, when Cole delivered his keynote speech at Kenyon.[39] He posed as a great champion of state development, but he advocated nothing that Johnson had not been urging for two years. And he had the added disadvantage of being an undistinguished speaker. Although the Twin Cities' newspapers lauded Cole's speech, the people were unimpressed. It is difficult to find any marked enthusiasm for Cole at any time during the whole campaign.

But the Democratic leaders could not foresee the ineffectiveness of Cole's efforts, and taking no chances, they planned a vigorous campaign for Johnson. His schedule consisted of a hundred and nineteen speeches to be delivered in seventy-eight counties in seven weeks. In his speeches, which were similar, he confined himself to state issues, for it was his belief that national issues had no place in a campaign for the governorship.[40]

The Democrats adopted the slogan "One good term deserves another," and they invited the voters to examine Johnson's record as governor. One group that early announced its support of Johnson was the Minnesota branch of the National Colored Personal Liberty League, which issued a circular letter to its members urging them to vote for Johnson.[41] In 1904 the labor element had supported Robert Dunn, but now William E. McEwen, owner and publisher of the *Duluth Labor World* and a leader of organized labor in Minnesota, maintained headquarters in the St. Louis Hotel in Duluth and organized a corps of political workers to stump St. Louis County for Johnson. Soon McEwen was to become one of Johnson's close advisers.[42]

Early in October Johnson made a record-breaking trip through St. Louis County, and with him were T. T. Hudson, William E. McEwen, and the veteran Democrat, Charles d'Autremont, all of

[38] *Duluth Evening Herald*, September 7, 8, 19, 25, 1906.
[39] *St. Paul Dispatch*, August 28, 1906; *St. Paul Pioneer Press*, August 28, 1906.
[40] Day and Knappen, p. 135; Executive Letters, Johnson to William Myers of Austin, September 18, 1906.
[41] *Ibid.*, Charles C. Curtis to Johnson, May 21, 1906.
[42] *Ibid.*, McEwen to Harvey Grimmer, October 8, 1906.

Duluth. McEwen reported that Johnson made a fine impression and that in every place he spoke he won several hundred new votes.[43]

The *Duluth Labor World* marveled at Johnson's way with people and told of an incident that occurred on the trip. At one of the Iron Range towns Johnson had just finished speaking from the rear platform of his train and was greeting men who came up to the car to meet him. A member of his party noticed a laborer who seemed anxious to get a glimpse of the governor and urged the man to come closer. The laborer hesitated, looking down at his grease-stained clothes and soiled hands, but Johnson called to him to come shake hands and greeted him by saying: "Don't be afraid. Those clothes are honestly worn. Without men who wear them this country would still be a barren wilderness." [44]

Something of the effect of this attitude of Johnson's appears, perhaps, in the humorous story of Ole, one of the governor's countrymen who had worked zealously against him in his first campaign but now was a devoted admirer. One of Ole's friends, wanting to tease him a bit, said, "I'm surprised at you, Ole — supporting Johnson now, when you opposed him so two years ago. You must think he's a great man."

"Ya, I do."

"Is he as great as Knute Nelson?"

"Ya, much greater."

"Is he greater than Roosevelt?"

"Ya, bigger."

"Is he bigger than God?"

"Well, Johnson's a young man yet." [45]

Johnson's trip proved to be so successful that the Republicans felt obliged to send out a circular letter to the voters of St. Louis County stating that Cole was a man from northern Minnesota and was especially interested in his section of the state. The Democrats replied that Johnson was interested in the whole state, that he never put any extra emphasis on his own section, because he tried to be the governor of all the people in all sections of Minnesota.[46]

[43] *Duluth Evening Herald*, October 4, 1906; Executive Letters, McEwen to Grimmer, October 8, 1906; *Duluth Labor World*, October 6, 1906.
[44] *Ibid.*    [45] Told to W. G. H. by Helen C. Barton of Minneapolis.
[46] *Duluth Labor World*, October 20, 1906.

*St. Paul Dispatch*, October 23, 1906

GOVERNOR JOHN — "Just look at the progress we have
made in the last two years!"

Johnson was more successful in this campaign than he had been in 1904, for now more people knew of him and wanted to hear him speak. The Republican *St. Paul Dispatch* had to admire his special ability of making speeches sufficiently local to reach the very hearts and homes of his listeners.[47] Yet it must be remembered that a great part of Johnson's popularity rested upon the recommendations he had made to the legislature and the campaign he was carrying on for reform in the fields of railroad and insurance legislation. Judge Torrance, who in this campaign was supporting Cole, went to a Democratic rally in Minneapolis to hear Johnson speak, and he wrote to his wife the following report: "Governor Johnson spoke for an hour and I never heard him speak so well. He sailed into the Railroads, timber thieves and the loose administration of the laws by former governors, hitting right and left." [48]

Johnson might have been spared the ordeal of such a strenuous campaign, for the Democrats had little to fear from their opponents. Robert Dunn charged that there were some Republicans on the state central committee and even on the state ticket who would vote for Johnson, and he poured scorn upon R. E. Thompson, chairman of the committee.[49] C. H. Warner, secretary of the committee, resigned after a disagreement with other members and was replaced by a Dunn man, Thomas Salmon of Minneapolis.[50]

This time it was Senator Knute Nelson instead of Clapp who was up for re-election. Heatwole in his newspaper kept up a systematic, bitter personal attack on Nelson, which the senator refused to dignify by reply.[51] Nelson regarded Cole's campaign committee as a very poor one which needed as much help as he could give it,[52] and he and Senator Clapp as well as Senator Albert Beveridge of Indiana went into the field to speak for Cole. Several Minnesota congressmen and, interestingly enough, Robert Dunn, Samuel Van Sant, and J. F. Jacobson campaigned for Cole. But none of the Republican leaders in 1906 were honestly convinced that the party was united, and Cole was not the leader to bring together opposing elements. Even a year later Congressman

[47] *St. Paul Dispatch,* October 20, 1906.
[48] Torrance Papers, Torrance to his wife, October 16, 1906.
[49] *Princeton Union,* August 16, 23, 1906.
[50] *St. Paul Dispatch,* September 29, October 5, 1906.
[51] Nelson Papers, Nelson to Theodore Roosevelt, July 18, 1906.
[52] *Ibid.,* Nelson to Soren Listoe, November 26, 1906.

*St. Paul Dispatch*, October 9, 1906

He's got his foot in it again.

James A. Tawney was concerned over the disorganization and demoralization which still existed within the party. He ascribed it to the assaults upon the party by the newspapers of the Twin Cities and to the woeful lack of leadership in the party.[53]

The only incident that caused some stir in the uninteresting campaign was the filing of one John W. Johnson for governor on the Socialist Labor ticket. The Democratic leaders immediately denounced this as a trick to confuse the voters. It was recalled that in the 1900 election Governor Lind lost some 20,000 votes because Tom Lucas was placed on the ballot as the Social Democrat candidate for governor, and some careless voters marked the ballot for every candidate designated as a "Democrat." Now the Democrats insisted upon an investigation of the petition which had placed John W. Johnson's name on the ballot. The Minnesota Supreme Court, after examining the petition and finding many names in duplicate, ordered the name of John W. Johnson to be taken off the ballot. John A. Johnson would be the only candidate for governor with the name of Johnson! [54]

Having no serious criticism to make of Johnson and his administration, the Republican orators — and it was claimed that there were thirty-two Republicans stumping the state for Cole[55] — could only warn the voters that the Democrats would have a strong party organization and the patronage for another two years if Johnson was re-elected. And the *St. Paul Pioneer Press* begged the voters not to vote for him merely because they liked him personally.[56] The country press gave Johnson more support than in 1904, and the Swedish newspapers, *Svenska Amerikanska Posten* and *Svenska Folkets Tidning*, were solidly behind him. The *Minnesota Stats Tidning*, however, announced that since there was a Republican legislature there would be more harmony if a Republican governor was elected.[57]

Johnson was on the verge of a collapse as the campaign drew to a close. After a great rally for him in Mankato on October 30

[53] James A. Tawney Papers, in Minnesota Historical Society, Tawney to J. P. Hurley, editor of the *Albert Lea Tribune*, September 3, 1907.
[54] *Jordan Independent*, October 11, 1906; *St. Paul Dispatch*, October 6, 9, 10, 11, 12, 1906.
[55] *Ibid.*, November 10, 1906.
[56] *St. Paul Pioneer Press*, October 31, November 1, 2, 1906.
[57] *Minnesota Stats Tidning*, October 17, 1906.

he was so ill with a severe cold that he was unable to mingle with the friendly crowd which gathered at the Saulpaugh Hotel after his speech.[58] On November 1 he spoke in Pine City, North Branch, and Duluth. When he arrived in Duluth to address a huge crowd in the Armory, his voice was almost gone, yet he delivered the speech and "thoroughly captivated his auditors," much to the amazement of his friends who knew his condition.[59] Johnson never failed to be impressed by the fact that so many people had gathered to hear him, and nothing could induce him to disappoint an audience. On November 3 he spoke in Cokato and in Minneapolis and on November 5 in St. Paul. Then he went home to St. Peter to vote.[60]

On election eve the odds were in favor of Johnson's re-election. The *Minneapolis Journal* noted that the men who had wanted to nominate J. F. Jacobson were still "sore" and were going to vote for Johnson, elect him, and get him out of the way for 1908, when the way would be clear for "Jake." [61] But no one, not even the optimistic Frank Day, was prepared for the overwhelming and unprecedented victory Johnson won. He swept the state, receiving 168,480 votes, a majority of 72,318 votes over Cole, who carried only five counties.[62] Such a majority would have pleased even a Republican candidate in Republican Minnesota.

Never at any moment during the campaign had Johnson thought he would lose this election, and when he learned the results, he said:

. . . I have never made any personal utterance concerning Mr. Cole during the campaign, and I have no regret for anything I have stated. I am proud to know I will have an opportunity to give my best efforts for the next two years to show my appreciation of this honor by doing all in my power to enforce the laws. I am especially obliged to the great army of Republican voters who have made some concessions in this contest.[63]

It was generally agreed that Johnson's victory was a personal

[58] *St. Peter Herald,* November 1, 1906; *Minneapolis Journal,* November 1, 1906.
[59] *Duluth Labor World,* November 3, 1906; *Duluth Evening Herald,* November 3, 1906.
[60] *Minneapolis Journal,* November 3, 4, 5, 1906.
[61] *Ibid.,* November 4, 1906.
[62] *Legislative Manual,* 1907, pp. 484–86.
[63] *St. Paul Dispatch,* November 7, 1906.

one. No other Democrat was elected to a state office. The people simply ignored the party label when they voted for the governor for whom they had developed a great affection and whose political ideals, methods, and achievements they admired. To them he had been the people's candidate, not the Democratic candidate.

Johnson's re-election was followed by rumors that he would next run for the United States Senate, for president or vice-president of the United States. In reply to such rumors he announced:

. . . all this nonsense about my future political career is not countenanced by me. The talk is entirely without my authority and is becoming ridiculous. I have no future political aspirations except to serve the state to the best of my ability for the next two years, and then I hope to be permitted to retire to my business. It is simply rot, this presidential and vice presidential talk. My friends are undoubtedly sincere in predicting nice things for me, and their well wishes are accepted in the spirit in which they are given, but I do not want anyone to think that my vanity prompts me to think they would be realized, or that I would even try to anticipate them by encouragement.[64]

He tried to make it clear that his duties as governor would keep him well occupied and that he would have no time for "silly fancies or dreams" of himself in the United States Senate or the White House. Feeling he had dispensed with rumors, he participated in the great reception given for him by St. Peter on November 14. A few days later he left Minnesota for New York City for a much needed rest.[65]

When Johnson returned to the capital from New York, he found himself faced with a crisis in the affairs of the Railroad and Warehouse Commission. The legislature of 1905, at the suggestion of the governor, had directed the commission to investigate railroad freight rates. So all during the summer of 1905 representatives of the railroads and the shippers of Minnesota had testified before the commission, which numbered three men: Judge Ira B. Mills, C. F. Staples, and W. E. Young. The railway companies, of course, held that freight rates, if anything, were too low in Minnesota, while James Manahan, a Minneapolis lawyer representing

[64] *Ibid.*, November 10, 1906.
[65] *St. Peter Herald*, November 16, 1906; Executive Letters, Johnson to F. G. Winston, November 16, 1906.

the Minnesota Shippers' Association, declared they were too high and demanded a reduction.

Manahan had requested permission to examine the books of the railway companies in an effort to prove that the companies could easily stand a reduction in rates, and when permission was granted by the commission, the railway companies immediately offered a compromise solution — a 10 per cent reduction in grain rates if the merchandise rates remained the same. Since this compromise would benefit the farmers but not the merchants and shippers, Manahan strongly opposed it and the proposal was rejected.

In a letter to the commission, Governor Johnson agreed that the proposal should have been rejected, but he suggested that since the railway companies had offered to reduce grain rates, the commission should compel them to do so without any reservations whatsoever. His letter served as a spur to the dilatory commission, and grain rates were reduced. Johnson, however, took no more chances with the commission. He ordered an expert to make a thorough investigation of freight rates for him, and having mastered the problem, he advised the commission from time to time and closely supervised its work. As a result, on September 6, 1905, the commission established a new schedule of lower freight rates on general merchandise shipped within the state.[66]

Then hearings on commodity rates began. Manahan tried to force the railway companies into disclosing the fact that they had contributed to political campaigns in Minnesota. He implied that the companies had worked to defeat "honest" candidates, and he added: "Who knows, to-day, whether the capital of Minnesota is located in this beautiful marble building, on the hills, or down in the valley on Fourth Street, in the sordid offices of the Great Northern or Omaha railroads?"[67] His question so shocked the members of the commission, Attorney General Young, who was present to represent the state, and the railroad lawyers that hearings were adjourned for the day.

Manahan next demanded a subpoena for J. J. Hill to force him to appear before the commission for questioning. It was issued,

[66] *Ibid.*, Johnson to the Board of Railroad and Warehouse Commissioners, August 16, 1906; *St. Paul Dispatch*, August 2, 14, 16, 23, 25, 1906; James Manahan, *Trials of a Lawyer: an Autobiography*, pp. 50–68.
[67] *Ibid.*, p. 70.

but Hill could not be found. Then the commission adjourned until after the November elections, much to Manahan's disgust. Later he wrote: "My efforts to compel railroad officials to disclose their political contributions were unbearable to the statehouse machine, leading members of which, at the time, were running for office." [68]

Elections over, the commission hearings began again and J. J. Hill appeared, but things were so managed that Attorney General Young examined all witnesses for the railroads and the shippers and the state. Manahan was furious and demanded the right to question the witness he had gone to so much trouble to produce. Angrily he reported: "The examination of Mr. Hill by Attorney General Young, lasting several hours, was a polite affair. . . . No attempt was made to show that the earnings and traffic of the Great Northern Railroad justified a reduction in rates. The inquisition was more like an informal gathering of friends, interested in railroading. . . ." [69] No one asked Hill whether he or any of the Great Northern officials had ever contributed money to political campaigns.

Finally Manahan made himself so objectionable by insisting on his right to examine Hill that he was disbarred from practicing before the commission.[70] He replied by appealing to Governor Johnson. He charged the commission with shielding and protecting the railway companies, thus being unfair to the people of the state, and declared that all three commissioners were guilty of neglect of duty and inefficiency in office.[71]

After considering Manahan's charges, Johnson refused to interfere, since the commission had disbarred Manahan upon the advice of Attorney General Young.[72] Manahan was thereafter a vigorous leader of the opposition to Johnson. But the whole fracas had the effect of urging the commission to action, and on December 29 it was announced that the Railroad and Warehouse Commission had ordered a general reduction in commodity rates throughout the state.[73]

[68] Ibid., p. 74.
[69] Ibid., p. 78.
[70] Ibid., pp. 80–81; St. Paul Dispatch, December 29, 1906.
[71] Ibid., December 10, 1906.
[72] Executive Letters, Johnson to Manahan and C. F. Hubbard, December 27, 1906.
[73] St. Paul Dispatch, December 29, 1906; The Republican Party in Minnesota: Its Achievements and Its Leaders, 1910 (a political pamphlet which has a brief account of this struggle to reduce railroad rates).

On January 9 Johnson was inaugurated for the second time. Present at the ceremony were three former Minnesota governors: L. F. Hubbard, John Lind, and Samuel Van Sant. As Johnson read his message, one of the longest ever delivered to a Minnesota legislature, his voice, strained and husky from the cold he had suffered since October, failed him altogether at one point and he had difficulty finishing.[74]

He began by stating that government was "not instituted for the protection of interests" or of individuals but for the "security, benefit, and protection of the people." Then he took up the issue of tax reform. In the recent election the people had adopted the "wide-open" tax amendment which was designed to give the legislature more power to regulate taxes. Johnson warned that it would be wise to make haste slowly in this particular field, and he advised the legislature that:

Inasmuch as all classes of property should bear a just proportion of the taxes for raising the public revenue, efforts should be made by you to increase the taxable property valuations upon those classes of property which hitherto have escaped payment of taxes either entirely or in large measure.

For example, since there was no taxation on mortgages, he suggested that a registry tax of one-twentieth of 1 per cent be paid into the treasury of the county in which the mortgage was recorded, and also that an income tax be placed upon mortgages. He recommended the creation of a permanent tax commission to make a careful study of taxes and report to the legislature and the governor from time to time, to see that the tax laws were strictly enforced, to make rules for and supervise the work of the local tax assessors and boards, and to see that assessments were free from discriminations.

The valuation placed upon the iron ore properties in Minnesota by the State Board of Equalization in 1906, he declared, was only a small fraction of the value the steel companies placed upon them, and he advised that those lands be revalued as soon as possible. The time had arrived, he said, for the legislature to adopt a system of taxation which would bring the state its just revenue from the great iron ore wealth it possessed. He suggested an in-

[74] Executive Letters, Johnson to Reverend Frank Doran of Winona, January 12, 1907; *St. Paul Pioneer Press*, January 10, 1907.

come tax of 5 or 10 per cent on the royalties for mineral rights and recommended that the tonnage of ore shipped be used as a basis of royalty values for tax purposes. To safeguard the mineral resources of the state and to watch leases, he urged the creation of a state department of mines. He condemned as absurd the law which provided that for all the iron ore taken from state lands the state should receive a fixed royalty of twenty-five cents a ton. He called this sum ridiculously small and asked for a law empowering the legislature to change this tax rate from time to time. Taxation of sleeping car companies, telephone companies, and express companies, he pointed out, ought to be revised so the companies could not in any way evade state taxes. He urged that corporations be made to pay an annual license tax and that all corporations delinquent in paying taxes to the state be heavily fined.

Again Johnson asked the legislature to abolish the free pass system, to reduce freight rates more than the Railroad and Warehouse Commission had reduced them, and to provide for a two-cent maximum passenger rate. A reciprocal demurrage law, he said, was demanded by the people and should be enacted.

He praised the Department of Public Instruction for its work, but he remarked that the University of Minnesota had not been able to keep some of its best faculty members because its salaries were so low. This situation he found deplorable: "Certainly Minnesota can afford to pay reasonable compensation for this class of service, and to provide means by which we can compete with any educational institution in the country in bidding for talent which would permanently endow our university."

Announcing that the lumber, grain, and livestock trusts had been violating the state laws, Johnson asked for appropriations to pay for additional staff members in the attorney general's office so that such companies could be prosecuted. He repeated his call for a law providing that the employer be made liable for injuries to employees while at work, and he informed the legislature that the newly created State Free Employment Bureau was highly successful. To prevent child labor and to enforce truancy laws he suggested that the number of labor inspectors be increased. Again he urged the legislature to provide for the building of a system of good roads and for the conservation of forest and mineral lands.

Declaring that the present primary election law was defective,

Johnson asked that it be revised so that party conventions could nominate several candidates for an office, one of which would be chosen by the people at the polls. He suggested that the law then be extended to include state officers. He asked the legislature to draw up a constitutional amendment providing for the initiative and referendum processes, and he endorsed municipal ownership of public utilities. Condemning as an American scandal the ease with which some states allowed divorces, he recommended the passage of a divorce law modeled on the suggestions made by the national divorce conference held in Philadelphia in 1906. In conclusion he condemned lobbying as "one of the greatest evils to political economy and political decency" and asked that all lobbyists be compelled to register and be required to submit all arguments to committees rather than to individuals.[75]

Johnson's message pleased the people and they were eager to see what the Republican legislature would do. The first thing it did was to re-elect the popular Knute Nelson to the United States Senate without any difficulty.[76] In the legislative action that followed, railroad issues were given primary attention. (The insurance legislation of this session has been reported in the preceding chapter, pages 177–81.) The year 1907 was a year of crusade against the railroad interests. More than thirty states considered or passed laws abolishing the free pass system, reducing freight and passenger rates, increasing the power of railroad and warehouse commissions, regulating service, and establishing reciprocal demurrage.

Most of the members of the Minnesota legislature were pledged to support an antipass bill, which, of course, the railroads did not oppose. Accordingly a bill forbidding public officials and officers of political parties to accept railroad passes became a law to go into effect December 31, 1908. Minnesota was one of thirteen states to outlaw the free pass system.[77]

After considerable discussion a law was passed providing for a maximum passenger rate of two cents a mile, and Minnesota

[75] *Inaugural Message,* 1907. Johnson's recommendations on insurance legislation were referred to in Chapter VII.

[76] *St. Paul Pioneer Press,* January 23, 1907; *St. Paul Dispatch,* January 23, 1907.

[77] *General Laws,* 1907, pp. 685–87; *Minneapolis Journal,* January 11, April 16, 17, 1907; *St. Paul Pioneer Press,* April 25, 1907; "The Legislatures and the Railroads," *American Review of Reviews,* vol. 36, July–December 1907, p. 220.

joined the ranks of eight other states which had such a law. Some reduction in passenger rates was effected in twenty-one states. Freight rates were lowered by a law which provided for an additional 10 per cent reduction of rates on grain, coal, lumber, and livestock. The Minnesota freight rate law was regarded as the "most scientific and equitable" of the laws passed by any state, and it was used by some states as a model for their own freight rate laws.

The railroads carried on a dogged fight against the reciprocal demurrage bill, but it finally passed the Minnesota legislature. Acts providing for an increased tax on sleeping cars and for the establishment of a maximum sixteen-hour day for railroad employees also became laws.[78]

Having witnessed the success of the national life insurance conference and the subsequent adoption of uniform life insurance laws in many states, Johnson wrote to President Roosevelt suggesting that a national conference be called to discuss railroad legislation, to try to bring about uniform railroad laws in the states, and to consider increasing the powers of the Interstate Commerce Commission. However, nothing came of his request.[79]

The Minnesota legislature rejected Johnson's recommendation for an employers' liability law, but passed bills making it illegal for children between the ages of fourteen and sixteen to work during school hours, providing for women inspectors to supervise girls working in shops and mercantile stores, establishing free public employment bureaus in cities of 50,000 or over, and creating a bureau of labor.[80] A State Board of Immigration and a Tax Commission were established. Laws were passed prohibiting telephone and telegraph companies from granting privileges to individuals or companies, allowing cities to own and operate public utilities, and providing for additional pure food regulations. A tax was assessed on the registry of mortgages, a $400,000 appropriation was made for the building of roads and bridges, salaries of the governor and supreme court judges were increased, the building

[78] *Ibid.*, pp. 219–20; *General Laws*, 1907, pp. 25–30, 109–11, 344–45, 694–96; *Minneapolis Journal*, February 6, 27, April 14, 24, 1907; *St. Paul Pioneer Press*, March 7, April 14, 25, 1907; *Minnesota in Three Centuries*, vol. 4, pp. 302–3.

[79] Executive Letters, Johnson to Theodore Roosevelt, March 16, 1907; Johnson to Governor Hoke Smith of Georgia, November 11, 1907.

[80] *General Laws*, 1907, pp. 205–6, 403–8, 493–96.

of a state hospital for inebriates was authorized to be paid for from liquor fees collected by the state, the Board of Equalization was directed to see that the companies operating iron mines paid their state taxes, and the campus of the University of Minnesota was extended. A bill providing for iniative and referendum was killed, and nothing was done to check the activities of lobbyists, to extend the direct primary system, or to rewrite Minnesota's divorce law.[81]

On the whole, the governor and the people of the state were satisfied with the work of the legislature. Johnson received high praise for his appointment of Samuel Lord, a Republican, O. M. Hall, a Democrat, and Dr. Franklin McVey, professor of economics of the University of Minnesota whose politics were unknown, to the newly created Tax Commission. In fact, the announcement of those appointments brought the Republican senate to a rising vote of confirmation and prompted the house of representatives to pass a resolution of appreciation.

T. D. O'Brien resigned as insurance commissioner to return to private law practice, but he was soon called back into the service of the state to assist Attorney General Young in defending the state in the Minnesota Rate Cases.[82] Stockholders of the railroad companies in Minnesota had brought suit against the state to restrain enforcement of the new schedule of freight and passenger rates. The cases attracted wide attention in railroad circles all over the United States and were not settled until 1913. When they reached the United States Supreme Court, the cases involving the Northern Pacific and the Great Northern railways were dismissed, but the small Minneapolis and St. Louis Railroad was granted a decision, which by that time meant very little, for the Minneapolis and St. Louis had been forced by competition to lower their rates in accordance with the current schedules.[83]

Johnson's second administration gave ample evidence of his remarkable capacity for growth and development. He had earlier moved around St. Peter and among the editors of Minnesota with

[81] *Ibid.*, pp. 361–62, 379–82, 586, 605–7, 686, 689–94, 703, 730–47; *St. Paul Pioneer Press*, April 25, 1907. The Minnesota primary law applied to congressional, judicial, county, and city officials; candidates could get on the ballot by their own affidavits and the payment of a ten- or twenty-dollar fee.

[82] *St. Paul Dispatch*, August 27, 28, 1907.

[83] O'Brien, *There Were Four of Us, or Was It Five*, pp. 63–68.

ease and assurance and had mastered the local and professional problems he faced. Now, with the same ease and assurance, he mastered the problems of state administration.

During the legislative session he remained in the capital, closely following the work of the legislature. On February 14 he took time off to escort William Jennings Bryan to the opening meeting of the Minnesota Editors' and Publishers' Association which Bryan addressed.[84] When in May Bryan again visited St. Paul to speak at Macalester College, he was asked by newspapermen what he thought of the rumor that Johnson would be a good running mate for him in 1908. Bryan refused to reply.[85]

On May 24, 1907, Johnson spoke at the ceremony dedicating the Minnesota monument in the national park at Vicksburg, Mississippi. There in a brief speech he reminded his audience that the citizens of the United States enjoyed many blessings and privileges but that with these came responsibilities. Then he made an appeal for the healing of relations between the North and the South and asked that all sections of the United States work together for the benefit of the Union.[86] According to the *Vicksburg Daily Herald*, all who met Governor Johnson were impressed and charmed.[87]

There was an unpleasant repercussion of the event, however. It was reported later that Governor Vardaman of Mississippi had asked Governor Johnson whether "the people of the South would be in any danger of harsh treatment at the hands of the people of the North if we asked them to assist us in repealing the fifteenth and modifying the fourteenth amendments," and Johnson was said to have replied that the people of the North and the Northwest felt that the white man must rule the South and that the South would be in no danger if it asked for such assistance. The *St. Paul Pioneer Press,* in an editorial, fiercely condemned Johnson for this statement, saying the North would never countenance any changes in or repeal of the two amendments, and accusing the governor of currying favor with the South for his future political aspirations.[88]

The truth of the incident is problematical. No other Twin

[84] *Proceedings of the Minnesota Editors' and Publishers' Association,* 1907, pp. 8–11.
[85] *St. Paul Dispatch,* May 18, 1908.
[86] Address by Governor John A. Johnson at Vicksburg Battlefield, May 25, 1907.
[87] *Vicksburg Daily Herald,* May 23, 24, 1907; *St. Paul Pioneer Press,* May 25, 1907.
[88] *Ibid.,* June 4, 1907.

Cities' newspaper mentioned it, nor did the *Vicksburg Daily Herald,* and no answer to the charge against Johnson was made. The *Pioneer Press* itself never again made any mention of the matter.

Johnson's party continued south from Vicksburg to New Orleans. There the governor was asked whether he was a candidate for the presidency in 1908, and with considerable annoyance he replied: "Well, that is hardly a fair question to put to a stranger, is it?" But he met the question and flatly announced that he was not a candidate and did not expect to be. He refused, however, to make any prophecy as to who the Democratic standard-bearer would be.[89]

Johnson was taken ill on the way home from this trip but recovered sufficiently to speak briefly at the ceremonies connected with the laying of the cornerstone for the Catholic Cathedral in St. Paul. When he was introduced as "our next president," the burst of applause could be heard a dozen blocks away. He was host to Secretary of War William Howard Taft, who came to Minneapolis on June 13 to deliver the commencement address at the University of Minnesota, and in a speech given at a banquet for Taft, Johnson declared that Minnesota was ready to help Taft win the presidency.[90] Then Johnson left Minnesota to be a commencement speaker himself.

When, in the preceding January, Johnson had been invited to give the commencement address and to receive an honorary degree at the University of Pennsylvania, he and his close advisers were tremendously pleased, for such an invitation had never before been extended to a governor from the Northwest. Although Johnson always had assistance in writing his speeches, he declined a number of speaking engagements in order to give more attention himself to the preparation of this address.[91]

On June 19 the tall, stooped Minnesotan, whose own back-

[89] *Minneapolis Journal,* May 25, 1907.

[90] *Ibid.,* June 13, 14, 1907; *St. Paul Pioneer Press,* May 31, June 4, 1907; *St. Paul Dispatch,* June 3, 14, 1907.

[91] Executive Letters, Charles C. Harrison, provost of University of Pennsylvania, to Johnson, January 18, June 6, 1907, and Johnson to A. E. Aarnes of Montevideo, March 20, 1907; *St. Peter Herald,* January 25, 1907. Only Robert Dunn could not bear to have Johnson so recognized; in the *Princeton Union* of February 7, 1907, he delivered one of his typically nasty blasts at Johnson: "Not satisfied, seemingly, with the natural gas flow of its own state, the University of Pennsylvania has invited Governor John to throw off a quantity of his particular brand of hot air at its commencement exercises — and the governor has condescendingly acceded to the request. The university is fortunate indeed, in securing the services of so noted a gasologist."

ground had denied him even a high school education, stood before the graduating class of the large eastern university and received the honorary degree of Doctor of Laws. Then he began his address, which he called "Opportunities and Responsibilities." To introduce it he pointed out some of the ties that bound together the two states of Pennsylvania and Minnesota — among them the stirring story of the First Minnesota Regiment, "the class of '61" of Minnesota boys in blue. Johnson told his audience how Minnesota's Governor Ramsey, a native of Harrisburg, Pennsylvania, raised the money to equip the First Minnesota Regiment among his Philadelphia friends, and

that class of '61 received their sheepskins in the shape of orders from Simon Cameron, again a son of Pennsylvania . . . to proceed to Harrisburg. . . . Forty-six years ago to-day they were passing through your state, and enlisting Pennsylvania boys in blue shouted to them along the route — "Go for them, boys of Minnesota, go for them; we'll be with you in a few days" . . . Scarcely two years later, July 2, 1863 . . . it was the second day of Gettysburg. Sickles' forces, defeated in the peach orchard, were fugitives before the superior forces of Longstreet and Hill. Eight companies of the First Minnesota, 262 men in all, stood guard over a battery on the hill at the Union center. General Hancock rode up at full speed, and after vainly trying to stop the fugitives, spurred to the spot where the First Minnesota stood firm. . . . "Charge those lines," shouted Hancock.

With fixed bayonets, first at double quick, and then at full speed, in the face of the concentrated Confederate fire, the brave 262 charged down the hill, broke through the first Confederate line, driving it back upon the second, thereby stopping the whole Confederate advance; then under cover of rocks and stumps held their ground in the dry creek below, until the Union reserve gained the positions above and turned Gettysburg into a Union victory.

Their duty done, the First Minnesota marched back victors to their position. But not the 262. There were 47 survivors — 215 dead or wounded on the field — not a man missing.

. . . If the young men and women of this class of 1907, of the University of Pennsylvania, desire from Minnesota a sign, a spirit of inspiration, a token of the qualities that command victory and success on earth, or an example of the achievements of fame and glory, I point you to the Minnesota class of '61, whose blood, shed for you and for all, has been part of the soil of Pennsylvania now for over forty years.

Turning to more general matters, Johnson warned the members of the graduating class that education was but one factor, and not the most important factor, in the production of a successful person:

A man is a man before he has had training, and no amount of schooling can inject honor and backbone into a creature that is born spineless. . . . The world wants educated men, but first of all it wants men — men of honor, men of character, men who are not prone to dethrone their own reason by excessive indulgence in those things which tear down and destroy, rather than those things which build up and create.

He urged his listeners to take their responsibilities as citizens seriously and suggested that some of them seek success in the field of government service, where good men were needed — needed because it would take the best brains in the country to solve such problems as the power of the trusts, the control of the huge railroad interests, the status and condition of the Negroes, and the rapid development of imperialism in the United States.

Johnson deplored the growing centralization of power in the federal government at the expense of the states, and he emphasized the desirability of maintaining the sovereign power of the states. In a plea for checking the "intoxicated money power," he declared that it was always the duty of citizens to protest against wrongs and oppressions and listed as some of the evils to be protested "the inflation of values, the creation of monopolies, the concentration of wealth in the hands of a few, conferring upon them the power to promote any industry, transportation, or commercial enterprise. . . ." He continued:

There has in the past been a tendency to evade and ignore the law, and this . . . has been promoted by public officials who have constituted themselves the discriminating power between the public policy and the law. . . .

If intoxicated money power, usurping the chariot reins of the nation, continues in its selfish and high-handed course, the American conscience, expressed in the law and ballot of an outraged people, will be driven to heroic means to arrest the mad flight and restore the country to its industrial and social equilibrium.

What the country was badly in need of, said Johnson, was a "national policy free from the domination of class, section and special interest — a fundamental policy which stands for liberty, security, growth and development of the whole country. . . ." He called for regulation and supervision of corporations and for "fair and humane treatment" for labor. In conclusion he repeated his call to social and civic responsibility: "Class of 1907, in the last analysis your state, your nation, your country is your alma mater, and the flag of the Republic is your class emblem." [92]

Even the *St. Paul Pioneer Press* praised Johnson for this speech and commented that he had shown a "breadth of view and a soundness of judgment which has been lacking in many a man who has been conspicuous enough in national affairs to be mentioned for the presidency." The paper also expressed the belief that he would be well equipped for the nomination in spite of his lack of experience in the national political field.[93]

The *St. Paul Dispatch* was much amused that Minnesota's Democratic governor should venture to beard the trusts in their own den, the trust-ridden state of Pennsylvania, a Republican stronghold; the paper solemnly called Johnson the "best harmonizer" of the Democratic party and observed: "It is this quality of evoking harmony which gives him his strong hold, backed as it is by excellent personal qualities that are being tested, being measured. The Democratic party may be wise enough to right its many mistakes, to weld its many warring factions, through the nomination of Governor Johnson." [94]

Writing to thank the governor for his address, Charles H. Harrison, provost of the University of Pennsylvania, commented on the way Johnson had held his audience: "It seems to me that the two elements which mark your power in such an Address are, first, that you know what to say; and second, that you believe every word that you say." [95] Harrison then expressed the wish that out of their meeting would develop a long-time friendship.

Back in Minnesota in July, Johnson soon had to deal with a major crisis in the form of a serious strike on the Mesabi Iron Range. Some sixteen thousand unskilled workers in the mines had recently been organized into unions, and they went out on a strike

[92] University of Pennsylvania commencement address, delivered by Governor John A. Johnson, June 19, 1907. Reprinted in full in Day and Knappen, pp. 324–58.

[93] *St. Paul Pioneer Press*, June 20, 1907.

[94] *St. Paul Dispatch*, June 20, 1907.

[95] Executive Letters, Harrison to Johnson, June 20, 1907.

which tied up almost every mine on the Mesabi Range, an area that shipped about 24,000,000 tons of ore in 1906, more than 30 per cent of the country's total supply.

The miners' unions were the result of dreadful living and working conditions rather than the work of agitators sent in from the West, as was charged by the mine operators. Most of the miners were Italian, Finnish, Polish, and Slavic immigrants who lived in crowded boardinghouses in cramped and filthy conditions, most of them unmarried because their wages were too low for them to support families. The standard wage was supposed to be two dollars a day, but in the two largest mines the average monthly pay was fifty dollars. There was no guarantee of work the year around, and no opportunity to save money. The regular working day was ten hours, but the men frequently worked twelve and fourteen hours. There were day and night shifts, and some of the mines operated on Sundays. The work was hard, dangerous, and tiresome so that two thirds of the miners could endure it only a year or two. Although each miner paid one dollar a month for doctor and hospital care, the list of injured who died because of lack of medical attention was long. In none of the mining towns was there a public library or night school or any other means by which an ambitious young miner might educate himself.

Watching the United States Steel Company amass huge profits while they labored long hours for a bare subsistence wage, the miners began to organize in 1905, and by 1907 there were fourteen unions all federated into a district union which was affiliated with the Western Federation of Miners. When first organized, the Western Federation of Miners had been affiliated with the American Federation of Labor, but when in 1905 one of its prominent leaders, William D. Haywood, took a leading part in the organization of the Industrial Workers of the World, the W.F. of M. left the American Federation of Labor to become connected with the I.W.W. In 1907, however, the W.F. of M. seceded from the I.W.W., though it did not rejoin the American Federation of Labor until 1911. Meanwhile, United States Steel Company officials watched the growth of unionism among the miners, used Pinkerton detectives to obtain the names of prominent union members, and then fired them.

On July 19 the miners demanded that the Oliver Iron Mining

Company abolish the contract system and the payment of bonuses and give them an eight-hour working day at a minimum wage of $2.50 for surface work and $3.00 for the more dangerous underground work. About ten days before the date set for the company to reply, the miners struck. This pleased the company, which declared it had not been given a full chance to answer the demands. The miners marched from town to town and from mine to mine calling others from work. They held mass meetings in the Range towns. Some of the miners were known to be armed and a critical situation rapidly developed since the mines were patrolled by faithful employees carrying rifles. The businessmen of the towns, the mine bosses, and the skilled workers despised the strikers and their leaders; citizens were enrolled as deputies and armed to protect themselves and to keep the peace.

The dock workers at Duluth and Two Harbors were already out on a strike of their own, so that all lake traffic was suspended and some forty-five thousand men in the mining region were idle. With no ore boats leaving the docks anyway, the miners' strike was not too serious for the mining companies, and knowing that the miners were not adequately prepared for a long strike, the companies decided this was a good chance to kill unionism once and for all. The chief issue became the right of the miners to organize and to protect themselves from the dictates of the mining companies. The United States Steel Company enlisted the aid of government officials, businessmen, the press, and the pulpit in this struggle with organized labor.

The most influential leader of the miners was a short, swarthy, well-educated, Italian-born Socialist, Teofilo Petriella, who had been sent by the Western Federation of Miners to organize the Range miners. He was accused of attempting to make Socialists of all the miners and of leading them to strike although they had no clear conception as to what would actually result from the strike. "It was currently reported among the men that they would win the strike in about six months, with the aid of money from the West, that the union would then come to own the mines and the railways, and every man's share would be good for $2500 a year." [96] As business was forced to suspend in the mining towns,

[96] Charles B. Cheney, "A Labor Crisis and a Governor," *Outlook*, May 2, 1908, pp. 25–26.

feeling against the miners and especially against Petriella became so high that the sheriff of St. Louis County, the local authorities, and the mining companies all appealed to Governor Johnson to send state troops to prevent bloodshed.

Johnson was in a difficult position. If he sent troops he could be accused of favoring the capitalists; if he did not, he could be charged with favoring the laborers. Johnson's treatment of the strike proved to be a splendid example of his policy of mastering the facts of a problem before acting and then proceeding slowly. It was an illustration also of his endeavor to be the governor of all the people of the state, favoring no one section and no one class.

Johnson first asked the sheriff of St. Louis County to write him a letter explaining the situation precisely, and then, armed with those facts, he went to the disaffected area to see the state of affairs for himself. In Duluth he conferred with the sheriff of St. Louis County, the mayor of Duluth, representatives of the United States Steel Company and the Oliver Iron Mining Company, delegations of the striking dock workers, who were accompanied by William McEwen, secretary of the Minnesota Federation of Labor, and John Maki, who represented the striking miners.

Thomas F. Cole, head of the Oliver Iron Mining Company, told Johnson that his company would not negotiate with the Western Federation of Miners "at any time" and would make no concessions as to wages, hours, or anything else. He warned that if the miners refused to return to work under the old terms, the company would find other men to replace them. George W. Perkins, chairman of the finance committee of the United States Steel Company, had stated earlier that his company would make no concessions to the miners. The representatives of the strikers from the mines and docks, however, left Johnson with the impression that they had real grievances but that they earnestly desired to respect law and order in their attempt to improve their working conditions.

Leaving Duluth, Governor Johnson went on a tour of the Iron Range. He stopped at Hibbing, Eveleth, and Virginia to talk with the miners, local officials, and citizens. Not standing on his official dignity, he went himself to Petriella's headquarters in Hibbing and conferred at length with the labor leader. The governor warned Petriella that the striking miners must respect law and order, and that he did not intend to send state troops to northern Minnesota unless the miners, by their own acts, made it necessary.

Petriella, nervous and voluble, spoke English brokenly and rapidly. He assured Johnson that the miners did not want violence and that he had forbidden them to carry arms or frequent saloons under pain of expulsion from the union. As a matter of fact, Petriella was anxious to do anything necessary to keep the Western Federation of Miners from gaining a bad name in Minnesota, for at that time three of the leaders of the federation were on trial for murder.[97] The acting president of the federation, C. E. Mahoney, who was also anxious to avoid any trouble, made a special trip to Minnesota to assist Petriella.

In Eveleth Johnson talked with John McNair, president of the local union, and with a delegation of miners. He also addressed the citizens in the town hall:

I do not see any occasion for the State to interfere at this time, and hope there will not be any. The men have a right to quit work. They have a right to organize and to persuade others to quit work. But if a man wants to work and he and his employer agree that he shall work, he has a right to work, and no one has any right to stop him. If necessary, the State will protect men in their right to work. I hope you will all keep cool, however, and regardless of your political beliefs, will respect the law and government. . . .[98]

When Johnson returned to St. Paul he had full knowledge of the situation on the Iron Range, and he assured the people of the state that there was no immediate danger of violence. After striking for two and a half weeks, the dock workers in Duluth returned to their jobs without gaining their demands for union recognition and increased pay. The miners, however, continued their strike. Petriella sent a telegram to Johnson demanding action from him which would allow the strikers to hold meetings in their own halls, for such meetings were being broken up by temporary deputies

---

[97] W. D. Haywood and two of his colleagues were tried on a murder charge which was proved to have been based upon perjured testimony, and they were acquitted. Their lawyer was the famous Clarence Darrow.

[98] Cheney, "A Labor Crisis and a Governor," *Outlook*, May 2, 1908, p. 29.

in the communities. In a violent speech made at this time, Petriella warned that if the governor did not act within twenty-four hours, he would not be responsible for what the miners might do. The mining companies were bringing in workers from outside the Range who, guarded by armed men, were putting one mine after another back into operation. Citizens still protested the marching of the miners from one town to another.

As appeals for state troops continued to come to Johnson, he decided to send a committee to the Iron Range to investigate further. He chose Lyle Day, T. D. O'Brien, and Harvey Grimmer, and before they left the capital Johnson, worried and anxious, said to O'Brien: "Damn politics! I'll never forgive myself if a single life is lost through my failure to perform my full public duty. I want you to go to the scene of the strike and let me know immediately the true situation. The militia will be held in the armory, and if you say troops are needed, they will entrain in fifteen minutes." [99]

The governor's committee toured the Iron Range, consulted the leaders of the strikers and the officials of the mining companies, then returned to St. Paul with their report. On the basis of their findings and his own earlier investigation, Johnson issued a proclamation to the people in the Range area. It stated that "all persons, irrespective of their affiliations with labor unions or otherwise," had a right to assemble peacefully in their own halls, and it directed public officials to see that such meetings were not disturbed in any way. The marching of the miners was prohibited on the grounds that it disturbed the peace, and the miners were warned against trespassing upon private mining property and attempting to keep anyone from going to work in the mines. Labor leaders were warned to guard against using inflammatory language "calculated to incite violence," and public officers were instructed to refrain from any action that might excite the citizens. If these terms were violated, state troops would be sent to the area. The proclamation concluded with these words:

These directions and this appeal to the people of that part of our state now affected by strike conditions is made in the hope that public

[99] O'Brien, *There Were Four of Us, or Was It Five*, p. 76. Lyle Day and Harvey Grimmer were trusted friends of Johnson's; Grimmer was a confidential executive clerk in Johnson's office.

peace will thereby be preserved, the lives and property of citizens of this state protected, and that, in the future, as in the past, the ordinary and usual course of the law will be sufficient to solve all questions which may arise affecting the public peace or the conduct of the citizens of this state.[1]

The strikers were pleased with the governor's proclamation even though it forbade them to prevent outsiders from replacing them in the mines. In that period, when most unskilled labor was unorganized, it would have been an impossibility, anyway, for strikers to keep the mining companies from importing laborers.

The companies, on the other hand, were not at all happy with the proclamation or with Governor Johnson's behavior during the strike. He had gained popularity among the strikers by appearing on the Iron Range without guards to protect his person; he had talked with the strikers and with their leaders; and he had treated the miners as respectable and responsible citizens. He had refused to accede to the mining companies' demands for state troops, so that the companies had to spend a great deal of their own money hiring armed guards to protect their mines. Most important, Johnson had demonstrated his belief that the law applied to both laborers and mine owners without distinction.

The strike ended almost immediately after the issuance of the governor's proclamation — not because of the proclamation, but because the miners were forced to go back to work or starve. They were bitter against the mining companies, but not against the state government. Not a life was lost, though the situation had been packed with elements that could have produced violence and bloodshed. It was generally conceded that Johnson's tactful handling of the situation had saved lives, protected property, and saved money for the state. For Johnson himself the strike was an experience that led him to give careful thought to the demands of labor, and his conduct won him the support of the labor element in the state.[2]

Thomas W. Lawson, Johnson's admirer and friend, wrote offering his assistance in attempting to settle the strike, but Johnson

[1] St. Paul Pioneer Press, August 3, 1907.
[2] Ibid., July 23, 24, 25, 26, 27, 28, 31, August 1, 2, 3, 1907; St. Paul Dispatch, July 23, 25, 26, 30, August 1, 2, 3, 1907; Duluth Labor World, August 31, 1907; O'Brien, There Were Four of Us, or Was It Five, pp. 76–77; Day and Knappen, pp. 161–63; Oppegard, pp. 85–91; Cheney, "A Labor Crisis and a Governor," Outlook, May 2, 1908.

was happy to be able to report that the strike was over and that he hoped for no more trouble. And he thanked H. L. Buck, one of the Democratic leaders of the state, for his expression of approval of the governor's actions — an approval that was shared by the majority of Minnesotans.[3]

By the end of the summer Johnson was tired out. On September 30 he left St. Paul to go to Keokuk, Iowa, where, upon the invitation of Governor Albert B. Cummins, he was to join a party of governors to accompany President Theodore Roosevelt on a boat trip down the Mississippi River to St. Louis to attend the Deep Waterways Convention. Upon his arrival in Keokuk, he was suddenly taken ill with an attack of his old ailment. He was in no condition to meet the party, so President Roosevelt's secretary, William Loeb, Jr., who was leaving Keokuk to go to Yellowstone Park, invited him to return to St. Paul in Loeb's private car.

Warned by his physician that he must have a complete rest, Johnson was forced to cancel all speeches scheduled for him in October. And to add to his burdens, Mrs. Johnson was seriously ill for some five weeks.[4]

So Johnson rested during October and November of 1907, doing only routine work. But his friends were busy with the task of launching him in the national political arena. A movement was developing to nominate him for president of the United States on the Democratic ticket.

[3] Executive Letters, Johnson to Lawson, August 13, 1907; Johnson to H. L. Buck, August 10, 1907.

[4] *Ibid.*, Johnson to Cummins, August 12, 20, 1907; Johnson to W. F. Saunders of St. Louis, October 18, 1907; Johnson to George B. Doty of Rochester, October 4, 1907. See also *St. Paul Pioneer Press,* September 29, 30, October 2, 3, 1907.

## CHAPTER IX

*Johnson for President?*

SINCE the emergence of William Jennings Bryan as the most prominent Democratic leader, the party had suffered from disharmony and disunion. When Bryan was the Democratic candidate for president of the United States in 1896 and 1900, there were some conservative Democrats who refused to vote, others who went over to support the Republican candidate, and some who halfheartedly supported Bryan only because of party loyalty. The majority of those who opposed Bryan came from the South and the East. The State of Maryland, for example, though traditionally Democratic, went Republican every time Bryan ran for president.

The conservative Democrats rejoiced at Bryan's second defeat and interpreted it to mean that the "Great Commoner" was forever removed from the list of presidential aspirants. Between 1900 and 1904 these Democrats endeavored to reorganize the party along traditional lines and prepared to nominate a man they could support in 1904. Successful in their efforts to control the Democratic National Convention, they nominated Judge Alton B. Parker of New York over Bryan's determined opposition. Although Bryan announced his support of Parker, he gave ample indication of his real feelings toward the Democratic candidate, and Parker's crushing defeat showed that many party members agreed with Bryan. Parker received a million and a half votes less than Bryan polled in 1900, and this was the worst defeat the Democrats had experienced in years. The great increase in votes cast for the Socialist and Populist parties was due to the revolt of Bryan Democrats rather than to growth in the two parties.[1]

Parker's decisive defeat gave Bryan and his followers encouragement and hope. Once again Bryan took command of the party,

[1] Edward Stanwood, *History of the Presidency from 1897 to 1916*, p. 133; Hibben, p. 258.

and with characteristic vigor, he set about organizing its progressive element. He sounded the call immediately after the election of 1904 in the headlines of the *Commoner*: "Prepare for 1908 — Democracy versus Plutocracy — The Election Lesson." But the conservative Democrats of the South and East did not give up; they began to search the country for a man who might successfully oppose Bryan for the leadership of the party. There seemed to be no one in sight in 1904, but they hoped to find such a man before 1908.

Johnson's victory in 1904 had been noted all over the United States. A Democratic governor in Republican Minnesota was unusual enough to draw the attention of the nation's political leaders. Even then there was some mention of him as a possible presidential candidate for the Democrats, but it was not taken seriously until the amazing vote he received in his second election proved beyond doubt that he was a remarkable campaigner. Soon after his re-election the Democrats of Cooper, Texas, held a mass meeting and started a movement for Johnson for president in 1908.[2] During the fall of 1906 and all through 1907, letters urging Johnson to consider running for the presidency poured into his office, and the number swelled during the first half of 1908.[3]

Professor Charles R. Boostrom, president of Southern Minnesota Normal College and of the Austin School of Commerce, was only one of several of Johnson's friends who urged him to consider the Democratic nomination seriously, and in a letter to the governor Boostrom expressed the feelings of many:

In one of my letters you told me that you didn't think there was much prospect in the broader field for national politics, but I tell you there is. All the people need is to have their attention directed to this especial fact, and there will be a landslide for you.

The only rational thing that the democrats can do is to nominate you providing they want to win. . . .

I don't think Bryan could be elected president even if he should receive a nomination, on account of his radical views on government ownership. . . . I think the people will recognize in you one who is

[2] Executive Letters, L. N. Cooper to Johnson, March 1, 1906, and August 5, 1907; *St. Paul Pioneer Press*, November 12, 1906; *Minnesota Stats Tidning*, November 14, 1906.
[3] Executive Letters, Frank Day to Arthur W. Dunn, February 14, 1907; Day to Seth Bottomley, April 29, 1907; Day to P. L. Boyden, February 7, 1907.

safe, sane and sound. The Lord knows I hope that they may do so.[4]

Johnson thanked Boostrom for his kind thoughts but explained that he did not think himself important enough to be considered for the presidency.[5] That some Minnesotans thought otherwise is suggested by a verse that appeared in the *St. Paul Dispatch* for February 13, 1907:

> *A Valentine to Governor John A. Johnson*
> You're a statesman with a velvety touch
> An artist at blarney and such
> As a candidate rare
> For the president's chair
> You'd help Old Democracy much.

In the spring of 1907 Henry Watterson, editor of the *Louisville Courier-Journal,* drew the nation's attention to his old friend, John A. Johnson. A Gold Democrat, Watterson had not supported Bryan in 1896, and he had been delighted with the nomination of Parker in 1904. Between 1904 and 1908 he was one of the leaders of the movement to head off Bryan's third nomination. In an editorial on May 6 Watterson said:

The democratic party might easily go farther for a presidential nominee, and fare worse, than the governor of Minnesota. He is a coming man upon the national steeplechase, having long ago arrived upon the field of the Queen of the States of the Northwest. . . . He grew up a typical new American. He has brains and enterprise, manhood and patriotism "to let" as it were, and would make a good president as surely as he has made a good governor. He would make a good candidate, too. He would run as they used to say . . . "like a skeerd deer."

During the summer and fall of 1907 Watterson hammered away at the fact that the national Democratic party was not united and accused Bryan of having done much to bring about that disunity. He urged the Democrats to search for a leader to replace Bryan, one who would unite the party and lead it to victory. With Theodore Roosevelt out of the running in 1908, Watterson declared, the Democrats had a fine chance to win — without Bryan. He admitted that Bryan would be nominated if he insisted on it, but

[4] *Ibid.,* Boostrom to Johnson, February 11, 1907.
[5] *Ibid.,* Johnson to Boostrom, February 18, 1907.

*St. Paul Dispatch*, July 16, 1907

"Oh, we knew it all the time."

he was sure the man stood no chance of becoming president of the United States. If Bryan considered the interests of the party, said Watterson, he would not run. And in that case, Watterson again suggested Governor Johnson of Minnesota as a "dark horse" who could unite the party and perhaps carry the election, a Democrat who did not live "east of the Alleghanies, nor south of the Potomac and the Ohio." [6] Watterson's advocacy of Johnson caused a great deal of comment, but it was generally agreed that the Minnesotan would be a good candidate only if Bryan approved of him.[7]

At the request of Ida Tarbell, Watterson wrote an introduction to an article about Johnson for the *American Magazine,* and Miss Tarbell thought he made Johnson appear both "attractive and convincing." [8] Writing to Johnson upon the publication of the article, Watterson said: [9]

You will have read in the *American Magazine* enough to assure you of my entire confidence and esteem. I have kept pretty close tab on you since my visit to St. Peter fifteen or sixteen years ago, partly through your public doings and partly through your brother Fred for whom and his interesting little family I entertain real affection.

As to the Presidency, reading the strange story of the White House from Jackson to Roosevelt, I am a fatalist. Whoever was born to it will get there; whoever wasn't won't. It does seem that, between Bryan and the Hearst and Belmont crowd, the Democratic party will have a slim chance next year; and yet . . . no man can safely prophesy.

But, I merely write to say, my dear Governor, that "I looks toward you." . . .

J. C. Hemphill, editor of the *Charleston News and Courier,* who had become acquainted with Johnson when they had served together on Thomas Lawson's insurance committee, wrote to remind him that the *News and Courier,* not Henry Watterson, was the real discoverer of John A. Johnson, presidential candidate. He added: "We have been talking about you here as a presidential possibility for months, and nothing would please me better, as you know, than to have you succeed that present impossible crea-

[6] *Louisville Courier-Journal,* July 10, 1907; *St. Paul Pioneer Press,* July 16, 1907.

[7] *Louisville Courier-Journal,* July 27, 1907. Reprints of editorial comments on Johnson's candidacy appear in this issue.

[8] Henry A. Watterson Papers, in Manuscript Division of the Library of Congress, Ida Tarbell to Watterson, June 18, August 2, 1907.

[9] Executive Letters, Watterson to Johnson, October 2, 1907.

ture in the White House." He then asked Johnson for his views on the tariff and states' rights issues.[10] Replying to Hemphill, Johnson said he would be satisfied to be allowed to retire to private life at the end of his term as governor, but he appreciated the fact that every citizen owed it to his country to perform political duties when called upon.[11]

In June Frank Day traveled to the Pacific Coast and back and was impressed by the enthusiasm for Johnson he found en route. Day was accused of launching a movement for Johnson's nomination, but both he and the governor denied any such intention. Yet, after a visit with Day, editor "Doc" Bixby of the *Nebraska State Journal* published the following:

> You have taken pains to state,
> > John A. Johnson
> That you're not a candidate,
> > John A. Johnson;
> But, now didn't Frank A. Day,
> In the words he had to say,
> Really give the snap away,
> > John A. Johnson?
>
> When the great convention meets,
> > John A. Johnson
> Occupying all the seats,
> > John A. Johnson;
> If the mention of your name
> Sets the hearts of men aflame,
> Will you then be in the game,
> > John A. Johnson?
>
> . . . . . . . . .
>
> If you want it, do not fear,
> > John A. Johnson.
> I will represent you here,
> > John A. Johnson.
> As for me, the die is cast,
> Bryan's day is long since past —
> I'm for Johnson, first and last,
> > John A. Johnson.[12]

[10] *Ibid.*, Hemphill to Johnson, July 20, 1907.
[11] *Ibid.*, Johnson to Hemphill, August 8, 1907.
[12] *St. Paul Pioneer Press*, June 24, 25, 1907; *Martin County Sentinel*, July 5, 1907.

Another member of Johnson's administration, John E. King, was closely questioned regarding Minnesota's governor when he was in North Carolina at a national convention of librarians. King found that many southerners were greatly interested in Johnson's possible candidacy and were surprisingly well informed about him.[13] Democrats in Sandusky, Ohio, organized the first "Johnson Club," [14] and John Dwan, city attorney in Two Harbors, was already actively working with political friends in Michigan for Johnson's nomination. He wrote to Johnson asking for copies of the University of Pennsylvania address and any other literature that he could distribute among his friends in Michigan.[15]

Those who were interested in Johnson's political future realized that he was handicapped by not being widely known and they welcomed invitations that promised to spread his acquaintance and reputation outside Minnesota. Samuel Untermeyer, a New York lawyer and political friend, invited him to come east on a quiet visit to see friends who were anxious to meet him. Untermeyer, however, suggested that Johnson be his guest so that he might meet people in his home, "where no political complexion" could be given the visit.[16] Roger Sullivan, member of the Democratic National Committee and political boss of Chicago, invited Johnson to address the Industrial Club in Chicago, because the people of that city wanted to hear him.[17] The chancellor of the University of Kansas requested Johnson to deliver the commencement address in June 1908 and was willing to wait until after January for his decision if he felt it might be possible for him to come.[18] From Seattle came an invitation for him to speak at a banquet to be held on either Jackson Day or Jefferson's birthday, whichever Johnson might find convenient. The president of the Democratic Club in Seattle wrote:

We have heard a great deal about you out here in the Northwest and most of us are desirous of meeting with you. You are one of the men being considered at the present time as a possible candidate for President of the United States, and many in this locality are favorable to you. . . .

[13] *Minneapolis Journal*, June 2, 1907.        [14] *Ibid.*, June 6, 1907.
[15] Executive Letters, Dwan to Johnson, July 17, 1907.
[16] *Ibid.*, Untermeyer to Johnson, October 27, 1907.
[17] *Ibid.*, Sullivan to Johnson, October 31, 1907.
[18] *Ibid.*, Frank Strong to Johnson, October 31, 1907.

Should you come here we will make arrangements to have you entertained by the Democrats of Spokane, Seattle, Tacoma, Everett, and Bellingham, the largest cities in the State and the Northwest.

Our Club also authorized me, in case you cannot come, to invite Tom L. Johnson, Governor Folk or William Jennings Bryan. I shall not communicate with them, however, until I hear from you. . . .[19]

Johnson had another political friend in Kentucky in the person of H. R. Prewitt, state insurance commissioner. Urging Johnson to come to Kentucky in the fall of 1907 to take part in the state political campaign, he promised:

I will see that the Campaign Committee properly invites you and will undertake to see that you get the best appointments in the State and good audiences. . . .

It is my candid judgment that the more the people see you and hear you, the better will be your chances. Kentucky is the gateway to the South. You have in this State, a friend in the leading Democratic paper of the South, the *Courier-Journal,* and I believe by your coming to the State and making a few speeches for the party this Fall, that you could do us great good in the State and great good would come out of it for you.[20]

Meanwhile, Bryan had not been idle. In 1906 he went on a triumphal world tour, returning to the United States late in the summer. Immediately after he arrived in New York, he delivered a major speech before a large and enthusiastic audience in Madison Square Garden. In this memorable speech he declared that the railroads must

ultimately become public property and be managed by public officials in the interests of the whole community in accordance with the well-defined theory that public ownership is necessary where competition becomes impossible. I do not know that the country is ready for this change; I do not know that a majority of my own party favor it, but I believe an increasing number of the members of all parties see in public ownership the only sure remedy for discrimination between persons and places and for extortionate rates for the carrying of freight and passengers.[21]

Since neither the people nor Bryan's party was ready for govern-

[19] *Ibid.,* C. A. Reynolds to Johnson, October 24, 1907.
[20] *Ibid.,* Prewitt to Johnson, August 6, 1907.
[21] *Speeches of William Jennings Bryan,* vol. 2, pp. 84–85.

ment ownership of railroads, this pronouncement caused considerable dismay among Democrats and delighted the Republicans.

Somewhat overwhelmed by the reaction, Bryan tried to explain. In the *Commoner* and in a speech delivered in Kentucky in September 1906, he pointed out that he had said government ownership must come *ultimately*, but that until the people were ready for it strict regulation of railroads should be the government policy. He also reminded his audiences that he had said he did not know whether the people or his party were ready for the issue, which he would never try to force upon them.

In February 1907 Bryan started on a three months' speaking tour of the West, and then went east to New England to stir up the progressive Democrats there. Everywhere he went, he found himself as popular as ever.[22]

Every political leader in the country knew that Bryan wanted the Democratic nomination, although he had made no formal announcement of his candidacy. He had no friendly feelings toward any Democrat who might be a serious contender for the nomination. The men most frequently mentioned as possible candidates were Governor Joseph Folk of Missouri, Judge George Gray of Delaware, Governor Judson Harmon of Ohio, Governor Hoke Smith of Georgia, and Governor Johnson of Minnesota. Then on November 14, 1907, Bryan made a formal announcement that he was willing to run for the presidency, but that if the Democratic party found a stronger candidate, he would support the choice of the party.[23] The die was cast — any aspirant to the nomination would have a struggle with the experienced Bryan.

Johnson persistently denied that he was a candidate for the nomination, but political leaders continued to regard him as one. Early in December he spoke before the National Rivers and Harbors Congress in Washington, and Senator Knute Nelson invited him to the Senate chamber, where he met and talked with the members.[24] Then on December 7 Johnson was one of the guests at a dinner given by the Gridiron Club, the famous organization of newspapermen in Washington. He had been invited by Walter W. Jermane, Washington correspondent for the *Minneapolis Journal*, and in reply he had written Jermane:

[22] Hibben, pp. 277–79.          [23] *St. Paul Pioneer Press*, November 15, 1907.
[24] *Ibid.*, December 5, 6, 1907.

It is not necessary to discuss any political feature of this particular proposition, because I am not a candidate for any office under the sun . . . but it has been my life ambition since I have attained to the years of discrimination, to attend a dinner of the Gridiron Club. . . .

I shall be happy to . . . attend . . . for no other purpose than to attend it, and attend it as your guest. . . .[25]

The dinner was given in the New Willard Hotel, and the two hundred and fifty guests included Vice-President Fairbanks, members of the Cabinet, the Supreme Court, and Congress, a few governors, and men who were prominent in state political affairs, in business, and in journalism. Johnson found his place at one of the side tables, and the dinner began when the club's president, Samuel Blythe, lighted the huge electric gridiron.

The evening's fun, as usual, turned largely on political matters and included witty jibes, in speech and song, directed at prominent leaders of both parties.[26] The Democrats, for example, were baited with the declaration that William Jennings Bryan, having been twice defeated, was the only logical candidate for the presidency, and they were urged to recall the old saying, "Three times and out." [27]

Johnson was introduced to the audience "rather far down" in the evening, when the guests were less interested in either individuals or speeches. The song to introduce him was called "Poor John" and was sung tearfully:

> There's a governor named Johnson,
> And his first name's John;
> To the front in politics he's always gone.
> Now his friends are shouting he's the man
> To run this country on the democratic plan.
> They've told a lot about him — say he's fine and big,
> And for fads and isms doesn't care a fig;
> But now there comes a change — things seem very cold.
> We asked them what had happened,
> And this sad, sad tale they told:
>
> Said John: "I won't be taken there again, no fear;

[25] Executive Letters, Johnson to Jermane, June 16, 1907.
[26] Some of the songs are quoted in the *New York Tribune,* December 8, 1907, and in the *Kansas City Star,* December 8, 1907.
[27] *Ibid.*

Bryan asked me questions til I felt so queer;
Thought I was too young to run for president just yet;
Told me William Jennings was the one best bet;
Said no one could help like John Johnson,
But told me pretty plainly not to run!"
It was warm at first, but it soon got mighty cold,
And back in Minnesota this sad, sad tale they told:

They took him 'round to see Mr. Bry-an, Mr. Bry-an,
    Billie Bryan,
And while they introduced him they were cryin'
"Here's the man we bet our money on."
Bryan put him through a cross-examination;
Johnson said he would like the nomination,
Then Bryan shook his head:
"Want it myself," he said,
Poor John! Poor John! [28]

At the conclusion of the song, the tall governor of Minnesota
rose to his feet. He stood for a moment saying nothing, a twinkle
in his eyes, a smile on his genial, friendly face. Then his deep,
warm voice rang out: "Poor John? I appreciate the honor; but
don't you think, when you look back at 1896, at 1900 and at 1904,
you ought to say 'Poor Bill'?" [29] This sally set the audience off
into laughter and applause, and Johnson, pleased that he had
made a hit, continued to speak once he could be heard.

The rules of the Gridiron Club forbade the publication of
speeches delivered before it, so his remarks were never recorded,
but the *Washington Post* compared it to the unreported speech
Lincoln delivered in 1856 which made him a prominent figure
among Republicans of the Middle West. Later Johnson's talk was
said to have been witty, amusing, and penetrating, "a fresh, vigorous, direct, typically western and yet broadly national review of
the political life of the time." [30] At one point Johnson, "in the
midst of a keen, clever eulogy of Minnesota, enumerated the products in which she excelled every other state, and concluded, with
a humorous glance at Vice President Fairbanks, 'And her produc-

---

[28] *Minneapolis Journal*, December 9, 1907.
[29] Day and Knappen, pp. 167–68. The account here is based upon the report of the
dinner in the *Washington Post*.
[30] Day and Knappen, p. 170.

tion of artificial ice exceeds even that of Indiana.'" That brought
Fairbanks laughing to his feet to applaud "while everybody else
roared and stamped."[31]

When Johnson concluded, such a scene took place as had never
before been witnessed at a Gridiron Club dinner. Guests left their
places and rushed to Johnson's table to congratulate him. "Uncle
Joe" Cannon was the first to reach him, to be followed by Senator
Foraker, Secretary Root, and others. Johnson, flushed and excited
but natural in manner, gracefully received the "compliments that
were showered upon him." His astounding performance that night
won him national attention as an outstanding and unique personality and gave impetus to the talk of him as a presidential
candidate.[32]

The *Kansas City Star* commented in an editorial that it was
not surprising that Minnesota's governor had made such a favorable impression in Washington and had become the leading topic
of conversation there. Johnson, the *Star* pointed out, needed only
to be seen, heard, and met for people to realize his worth, and the
paper advised the Democrats to rally the party about him.[33] Editor Hemphill of the *Charleston News and Courier* was pleased
that Johnson had aroused so much attention, and Charles H.
Grasty, owner of the *Baltimore News,* became an influential Johnson admirer as a result of the Gridiron dinner. An article on "Johnson of Minnesota" as well as a long editorial on the situation
within the Democratic party appeared in the *News* for December 9.

In the editorial Grasty reminded his readers of the Democrats'
crying need for a new candidate. (It must be remembered that the
normally Democratic state of Maryland had repudiated Bryan
in 1896 and again in 1900. Maryland Democrats saw no hope of
carrying the state in 1908 if Bryan was the nominee.) Grasty ag-
gressively urged the nomination of Johnson, "a man who is not
associated in the public mind with any of the party's troubles,
who represents personal vigor, force and ability, but is not ex-

[31] *Ibid.,* p. 169.
[32] *Ibid.,* pp. 165–75; *Baltimore News,* December 9, 1907; *Atlanta Constitution,* December 8, 1907; *Charleston News and Courier,* December 8, 1907; *Minneapolis Journal,*
December 9, 1907; *New York Tribune,* December 8, 1907; *New York Times,* December 8, 1907; *Washington Post,* December 8, 1907; *Kansas City Star,* December 8, 1907.
[33] *Ibid.,* December 9, 1907.

pressly identified with any aspect of the party's national record." [34] Grasty presented Johnson as a man of shrewdness and common sense, a democrat in the large sense of the word, and not a reformer or "savior of society" like William Jennings Bryan.

The *Baltimore News* article on Johnson began:

After all, Henry Watterson is a pretty good judge of colts. Six or eight months ago, when it looked as if the next election would go by default to the Republican because of the poverty of presidential material in the Democratic party, the Louisville editor announced that he had made a discovery.

The discovery, the *News* continued, was an unknown man with the uninspiring name of John Johnson, a name which meant so little that few bothered to find out where the man came from. Then —

He attended the Gridiron dinner. He made a speech. A barnyard rooster never goes through that experience without losing his tail feathers. A mere prairie phenomenon would have been exploded. A demagogue would have been found out. Any word of buncombe would have made the gridiron sizzle. . . .

Here is a Democrat without demagogy. A leader whose head is not in the clouds. A sober thinker with the saving grace of humor. A right-doer whose temperature is perfectly normal. A man of action without strenuosity. A young man of seasoned judgment. A man of the people who looks well in evening clothes. The possessor of that greatest gift of the gods, sense — which means judgment and taste — but all the while a virile son of the West with every red corpuscle intact.

The next day the *Baltimore News* published a cartoon picturing a scowling Bryan looking on as "Uncle Sam" shook Johnson by the hand and remarked: "Well, John, I'm glad to have met you, and the more I see you, the more I like you."

At the White House, where he had visited President Roosevelt, Johnson was questioned by a group of reporters. He swung one leg informally over the corner of a table near him and answered all their questions, enjoying his talk with them as much as he liked to talk with the Minnesota editors. His interviewers went away impressed by his simplicity of manner, his honesty and frankness, and his utter sincerity.[35]

[34] *Baltimore News,* December 9, 1907.
[35] *Ibid.,* December 10, 1907.

On December 12, while Johnson was still in Washington, the Democratic National Committee met in that city and unanimously endorsed the candidacy of William Jennings Bryan — although the *New York Herald* reported that there was an undercurrent of feeling against Bryan among the committee members which was not expressed because no popular sentiment had crystallized around any other potential candidate. Members of the committee were Thomas Taggert of Indiana, chairman, Urey Woodson of Kentucky, Roger Sullivan of Illinois, Norman E. Mack of New York, Tom Johnson of Ohio, and C. G. Heifner of Washington.[36]

The committee also accepted the invitation of the city of Denver to hold the national convention there. The *Charleston News and Courier* deplored this choice, pointing out that Denver was in the area of strong free-silver sentiment, which would in itself increase the menace of radicalism in the Democratic party.[37] The *Atlanta Constitution* noted that the choice of Denver made it certain that Bryan would be nominated.[38]

Accepting the endorsement of the national committee, Henry Watterson began to write editorials urging Bryan's election, and the *New York Tribune* commented that Watterson had no other recourse since Johnson had not responded to the colonel's suggestion that he become an active candidate.[39] Some Democratic newspapers were urging the nomination of Judge George Gray of Delaware. Thomas Lawson, however, made a characteristically unorthodox suggestion; he said he thought Theodore Roosevelt and John A. Johnson would make a perfect team for the people to choose. And the *Charleston News and Courier* replied that such a combination would be acceptable if Johnson ran in first place.[40]

The *New York Tribune* accepted Bryan's nomination as a foregone conclusion but poked fun at his candidacy by publishing some verses entitled "Wanted, an Issue for William Jennings Bryan":

> My kingdom for an issue,
> Said Bryan of Nebraska,

[36] *New York Herald*, December 12, 13, 1907.
[37] *Charleston News and Courier*, December 14, 1907.
[38] *Atlanta Constitution*, December 13, 1907.
[39] *New York Tribune*, December 9, 1907.
[40] *Charleston News and Courier*, December 27, 1907.

I've tramped this country
Up and down from Jersey to Alaska,
I've even ransacked Europe, and
Searched Asia in vain,
And now I am in desperate
Straits, for one I must obtain.

For I've lured them with Free Silver,
And I've tried them with Free Trade,
And said I'd knock the tariff
Off everything that's made.
Railed with demagogic unction
Against government by Injunction,
But they snowed me under on Election morning.

When I came last year from Europe, they
Turned out fifes and drums,
And they met me down the harbor
With "The Conquering Hero Comes."
But when I said that Railroads
To the Nation must belong,
They changed their tune, and from
That day they've sung another song.

I have preached the Rights of Labor,
And the poor man's wrongs bewailed,
The greed of Corporations
I've unmercifully assailed,
And the dangers of Expansion
Our enemies would launch on,
But they wiped me off the slate Election morning.

I admit I'm getting nervous,
For the months are slipping past,
Convention's coming, and I fear,
This chance will be my last,
And playing second fiddle
Is a part I always hate,
And yet, I know if I can't fish
They'll set me cutting bait.

.   .   .   .   .   .   .   .   .   .

So send along your issues,
Even second hand will do,
By practice I have learned to
Make old issues seem like new;
Some Democratic varnish, mixed
With Demagogic Bluff,
And if ancient rust shows through,
Just dodge it, that's enough.

But I've got to have that Issue,
And that at no late date,
Or else I fear I'll lose the job
Of Steady Candidate,
The Nomination, I must have,
The rest — it's Kismet, Fate,
For I know what's coming on Election morning.[41]

Amid speculation as to Bryan's chances for the nomination and his possible opponents, Johnson left Washington and returned to Minnesota. There an incident occurred which caused a minor flurry among Democrats both within and outside the state. Dr. W. W. Mayo, the "old doctor" and father of the famous Mayo brothers, returning from a trip to St. Louis, stopped off in St. Paul and spent some time with Johnson. The doctor was a veteran Democrat and a long-time friend of the governor, in whom he took a fatherly interest. The two men settled down to talk about the current political situation and to exchange accounts of their recent trips.

Johnson later admitted that in telling Dr. Mayo of his experiences in Washington, he had talked more freely than he realized, but it never occurred to him that Dr. Mayo would get the impression that he was actively a candidate for the Democratic nomination. As a result, no one was more amazed than Johnson to read that Dr. Mayo, in an interview with A. W. Blakely, editor of the *Rochester Post-Record*, had reported that the governor had said he was a candidate for the Democratic nomination and did not care who knew it. Dr. Mayo also wrote the news to Governor Folk of Missouri, whom he had met on his visit to St. Louis.

Minnesota and Missouri newspapers took up the Mayo an-

[41] Reprinted in the *St. Paul Pioneer Press*, December 19, 1907.

nouncement at once. The *Long Prairie Leader* commented: "The Johnson presidential candidacy has reached the diagnosis state. Dr. Mayo, the famous Rochester surgeon, has been called in and pronounces the candidacy as genuine." [42]

Johnson, of course, immediately issued a denial of the statement attributed to him and implied that Dr. Mayo had been misquoted. But the peppery little doctor indignantly replied that he had not been misquoted, nor had he misquoted the governor. Johnson was then forced to say that Dr. Mayo had misunderstood him, that he had told the doctor he did not expect to be a candidate, and that there was only a bare chance of such a thing if Bryan retired from the field, which did not seem even a remote possibility.

Talking by telephone with one of Dr. Mayo's sons, Johnson learned that the doctor had returned to Rochester full of excitement at the idea of Johnson's being considered for the presidency. And with characteristic impulsiveness, he had tried to do something to speed up the process.

After Johnson's emphatic denial, no further mention of the incident was made in the newspapers. But the whole episode had heightened the impression that Johnson was taking the presidential talk very seriously.[43]

Interest in Johnson was now widespread enough that newspaper reporters and magazine writers journeyed to Minnesota to see, interview, and make estimates of Governor Johnson. They saw a tall, stooped, angular man in his middle forties whose face impressed them with its fine, clear eyes and its deep lines — lines on his cheeks, lines around his mouth, and particularly lines around his eyes. He had a very expressive face which changed constantly as he talked, and when he listened or observed, the intensity of the man showed as his eyes narrowed and his face set in tense lines.

The numerous small lines around his eyes were caused by his ready smile, but the deep, hard lines in his face came from his patient endurance of physical pain. In repose Johnson's face had strength, dignity, and a touch of sadness. His brown hair was get-

---

[42] Quoted in the *Princeton Union*, December 26, 1907.
[43] Executive Letters, Johnson to Charles Holdridge of St. Louis, December 17, 1907, and Johnson to A. T. Ankeny of Minneapolis, December 23, 1907; *St. Paul Pioneer Press*, December 16, 19, 1907; *Princeton Union*, December 19, 1907.

ting thin and slightly gray above his ears, and he had acquired the habit of running his fingers through his hair as he talked. Not at all effusive and completely without affectation or undue deference, he had a natural simplicity of manner which set at ease all who came to talk with him. One magazine writer noted that "Johnson makes you feel very familiar with him, but he is very dignified with you." [44] Another wrote:

To meet him is to like him. To talk with him is to become his friend. To know him well is to join the ranks of his admirers. He is possessed of a compelling power, which may be personal magnetism, or maybe the attraction of inherent manliness, deep seated sincerity and absolute integrity, that draws to him everyone with whom he comes in contact.[45]

Johnson often surprised visitors who did not know him by his unconventional positions and his restlessness. Sitting in his office, he either placed his long legs on the desk in front of him or sat with one leg doubled up under him. A woman reporter wrote of him: "Seated, his legs are in the way, he winds them around his chair and in the midst of an argument startles you by depositing one of them in an impersonal way on the table in front of him." [46] Most often when receiving callers he sat on the edge of his desk or a table on his hands, palms down, and swung his legs in space. At times he would pace nervously up and down the room.

Forceful and intense when he was really interested in a subject, he gestured freely as he talked, pointing with his long forefinger, striking his open palm with his fist for emphasis, or using his outspread hand in accepting or rejecting a point. On days when things were relatively quiet in his office, Johnson "would restlessly stroll into the press room in the capitol, sit on the corner of the table, swinging his legs and inquire: 'Well, boys, can I do anything for you?' " [47] The newspapermen had the run of his office, and he liked nothing better than a session with them.

Johnson had made it a rule that anyone who came to see him should be admitted. Once when an elderly laborer was sitting in the governor's office telling him about his difficulties with a son

[44] Hard, p. 569.
[45] Don E. Giffin, "Governor Johnson, A Character Sketch," *Independent*, May 14, 1908, p. 1070.
[46] *St. Paul Dispatch*, September 21, 1909.  [47] Day and Knappen, pp. 191–92.

who was then in a reformatory, Frank Day came in to tell the governor that J. J. Hill was in the reception room and was getting impatient because he could not see the governor at once. The old man promptly grabbed his hat and rose to leave, but Johnson stopped him with the words, "Sit down. You are as important as J. J. Hill," and the old man stayed and finished what he had to say.[48] Another time a fellow townsman from St. Peter, a coal heaver whom Johnson knew, called upon the governor to pay his respects. Johnson was very busy at his desk, but he stopped his work, greeted his friend, and talked with him for an hour about old times.[49]

C. E. Russell, a writer for *Everybody's Magazine,* was impressed by Johnson's conception of his position. He wrote of Johnson as a new type of public servant, who "acts and talks at all times as if he thought himself only the hired man of the State of Minnesota. . . . It seems never to have occurred to him that he is in a position in any way superior to the position held by his fellow citizens; he seems only to think he has been employed by the State to do a certain job, and he is trying to do it." [50]

As the state's chief "hired man," Johnson tried to be considerate of those in positions below his, and his office staff was devoted to him. One Saturday everyone in the governor's office was planning to attend a football game on the University of Minnesota campus, and Johnson was as eager to see the game as the rest. But just as they were about to close the office for the day, important extradition papers arrived, with word that an officer was coming that afternoon to get them. Any clerk could have stayed in the office to deliver the papers to the officer, but Johnson knew how they had all been looking forward to attending the game. So he said nothing about the papers, told the others that he would be along a little later, and remained in his office waiting for the officer. He did not see the football game, but his office staff did.[51]

The men closest to Johnson, the men who were his political advisers and who often were referred to as his "Kitchen Cabinet,"

[48] Elinor Johnson Smith to W. G. H.
[49] William F. Williams to W. G. H. "Billy" Williams, long a well-known figure to men in political life in Minnesota, was first appointed governor's messenger by Johnson, who greatly admired Williams' skill in baseball.
[50] Charles Edward Russell, "Governor Johnson — New Style Politician," *Everybody's Magazine,* vol. 18, April 1908, p. 494.
[51] William F. Williams to W. G. H.

were Frank Day, T. D. O'Brien, John E. King, William McEwen, Theodore Knappen, once a newspaperman, Harvey Grimmer, formerly with the *St. Paul Globe*, W. H. Williams, state labor commissioner, and John McDermott, state oil commissioner. After working hours these men would meet with Johnson at one of the hotels in St. Paul and discuss political affairs and problems. King, Grimmer, and Johnson's brother Fred, who lived in New Ulm, did much of the writing of the governor's state papers, addresses, and campaign speeches.[52]

Political friends, reporters, and magazine writers, as well as his personal friends, agreed that Johnson was an independent in thought and action. J. G. Pyle, onetime political writer for the *St. Paul Globe* and biographer of James J. Hill, thought that Johnson would be unsafe in a party emergency, for he felt the governor had little regard for the sanctity of party relations and would act always according to the dictates of his conscience.[53] Lincoln Steffens interviewed Johnson for *Everybody's Magazine* and was impressed with his integrity.[54] H. N. Benson, Arthur Evenson, and George Nutter, all of St. Peter, as well as Julius Schmahl, both a political and a personal friend, knew Johnson most of his life, and it was their belief that he had too much intelligence and integrity to be run or used by anyone.

At times during Johnson's political career charges were made by his political enemies, especially by Robert Dunn, that he was influenced by Richard T. O'Connor, the Democratic boss of St. Paul, who was declared to be tied up with J. J. Hill. But those who knew Johnson well believed that no one could influence him to do something he did not want to do, nor could anyone "pull the wool over his eyes." His friends agreed that he could be agreeable to those who tried to influence him, but that he made his own decisions. Not even Frank Day, his closest adviser, could move him once his mind was made up on a question. Johnson felt responsible for his actions as governor only to the people of Minnesota.[55]

[52] *Ibid.*

[53] Joseph Gilpin Pyle, "John A. Johnson, the Democratic Governor of a Republican State," *Putnam's Monthly*, vol. 4, May 1908, pp. 208–13.

[54] Lincoln Steffens, "Bryan–Johnson on What the Matter Is in America and What to Do About It," *Everybody's Magazine*, vol. 19, July 1908.

[55] This impression comes from interviews with the friends of Johnson mentioned in the text, from the reactions of magazine writers and newspaper reporters, and from the columns of Minnesota newspapers, both Democratic and Republican, most of which never questioned Johnson's integrity.

Lincoln Steffens reported that Johnson's grasp of national and world affairs was "neither broad nor deep," that his outlook was somewhat provincial, but, said Steffens, "his is not a mind made up, like Taft's and Bryan's. He is teachable, and, like Roosevelt, he learns cheerfully and fast, from everybody." [56] Steffens also noted that Johnson surprised some and puzzled others by frankly admitting he did not know the answers to some questions or the solutions for some problems. William Hard of the *American Magazine* concluded that Johnson's was "a curious character, a kind of waiting character . . . [which] expands only when the necessity of expansion comes." [57] Johnson, Hard wrote,

moves forward where common sense takes him, but he moves cautiously and deliberately. It is like that queer walk of his. It is so easy, so sprawly, so comfortable, that it is some time before you notice how long his strides are and how much ground he has covered while you have been looking at him. . . .

This faculty of development, of development through human experience, through a wider and wider acquaintance with human beings in an expanding circle . . . this faculty is deeply characteristic of the man, and the man, in that respect, is deeply characteristic of his state.[58]

Probably one of the main reasons for Johnson's success and power was that he was attuned to the popular mind. He seemed to know instinctively what the majority of the people favored, demanded, or opposed. As a result, Johnson was a conservative, but one who, realizing that changes must be made, favored slow and gradual development and was shocked at the idea of any sudden or basic change. He was progressive in that he favored such measures as the initiative and referendum, direct election of senators, a graduated income tax, an inheritance tax, and woman suffrage. He opposed government ownership of railroads until all other remedies for the railroad problem had been tried. He was not a free trader, but favored a lower tariff and reciprocal tariffs with Canada. Both state and federal governments, he believed, should regulate the huge corporations, and he was strongly opposed to the increasing centralization of power, both commercial and po-

[56] Steffens, p. 13.
[57] Hard, p. 571.
[58] *Ibid.*, pp. 575–76.

litical, in the hands of relatively few men. Attacking the close connection between corporate wealth and government — local, state, and federal — Johnson deplored the indifference of the average American citizen to his individual political power and implored the voter to defy the entrenched political machines, ignore party loyalties, and cast his vote to free the country of all politicians who served special interests rather than their country. To Lincoln Steffens Johnson said:

I would have the people take back their political power and then use it gradually (as they would), fairly, cautiously, but firmly, to save our civilization. . . .

We *must* make the government represent humanity instead of interests. But by "we" I mean "we the people," not me.[59]

His emphasis upon "we the people" certainly was one of the elements of Johnson's popularity. In addition to urging the people to use their political rights and powers, he advised the states to guard against the encroachment of the federal government, which he felt was taking over more and more powers that rightfully belonged to the states.[60]

There is no doubt that Johnson enjoyed being governor of Minnesota. The position never oppressed him. Although he took his responsibilities seriously, his sense of humor kept him from losing his perspective. Meeting numbers of people constantly was not a burden, but a pleasure, and he delighted in the travel connected with his official duties. Devoted to his country, he wanted to see all of it; interested in everybody and everything, he learned a great deal on the official trips which took him all over the United States.[61]

When he had time, he slipped away from his office for a game of poker with some of his friends, and when he returned to St. Peter for brief visits he usually rejoined his poker-playing friends there in a game. The last time he played poker in St. Peter, he lost some money, and when the game broke up and he was ready to leave, he said jokingly, "It's mighty humiliating to have you people from the sticks take us city folk. I'll be back. This is only a loan!" [62]

[59] Steffens, p. 15.　　　　[60] *Ibid.*; Day and Knappen, pp. 227–38.
[61] Elinor Johnson Smith to W. G. H.　　　　[62] George Nutter to W. G. H.

He attended as many of the University of Minnesota football games as he had time for, and he also went to baseball games. He had a pass for the latter, but he never used it himself. He gave it to various friends who otherwise could not afford to go, while he bought his ticket to the bleachers, where he sat with the newsboys. Fond of walking, he usually walked from his home in the Aberdeen Hotel to the capitol every day. Taking various routes between the two places, he counted his footsteps to see which was the shortest and found that one route took twenty-five steps less than the others because he had cut through a vacant lot and climbed over a fence! [63]

Whenever Johnson rode on the streetcar, he stood on the rear platform and talked with the men about him.[64] Shortly before he died, he purchased an automobile, a new, shining, red touring car, with which he was as pleased as a child with a new toy. The *St. Paul Dispatch* published a picture of the governor sitting in his new car before the capitol, and the caption underneath read: "And when the governor starts away, the building sags toward the front, with the weight of the state employees rushing forward to see him start." [65]

The governor and his wife were regular attendants at the theater, and both enjoyed dining out at restaurants, where Johnson delighted in sampling unusual dishes. Especially fond of Chinese food, he frequently patronized a St. Paul restaurant operated by a Chinese named Moihee, who was devoted to Johnson and went to great trouble to prepare special oriental foods for him.[66]

Johnson had plans for his immediate future that were only indirectly political. Since 1905 George E. Vincent, president of the Chautauqua Institution, had tried to engage him as one of the speakers on the Chautauqua's summer program, and the directors of several other chautauqua and lyceum bureaus had invited him to take part in their programs.[67] Johnson had never been able to

[63] William F. Williams to W. G. H.
[64] Giffin, p. 1072.
[65] *St. Paul Dispatch,* May 29, 1909.
[66] H. G. McCall to W. G. H.
[67] Executive Letters, Vincent to Johnson, June 2, 1905, February 28, 1906, February 5, April 4, 1907; Johnson to Vincent, April 6, 1907; S. B. Hershey of the American Lyceum Union to Johnson, September 13, 1907; F. L. Rainey of the Fairfield Chautauqua Association to Johnson, October 7, 1907; Frank Hageman of the Salina Chautauqua Association to Johnson, May 6, December 30, 1907.

accept these offers because of the pressure of public business, but as he traveled around the country on official trips, the idea of becoming a chautauqua speaker appealed to him more and more. He was happy on the platform, he felt he had something to say, and he knew that public lecturing was one way to travel around the United States and be well paid for doing it.

When Johnson was re-elected in 1906, he took it for granted that he would retire at the end of his term and return to his editorial desk in St. Peter, but the demand for him as a chautauqua speaker and the talk of his being a presidential candidate gradually changed his mind. He began to take seriously the idea that he might be nominated for president of the United States, but he did not think 1908 was the time. It was his firm belief that he was not well enough known — and what better way was there to become a well-known figure than to follow the example of the popular William Jennings Bryan? So Johnson decided to retire temporarily from politics at the end of his term in 1908 and take to the lecture platform.[68]

He then talked with Charles L. Wagner, the manager of the Slayton Lyceum Bureau, who had tried repeatedly to engage him, and all arrangements were completed in February 1908. Johnson was to receive two hundred dollars for each lecture, and he prepared addresses on two topics: "Landmarks of American Liberty" and "The Majesty of the Law." He was scheduled to give a few lectures scattered through the summer of 1908 and then to embark upon a continuous lecture tour which would take him from coast to coast from January until May in 1909. He and his wife planned to go to Europe for the months of May and June to satisfy an old ambition, and then he would return to the lecture platform in July. When making these plans, Johnson assured Wagner that he had no intention of running for governor for a third term and insisted that he was not a candidate for the presidency.[69]

But Johnson's friends had no thought of allowing him to retire from active politics even temporarily. They made plans to present him to the Democratic National Convention at Denver in July, and they persuaded him to make his summer lecture engage-

<hr/>

[68] Elinor Johnson Smith, Henry N. Benson, George Nutter, and Julius Schmahl to W. G. H.
[69] Elinor Johnson Smith to W. G. H.; Day and Knappen, pp. 204–12.

ments contingent upon the outcome at the convention. His attitude toward their activities in his behalf he expressed in a letter to a political friend on January 23, 1908. He said he had no desire to work to "beat Bryan," but

My friends feel, and I can with all modesty say that I also feel that since no man has ever declined the presidency, and that should a situation present itself at Denver which can be advantageously used, the democrats of Minnesota owe it to me to be in a position to take advantage of such a situation. That is my position at this time.[70]

While scores of letters urging Johnson to run came to the governor's office, his Minnesota friends faced some concentrated and vigorous opposition led by the fiery, red-haired James Manahan of Minneapolis, the lawyer whose hostility Johnson had incurred in the Railroad and Warehouse Commission episode in 1906. Manahan, an ardent Bryanite, returned early in January 1908 from a visit with his hero in Lincoln, Nebraska, and reported that Bryan had said Johnson was the candidate of the "interests" in the Democratic party. Manahan himself declared sarcastically that he thought the presidency was too big a position for a man whose reputation rested on the fact that he was a jolly good fellow, and he charged that the attention given to Johnson by Tom Taggert of Indiana, Roger Sullivan of Chicago, and the Tammany Hall bosses was evidence that the "interests" were back of him.[71]

During the first weeks of January a round-robin letter endorsing Bryan for president was sent out from Duluth by such Bryan Democrats as Manahan, T. T. Hudson and Albert Fessler of Duluth, H. L. Buck of Winona, and C. E. Vasaly of Little Falls. Some Democrats who signed the letter later removed their signatures when they realized that Johnson might be an active candidate. But Duluth continued to be a sore spot in the state for the Johnson forces.

Manahan constantly reminded the Minnesota Bryan Democrats that Johnson had never endorsed the views of the "Peerless Leader" and never would.[72] He regarded Johnson as a "lovable

[70] Executive Letters, Johnson to W. J. Whipple, January 23, 1908.
[71] St. Paul Pioneer Press, January 11, 1908; Manahan, pp. 95–96. For the episode involving Manahan and the Railroad and Warehouse Commission, see above, pp. 206–8.
[72] Executive Letters, Frank Day to John Skrogand of Watson, January 20, 1908; Day to John Jenswold, Jr., of Duluth, January 20, 1908; Day to C. L. Eaton, January

and tactful man, a brilliant and adaptable politician," whose followers were "ardent young men, without any knowledge of government or economics, who automatically fell under the spell of his magnetic oratory." Maintaining that Johnson was closely connected with the "Dick" O'Connor-J. J. Hill machine, "which reached the front door of Wall Street and the back door of Tammany Hall," Manahan declared that O'Connor saw in Johnson an excellent candidate for the conservative forces of the Democratic party, a man conservative enough to suit J. J. Hill and to be an "antidote" for Bryanism. Considering this combination of Johnson, O'Connor, and Hill a "sinister triangle," Manahan said he felt it was his duty to fight the Johnson boom.

From this time forth Johnson had to make repeated denials that he was receiving any support from Hill or any other representative of an "interest." [73] He felt that the efforts of Manahan and his friends injured his candidacy somewhat, but he wrote, "It has not resulted as its promoters possibly hoped, in making me an avowed candidate for the presidency, and thus draw all the concentrated fire of Mr. Bryan's active campaign managers." [74]

There was some fun at the expense of both Bryan and Johnson at the annual Gridiron dinner, which Johnson was unable to attend. In the midst of the proceedings "Miss Democracy" appeared at the door of the banquet hall and asked for Governor Johnson of Minnesota. She was told he was not present and was asked if any other man, Bryan, for example, would do, but she rejected him and said sadly, "I accepted him in '96 and again in 1900, and he jilted me both times." Then as Miss Democracy prepared to leave, she announced she would continue her search for Johnson and said shyly, "This is leap year, you know." [75]

Attention was drawn to Johnson also by the *New York World,* which on January 3, in an article written by S. M. Williams, presented Johnson as an available candidate for the Democratic presidential nomination. On January 20 Williams, in a confidential letter to Johnson, wrote:

While in Washington during the past week I heard many compli-

30, 1908. See also *St. Paul Pioneer Press,* January 11, 18, 1908, and *Martin County Sentinel,* January 31, 1908.

[73] Manahan, pp. 95–97.

[74] Executive Letters, Johnson to W. W. Baldwin of Burlington, Iowa, January 18, 1908.

[75] *St. Paul Pioneer Press,* January 26, 1908.

mentary expressions regarding you personally and your possible candidacy. President Roosevelt said: "If the Democrats nominate Mr. Bryan, Mr. Taft will have a walk-over, but if they should nominate Governor Johnson, while Taft could beat him, yet it would be a hard fight." Secretary Cortelyou said: "Johnson would be the strongest candidate the Democrats could name." Senators Culberson, Bacon, and Daniel said that they believed Mr. Bryan could not be elected, if nominated, but that you could carry all the states that Bryan could with the addition of several northern states.[76]

The *World* continued to advocate Johnson's nomination and, in reply to the charges of the Bryan men, declared that after a careful examination of Johnson's record it could not find any evidence that either J. J. Hill or Wall Street was backing him.

To New York in January went St. Paul's Democratic boss, Richard T. O'Connor, usually referred to in Minnesota newspapers as "the Cardinal." The purpose of his trip was to discuss Johnson's prospects with his political friends in New York and to try to line up state delegations to the Denver convention for Johnson. O'Connor and his friends had several conferences with Senator Daniel of Virginia, who had once been allied with Bryan in the cause of free silver but who now promised to get an uninstructed delegation from Virginia which would be favorable to Johnson. A Democrat named Dickey from Baltimore insisted that he could guarantee an uninstructed delegation from Maryland, where there was strong sentiment for Johnson. As early as the end of January the Johnson organizers counted Maryland, New York, Virginia, Illinois, and Minnesota as Johnson states. But there never was any systematic organizing of each state for Johnson, and he was advised again and again to allow his friends to do more than volunteer work for him, to let them receive contributions and organize the country from the smallest town to the great cities.

[76] Executive Letters, Williams to Johnson, January 20, 1908. It was a call from Williams, perhaps, that led to an amusing incident one day when Governor Johnson was being entertained at the home of John Dwan, of Two Harbors, Minnesota. In the living room a small group of nonpartisan guests was awaiting his appearance, while he was upstairs shaving. A long-distance call came through from the *New York World* and the governor was asked to step to the phone. He came downstairs immediately, his face still covered with lather and the safety razor in his hand.

As he entered the room, he remarked, "Isn't this a fine appearing candidate for president?" And he continued to shave as he discussed the presidential outlook over the phone and in the presence of the guests. (Helen C. Barton of Minneapolis to W. G. H.)

Samuel Untermeyer again advised Johnson to come to New York to meet political friends and informed him that on a trip south Untermeyer had been amazed at the amount of discussion there was about him. Untermeyer also urged Johnson to announce his candidacy so that Democratic leaders would know his intentions before they made any commitments. He suggested that Johnson make his announcement in the form of a letter, answering the question as to whether or not he would accept the nomination if it was offered. After such a formal announcement, said Untermeyer, "Johnson Clubs" could be organized all over the country.[77]

In spite of the fact that Johnson refused to sanction any organized effort on a nationwide scale involving financial contributions, a few "Johnson Clubs" sprang up here and there. For example, the chairman of a committee that organized a "Johnson Club" at Harvard University wrote to Frank Day asking for literature on Johnson which the club might have printed and circulate, and he explained: "Johnson sentiment here is strong. There are many Republicans here that would vote for Johnson; there are many Democrats that would not vote for Bryan. Such a club as we have in mind can do Johnson no harm and likely will do a little good." [78]

On March 6 the Minnesota Democratic state central committee met and passed a resolution endorsing Johnson as a candidate for the presidential nomination. Although Frank Day had done considerable work to line up Johnson's friends before the committee met, there was a four-hour struggle with the Bryanite members, and the final vote on the resolution was 68 to 23, the Bryanites refusing to make the vote unanimous. After the meeting some two hundred Bryan followers gathered at the Ryan Hotel in St. Paul, organized the Minnesota Bryan Volunteers, and announced that they would work to stop the movement to send a Johnson delegation to Denver.[79] Nevertheless the Democratic state central committee under the leadership of Frank Day put Johnson in the field as an active candidate. Johnson himself, however, did not

[77] Executive Letters, Crawford Livingston to Johnson, January 31, 1908; L. P. Covington of Boston to Johnson, February 26, 1908; Samuel Untermeyer to Johnson, February 9, 21, 1908. See also St. Paul Pioneer Press, January 29, 1908.

[78] Executive Letters, F. E. Biermann to Day, March 11, 1908.

[79] St. Paul Pioneer Press, March 7, 1908; Martin County Sentinel, January 31, March 3, 1908.

give the committee any encouragement and refused to accept money which was sent to him to help finance a campaign.

T. D. O'Brien was convinced that Johnson had no chance for the nomination in 1908. Tammany Hall had indicated its interest in Johnson's candidacy, and O'Brien believed that anyone supported by Tammany Hall would be defeated. O'Brien told Johnson what he thought, and Johnson agreed but said he intended to let his friends "amuse themselves" with their plans for him. "What I did not appreciate," wrote O'Brien, "was that the governor shrewdly understood the publicity he was receiving and knew how much it would enhance the value of his services upon the lecture platform." (O'Brien's brother, C. D. O'Brien, was a devoted follower of William Jennings Bryan, and although T. D. O'Brien did not share his brother's political feelings, he was well informed as to the strength of the Bryan movement.) [80]

Johnson campaign headquarters were established in Washington, Chicago, and Denver under the direction of F. B. Lynch, who had been treasurer of the Democratic state central committee during both of Johnson's administrations. The New York Democrats encouraged the Johnson forces by voting to send an uninstructed delegation to Denver.[81] Johnson men went to North Dakota to try to persuade the Democrats of that state to send a delegation for Johnson — but James Manahan went too. And in spite of Governor John Burke's strong support of Johnson, Manahan and the Bryan men finally succeeded in electing a North Dakota delegation pledged to Bryan.[82]

Aloof, but interested in the affairs of the Democratic party, former President Grover Cleveland, still detesting Bryan, watched closely the efforts of the conservative Democrats to find a candidate. On March 14 he expressed himself on the situation in a letter:

I have lately come to the conclusion that our best hope rests upon the nomination of Johnson of Minnesota. The prospects to my mind appear as bright with him as our leader as with any other, and whether

[80] Executive Letters, Frank Day to J. A. Nowell of Spokane, October 30, 1907; Frank Day to George Canfield of Spokane, March 19, 1908; Harvey Grimmer to A. S. White of New York, March 18, 1908; Johnson to C. A. Meacham of Warren, Pa., March 25, 1908. Also O'Brien, *There Were Four of Us, or Was It Five,* pp. 80–81.

[81] *St. Paul Pioneer Press,* March 16, 18, 20, 1908.

[82] Manahan, pp. 98–102.

we meet with success or not, I believe with such a leader we shall take a long step in the way of returning to our old creed and the old policies. . . .[83]

There had been some effort to persuade Johnson to run for vice-president, but he flatly refused to consider the proposition and announced that he would not accept the nomination if it came to him.[84] He finally followed Untermeyer's advice and stated his position clearly in a letter replying to an inquiry as to whether he would accept the nomination for the presidency if it was offered to him. On March 27 he wrote the letter to Swan J. Turnblad, editor of the Swedish newspaper, *Svenska Amerikanska Posten*:

. . . I do not believe that any American citizen should be an active, open candidate for the nomination for the presidency. Any American would appreciate the high honor which could come to him in being selected as standard bearer of his party. While I recognize that the press has had much to say of me in connection with this high office, I have hitherto avoided any public or private expression regarding my position. Matters have progressed so far, however, that it seems to me that I could at least say, in answer to your interrogation, that if the Democratic party of the nation believed me to be more available than any other man, and felt that by my nomination I could contribute any service to the party and to the nation, I should be happy to be the recipient of the honor. . . .

I have done nothing and will do nothing in the way of organization to bring about this end and shall not be a candidate in a sense of seeking the nomination. . . . I desire it to be understood that in no sense am I to be a candidate for the purpose of defeating Mr. Bryan or any other man. . . . In order that there be no doubt I would say . . . that if a nomination came to me, I certainly should not refuse it.[85]

Having put himself on record, Johnson prepared to leave Minnesota to make several official speeches and to begin his schedule of chautauqua lectures. Everywhere he went he was interviewed by newspaper reporters. En route to Shiloh, Tennessee, where he was to dedicate the Minnesota monument on the battlefield on

---

[83] Cleveland to E. Prentiss Bailey, March 14, 1908 (letter in full in *Letters of Grover Cleveland, 1850–1908*, edited by Allan Nevins).

[84] O'Brien, *There Were Four of Us, or Was It Five*, p. 62; *St. Paul Pioneer Press*, March 16, 1908; Executive Letters, Johnson to F. A. Partlow of Clear Lake, Wis., February 10, 1908.

[85] *Ibid.*, Johnson to Turnblad, March 27, 1908.

April 10, he stopped off in Chicago, where reporters asked him what he thought of the charge that he was a candidate of the "interests." He replied that the accusation was "absolutely false" and that he had never received encouragement of any kind from James J. Hill.[86]

At Shiloh he delivered a speech which in its tone sounded as if it had been modeled on Lincoln's Gettysburg Address. In it he again made a strong plea for the preservation of the powers conferred upon the states by the Constitution and protested against the increase of the power of the federal government at the expense of the states.[87] From Shiloh he went to Louisville, Kentucky, where he gave the main address at a Jefferson Club dinner, and the next day he was the luncheon guest of the Chicago Press Club.[88] Stopping at Omaha on his way to Lindsborg, Kansas, to speak to the students at Bethany College, he told reporters that Bryan was "a has been" whose popularity had reached its height and had begun to decline.[89]

Johnson's first chautauqua lecture was delivered on April 27 at Houghton, Michigan, where he talked on "Landmarks of American Liberty." After discussing the historic documents on which the American Constitution and system of laws were based, he declared that the progress of the United States "as guided by the landmarks of constitutional liberty" was threatened by two dangers: the increasing centralization of power in the federal government and the increasing power of centralized and predatory wealth, defiant of the public welfare and the law of the land. He condemned the high tariff laws which the Republican administrations had refused to revise and the "gross favoritism" shown in the enforcement of the laws. The next day he repeated this lecture in Detroit, and the day following gave it at Ann Arbor before the students of the University of Michigan.[90]

In May Johnson attended the Governors' Conservation Conference in Washington, D.C. With him as a delegate went Cyrus Northrop, president of the University of Minnesota, and from

[86] *St. Paul Pioneer Press*, April 8, 1908.
[87] Address by Governor John A. Johnson at the dedication of the Minnesota monument on Shiloh Battlefield, April 10, 1908.
[88] *St. Paul Dispatch*, April 14, 1908.
[89] *St. Paul Pioneer Press*, April 18, 1908.
[90] *Ibid.*, April 28, 1908; Day and Knappen, p. 210.

Chicago east the two men found themselves traveling on the same train with Vice-President Fairbanks and William Jennings Bryan. It was reported that they all avoided talking politics!

The governors of forty-four states and their advisers, federal conservation experts, and some Cabinet members gathered in Washington at the invitation of President Roosevelt. Special guests of the conference were Bryan, Andrew Carnegie, John Mitchell, and J. J. Hill. President Roosevelt opened the conference with a speech and presided at the first day's meetings, then he suggested that Governor Johnson preside at the morning meeting of the second day's session. There were speeches by all the special guests and by Secretary of State Elihu Root, Secretary of the Treasury George B. Cortelyou, Samuel Gompers, and Governor Johnson. Minnesota's governor spoke about the elimination of wasteful methods in the mining of iron ore on the great Mesabi Range.

For three days Johnson took an active part in the discussions of the conference,[91] and Archie Butt, aide to President Roosevelt, decided that the governor most observed by all present was Johnson of Minnesota, about whom he wrote:

He is smooth shaven, but has none of that Pharisaical Methodistical manner of the Peerless Leader and never seems to pose or be self-conscious, even when he must know that he is the cynosure of all eyes — official ones at least. He is most direct in conversation, and never leaves you in doubt for a moment as to what he thinks. I suppose the Democracy must be afflicted with Bryan once more, but it is good to feel that we are training up a few leading men to take his place. . . . I believe if Johnson primarily had been known a year earlier that he would have been nominated, with every chance for election.[92]

Johnson delivered two more official speeches during May. He spoke before the Cotton Manufacturers' Association in Richmond, Virginia, and the Commercial Club in Birmingham, Alabama, where there was already a strong Johnson feeling. Then he went

[91] Executive Letters, Theodore Roosevelt to Johnson, November 11, 1907, and Johnson to the *New York Times*, November 25, 1907; Newton C. Blanchard, ed., *Proceedings of a Conference of Governors in the White House, Washington, D.C.*, pp. 1–75; *St. Paul Pioneer Press*, May 13, 15, 1908; *Martin County Sentinel*, May 22, 1908.

[92] Butt to his mother, May 15, 1908 (letter in full in Lawrence F. Abbott, ed., *Letters of Archie Butt*, pp. 6–7).

on to Tuscaloosa, where he had been invited to deliver the commencement address. Senator J. H. Bankhead had written several letters saying it would give him great personal satisfaction to have Johnson make the address.

Johnson stood before the commencement audience of the University of Alabama and began to read his address, "The New Federalism." The day was intensely hot, and a storm raged outside the hall. The audience was restive, and Johnson realized that they were not attending to his words. So he put his manuscript to one side and began to talk. His audience sat up then and listened intently as he "struck blow after blow for the rights of the states." He lambasted the tariff policy of the Republicans and attacked the power of the great corporations. When he concluded, the audience was wild with enthusiasm and applauded loudly and at length. There was no doubt about the popularity of Johnson's views on these issues.[93]

While Johnson was out of the state speaking, the Minnesota Democrats in their state convention succeeded in electing a solidly Johnson delegation to the Denver convention. Two of the outstanding Bryan men who attempted to block the convention's vote for Johnson were James Manahan and Fred Pike, and Frank Day, in a final plea for a solid Johnson delegation, said: "No Pike or piker, no man or Manahan can stand in the triumphant way of Governor John Albert Johnson." John Lind, a good friend to Bryan, remained silent until after the state convention, then reluctantly came out in support of Johnson's candidacy.[94]

Further clearing the way for Johnson's nomination at Denver, Frank Day announced that the governor would not run for a third term. Three days later, on June 12, Johnson himself issued a formal statement that under no circumstances would he accept the nomination for governor in 1908.[95]

But in spite of all their plans and efforts, by the middle of June

[93] Executive Letters, Bankhead to Johnson, February 6, March 9, 1908; John W. Abercrombie, president of the University of Alabama, to Johnson, February 25, 1908; Johnson to Bankhead, March 19, 1908. See also *Birmingham Age-Herald*, May 26, 27, 1908; *St. Paul Pioneer Press*, May 22, 1908; and "Governor Johnson's Birmingham Speech," *Outlook*, June 13, 1908, pp. 322-23.

[94] Executive Letters, Day to Dr. George S. Brown of Birmingham, Ala., May 15, 1908; *Minneapolis Journal*, May 6, 7, 9, 1908; Manahan, p. 104; *St. Paul Pioneer Press*, May 7, 10, 14, 1908.

[95] *Ibid.*, June 10, 13, 1908.

*St. Paul Dispatch*, July 6, 1908

BRYAN — "I'm not afraid of storms, but I do wish
it would clear up."

the Johnson forces realized their cause was hopeless. As state after state elected delegations pledged to Bryan, there was little doubt as to who would become the Democratic nominee, even though some states, such as New York and Georgia, elected delegations which were ready to vote against Bryan if there seemed to be any chance of defeating him. In Alabama the battle between the Bryan and Johnson forces was hard fought. Johnson's strength lay in the three chief cities, Birmingham, Mobile, and Montgomery, but the Bryan men of the state outvoted the Democrats from the cities, and a delegation pledged to Bryan was elected.

Knowing they had little if any chance for success, Frank Day and his followers nevertheless decided to carry through the movement for Johnson, bearing in mind the fact that no one can foresee positively the results of any nominating convention. It is to their credit that they did it with spirit.[96]

The Johnson headquarters in Denver buzzed with activity. Sixty-two sleeping rooms and twenty-two headquarters rooms had been leased by the Johnson men, and the most colorful figure among them was R. T. O'Connor, who became the "sartorial feature of the convention crowd" by appearing in a new suit of clothes each day in the week. Campaign literature and buttons were distributed, and the words for Johnson songs were passed around.[97] The first verse and chorus of one of the songs, sung to the tune of "Glory, Glory Hallelujah," went like this:

> From the wash tub to the White House
> John Johnson is bound to go.
> From printer's devil to President,
> The People want it so.
> With grit and brains and character
> Our Johnson is not slow.
> Yes, Johnson is our man.
>
> CHORUS:
> We'll all vote for John A. Johnson,

[96] Executive Letters, Frank Day to H. W. Rudd of Alexandria, Va., June 13, 1908; Day to P. F. Butler of Hartford, Conn., June 19, 1908; Harvey Grimmer to W. R. Swartout of Oklahoma City, July 2, 1908. See also *Minneapolis Journal*, May 19, 1908; *Atlanta Constitution*, July 7, 1908; *New York Herald*, July 7, 1908; and *New Orleans Picayune*, July 7, 1908.

[97] *St. Paul Dispatch*, July 1, 2, 1908. The words of the song are taken from a manuscript version in the archives of the Minnesota Historical Society.

We'll all vote for John A. Johnson,
We'll all vote for John A. Johnson,
For Johnson is our man.

In the *Louisville Courier-Journal* on July 1 Henry Watterson took stock of the situation. He reminded the Democratic party that in 1907 he had made great efforts to sidetrack Bryan and push forward Johnson. He explained that he had hoped to create a positive movement for Johnson rather than an anti-Bryan movement with Johnson at its head. That attempt, declared Watterson somewhat sadly, had failed and the Johnson followers had responded too late to work up real popular support. So Watterson had reluctantly gone over to Bryan because there was nothing else to do. He did not think an anti-Bryan movement would ever become as strong as the pro-Bryan sentiment in the country, at least not in 1908.

Watterson had suggested to Bryan that Johnson might become the vice-presidential nominee, but Bryan repudiated the suggestion. In a talk with Watterson in Lincoln before the convention opened in Denver, Bryan indicated that he would never accept as a running mate one who "is suspected of intimate connections with the Wall Street crowd." On July 2 Bryan wrote Watterson that he had decided that Judge George Gray of Delaware would be the best representative of the conservative Democrats for the vice-presidency, and on July 6 he again wrote to repeat this opinion, adding: "I note what you say in regard to Mr. Johnson. I still feel as I did when I talked with you, and believe that such a nomination would be unfortunate, in that it would lay us open to the charge of putting expediency above principle." [98]

A few days before the Denver convention T. D. O'Brien received a telegram from Bryan asking him to stop off in Lincoln on his way to Denver. O'Brien did so, and Bryan told him that Johnson's followers had so bitterly attacked him that he would never consent to Johnson as his running mate. In any case, Johnson and his friends had already announced repeatedly that he would not consider the nomination for the vice-presidency.[99]

[98] Watterson Papers, Bryan to Watterson, May 26, July 2, 6, 1908; *Louisville Courier-Journal*, July 1, 1908.
[99] Executive Letters, Frank Day to George Miller of Shippensberg, Pa., July 1, 1908, and Grimmer to George Lanz of Chicago, July 7, 1908. See also O'Brien, *There*

Walter Wellman, political writer for the *Chicago Record-Herald,* reported that the "feud that has sprung up between Bryan and Johnson and their followers" was "one of the features of the day." Wellman accused the Bryan men of circulating the story that Johnson was the tool of the J. J. Hill-Wall Street crowd, and Watterson declared that the Johnson men had spread stories derogatory to Bryan. Wellman also said that Bryan was "exceedingly jealous" of Johnson and had, from the first, feared Johnson's popularity and resented his actual candidacy.

The *New York Herald* commented that the Johnson delegates had expected to experience a coolness at Denver but not a frigidity from the Bryan forces. James Manahan, who was not a delegate to the convention, was in Denver working against Johnson and attacked him publicly in a long interview published by the *Rocky Mountain News.* The *Washington Post,* regretting that the anti-Bryan faction seemed to be doing little at Denver except to produce evidence that Bryan would never be elected if nominated, declared that it was too late for the Democratic leaders to rally around another candidate.[1]

On July 6, the day before the Denver convention opened, the anti-Bryan leaders met in a last minute attempt to think of some way of defeating Bryan. Present were D. F. Cohan and W. F. Sheehan of New York, James Guffey of Pennsylvania, J. J. Smith of New Jersey, A. F. Cox of Georgia, I. L. Straus of Maryland, J. M. Marvel of Delaware, and F. B. Lynch of Minnesota. They reluctantly came to the conclusion that it was too late to stop Bryan, and thereafter only a few who were definitely pledged to Johnson or to Judge Gray of Delaware continued the attempt to wrest the nomination from Bryan. Consequently the distribution of votes in the balloting of the convention did not show the real strength of either Johnson or Gray. Both had been equally emphatic in refusing to be considered for the vice-presidency.[2]

*Were Four of Us, or Was It Five,* p. 62; *New Orleans Picayune,* July 2, 1908; *San Francisco Chronicle,* July 2, 1908; *St. Paul Dispatch,* July 3, 1908; *St. Paul Pioneer Press,* July 2, 1908; and *Chicago Record-Herald,* July 2, 3, 1908.

[1] *Ibid.,* July 3, 6, 1908; Manahan, pp. 104–6; *Washington Post,* July 3, 1908; *New York Herald,* July 7, 1908; *Louisville Courier-Journal,* July 4, 1908.

[2] *Ibid.,* July 7, 1908; *New York Tribune,* July 11, 1908; *San Francisco Chronicle,* July 7, 1908. There may have been others present at the July 6 meeting, for among the anti-Bryan men at the convention were Charles F. Murphy, Tammany Hall leader, Senators Rayner of Maryland, Daniel and Martin of Virginia, Simmons of North Caro-

The Bryan men were ready when the convention opened on July 7. Bryan himself remained at home, keeping in touch with the proceedings through his brother Charles by telegraph and telephone. Thomas H. Taggert called the convention to order, Theodore A. Bell of California delivered the keynote speech, and Henry D. Clayton of Alabama became the permanent chairman.

Two problems of importance were settled that first day, and settled to Bryan's satisfaction. Judge Parker had planned to present a resolution in eulogy of ex-President Cleveland, who had died on June 24, but the resolution, which had been published before the convention met, was objectionable to Bryan, who resented as a reflection upon his own policy Parker's praise of Cleveland's sound money principles. Bryan therefore arranged to have one of his followers deliver a tribute to Cleveland before Parker got the floor. Parker's resolution then came as an anticlimax.

Next came the question of deciding upon the two contesting delegations from Pennsylvania, one of them led by Bryan's political enemy, Colonel James M. Guffey, whose leadership of the Pennsylvania Democrats was at stake. Bryan won again when Guffey's delegation was excluded by the credentials committee.

On the second day of the convention the blind Senator Gore of Oklahoma began a demonstration for Bryan which lasted eighty-seven minutes, twice as long as the one which the Republican National Convention had just given for Theodore Roosevelt and the longest such demonstration on record. Bryan's daughter Ruth and Roosevelt's daughter, Alice Longworth, were in the gallery, both clocking the ovation, and it was reported that Mrs. Longworth left the auditorium when it became apparent that the demonstration for Bryan exceeded that for her father. The delegates from Minnesota, New York, New Jersey, Delaware, Georgia, and Connecticut refused to take any part in the furor, but their inactivity did not dampen the ardor of the Bryan delegates.

The party platform was adopted without any opposition, and then the nominations for the presidential candidate began. Ignatius Dunn of Nebraska nominated William Jennings Bryan and pandemonium broke out again. Bryan, in his home, listened to the cheering and stamping over the telephone.

lina, Johnston of Alabama, Foster and McEnery of Louisiana, and Bailey and Culberson of Texas.

Meanwhile the Minnesota delegation, seated far in the rear of the auditorium, prepared for their presentation of Johnson. The governor's friends, T. D. O'Brien, F. A. Day, F. C. Winston, Daniel Lawler, W. S. Hammond, and Swan J. Turnblad, were among the delegates. Winfield S. Hammond, who had twice nominated Johnson for governor, now took his place on the platform and delivered the nominating speech for Johnson, and the nomination was seconded by Isaac L. Straus, attorney general of Maryland. There followed a half-hour demonstration led by the Minnesota delegation.

Levin Irving of Delaware next presented Judge Gray as a candidate. Then the balloting started. Bryan received 888½ votes, Judge Gray 59½ votes, and Johnson 46 votes — whereupon the convention voted to make Bryan's nomination unanimous. John W. Kern of Indiana was nominated for the vice-presidency by acclamation, and soon afterward the convention adjourned. Bryan and his followers, delighted with their success, prepared for the coming campaign against William Howard Taft, who, as Roosevelt's choice, had been nominated by the Republicans at their convention in June.[3]

For the Johnson forces the action of the convention had been a disappointment, although not a surprise. Johnson had received twenty-two votes from Minnesota, five from Connecticut, nine from Maryland, one from New Hampshire, three from Pennsylvania, three from Rhode Island, two from Georgia, and one from Maine. On July 10 the *Baltimore News* stated: "For the honor of the State and the credit of the Democratic party, let it be said at once that nine [votes for Johnson] were cast by delegates from Maryland."

Begun too late and badly managed, the campaign for Johnson had stirred up a great deal of publicity for him, which even reached overseas to the land of his parents' birth. But the campaign had also produced ill-feeling among the Bryan men, a thing which could have been avoided. Johnson himself had tried to keep his followers from antagonizing Bryan. Again and again he an-

[3] *Ibid.*, July 8, 1908; *St. Paul Dispatch*, July 7, 8, 9, 10, 1908; *St. Paul Pioneer Press*, July 8, 9, 10, 11, 1908; *New York Herald*, July 8, 1908; *Charleston News and Courier*, July 4, 10, 11, 1908; *Louisville Courier-Journal*, July 9, 10, 11, 1908; *Baltimore News*, July 10, 1908; *Baltimore Sun*, July 9, 10, 11, 1908; *Atlanta Constitution*, July 9, 10, 1908; Stanwood, pp. 182–97.

nounced that he was not a candidate to "beat Bryan"; nevertheless the Johnson movement attracted the anti-Bryan Democrats,
and the Johnson organizers did not repudiate them.

Johnson himself was not disappointed with the results of the
convention. He had never been a willing candidate and had never
expected the nomination. He had been convinced from the start
that he was not well enough known to have any chance of success. Now he sent a telegram of congratulation to Bryan, pledging
his support during the coming campaign.

On the whole both Johnson and his followers were sufficiently
encouraged by the 1908 experience to begin thinking seriously in
terms of 1912. In a sense Johnson had now been discovered by the
nation, and as the months went by in 1908 his popularity increased. There were so many demands for him to speak in all parts
of the country that he could not hope to accept the half of them.
On July 11 he started out on a two weeks' lecture tour which took
him into Oklahoma and Arkansas. He was anticipating with eager-
ness his retirement to private life and to a year on the lecture
platform.

MINNESOTA's Democratic leaders were so involved in campaigning for Johnson's nomination for the presidency that they gave little attention to the state campaign until after the Denver convention. Johnson had never considered running for a third term, and his attention had been centered on national affairs and on his plans for lecturing. When the time came, therefore, for the Democrats to prepare for the gubernatorial campaign, they were at a loss for a candidate.

The Republicans, on the other hand, were sure of at least one strong candidate for governor. Since the election day that saw the defeat of A. L. Cole, the friends of J. F. Jacobson had been planning to have him nominated in 1908. As early as January 1908, however, another aspirant for the governor's chair, Attorney General E. T. Young, formally announced his candidacy on the Republican ticket. Jacobson and his friends were more than a little annoyed, for they felt the time had come for Jacobson to be accorded the honor of the nomination and that all Republicans should recognize that fact.

Jacobson had been a good loser in 1906 and had campaigned vigorously for Cole. Also, between 1906 and 1908 he had made his peace with the opposing element within the Republican party. Recognized as the leader of the anti-Jacobson forces in 1906, Robert Dunn created a sensation at a Republican "harmony" dinner in February 1908 by urging the nomination of Jacobson and suggesting that all other aspirants step aside for the man from Lac qui Parle County. He made a strong plea that a united Republican party support Jacobson. E. T. Young was displeased with Dunn's speech and said that if "harmony" meant the suppression of rivalry among candidates, he was not in favor of it. He thought a good, free fight for the nomination, a fight without rancor and bitterness, would be healthier for the party.[1]

In February Jacobson formally announced his candidacy for the governorship and Joel Heatwole let it be known that he too was an active aspirant. So the Republicans had three men in the field.

The Democrats were silent. As yet only the party leaders knew that Johnson did not intend to run.[2] Next to Johnson, T. D. O'Brien was regarded as the state's leading Democrat, but he appeared to be satisfied with his private practice. Also, being Irish and a Catholic, O'Brien was not likely to appeal to any large number of the Scandinavians and Protestants in Minnesota. Leonard Rosing's one experience as the Democratic nominee had been an unhappy one, and Rosing was now a sick man.

While the Democrats were trying to find a candidate, Robert Dunn, in the *Princeton Union* on February 20, prophesied that Taft and Bryan would become the presidential nominees and that Jacobson and Johnson would run against each other for governor of Minnesota. Taft and Jacobson would win, he said, Jacobson by a majority of 20,000 votes.

It was on June 9 that Frank Day announced that Johnson would not run for a third term. Reporting the announcement, the *Minneapolis Journal* said it had sent a chill through the bones of the Democratic officeholders, who were sure no one but Johnson could be elected on the Democratic ticket. These officeholders, said the *Journal*, were sitting up nights trying to think how they could force Johnson to run again. The Republicans rejoiced over the announcement, and the *St. Paul Pioneer Press* observed that Johnson was wise in refusing to run in 1908. Rather than risk defeat, which was certain with a united Republican party behind its candidate, the *Pioneer Press* declared, it was best for Johnson to retire gracefully, by his own action, "so that Johnson prestige and dignity may sustain as little injury as possible."[3]

Johnson's own statement that he would not be a candidate in 1908 was very clear. No one could misunderstand when he said:

[1] *Princeton Union*, February 27, 1908; *St. Paul Pioneer Press*, January 19, 23, February 11, 1908.

[2] *Ibid.*, January 19, 23, February 15, 1908. The death of A. L. Cole was reported in the *Princeton Union*, March 12, 1908.

[3] *Minneapolis Journal*, June 10, 1908; *St. Paul Pioneer Press*, June 10, 1908.

"Under no circumstances will I be a candidate for renomination."
There were some Republicans, nevertheless, who refused to take
his statement seriously. Two of them were Robert Dunn and J. F.
Jacobson, who believed that Johnson would be forced to run by
his own party.[4]

On July 1 the Republican state convention met in St. Paul.
A. B. Cole called the convention to order and in his opening speech
asked for unity in the party. He reminded the Republicans that
defeat had been the result of division in both 1904 and 1906. He
pledged the "Cole" forces to support Jacobson, the man whose
friends had helped defeat his brother, A. L. Cole, in 1906. Then
Frank Eddy, a veteran Republican, delivered the nomination
speech for Jacobson. Referring to "Jake," Eddy said:

He was a rough rider when the man who made that a synonym for
honesty in politics was riding a hobby horse. He stood for the "square
deal" long before the man who has made that phrase famous had quit
playing in alleys. He not only stood for the "square deal," but for an
honest shuffle and a straight cut, without which a "square deal" is not
possible. . . .

The choice of the Minnesota Republicans has already been made
in their hearts. The only charge that his opponents have been able to
make against him is that he eats pie with his knife.

May we not hope that a working representative of the workers will
accomplish results in great contrast to the three-suited, kid-gloved
apostle of masterly inactivity. We offer him just as God made him for
a rough, rugged sort of man, and we would not have him different if
we could. . . .

It is superfluous to name him. You all know who he is. I will only
paraphrase a famous couplet, and say,

> If you ask us where he hails from
> We've only one reply to make
> He comes from Minnesota,
> And the people call him Jake.[5]

Roars of applause and the waving of hats followed Eddy's
speech, and when the demonstration died down, E. T. Young seconded the nomination. Joel Heatwole was called upon to do likewise, but he did not appear, and it was not until the next day that

[4] *St. Paul Dispatch*, July 18, 1908; *Princeton Union*, July 16, 1908.
[5] *Minneapolis Journal*, July 1, 1908.

Heatwole, disappointed, pledged his support for "Jake." The nomination was made by acclamation, and A. O. Eberhart of Mankato was nominated for lieutenant governor.[6]

Jacobson's nomination received national attention. The statement that "he eats pie with his knife" was lifted out of Eddy's nomination speech and made headlines on the first pages of newspapers all over the country. The *Chicago Record-Herald* announced that the Minnesota Republicans had nominated a man they called "Jake," a "hirsute, uncouth implement dealer" who eats pie with his knife, and the paper commented that the nomination did not reflect any credit upon the party. "Jake" made the front page of the *San Francisco Chronicle* and also of the *Baltimore News*, which was amused that one of his personal habits should become a campaign issue.[7]

Many Minnesotans were acutely sensitive to such publicity. The *Minneapolis Journal* deplored the whole thing, but had to admit that the damage was done even if it could be proved that Jacobson did not eat pie at all, as his wife claimed. The *St. Paul Pioneer Press* came to Jacobson's defense by saying that Frank Eddy was simply paying a compliment to the candidate's "sturdy character and vigorous methods which are devoid of sham and pretense." Mr. Eddy, explained the *Pioneer Press*, never intended his remark to be taken literally.[8] But the Republican *Brown County Journal* had to admit that "Jake" was the "rugged type in public life" who was not very refined but had honesty and integrity, which were more important.[9] The *St. Peter Herald* enjoyed the whole situation and remarked that "Just so Jake hands out the pie; it makes no difference how he eats it." [10]

There is no doubt that Jacobson was a rough, unpolished individual who, like Robert Dunn, did not care how he looked. Judge Torrance wrote to his wife: "I had a call from Jacobson, the Republican nominee for governor. If he would brush himself up a little and look more like [other] folks he would not be so bad be-

[6] *Ibid.*, July 1, 2, 1908; *St. Paul Pioneer Press*, July 1, 2, 1908.
[7] *Ibid.*, July 2, 8, 24, 1908; *San Francisco Chronicle*, July 2, 1908; *Chicago Record-Herald*, July 2, 1908; *Baltimore News*, July 1, 7, 1908; *Martin County Sentinel*, July 31, 1908; *Brown County Journal*, July 4, 1908; *St. Peter Herald*, July 24, 31, 1908.
[8] *St. Paul Pioneer Press*, July 8, 1908.
[9] *Brown County Journal*, July 4, 1908.
[10] *St. Peter Herald*, July 24, 1908.

cause he is a man of considerable native ability." [11] "Jake," however, did not "brush himself up." He went through the gubernatorial campaign being himself.

The platform adopted by the Minnesota Republicans endorsed the party's national platform and urged the regulation and control of the liquor traffic within the state and the building of a system of good roads. As in 1904, the Republicans were relying on the national platform to see them through.[12]

It was reported that the Democrats had asked John Lind to be their candidate but had been refused. Johnson, off on his lecture tour, repeated that he would not consider running for a third term. The Democratic leaders, however, went ahead and encouraged Johnson sentiment in the state, feeling that they might be able to argue or force Johnson into accepting the nomination. Both Johnson and R. T. O'Connor suggested Mayor John G. Armson of Stillwater as a candidate, but no one, not even Armson, seemed to take kindly to the suggestion.[13] Most of the county delegations elected to the state Democratic convention were uninstructed but hoped to vote for Johnson.

Up to the eve of the convention, pressure was applied to Johnson to obtain his consent to run, but he flatly refused. He had never been a man of means, and now he had a chance to make more money lecturing than he received as governor, more than he had ever thought he would earn. He fully realized that he was in precarious health, and he felt he owed it to his wife to accumulate some money when he could. He felt he had performed his duty to his state and party by serving two terms as governor and thought his party should recognize that fact. Mrs. Johnson was also strongly opposed to his continuing in office, and her feelings carried considerable weight in Johnson's decision.

The lecture platform was a new experience for Johnson, and one that greatly appealed to him. In addition, he knew that it would make him more widely known and so would better his chances for the presidential nomination in 1912. On the lecture platform, Johnson was making up his mind, aloud, on national issues and problems. It was stimulating and fruitful. Then, too,

[11] Torrance Papers, Torrance to his wife, July 10, 1908.
[12] *St. Paul Pioneer Press*, July 2, 24, 1908.
[13] *Ibid.*, July 24, August 1, 13, 14, 15, 1908.

*St. Paul Dispatch*, July 20, 1908

Weary of the burden

271

his commitments had to be considered. He had assured Mr. Wagner of the Slayton Lyceum Bureau that he was retiring from politics at the end of his term and so could meet his lecture schedule for the following months. And finally, some of his political advisers, such as R. T. O'Connor and Samuel Untermeyer, had advised him not to run a third time. They felt the prestige of two terms was sufficient and that there was too much risk involved in trying for a third.[14]

Asked what he would do if the Democratic state convention forced the nomination upon him, Johnson replied: "I do not consider that probable. I think my friends throughout the state will respect my wishes in this matter, but I shall decline the honor if nominated. I couldn't accept it without stultifying every sense of honor and belying all my declarations." [15] He then suggested that Frank Day become the Democratic candidate. But Day and other Democratic leaders still worked to persuade Johnson to change his mind.

As the meeting of the Democratic state convention approached, the party was threatened with demoralization. In desperation the leaders finally decided to present to the convention Congressman Winfield S. Hammond as the only candidate for governor. But Hammond himself was opposed to this, because he felt that only Johnson would satisfy the Democrats of the state. As the delegates assembled in Minneapolis, there was a pronounced feeling among them that Johnson must sacrifice his personal desires to the will of the party. The day before the convention opened, the *Minneapolis Journal* published a cartoon of Johnson astride the Democratic donkey, the donkey looking at him and saying: "Say, John, I've carried you quite a spell — Now you carry me this trip." It was said that the delegates not only planned to nominate Johnson, but that should he refuse the nomination, they planned to have his name put on the ballot anyway.[16]

Frank Day called the Democratic state convention to order on August 19. In a short speech he asked the convention not to con-

[14] Elinor Johnson Smith, Julius Schmahl, and Henry N. Benson to W. G. H.; O'Brien, *There Were Four of Us, or Was It Five,* p. 80; *St. Paul Dispatch,* August 17, 1908; *Brown County Journal,* August 15, 1908; *St. Paul Pioneer Press,* August 15, 17, 1908.

[15] *Ibid.,* August 18, 1908; *St. Paul Dispatch,* August 18, 1908.

[16] *Ibid.; Minneapolis Journal,* July 15, 16, August 1, 4, 14, 18, 1908; *St. Paul Pioneer Press,* August 18, 19, 1908; Day and Knappen, pp. 138–39.

*Minneapolis Journal*, August 19, 1908

John's turn to carry the donkey

sider Johnson a candidate but to allow him to retire as he wanted
to do. Day then denounced Jacobson as a man who had been a
tribune of the people but had compromised his principles and sold
out to the "interests" in order to obtain the nomination for
governor.

Next the platform was adopted. It supported the national
Democratic platform; it declared a tonnage tax on iron ore desirable if the tax amendment was declared ratified by the Minnesota Supreme Court; it recommended a nonpartisan judiciary for
the state, the initiative and referendum, the extension of the direct primary law to include all state offices, a law providing for
state guarantee of deposits in state banks, and an employers' liability law.

Then the main business of nominating a candidate for governor
came before the convention. Mayor Daniel Lawler of St. Paul
mounted the platform and began a nominating speech for Johnson, but he did not progress very far with it. A great spontaneous
cheer interrupted him at the first mention of Johnson's name. All
the pent-up feeling for Johnson burst forth, and the "wildest political demonstration ever witnessed in the state" broke out. For
sixty-five minutes about one thousand delegates cheered and
shouted and marched up and down the convention hall and out
into the streets, carrying the governor's picture with them and
demanding Johnson and no one but Johnson.

When Lawler had finally been allowed to finish his speech, the
convention nominated Johnson by acclamation. It then adjourned
without giving the governor a chance to refuse the nomination. A
"Democratic tornado" had swept Johnson into an extremely difficult situation.[17]

Johnson had remained in his office all day. When he was informed of the convention's action, he was very much disturbed.
What was he to do? If he refused the nomination, he would be regarded as "a recreant to the interests of his party." If he accepted
it, he would be accused of both insincerity and weakness.

Frank Day and others did their best to convince him that he
owed it to his party to accept the nomination in return for what
his political friends and the party had done for him. Day pointed

[17] *St. Paul Dispatch,* August 20, 1908; *Minneapolis Journal,* August 19, 20, 1908; *St.
Paul Pioneer Press,* August 19, 20, 1908.

out that the Bryan Democrats had eagerly supported his nomination once they heard that he intended to support Bryan in
the coming campaign. This meant a united Democracy behind
Johnson.

After a very difficult night, Johnson called in newspapermen about noon the next day and announced that, reluctantly
and against his better judgment, he had decided to accept the
nomination.

Mrs. Johnson was furious, and in no uncertain terms she told
Frank Day what she thought of him and his fellow conspirators
for what they had managed. Day claimed that it had been impossible for him to control the convention because the Johnson
feeling was so strong and because with the Bryan Democrats
working for Johnson's nomination, there was no opposition to it.
But it was evident that Day was completely happy with the work
of the convention.[18]

In general, Johnson's intention of retiring at the end of the term
was accepted as sincere, and few editors questioned the fact that
he accepted the nomination as a duty forced upon him rather than
willingly. Even the St. Paul Pioneer Press, which had fought Johnson as hard as possible during two campaigns and was to put up
a fight against him once more, accepted his word. Commenting
upon his decision to accept the nomination, the Pioneer Press
said: "The governor honestly wanted someone else to sit in his
chair for the next two years, and John A. Johnson was not a triumphant, joyful man when he told reporters . . . that he had
decided to accept the nomination which the party had forced
upon him." [19]

The St. Peter Herald observed: "The delegates to the state convention have made Governor Johnson's duty plain, and unless we
know nothing of the man, he will not shirk that duty." [20] The Jordan Independent explained that the ovation given Johnson at the
convention was an expression of love and esteem and was "so
unanimous and so spontaneous and so sustained that it overthrew
all the work of the Governor and his friends." [21] But Robert Dunn

---

[18] Ibid., August 21, 1908; Elinor Johnson Smith to W. G. H.; Executive Letters, Johnson to R. C. Larrabee of LeRoy, August 20, 1908; Martin County Sentinel, August 28,
1908; Day and Knappen, p. 140.

[19] St. Paul Pioneer Press, August 21, 1908.

[20] St. Peter Herald, August 21, 1908.      [21] Jordan Independent, August 27, 1908.

scoffed at the "spontaneous demand" for Johnson, asserting that Johnson's "Kitchen Cabinet" realized that the only way for them to remain in power was to renominate him, so they organized the Johnson movement for the presidency, allowed him to gain more publicity by lecturing, and then created the "spontaneous demand" for him in the state convention.[22]

Johnson's acceptance of the nomination was cause for great rejoicing among the Democrats of the state, but the Republicans rather grimly began to prepare for the tremendous efforts they knew it would take to defeat the popular Johnson.

Jacobson, in fact, was already campaigning informally, but Johnson left Minnesota on August 20 to deliver one of the chautauqua lectures he had scheduled for the summer. The heavy speaking program he had borne since the first of the year began to have its effect upon him. In March he had suffered an attack of his chronic malady, and now he had another attack. On August 26 he and Mrs. Johnson went to Lake Pepin for a few days of rest and relaxation. He had to refuse engagements at any of the county or state fairs, for speaking in the open air, he found, caused him considerable difficulty with his throat. Nevertheless, when the *St. Paul Pioneer Press* published a cartoon of the governor lecturing and fishing and giving little time to his campaign, it was indulging in wishful thinking, for when Johnson began to campaign he did so in true Johnson fashion.[23] But the *Brown County Journal* advised its readers:

Why elect a governor to go on a lecture platform? Governor Johnson is admittedly contracted for lectures in various parts of the United States. . . . Vote for a man who will stay at home and attend to the important business of the office of chief executive. . . . Do you favor voting for a man who doesn't want the position he is nominated for, in order to continue in office an army of hungry office holders? It's up to you, Mr. Voter.[24]

On August 31 William Jennings Bryan came to St. Paul, and F. B. Lynch, national Democratic committeeman from Minnesota, entertained him at a luncheon where he met many of the

    [22] *Princeton Union,* August 27, 1908.
    [23] Executive Letters, Frank Day to George Miller of Minneapolis, August 26, 1908, and Harvey Grimmer to Frank Tolman of Paynesville, August 31, 1908; *St. Paul Pioneer Press,* August 28, 1908.
    [24] *Brown County Journal,* September 19, 1908.

leading Democrats of the state. Governor Johnson attended the luncheon, of course, and that night at the state fair grounds before a crowd of 20,000 people Johnson introduced Bryan and urged the people of Minnesota to vote for him. Bryan, who mounted a chair to be seen and heard, delivered a campaign speech in which he, in return, asked for the re-election of Johnson. In public at least, Johnson and Bryan were the best of political friends.[25]

Both Johnson and Jacobson opened their campaigns formally in September, Jacobson at Clarkfield on September 21 and Johnson in Montevideo the next day. Before an audience of about three hundred people, Jacobson announced that he intended to stand for election upon his record in the Minnesota legislature and on the State Board of Control. He told his listeners of his part in framing a state prison labor law, of his work in the investigation of the pineland frauds, of his efforts to obtain railroad legislation which would provide for more government regulation of railway companies, and of his long fight to increase the tax on the gross earnings of railways.

Jacobson denounced as entirely false the charge that, in order to obtain the nomination, he had yielded to the "interests," especially the liquor interests of the state. He said with emphasis that he stood for county option then as he always had in the past. In criticism of Johnson's absence on the lecture tour, Jacobson assured the voters that he would spend all his time being governor of the state if he was elected.

On the whole, the speech was a disappointment. Jacobson dwelt too much upon what he had done and said too little about what he intended to accomplish as governor. It did not sound at all like the man who had earned a reputation for being an aggressive, hard-hitting individual with radical tendencies. Rather it sounded like a man on the defensive.[26]

The following night at Montevideo Johnson began his campaign with a two-hour speech before an audience three times larger than Jacobson's at Clarkfield. He accused the Republican candidate of compromising his principles by accepting the support of the "interests," which, after opposing him in 1906, had helped win his nomination for governor in 1908. Johnson based this charge on

[25] St. Paul Pioneer Press, September 1, 1908.
[26] Minneapolis Journal, September 22, 1908; Princeton Union, September 24, 1908.

the statements made by Republican leaders E. T. Young and Joel Heatwole just before Jacobson was nominated; in fact, Johnson carefully quoted the words of these men, so that actually two leading Republicans were criticizing Jacobson rather than his Democratic opponent.

Sometime in August Jacobson, in a speech at Duluth, had accused Johnson's administration of extravagance. This was a serious error, and the *St. Paul Dispatch,* a Jacobson organ, condemned him for it, pointing out that all appropriations had been voted by a Republican legislature, not by the governor.[27] Now, in his Montevideo speech, Johnson defended himself against Jacobson's accusation. Deliberately and clearly he read all the appropriations that had been made by the legislature and showed that the total did not add up to extravagance. Then he remarked, with a touch of humor, that it was a queer thing that the Democratic candidate for governor had to defend the Republican legislature from the censure of the Republican candidate.

Turning from defense to attack, Johnson asked Jacobson to deny that he had ridden on a railroad pass when he campaigned for Cole in 1906. This was a fact, said Johnson, about a man who was posing as a reformer, a leader of the people in opposition to the railroad interests. In addition, he condemned Jacobson for urging all Republicans to vote a straight ticket. Johnson advised his hearers to study the issues and the candidates and to vote for the best man. This habit, said Johnson, was an excellent one to form.

Because of the criticism about his absence from the state, Johnson felt obliged to explain his chautauqua contract. Without apology and in a light and joking manner, he told about his summer lecture schedule, arranged earlier in the year, and declared he had done a good bit of advertising of the beauties of Minnesota. Claiming that he was doing only what the governors of Iowa, Nebraska, Colorado, and Indiana were doing, he explained that he used his vacation time for the lectures.

Then he compared the national Democratic and Republican platforms, urged the voters to support William Jennings Bryan, reviewed his own record as governor, and pointed out how

[27] *St. Paul Dispatch,* August 16, 1908.

many of his recommendations had been made into laws by the legislature.[28]

The governor's speech was far more effective than Jacobson's. Johnson had talked about his record with pride, never with apology, never on the defensive, and he had emphasized the planks of the Democratic platform that presented a positive program to the voters. Disappointed in Jacobson, the *Minneapolis Journal* regretted that its candidate had made the grave error of accusing the governor of extravagance and admitted that Johnson was right in defending the Republican legislature.[29] And there were some Republicans who were not convinced that Jacobson had not surrendered to the "interests" in order to secure the nomination.[30]

On September 23 Johnson spoke in Willmar, where he stated that he would sign a county option bill if the legislature passed one. That put the responsibility directly upon the new legislature, but it was no new declaration for the governor, who had put himself on record with regard to county option in the preceding legislative session. Three days later at a rally in Stillwater Johnson was stricken ill with ptomaine poisoning and was forced to take to his bed for two days. As a result, he missed a dinner party given for Bryan by John Lind. But he returned to his campaigning as soon as he could, and in Rochester on September 29 he accused his opponent of avoiding the issues of the day. The Republican candidate, he said, was not the reforming, crusading Jacobson of the old days when they were both serving in the legislature. Referring again to his lecture program, he made the point that, after all, he was sacrificing $40,000 a year on the chautauqua circuit for the privilege of being governor at $7000 a year.

As before, Johnson carried the burden of his campaign alone. Lind was out of the state campaigning for Bryan, and when he did return it was to speak for Winfield S. Hammond, who was running for re-election to Congress. On the other side there were about twenty-five speakers in the field for Jacobson, including

[28] *St. Paul Pioneer Press*, September 23, 1908; *Minneapolis Journal*, September 23, 1908.

[29] *Ibid.*

[30] Dr. George Orr to W. G. H. Dr. Orr had been chairman of the Scott County Republican delegation but had resigned on June 25, 1908. His delegation was pledged to Jacobson. For his work in connection with dental legislation passed by the legislature of 1907, Dr. Orr was awarded a loving cup by the state dental association. He was active in the Republican party until his death in 1945.

Senators Nelson, Clapp, and Dolliver, Governor Hughes of New York, Governor Cummins of Iowa, and the Republican presidential candidate, William Howard Taft. It is true that most of the outside speakers came to Minnesota to campaign for the national Republican ticket, but they usually spent some time urging the people to vote for the Republican candidate for governor as well.[31]

On October 10 Johnson spoke in the St. Paul Auditorium, and that night he produced a welcome surprise, especially for the people of St. Peter, when he announced that Andrew Carnegie was giving $32,500 to Gustavus Adolphus College without requiring the college to raise an equal amount. This was exciting news for the Swedish element in the state and for all those interested in education.[32]

Early in 1905 Johnson, learning that Carnegie was planning to give financial assistance to small colleges all over the country, had written him to request aid for the little college in St. Peter, and also for Hamline University and Macalester College. Sometime in May 1906 Johnson called on Carnegie to present in person the needs of Gustavus Adolphus College. Carnegie's only objection to giving the college a grant of money was that the school allowed the sons and daughters of clergymen to enter tuition free. When the college board finally voted to rescind the rule giving this special privilege to one class of students, Carnegie offered a gift of $32,500 provided the college would raise a similar amount. Johnson interceded once more, and it was through his efforts that Gustavus Adolphus received its gift free of the condition.[33]

Carnegie himself was much impressed with Johnson. He considered him "one of those rare men who would not help making an impression upon one instantly; a few words and you felt your brain say to itself, as it were, 'This is no ordinary man. He has a future before him if he is spared.' "[34] The wealthy industrialist

[31] Executive Letters, H. Grimmer to E. A. Smith of Lake City, October 13, 1908, and Johnson to E. J. Buehler, September 28, 1908; *St. Paul Pioneer Press*, September 22, 28, 29, 30, October 20, 1908; *Minneapolis Journal*, October 7, 8, 1908.

[32] *St. Peter Herald*, October 16, 1908.

[33] Andrew Carnegie Papers, in Manuscript Division of the Library of Congress, Johnson to Carnegie, April 3, 4, 21, 1905. See also Executive Letters, Johnson to Carnegie, May 14, 1906; L. G. Almen to Johnson, May 25, 1906; Johnson to H. N. Benson, November 30, 1907; Benson to Johnson, February 18, 1908; Johnson to Carnegie, February 24, 1908; Johnson to James Bertram, March 4, 1908; P. A. Mattson to Johnson, March 3, 1908; and *St. Peter Herald*, March 6, 1908.

[34] Carnegie's tribute to Johnson upon Johnson's death, reprinted in Day and Knappen, p. 413.

became one of those who hoped to see Johnson elected president of the United States.

When Johnson appeared at a rally in Mankato soon after the Carnegie gift was announced, he was greeted with a record-breaking demonstration. Citizens from St. Peter and a delegation of Gustavus Adolphus students were present, along with many others from the country round about, and the students led the cheering and sang a campaign song written for the occasion. Johnson felt at home in southern Minnesota, and the people of the section claimed him as their own.[35]

Once again Johnson made a successful campaign tour of the Mesabi Range. In Duluth he addressed a huge crowd which packed the Armory. His stand against a tonnage tax on iron ore, which he had declared in his message to the 1907 legislature, was popular with the people of St. Louis County, whereas Jacobson's pronouncement in favor of a tonnage tax did not win him many votes in that area. Both the *Duluth Labor World* and the *Duluth Evening Herald* supported Johnson, although the *Duluth News Tribune* remained loyal to Jacobson. The *Evening Herald* lauded Johnson and attacked Jacobson again and again, referring to Johnson always as "the people's governor." [36]

Unfortunately for the Republicans, they had chosen as their nominee for governor a man whose appearance and manners called forth too much apology. They could compare Jacobson to Lincoln and sneer that "aristocratic" Minnesotans shrank from Jacobson even as Washington society shrank from Lincoln, they could try to explain away "Jake's" lack of culture and refinement, they could picture "Governor John" as a "dude" and a "society man" living in the best hotel in St. Paul and frequenting the exclusive University Club — but the people of Minnesota had had more than enough of that kind of defensive approach in 1904. The better class of Norwegians did not consider Jacobson a good representative of their nationality, and the Scandinavians as a whole were satisfied with Johnson.[37] All three of the Swedish newspapers,

[35] *St. Peter Herald,* October 30, 1908.

[36] *St. Paul Pioneer Press,* October 15, November 1, 2, 1908; *Duluth Evening Herald,* October 14, 15, 1908.

[37] Nelson Papers, Nelson to Soren Listoe, December 22, 1908; *Brown County Journal,* September 26, October 24, 31, 1908; *St. Paul Dispatch,* October 26, 1908; *Princeton Union,* October 15, 1908.

the *Svenska Amerikanska Posten*, the *Minnesota Stats Tidning*, and the *Svenska Folkets Tidning*, vigorously supported Johnson.[38]

On October 31 Johnson delivered seven speeches in Minneapolis and could not deliver the eighth because his voice failed him. Nor could he do all the speaking scheduled for him in St. Paul the next day. On election eve he collapsed from fatigue and illness. During the whole campaign he had suffered from attacks of his old malady, and his voice was in such a condition at the end of the campaign that his physician ordered him to take a complete rest for several weeks.[39]

As election day approached, the betting odds were on Taft and Johnson. And when the returns were in, Frank Eddy, who had nominated Jacobson, wrote to Senator Knute Nelson: "Well, we got cleaned up. It was only what I expected although towards the last of the campaign I had hopes." [40] Those who had bet their money on Johnson collected, for he received 175,136 votes to Jacobson's 147,997, a majority of more than 27,000. Taft carried Minnesota by a majority of 84,442 votes over Bryan.[41]

The *Svenska Amerikanska Posten* hailed Johnson's victory as the people's victory, and the *Northfield News*, the *Minneapolis Journal*, and the *St. Paul Dispatch* declared it to be a personal triumph for Johnson himself. The *Dispatch* referred to Johnson as the "best representative, the best advertising force" the state possessed, and the *Journal* stated that the governor emerged from his third campaign a greater figure than ever, and better prepared for the presidential race in 1912.

The *St. Paul Pioneer Press* mournfully admitted that the Republican leaders had "known all the time that they were fighting against odds." But Robert Dunn in his *Princeton Union*, Sam Langum in his *Preston Times*, and Philip Liesch in his *Brown County Journal* maintained that the election of Johnson was due to the support he received from the liquor and steel interests,

[38] *Svenska Amerikanska Posten*, October 13, 20, 27, 1908; *Minnesota Stats Tidning*, October 28, 1908; *Svenska Folkets Tidning*, October 7, 14, 21, 28, 1908.
[39] Executive Letters, Grimmer to G. F. Hughes of Mason City, Iowa, October 20, 1908; Johnson to Dr. J. Y. Ernst of Faribault, November 7, 1908; Johnson to A. W. Frederickson of Chicago, November 1, 3, 1908; Grimmer to J. J. Heinrich of Minneapolis, November 30, 1908. See also *Minneapolis Journal*, November 1, 4, 1908, and *St. Paul Pioneer Press*, November 1, 1908.
[40] Nelson Papers, Eddy to Nelson, November 10, 1908.
[41] *Legislative Manual*, 1909, pp. 556–57.

which feared Jacobson. "Jake," they said, with his advocacy of county option and a tonnage tax, was still too radical for the "interests." [42] Everyone agreed that it had been a hard campaign for both parties, and that Jacobson had proved a worthier opponent for Johnson than either Dunn or Cole.

The *Baltimore Sun* published an editorial under the caption "If — " which recounted the story of Johnson's third election and stressed the fact that he had carried a Republican state during two national elections in which Republican presidents had been elected. "If John Johnson had been nominated by the Democratic National Convention last July," mused the *Sun*, "might not the result of the Presidential election . . . have been different . . . ?" Both the *Sun* and the *Baltimore News* had refused to support Bryan and had reluctantly advised their readers to vote for Taft. [43] The *Charleston News and Courier* was relieved that the campaign was over and suggested that Southern Democrats begin to make plans for 1912 while the party was getting over its "Bryan infatuation." [44]

A long article by Henry Watterson on Johnson's re-election and his achievements in office appeared on the front page of the *Courier-Journal*; it noted that Minnesota believed the nation would call upon Johnson for a higher office. [45] The *New York World* and the *Washington Post*, in righteous indignation, told their readers they had warned the Democrats that the people of the nation did not want Bryan and had prophesied defeat if he was permitted to run again. [46]

In reply to a telegram of congratulation from Bryan Johnson expressed his regret at Bryan's defeat, which, he said, was not a "personal defeat, but was due to the fact that the country even yet seems not ready" for the reforms Bryan championed. [47] From the East came a letter from Samuel Untermeyer expressing his delight over Johnson's victory but also his regret that Johnson had

[42] *Svenska Amerikanska Posten*, November 4, 10, 1908; *Northfield News*, November 7, 1908; *St. Paul Dispatch*, November 4, 1908; *Minneapolis Journal*, November 5, 1908; *St. Paul Pioneer Press*, November 5, 1908; *Princeton Union*, November 5, 1908; *Preston Times*, November 11, 1908; *Brown County Journal*, November 14, 1908.
[43] *Baltimore Sun*, November 4, 5, 1908; *Baltimore News*, November 5, 7, 1908.
[44] *Charleston News and Courier*, November 21, 1908.
[45] *Louisville Courier-Journal*, November 5, 1908.
[46] *New York World*, November 4, 1908; *Washington Post*, November 4, 1908.
[47] Executive Letters, Johnson to Bryan, November 6, 1908.

not allowed his friends to press his candidacy for the presidency sooner than he did. "But the past is buried and we are looking to you for the future," wrote Untermeyer.[48]

Richard Lloyd Jones of *Colliers' National Weekly* also wrote to Johnson, saying the Democrats certainly would not have suffered such a defeat had they nominated the governor of Minnesota, and asking Johnson to "gossip" a bit with Norman Hapgood, his chief editorial writer, whom he was sending out to talk with Johnson.[49]

During the national campaign some people came mistakenly to believe that Taft had bargained with the Catholics and won the election with their support. As a matter of fact, Taft, a Unitarian, was accused by some of being an infidel and by others of being a Catholic, and even though his campaign managers assured the voters that he was a good Protestant, the rumors persisted. And from them grew another rumor in Minnesota. It was whispered that Johnson's wife was a Catholic and that he would for this reason obtain the solid Catholic vote. Mrs. Johnson was not a Catholic and never had been. The rumor probably had its foundation in the fact that she was educated in the Lady of Lourdes Academy in Rochester, Minnesota, where she was placed by her aunt, who was a Catholic. Johnson undoubtedly did receive a heavy Catholic vote, but he did so because two of his associates, T. D. O'Brien and R. T. O'Connor, had strong Catholic followings and because most Minnesota Catholics were inclined to be Democrats anyway.[50]

The election was over. The Republicans, now that Jacobson had been defeated, began to think about new men to offer two years hence.[51] Johnson was allowed a week's rest, and then he went to St. Peter to attend the town's third celebration for its native son. On the morning of November 12 he and his wife, accompanied by Madame Olive Fremstad, a former St. Peter resident who was now a famous opera star, and by a party of some two hundred and

---

[48] *Ibid.*, Untermeyer to Johnson, November 9, 1908.

[49] *Ibid.*, Jones to Johnson, November 10, 1908.

[50] William Jennings Bryan Papers, in Manuscript Division of the Library of Congress, D. L. Savage of Minneapolis to Bryan, November 9, 1908; E. Garrison of Hudson, Mich., to Bryan, November 7, 1908; and numerous other such letters to Bryan on the subject of his defeat by the Catholics. See also Elinor Johnson Smith to W. G. H.; and Henry F. Pringle, *Life and Times of William Howard Taft*, vol. 1, pp. 373–74.

[51] Nelson Papers, Nelson to Listoe, December 22, 1908; Dr. George Orr to W. G. H. Both these men expressed the opinion that the Republicans had had to run Jacobson, who was "bound to run," in order to keep peace in the Republican party.

fifty prominent Democrats from all over the state, journeyed to St. Peter from St. Paul on the governor's special train. They were met at the station in St. Peter by a band, the public school children, and the students of Gustavus Adolphus College. Johnson spoke a few words to the students, small and large, and then he and Mrs. Johnson went to Henry Essler's home, where they were to be guests for their brief visit.

The little town of St. Peter was gaily decorated, and there were pictures of Johnson everywhere. Some of the trains bringing friends of the governor to St. Peter bore maroon and gold banners with "Johnson 1912" on them, and people carried such banners along the street or wore badges printed with the same sentiment. It was a holiday for everyone in the town, and the air was filled with excitement and good feeling.

At three o'clock in the afternoon people crowded into the auditorium of Gustavus Adolphus College to attend the reception for Governor Johnson and Madame Fremstad. Ex-Governor John Lind, Frank Day, T. D. O'Brien, R. T. O'Connor, and Lieutenant Governor A. O. Eberhart were among those present, as were Johnson's brother Fred and his family from New Ulm and his sister Hattie, who taught school in St. Peter. Madame Fremstad was persuaded to sing a few songs, and when she had finished Johnson went to her side, seized her hand, and led her out onto the stage to receive the applause. The audience stood and cheered both the singer and the governor until everyone was exhausted. Johnson thanked his fellow townsmen and friends for their kindness to him; then Winfield S. Hammond spoke, predicting a bright political future for Johnson. The celebration continued on into the evening, when there was a parade and speeches and much merrymaking.[52]

Johnson returned to St. Paul to rest before he resumed his heavy schedule of activities for December. President Roosevelt had appointed him a member of the National Conservation Commission, so on December 8 Johnson was in Washington to attend a meeting of the commission and also a national conservation conference at which he was one of the main speakers. On December 12 he was a guest speaker at the Gridiron Club dinner, and a

[52] St. Peter Herald, November 13, 20, 1908; Minneapolis Journal, November 12, 13, 1908.

week later he was in Montclair, New Jersey, delivering a chautauqua lecture, "The Majesty of the Law." [53]

Back in Minnesota for the holidays, Johnson faced some sharp criticism for interfering in an appointment at the university. At a meeting on December 29 all members of the Board of Regents of the University of Minnesota were present to consider the selection of a man to succeed E. W. Randall, who had resigned as dean of the College of Agriculture. There were four candidates for the position. One was William H. Hayes, assistant secretary of agriculture, who at one time had been a member of the University of Minnesota faculty and was eminently qualified for the position. Another was J. W. Olsen, state superintendent of public instruction, whose candidacy had Governor Johnson's active support. Johnson wanted to appoint C. G. Schulz, former superintendent of schools for Nicollet County and assistant superintendent of public instruction, to Olsen's position, and to do this he had to move Olsen out.

The Board of Regents, influenced by Johnson, who was very popular with the members and especially with Cyrus Northrop, president of the university, voted to appoint Olsen to the vacant deanship. Three of the regents refused to vote, and one of these was probably John Lind, whom Johnson had named to serve on the board. Lind was violently opposed to Olsen's appointment because he did not consider the man qualified for the job. The faculty of the university also strongly disapproved of the appointment, as did many of the friends of the university.

At any rate, when the announcement of Olsen's appointment was made, there was an immediate repercussion. The *St. Paul Pioneer Press*, calling the appointment of Olsen a personal victory for the governor, angrily charged Johnson with playing politics with the educational institutions of the state. Condemning the "indecent haste" with which the Board of Regents had filled Dean Randall's position, the *Minneapolis Journal* examined Olsen's training and career and found that he had neither the knowledge nor the qualifications necessary for the position.

[53] Executive Letters, Theodore Roosevelt to Johnson, June 18, 1908; Gifford Pinchot to Johnson, November 27, 1908; W. W. Jermane to Johnson, November 9, 1908; J. S. Shriver, secretary of the Gridiron Club, to Johnson, November 25, 1908. See also *St. Paul Pioneer Press*, December 6, 9, 10, 13, 19, 25, 1908.

Undoubtedly the appointment of Olsen was injudicious, but Johnson could be charged only with an error in judgment. To him the deanship was an administrative position, and since Olsen had done administrative work as state superintendent of public instruction, Johnson felt he would be quite adequate to the new position. But there was so much criticism of the appointment that Olsen, in accepting the position, promised to resign when a better qualified man was found. And John Lind did not rest until Olsen had resigned. This was the only time in his career as governor that Johnson was severely censured for an appointment.[54]

In the midst of the furor over Olsen Johnson was inaugurated, the second governor, and the only Democratic governor, of Minnesota ever to be inaugurated three times. It was a quiet, simple ceremony on a severely cold day, the thermometer registering twenty-seven degrees below zero. The governor read his message, which was very long, and because he was still having serious difficulty with his throat he was obliged to omit parts of it.[55]

It was immediately apparent that Johnson had learned much from the conservation conferences he had attended, for he launched into a recital of the natural resources of northern Minnesota and urged the conservation of those resources and the development of that area. He suggested that the activities of the Timber Board, Forestry Board, Drainage Commission, Land Commission, and Highway Commission be consolidated into one state department of mines, public lands, and forests devoted to the conservation and development of Minnesota's natural resources.

Turning to the subject of taxation, Johnson recommended that the county assessor system be adopted to replace the current slipshod township assessor system. On the grounds that the Minnesota Supreme Court was still in the process of deciding whether or not the "wide-open" tax amendment had been ratified by the people in 1906, he said there was no need of his discussing the question of taxing the iron mines in Minnesota, for until it was decided that the amendment had been approved, the legislature would not have the power to enact any drastic changes in the

[54] George M. Stephenson and Henry N. Benson to W. G. H.; *Minutes of the Board of Regents, University of Minnesota*, December 8, 29, 1908; *St. Paul Pioneer Press*, December 30, 31, 1908, January 2, 1909; *Minneapolis Journal*, December 30, 1908.

[55] *Ibid.*, January 6, 1909; *St. Paul Dispatch*, January 6, 1909; *St. Paul Pioneer Press*, January 6, 7, 1909.

taxation system. Nevertheless, once again he stressed the fact that the mining interests must pay their "full and just" share of taxes to the state.

Reviewing the railroad legislation passed in the preceding session, Johnson indicated that additional railroad regulation was necessary, and he brushed aside the claim of the railroad companies that federal control and state control of railroads were incompatible. In this connection, he expressed his states' rights sentiments when he said: "The dignity and character of the duties devolving upon the officers of the state are as great as those devolving upon any officer, and are generally performed with as high a sense of public duty and with as much intelligence as are to be found in any governmental department." He summarized the Minnesota Rate Cases, which challenged the power of a state to regulate railroad rates, and raised the question as to whether a railroad company could sue a state in a federal court.[56]

He renewed his recommendations that laws be passed to provide for officers who would enforce compulsory attendance in the county schools and to establish a county board of education which would appoint the county superintendent of schools. He urged that a definite professional standard be established for teachers and superintendents and that a minimum salary law for teachers be passed.

For the third time he asked for an employers' liability law, a revision of the primary election law and its extension to all state offices, and an initiative and referendum law. Because of the remarkable increase in the number of state banks, he recommended, at the behest of the bankers of the state, that a state banking department be established and that a law be enacted to require all state bank examiners to qualify for their positions by passing a rigid examination. He called the attention of the legislature to the progressive legislation of Ohio, Massachusetts, and Iowa with regard to a uniform system of accounting for cities, villages, and counties and suggested that Minnesota follow their example.

[56] The chief railroad companies in Minnesota, acting together, claimed that only the federal government had the right to regulate rates and brought suits against the state to prevent the enforcement of the revised freight and passenger rates, declaring them to be confiscatory and depriving the railroad companies of a "reasonable income" on business done in the state. Attorney General E. T. Young, T. D. O'Brien, E. S. Durment, and Royal A. Stone defended the state, and the attorneys for the railroad companies included Frank B. Kellogg, C. A. Severance, and Pierce Butler.

Johnson had always had a special interest in institutions for unfortunates. He did not neglect them now. He asked the legislature for an appropriation for a new building at the State Hospital for Consumptives at Walker and said there was need for an industrial school to train the children at the Phalen Crippled Children's Hospital. He reported that the State Board of Visitors had studied provisions made for the care of the insane and had found that Minnesota was woefully lacking in adequate means of caring for these unfortunates. It would take one million dollars, said Johnson, to provide adequate buildings and equipment at the three state hospitals for the insane. Until more space was available at these hospitals, Johnson suggested that patients be placed in county asylums and that the state pay three dollars a week for each patient so placed.

Laws were needed, he stated, to provide for state regulation of city streetcar companies, telephone companies, and light and power companies. Then he concluded his message with these words:

Whatever may be our respective personal and political affiliations and ideas, our duties and our purposes, I am sure, are one: namely, the protection and advancement of the highest public interests of our commonwealth. . . . There is surely no obligation to party, class or section, paramount to our own sworn obligation to the state as a whole which includes all parties, classes and sections.[57]

The *St. Paul Pioneer Press* approved of everything in the message except Johnson's request for the extension of the direct primary law and for the initiative and referendum; both these measures the paper considered too radical. Lauding Johnson as one who "sinks the party leader in the public servant," the *St. Paul Dispatch* found nothing to criticize. But Robert Dunn, in true Dunn style, bluntly stated that there was not much in the whole message and noticed that Johnson made no mention of the county option issue.[58] Dunn himself was opposed to any kind of tonnage tax, so he had no criticism to offer about Johnson's declaration on that matter.

The thirty-sixth Minnesota legislature did not prove to be as

[57] *Inaugural Message*, 1909.
[58] *St. Paul Dispatch*, January 6, 1909; *Princeton Union*, January 7, 1909; *St. Paul Pioneer Press*, January 7, 1909.

cooperative as its predecessors with the chief executive. Again it was a predominantly Republican body, and some of its leading members decided to make a systematic scrutiny of all legislation to be sure that no bill passed would add to the governor's popularity. They were reported to be extremely annoyed with Johnson for taking so much credit in the recent campaign for what the Republican legislatures of 1905 and 1907 had accomplished. Some of the members claimed that Johnson was eager to have the state adopt a preferential primary law, by which the people could direct the legislature in the election of senators, because he was getting ready to become a candidate for the United States Senate.[59]

In January the Minnesota Supreme Court decreed that the "wide-open" tax amendment had been properly ratified in the election of 1906, so the legislature could, if it chose, work out a more modern and equitable system of taxation for the state. This brought to the fore the whole issue of a tonnage tax on iron ore, and upon that issue there developed a mighty battle between the progressive element in the legislature and those who represented various special interests.[60]

In the legislature of 1907 Representative H. O. Bjorge had introduced a bill providing for a tonnage tax on iron ore, and the bill passed the house, where the representatives from the rural areas voted for it. However, it was defeated in the senate. The fact that the United States Steel Company was considering establishing a $20,000,000 plant at Duluth played a great part in

[59] *Ibid.*, January 12, 1909; *St. Paul Dispatch*, March 5, 6, 1909; *St. Peter Herald*, February 5, 12, 1909; *Minneapolis Journal*, January 8, 1909; *Jordan Independent*, April 22, 1909. The only major political appointment Johnson made was to replace W. H. Williams with William E. McEwen as labor commissioner. Williams was forced to resign when it was found that he had taken some funds from his official treasury; the Democrats insisted that he return the money in full. As to the preferential primary system, such a law was passed by the Oregon legislature, and as a result, Senator Chamberlain, a Democrat, was elected by a Republican legislature.

[60] Among the progressive and public-spirited legislators were Senators Sundberg, Cashman, Sageng, A. L. Hanson, Dale, Bedford, Victor Johnson, S. A. Nelson, Elwell, Fosseen, Naeseth, Ahman, and F. H. Peterson, and Representatives Bjorge, Burnquist, Ware, E. E. Adams, C. E. Johnson, Haugland, Washburn, Kneeland, Noble, and Rockne. The chief of all the legislators representing special interests was Senator E. E. Smith of Minneapolis, chairman of the tax committee, who virtually ran the senate. Senator Sullivan represented the Twin City Rapid Transit Company, Senator W. W. Dunn the liquor interests, Senator Laybourne the steel interests, and Senator Hall the railroad interests. In the house of representatives those who represented special interests included Representatives Brady, Dalzell, Dorsey, Doyle, L. H. Johnson, W. H. Nolan, Rodenberg, and others. Fortunately the speaker of the house was A. J. Rockne of Zumbrota, who proved to be a fair and able man. (Lynn Haines, *Minnesota Legislature of 1909*, pp. 1–35.)

the defeat of the bill, for the company, of course, strongly opposed such a measure. Lynn Haines, who was secretary of the Minnesota Citizens' League at this time, accused Johnson's political advisers of urging the Democrats in the house to vote for the bill while they worked to have it defeated in the senate. The reason for their action, according to Haines, was to spare Johnson any unpopularity that might result from his vetoing the bill, which they knew he opposed.[61]

Be that as it may, there probably was not sufficient sentiment in favor of a tonnage tax bill in 1907 to secure its enactment. However, the new State Tax Commission, set up by the legislature in accordance with Johnson's recommendation, raised the valuation of the iron mines from $32,000,000 to $180,000,000. But this was not enough to satisfy the proponents of a tonnage tax.

When the legislative session began in 1909, Bjorge was ready. He introduced a bill that provided for a tax of two to five cents on every ton of iron ore taken from the mines in Minnesota. Whether the tax should be two cents or more was to depend on the quality of the ore.

The United States Steel Company bitterly fought the Bjorge bill through their representatives in the legislature, and the people of St. Louis and Itasca counties were desperately anxious to have it defeated. From the Iron Range came a delegation of two hundred and fifty men to bring pressure upon the legislature to kill the bill. They all wore badges printed with the words "No Tonnage Tax." But the citizens of the rest of the state were just as vehement in demanding that the Bjorge bill be made into law.

In the midst of pressure from all sides, the house of representatives passed the bill, and on April 16 it passed the senate by a vote of thirty-eight to twenty-four. Almost immediately three thousand telegrams demanding that he veto the bill came to Governor Johnson from the Iron Range.[62]

After considerable deliberation, Johnson did veto the bill. In his veto message he referred to the measure as an "uncertain and ill-digested experiment, not fully understood by its friends, and intensely feared by the sections of the state" to which it applied.

[61] *Ibid.*, p. 40; *St. Paul Pioneer Press*, March 13, 14, 1907.
[62] *Ibid.*, March 22, April 8, 17, 20, 1909; *St. Paul Dispatch*, April 21, 1909; *St. Peter Herald*, April 16, 1909; *Jordan Independent*, April 8, 1909; Haines, pp. 35–44; Day and Knappen, pp. 157–58.

He declared that in its application the bill tended to "violate the fundamental principle of taxation, that of equality" and at the same time it failed "to meet the constitutional requirement of uniformity in taxing the same class of subjects." The practical effects of the bill, he stressed, would be "to strike a severe blow at the development and prosperity of all the great mineral bearing counties in northeastern and north central Minnesota." These sections, he said, had just emerged from an industrial depression which would return under the provisions of the Bjorge bill. He maintained that if the tonnage tax bill became law, "so little understood and . . . so generally misunderstood" as it was, the whole subject of taxation would be plunged into "a sea of political and sectional feeling and prejudice," which not only "would make a just and scientific measure impossible of enactment" but would tend to arouse sectional hatreds that could endanger the future development of the state and make the subject of state taxation "the mere football of partisan and sectional politics."

Declaring that the current ad valorem system of assessing and taxing the iron ore properties was successful, Johnson held that there was no "urgent and vital" need for a tonnage tax at that time, and he advised the legislature to take more time to study the whole problem of taxation in conjunction with the State Tax Commission. If the legislators felt that the revenue coming from the mines was insufficient, they could increase the assessments "without plunging any section of the state into panic." Since northern Minnesota felt so strongly that the tonnage tax was unfair sectional discrimination and since it constituted a double system of taxation on one class of property, Johnson declared the bill to be wrong in principle.[63]

The Bjorge bill was not passed over Johnson's veto, and the legislature adjourned the day after it received his veto message.

Johnson's action provoked much comment. Joel Heatwole vigorously charged Johnson with favoring the corporations, since a majority of the people wanted the tonnage tax bill to become law. The *Minneapolis Tribune*, on the other hand, was certain that the governor had saved Minnesota "from a sectional division more bitter at the beginning than that which separated North and

[63] *Message of Governor Johnson Accompanying His Veto of the Tonnage Tax Bill,* April 20, 1909.

South before the Civil War," and the *Minneapolis Journal* congratulated him for doing a noble and courageous thing and refusing to play politics. Both the *St. Paul Pioneer Press* and the *St.
Paul Dispatch* had favored the Bjorge bill; but Robert Dunn not
only lauded Johnson in the *Princeton Union* for his brave and
righteous action but also sent him a wire of congratulations. The
*Duluth Labor World* commented as follows:

> And hotter did the battle wax,
> On that infamous tonnage tax,
> Till the vote upon the senate floor,
> Stood thirty-eight to twenty-four.

> When of justice we had lost command,
> Then John A. Johnson took a hand,
> And proved that he at heart was fair
> And fit to fill the Governor's chair.[64]

In choosing the unpopular course by vetoing the tonnage tax
bill, Johnson again asserted his independence. And it was probably well that he did so, for undoubtedly the imposition of a tonnage tax at that time would have caused a great deal of bitterness
among the people of northern Minnesota. Certainly they would
have begun to work at once for the repeal of the law, and the
whole issue of taxation might very well have become, as Johnson
predicted, "the mere football of partisan and sectional politics." The problem of exacting the proper amount of compensation from the owners of the iron mines remained unsolved for
years afterward.[65]

Also charged with feeling in the 1909 legislature was the
struggle over a county option bill introduced by Representative
A. K. Ware of Northfield. It provided that the voters of each
county should have the right to choose whether their county

[64] *St. Peter Herald,* April 30, 1909; *Minneapolis Tribune,* April 21, 1909; *Minneapolis
Journal,* April 21, 1909; *Princeton Union,* April 22, 1909; *Duluth Labor World,* April 24,
1909.

[65] Out of this whole episode came the rumor that at Johnson's death he was found
to have left some $10,000 in United States Steel stock, supposedly a gift from the com-
pany for his veto of the tonnage bill. His widow insists that he had no such stock at
any time, and H. N. Benson and Arthur Evenson, who knew Johnson intimately, say
that he had some copper stock, which was worth little, but no steel stock. Julius
Schmahl, who had known Johnson since they were boys, states that he is certain Johnson never had steel stock but that if he did he had paid for it himself. These three
men, all of whom were so well acquainted with Johnson, reject entirely the idea that
he could have been bribed or would have accepted such a gift.

should be "wet" or "dry." Ten of the fifteen members of the so-called Temperance Committee voted for an indefinite postponement of the bill, which satisfied the Minnesota Liquor Dealers' Association, a powerful force in Minnesota politics. An attempt was made too to place the street railways under the jurisdiction of the Railroad and Warehouse Commission, but that bill also was indefinitely postponed. And bills providing for initiative and referendum, the extension of the direct primary system, woman suffrage, and the direct election of senators were defeated. All four of these bills Johnson favored.[66]

Having spent much of the session on bills which ultimately were defeated, the legislature accomplished little of real importance. Laws were passed providing for a women's and children's department in the State Bureau of Labor, for a woman to be appointed assistant commissioner of labor, and for the establishment of a maximum of fifty-eight hours a week for women working in industry. An investigating committee was created to draw up an employers' liability bill to be presented to the next legislature, and a bill was passed providing that all employees injured while at work report to the commissioner of labor. A million-acre game preserve in northern Minnesota was established, and a fund was set up to maintain forest reserves. School attendance was made compulsory for all children between the ages of eight and sixteen years.

A law was passed to permit Sunday baseball between the hours of one and six o'clock in the afternoon provided the games were conducted "in a quiet and orderly manner so as not to interfere with the peace, repose and comfort of the community." Governor Johnson brought upon himself some criticism from the churches for signing this bill. One law which the governor found it difficult to accept was that forbidding the manufacture, sale, or giving away of cigarettes or cigarette paper. He was a heavy smoker of cigarettes, preferring them to pipes or cigars, but now he felt morally obligated to give them up.[67]

For Governor Johnson the legislative session had been arduous,

[66] Haines, pp. 59–83.
[67] General Laws, 1909, pp. 78, 184, 219, 250, 275–78, 338–39, 364, 476–79, 622–26; St. Peter Herald, April 23, 30, 1909; Princeton Union, April 22, 1909; St. Paul Dispatch, May 13, 1909; Elinor Johnson Smith to W. G. H.

and personal troubles were added to his heavy official duties. At the outset of the session, Mrs. Johnson underwent a serious operation performed by Dr. William J. Mayo in St. Mary's Hospital in Rochester. For some time the governor went back and forth from his desk in the capitol to the hospital in Rochester. A month later he became ill himself and was forced to remain away from his office for several days. Under orders from his physician, he was obliged to cancel all the chautauqua lectures he had been scheduled to deliver as soon as the legislature adjourned. Both he and Mrs. Johnson needed a rest, so they went with friends to Old Point Comfort, Virginia, for the first two weeks in May. The relaxation seemed to restore him and he looked well when he and his party journeyed on to Washington.[68]

In an interview with Washington newspapermen Johnson did his best to squelch the rumor that his health was almost completely shattered. Admitting that he had been ill and tired when he went to Virginia, he insisted that the rest there was all he needed. He also tried to kill the rumor that he intended to be a candidate for the United States Senate when Moses Clapp finished his term.

When Johnson and his party called at the White House, President Taft greeted him as an old friend, slapping him heartily on the back and expressing delight at seeing him again. Before he left, Johnson assured Taft that he would be waiting to greet the president personally when he visited Minnesota in the late summer.[69]

[68] Executive Letters, Day to B. F. Williams of Milwaukee, January 25, 1909; Grimmer to Bess Howard of Mitchell, S.D., February 26, 1909; Day to Dr. C. L. Chambers of Bismarck, N.D., April 25, 1909; Day to Professor E. B. Gault, University of S.D., April 27, 1909. See also *Minneapolis Journal,* January 27, 1909, and *St. Paul Dispatch,* January 26, 1909.

[69] H. G. McCall to W. G. H. Mr. McCall and his wife were in Johnson's party on this vacation trip. See also *Minneapolis Journal,* May 16, 1909; *St. Paul Dispatch,* May 14, 15, 1909; and *Martin County Sentinel,* April 9, 1909.

WHILE Johnson was in Washington, the Payne-Aldrich tariff bill was being debated in Congress and discussed by the country at large. This bill was the result of a Republican pledge made in the national platform in 1908 — a pledge, as it was popularly understood, to revise the tariff downward, and President Taft had committed himself to this interpretation during the campaign.

The president called a special session of Congress to revise the tariff, but his message opening the session was brief and contained no militant call, no urgent request, for the downward revision the people were demanding. The Republican congressmen who were anxious to see the tariff reduced in compliance with the wishes of the people were sadly disappointed with the president's message.

But the high tariff men in Congress were ready for Taft's message. As a matter of fact, the House Ways and Means Committee had a tariff bill all ready to submit, a bill fathered by Representative Sereno Payne of New York, "an honest devotee of privilege." The Payne bill was easily put through the House under the guidance of its friends, particularly Speaker "Uncle Joe" Cannon, who highly approved of it. It was then sent on to the Senate, where Senator Nelson W. Aldrich of Rhode Island undertook to direct its course. Within forty-eight hours the Finance Committee had made more than eight hundred changes in the bill, six hundred of them increasing rather than decreasing rates, and then the bill was submitted to the Senate for its consideration.

At this juncture the bewildered Taft, who had expected Congress to reduce tariff rates even though he had not stressed the point, asked the progressive Republican Senators Beveridge, La Follette, and Dolliver to fight the bill. They secured the expert assistance of Senators Clapp, Cummins, and Bristow, and the six senators made ready to attack the bill item by item. These six men all represented the Middle West; Beveridge was from Indiana, La Follette from Wisconsin, Dolliver and Cummins from Iowa, Clapp from Minnesota, and Bristow from Kansas. From the first week in May until the first week of August these "insurgents" worked day and night to master tariff schedules and to defeat the Payne-Aldrich bill.[1]

The open revolt of the insurgents was announced just at the time Johnson was paying his visit to President Taft, and it was inevitable that newspaper reporters would ask him what he thought of the Payne-Aldrich bill. He, of course, condemned it, saying it violated the pledge the Republican party had made to the people:

The Republican party promised the people a thorough, honest and downward revision of the tariff. There is no doubt of that. The people expect that party to redeem that pledge. If that party does not keep faith with the people, the Middle West is lost to the Republicans for years hence. The national administration cannot escape responsibility for the action of congress on the tariff. . . . Out in my country the people — the masses of people have no faith in the leadership of Mr. Cannon and Senator Aldrich. They have heard so much of this combination and its control of congress that they regard this control as being in the interest of the interests. The people believe the interests control congress. I don't know how the senators and leading Republican papers are going to defend this tariff bill.[2]

Johnson highly approved of Moses Clapp's action in joining the insurgents and attacking the bill. As the Aldrich forces battled with the insurgents during the hot summer months of June and July, Johnson, back in Minnesota, watched the progress of events closely. To a friend he wrote:

They are certainly making history very fast down in Washington, and it is history which I believe will arouse the country to a political revolution which will surely bring Democratic victory in the next presidential campaign. Whatever the outcome of the next presidential convention, I hope to be in the fight to help overthrow the party that, through legislation, seems to be heaping the burdens upon the masses instead of trying to relieve them.[3]

[1] Claude G. Bowers, *Beveridge and the Progressive Era*, pp. 333–51; Pringle, pp. 425–51.
[2] *St. Paul Pioneer Press*, May 16, 1909.
[3] Executive Letters, Johnson to X. F. Beidler of Lincoln, Ill., July 8, 1909.

When the Senate finally passed the Payne-Aldrich tariff bill despite the herculean efforts of the six senators, the nation watched to see what Taft would do. He had assured the insurgents he would veto the bill, but on August 5 he signed it instead. Apparently he had been repelled by the tactics of the insurgents and completely won over by Cannon and Aldrich.

From all over the country came loud cries of protest against the action of the Congress and the president.[4] And when Johnson heard that Taft had signed the bill, he gravely announced that he thought the Payne-Aldrich tariff would prove disastrous to the Republican party. "When such men as Dolliver, Beveridge, Nelson, and Clapp vote against it," he said, "there must be something radically wrong." Again he prophesied that the Republican party would pay for its action in the next presidential election.[5]

There is no question but that Johnson took very seriously the prospect of his winning the presidential nomination on the Democratic ticket in 1912. He now made up his mind not to return to St. Peter when his third term as governor came to an end. He sold his home in St. Peter and purchased one on Lincoln Avenue in St. Paul, where he and Mrs. Johnson decided to make their permanent home. His plans for the future included both the lecture platform and active participation in the affairs, probably the national affairs, of the Democratic party.

But on July 12 Johnson collapsed from such a serious attack of his chronic ailment that he was confined to his bed for several days and Dr. William J. Mayo came from Rochester to see him. His attacks had been getting more and more frequent and severe, and Dr. Mayo advised him to submit to a fourth operation. Johnson agreed, but within ten days, after taking care of some official duties, he was off on another chautauqua lecture tour.[6]

Johnson also insisted on making an official visit to Seattle, where he had been invited to represent Minnesota on "Minnesota

[4] The ten Republican senators who voted against the bill were Beveridge, Burkett, Bristow, Clapp, Crawford, Cummins, Dolliver, Brown, La Follette, and Knute Nelson.
[5] *Minneapolis Journal*, August 10, 1909.
[6] Executive Letters, Frank Day to F. H. Milham of Kalamazoo, Mich., July 14, 1909; Day to C. J. Swift of Columbus, Ga., July 15, 1909; Day to Jessie Spicer of Spicer, Minn., July 16, 1909; Day to O. L. Wilson of Aurora, Ill., July 29, 1909. See also *St. Paul Pioneer Press*, July 14, 16, 18, 26, 1909, and *St. Paul Dispatch*, July 17, 19, 1909. Johnson received numerous letters from people all over the country suggesting a variety of "cures" for appendicitis and indigestion.

Day" at the Alaska-Yukon-Pacific Exposition. On the way to Seattle the governor stopped off at Spokane to attend an irrigation congress on July 31, and by so doing he disappointed about fifty thousand people who that same day attended the exposition in Seattle. Through some misunderstanding, the president of the exposition had expected Governor Johnson to be in Seattle that day, designated "Swedish Day," and had arranged a banquet in his honor. When Johnson did not arrive, Governor Hay of Washington spoke in his place. As a matter of fact, Johnson had promised to be in Seattle only for "Minnesota Day" on August 3, and he had explained by letter that he planned to be in Spokane on July 31. He suggested that J. E. Chilberg, the president of the exposition invite John Lind to represent Minnesota on "Swedish Day." But Chilberg had not understood, or Johnson had not been clear, and Chilberg was so annoyed that he ignored Johnson when the governor arrived in Seattle. Johnson, however, refused to let the incident upset him and soon had the whole thing cleared up to the satisfaction of everyone concerned.[7]

Upon his arrival in Seattle, Johnson was met by the press. Again he announced that he would not be a candidate for governor in 1910 or for the United States Senate at any time in the future, and, in reply to a query as to whether he would be a presidential candidate in 1912, he said, "Well, it is just a little too far ahead to answer such a question yes or no, and really I do not care to enter into a discussion of the matter." [8]

On "Minnesota Day" Mr. Chilberg entertained Governor and Mrs. Johnson at a luncheon in their honor, and in the afternoon Johnson delivered a speech in the auditorium. The crowd cheered Johnson for more than ten minutes. From the auditorium the party proceeded to "Klondike Circle," where Johnson unveiled a bust of James J. Hill, "The Colossus of the Roads," and spoke briefly in praise of the "Empire Builder." That evening there was a banquet for the Minnesota guests, followed by a reception.[9]

Johnson's Seattle speech, "The Call of the West," became one of the most controversial addresses he ever made. In it he condemned President Taft and the Congress for the "sham tariff re-

[7] *St. Paul Pioneer Press*, July 29, August 4, 1909; *Minneapolis Journal*, August 1, 14, 1909.
[8] *Ibid.*, August 2, 1909.　　　　[9] *Ibid.*, August 4, 1909.

vision" of the iniquitous Payne-Aldrich bill. The West, he declared, bitterly opposed the bill, and he called upon the West to
assert itself in the councils of the nation against the domination
of the East. He urged the West to awake and take the lead as
some of its congressmen had done in their fight on the Payne-
Aldrich bill. Here he identified himself with the progressives, and
since he spoke as a Democrat with a national reputation, it was
understood that he was ready to lead the progressive Democrats
of the country.

The *Minneapolis Journal* suggested that Johnson's speech might
very well have been a keynote speech for the presidential nomination in 1912, and the paper urged the Republicans to bring about
a regeneration within the national party rather than allow the
Democrats to begin a campaign to overthrow Republican su-
premacy.[10] The *New York American* hailed the speech and stated
in an editorial:

If the disintegrated and drifting democracy has any chance of revival and reunion, it must be behind some leader clear and definite
like Johnson of Minnesota.

He is the only governor calling himself a democrat who has convictions and the courage of them. He does not fear to take positions.
He does not hesitate to challenge prejudices. He even dares to point
his party beyond the line of tradition to the goal of independence and
common sense.

There is good stuff in Johnson and a good ring to his voice, and a
clear head on his shoulders and a good, stout heart in his bosom.[11]

"The Call of the West" also brought down upon Johnson abun-
dant and sharp criticism for his appeal to sectionalism. He insisted that he had no intention of stirring up one section of the
country against another, but he did see good reason for prodding
the West to assert itself and, with the South, begin an active
movement to wrest control of the government from those who afflicted the country with the Payne-Aldrich tariff. Nevertheless,
the East smarted under Johnson's attack. If there had been some
eastern newspapers that were unaware of Johnson, there were
none any longer. The South highly approved of his speech.[12]

[10] *Ibid.*, August 3, 4, 1909.
[11] Quoted in the *Minneapolis Journal*, August 5, 1909.
[12] *Ibid.*, August 11, 14, 1909.

From Seattle, in the company of Governors Marion E. Hay of Washington and Charles Evans Hughes of New York, Johnson went on to Vancouver Island and Victoria, then traveled back to Minnesota by way of Winnipeg. During the remainder of August he was off on a lecture tour in Ohio, Illinois, Iowa, Missouri, and Nebraska. On the tour, which was strenuous and involved irregular hours and meals, Johnson suffered great pain, but he refused to cancel the lectures at such a late date.[13]

He was on the verge of a physical collapse when he returned to St. Paul, but he tried to keep going until after President Taft's projected visit on September 19. He was forced, however, to submit to an operation on his throat, and all his speaking engagements for a month were canceled — with no assurance that he would be able to do much public speaking at the end of that time. Nevertheless, he refused to discuss his health except to insist that he felt fine. "Billy" Williams, the governor's young messenger, saw Johnson daily when he was not out of town, and Williams has said that on days when Johnson was in such pain that he could hardly sit up behind his desk, he always replied to the query as to how he was feeling by saying, "Fine, fine. I never felt better in my life!" [14]

The Minnesota State Fair began on September 6, and Senator Knute Nelson delivered the main address to the fair crowd on the opening day. Both Senator Clapp and Governor Johnson spent the day at the fair and sat on the platform when Nelson spoke. The crowd called for the popular Johnson to speak, but he was unable to respond because of the serious condition of his throat. His friend, Arthur Evenson, saw him at the fair and was shocked by his appearance. The day proved to be more than he could stand. He developed a severe cold and by the end of the week was a very sick man.[15]

On Sunday, September 12, Johnson suffered such terrible pain from his old ailment that he decided he could put off an operation no longer. Arrangements were made for him to go to Rochester the next day. But by Monday morning the attack had passed, and

---

[13] *Ibid.*, August 24, 1909; *St. Paul Dispatch*, August 20, 1909.

[14] Executive Letters, Johnson to C. F. Sandahl of Oakland, Neb., September 1, 1909, and Johnson to Dr. D. B. Miller of Bird Island, September 8, 1909; *St. Paul Dispatch*, August 31, 1909; *St. Paul Pioneer Press*, September 2, 1909; "Billy" Williams to W. G. H.

[15] Arthur Evenson to W. G. H.; *Minneapolis Journal*, September 6, 13, 1909; *St. Paul Pioneer Press*, September 6, 1909; *St. Paul Dispatch*, September 6, 1909.

he felt well enough to go to his office to clear his desk before he left.

At the capitol his friends came to wish him well, and they did not conceal the fact that they were seriously worried about him. Johnson, however, insisted on making light of his condition and of the operation before him. When one friend gravely wished him luck, Johnson replied, "Oh! don't put it so seriously. I am used to this sort of thing, and I regard a stay in a hospital as a vacation. I will be well enough to read within a few days and then I am going to break my record. The last time I was in the hospital I read fourteen books. Why, the best chance I get for reading nowadays is when I am in the hospital." [16]

Johnson and Frank Day went to Carling's restaurant for lunch that noon, and there a friend of the governor's remarked that he would gladly go to Rochester in the governor's place, and Johnson answered, "You would be foolish. . . . I am used to these operations. It will be over in twenty or thirty minutes, and I do not even dread it. It will be much easier for me than for you." [17]

During the luncheon Johnson was gay and talkative. He seemed to feel very well. As he and Frank Day walked back to the capitol, Day suggested that the governor express himself clearly as to his attitude toward the governorship in 1910 and the presidential candidacy in 1912. Johnson remarked that the pressure on him to run for the presidency in 1912 was great enough even then to make it seem doubtful that he could do otherwise. In view of that, he felt he might be forced to run for a fourth term as governor.[18]

Johnson was not really so optimistic about his health as he appeared to be. He admitted to Secretary of State Julius Schmahl, whom he had known all his life, that he knew he was a very sick man, that he realized the operation would be a serious one, and that he had no assurance he would return to his desk in the capitol. Three times before he had undergone the same kind of operation, each time there had been real danger of his not surviving, and never had he been in such poor physical condition before the operation as he was now.[19]

[16] Day and Knappen, p. 249.        [17] *Ibid.*
[18] *Ibid.*, p. 250.
[19] Julius Schmahl to W. G. H. Mr. Schmahl said that Johnson was far from optimistic about his condition and that he did not hesitate to express his concern to his close friends.

He had scarcely returned to the capitol with Frank Day on that September afternoon when he was seized by another attack and had to be taken home. At five o'clock he and Mrs. Johnson boarded the train for Rochester. The trip was a nightmare for Johnson, for the motion of the train aggravated his condition. When they arrived that night, Dr. Will Mayo, with a trained nurse, met them at the station, and the governor, too weak to stand alone, leaned upon his friend's arm.

The party went directly to the home of John Sullivan, whose daughter was an intimate friend of Mrs. Johnson's, and there Johnson was put to bed. He had a restless night, and the next day he was moved to St. Mary's Hospital.[20]

The people of Minnesota were already deeply concerned about the condition of their governor, and newspaper reporters from the Twin Cities and Chicago gathered in Rochester to keep them informed of the daily progress of the distinguished patient. A newspaperman whom he had known for many years was admitted to see Johnson the night before his operation. The governor was cordial, friendly, and optimistic, and the reporter went away convinced that Johnson was sure in his own mind that there was no danger.[21]

It was not until the day of the operation that the news of Johnson's illness became national. President Taft was then on his swing around the country defending his signing of the Payne-Aldrich tariff. On September 14 he spoke in Boston, and, unaware of Johnson's condition, he condemned the Minnesota governor's Seattle speech, "The Call of the West," declaring that it was difficult to take seriously Johnson's attempt to stir up sectional strife by calling upon the West to organize against the East.[22]

The next day, Wednesday, September 15, Johnson was taken to surgery. With his brother's assistance, Dr. Will Mayo performed the delicate operation, which revealed intestinal adhesions and an obstruction of the bowels. For almost three hours the doctors worked, while members of the Surgeons' Club, including Si-

[20] *St. Paul Pioneer Press*, September 13, 14, 1909; *Minneapolis Journal*, September 13, 15, 1909; *St. Paul Dispatch*, September 13, 14, 1909; *Rochester Post and Record*, September 14, 1909; Day and Knappen, p. 250.

[21] *Ibid.*, pp. 251–53; Clapesattle, pp. 488–89; *Minneapolis Journal*, September 16, 1909; *St. Paul Pioneer Press*, September 15, 1909.

[22] *Ibid.*; *Rochester Post and Record*, September 15, 1909.

gnor Bastianelli, surgeon to the King of Italy, witnessed the operation. The shock to the patient was so great that from the start there was some doubt that Johnson would rally from it. That night he suffered a sinking spell which brought him close to death, but Dr. Charles T. McNevin, who was assigned to his case, was with him and helped bring him through it.

On Thursday morning Johnson indicated that he knew just how serious his condition was by remarking to Dr. McNevin, "Well, Mac, we had a pretty close shave last night, didn't we?" But he insisted he would be all right and by his courage and determination encouraged those around him. On Friday night, September 17, however, he had another sinking spell that brought Dr. Will and Dr. Charlie Mayo, Dr. Judd, and Dr. McNevin to his bedside.

Asked by newspaper reporters what chances the governor had to recover, Dr. Will Mayo cautiously replied that he was not expecting Johnson to die but that the next three days would be critical ones. The people of Minnesota were so anxious for the most recent reports of the governor's condition that "the twenty telephone lines of the *St. Paul Pioneer Press* were busy all day answering inquiries."

Suffering as he was, Johnson remembered that President Taft was to be in St. Paul on September 18, and he insisted upon dictating a message of welcome, in which he also expressed his regret at being unable to greet the president personally. Taft replied that he was greatly distressed to hear of Johnson's serious illness and said, "I miss your smiling and courteous personal greeting, which I have had every time I have come to the state heretofore, and I thank you from the bottom of my heart for your message, sent when you are on a bed of pain. I fervently hope and pray that your wonderful strength and fortitude will make your recovery speedy. . . ." [23]

Before he began his speech in St. Paul that day, Taft told his audience how deeply touched he was by Johnson's message and expressed his wish that their governor would be spared. "With his courage and his great common sense he cannot be taken away," said Taft. "He is too valuable, not alone to the people of Minnesota, but to the people of the whole nation, who doubtless will in-

[23] *St. Paul Dispatch,* September 18, 1909.

sist in time that he serve them." [24] Wild cheering followed these remarks. No one had ever been as popular with the people of Minnesota as Governor Johnson.

During Saturday and Sunday, although suffering constant and excruciating pain, Johnson seemed to improve, and Dr. Will Mayo felt that if he held his own on Monday, his recovery would be certain and speedy. But by three o'clock Monday afternoon Johnson was exhausted. He no longer had the strength to fight on. Although the doctors worked desperately hard to save him, their efforts were in vain. This was no sinking spell; it was a "wearing out."

Conscious almost until the end, Johnson felt his strength ebbing away and knew he was dying. Just past midnight he shook hands with Dr. Will, Dr. Charlie, Dr. McNevin, and his nurses and murmured his appreciation for all they had done for him and said goodbye. Then everyone but Mrs. Johnson withdrew, and he said to her, "Well, Nora, I guess I am going, but I've made a good fight." From then on until he died, quietly and in no pain at 3:25 A.M. Tuesday morning, Mrs. Johnson, Dr. Will, and Dr. McNevin were with him, and his brother Fred, Frank Day, and F. B. Lynch were waiting outside his room.

In Rochester the tolling of the bells told the people of the town that Johnson had lost his heroic struggle.[25] The word spread rapidly and the whole state was plunged into deep gloom. Men and women wept on the streets, and some fifty thousand people viewed the body as it lay in state in the capitol all day Wednesday.

The next day the remains of John A. Johnson were taken home to St. Peter for burial. All Minnesota suspended its activities to mourn the loss of its chief executive, a young man only forty-eight years of age, whose life had so tragically ended in mid-career. "The war ships in New York harbor dropped their flags to half mast," and hundreds of memorial services were held throughout the country. But the greatest tribute to John A. Johnson was the fact that

[24] *Minneapolis Journal,* September 19, 1909.
[25] *Ibid.,* September 16, 17, 18, 19, 20, 21, 1909; *Baltimore News,* September 16, 17, 18, 19, 21, 1909; *Chicago Record-Herald,* September 18, 20, 21, 22, 1909; *St. Paul Pioneer Press,* September 16, 18, 19, 21, 1909; *St. Paul Dispatch,* September 16, 18, 21, 1909; *Rochester Post and Record,* September 16, 17, 18, 19, 20, 21, 1909; *Martin County Sentinel,* September 17, 1909; *St. Peter Herald,* September 17, 1909; Day and Knappen, pp. 253–56; Clapesattle, pp. 488–89; Torrance Papers, Torrance to his son, September 16, 1909.

so many Minnesotans felt a great personal loss in his death. He had been peculiarly dear to the hearts of the people of his state. They had loved him as they had never before loved any man in public life.

The *St. Paul Pioneer Press*, the paper which had taken the lead in opposing Johnson in three gubernatorial campaigns and had kept up a steady criticism of his actions as governor, confessed that Johnson had been a man with political opponents but no enemies. Even those who had criticized his political actions had found it impossible to dislike the man, admitted the *Pioneer Press*. Robert Dunn, whose pungent and vitriolic pen always lambasted his political opponents, Johnson among them, declared that he had never known anything which reflected discreditably upon Johnson, who had possessed the genius of friendship and leadership. During most of the time that Dunn was attacking Johnson as the leader of the Democrats, the two men personally had been on friendly terms. Johnson's legacy to the people of Minnesota, according to the *Minneapolis Journal*, was the inspiration of his life. Possessed of a kind heart, high ideals, and a strong will, Johnson "proved by his own life that the battle with obscurity and poverty, while always hard, is never hopeless." [26]

The editors of Minnesota certainly knew Johnson as well as any group of men, except perhaps the small circle of his close political friends and advisers. He had mingled with them for twenty-one years. They were critical men, not easily satisfied, and yet, reading the country newspapers, one cannot help being impressed by the good will, warmth, and enthusiasm there was for Johnson. No other editor received that kind of treatment from the rest of his fraternity.

Johnson's life was a typical American success story. Born in poverty, never possessing any material advantages and with little education, he had faced life fearlessly, courageously, optimistically. He was always willing to learn, a thing he did with an amazing quickness. Opportunities seemed to seek the man, probably because he possessed the gift of a magnetic personality which drew people to him and made them remember him. Probably Johnson represented the average man's ideal of American citizenship. Like

[26] *St. Paul Pioneer Press*, September 22, 1909; *Princeton Union*, September 23, 1909; *Minneapolis Journal*, September 21, 1909.

others who had worked their way up from poverty to success, Johnson firmly believed that anyone with ability, determination, and hard work could rise to the top in his particular field of endeavor.

Still, these things alone did not make Johnson the successful and beloved governor he became. Nor did the blessing of an unusually attractive personality account for his popularity. These achievements and qualifications helped, but Johnson had more than this to offer. He possessed ideals, high ideals; strong convictions and the courage of those convictions; integrity, sincerity, independence of action, and a high sense of duty. His optimism, quick sympathy, impulsive generosity, and keen sense of humor gave him a balance which was remarkable and rare. One of the common people, he was an uncommon man.

One cannot minimize the effect upon Johnson of almost constant physical suffering. Certainly the patience, sympathy with others, and disciplined character of the man were in part due to that. And more than in anything else, Johnson's power seemed to lie in the moral force of his character.

His insistence that all citizens must assume their duties and responsibilities as well as enjoy their privileges; his emphasis upon fair play in politics; his stress upon government "of the people, by the people and for the people" — in short, all his reiterated principles were underscored by the moral force of the man behind his words. And he followed up his words by example. He believed that the man, not the dollar, was the important factor in the building of a great country, and in the era of materialism in which he lived this was refreshing.

Calling himself "the first class hired man of the people," he was looked upon as a man of the people who had their interests at heart. He was considered a man of stability and common sense who could best serve the people by assuming the role of the pacifier rather than that of the agitator. Cautious and unemotional, he thought out a problem before he acted upon it, and he tried always to secure the counsel of the ablest men around him.

Without experience in the national political field, Johnson had become a nationally known figure, and when he died so unexpectedly, it was generally felt that the country had lost a leader it could ill afford to lose, a man who had seemed destined for use-

ful and distinguished national service and one whose personal life
and career were an inspiration to the young men of the country.
To many in the nation, as well as in Minnesota, he had appeared
to be the sane, sober, constructive leader for whom many in the
Democratic party were seeking to replace William Jennings Bryan,
and the romance of his rise from a humble background had enhanced his appeal and reputation.[27]

Johnson stood with the progressives of both political parties in
their demands for a downward revision of the tariff, direct election of senators, extension of the direct primary system, woman
suffrage, initiative and referendum, and increased regulation of
corporations. Already an amazingly popular figure by 1909, he
might easily have qualified for the leadership of a popular movement against the entrenched Republican administration. True, he
needed more experience in national affairs. He never had studied
to any serious degree the foreign policies and problems of the
United States, but his record indicated that he had abilities and
capacities which developed as he met expanding responsibilities.
Most of all he had a largeness of spirit and a moral force which he
exerted for the ends of political decency and the faithful performance of duty in the maintenance of good government. American politics stood much in need of men like John A. Johnson of
Minnesota.

[27] Executive Letters, Lyman Abbott to Mrs. Johnson, September 16, 1909; President Taft to Mrs. Johnson, September 21, 1909; Mrs. Grover Cleveland to Mrs. Johnson, September 23, 1909; Andrew Carnegie to Mrs. Johnson, November 6, 1911. See
also "Pollock's Clippings," six volumes of clippings regarding the death of Johnson and
comments on his career from newspapers of the nation; *Baltimore Sun,* September 22,
1909; *Baltimore News,* September 19, 21, 1909; *Chicago Record-Herald,* September 22,
1909; *Washington Post,* September 20, 22, 1909; *Charleston News and Courier,* September 22, 1909; *New York Herald,* September 23, 1909; *New York Times,* September
22, 23, 1909; and *Louisville Courier,* September 22, 1909.

# Bibliography

INFORMATION was offered to the author by several individuals who knew Governor Johnson well. Most helpful was Elinor Johnson Smith (Mrs. William A.), Johnson's widow, who not only submitted for examination a box of letters received by Johnson but also spent considerable time in conversation. Hattie Johnson, Johnson's sister, was also very cooperative. Information was gathered in personal interviews with Henry N. Benson, attorney and veteran Republican in St. Peter; Mr. and Mrs. George Nutter, personal friends of Johnson's in St. Peter; Adolph Holmstead, long-time printer in the *St. Peter Herald* office; Mr. and Mrs. Arthur Evenson of St. Paul and formerly of St. Peter, personal friends of Johnson's; Mrs. Fred W. Johnson of New Ulm, Johnson's sister-in-law; Mrs. C. H. Helmes of St. Paul and Long Beach, California, sister of Mrs. Fred Johnson; Dr. George Orr of St. Paul, a veteran Republican who during Johnson's time was active in Scott County Republican affairs; Julius Schmahl, state treasurer of Minnesota (secretary of state during Johnson's administrations); H. G. McCall of St. Paul; William F. Williams, the governor's messenger appointed by Johnson; and Denny Donahue of Mankato. A letter from Harvey Grimmer of St. Cloud substantiated some information already gathered.

The Executive Letters of Governor Johnson were examined in the Minnesota Historical Society. These include twenty volumes of letters, each volume containing about a thousand letters, and seventeen boxes of letters which were sent to the governor. Of particular value among other sources in the Minnesota Historical Society were the John Lind Papers, Knute Nelson Papers, Leonard A. Rosing Papers, James A. Tawney Papers, and Ell Torrance Papers. Permission was granted by the director of the Manuscript Division of the Library of Congress for the examination of the William Jennings Bryan Papers, Henry A. Watterson Papers, Andrew Carnegie Papers, and William Howard Taft Papers. For the purpose of this biography there was little in the Carnegie and the Taft papers, and the Clapp Collection in the Minnesota Historical Society was of no value.

The *Proceedings of the Minnesota Editors' and Publishers' Association* meetings from 1888 to 1910 (three volumes), the *Official Proceedings of the Thirty-Second Annual Convention of the National Editorial Association, July 9–12, 1917,* and the *Minutes of the Board of Regents, University of Minnesota, 1904–1909* (incomplete) were examined, as were volumes of newspaper clippings about Johnson's career and death taken from the newspapers of the country and designated as "Pollock's Clippings, a Memorial to John A. Johnson."

## Government Publications

BLANCHARD, NEWTON C., ed. *Proceedings of a Conference of Governors in the White House, Washington, D.C., May 13–15, 1908.* Washington, 1909.

*Final Report of the Governor John Albert Johnson Memorial Commission.* St. Paul, 1913.

*General Laws of the State of Minnesota,* 1905, 1907, 1909.

*Inaugural Message of Governor John A. Johnson to the Legislature of Minnesota,* 1905, 1907, 1909.

*Legislative Manual of the State of Minnesota,* 1895, 1897, 1899, 1901, 1903, 1905, 1907, 1909.

*Message of Governor Johnson Accompanying His Veto of the Tonnage Tax Bill,* April 20, 1909.

RICHARDSON, JAMES D. *A Compilation of the Messages and Papers of the Presidents,* vols. 9 and 11. Washington, 1909.

## Newspapers

In the Minnesota Historical Society there are six bound volumes of clippings on the death of John A. Johnson, taken from newspapers all over the United States.

*Albert Lea Standard (Freeborn County Standard)*, 1904, 1906, 1908.
*Albert Lea Tribune*, 1904.
*Appleton Press*, September to November 1904, November 1906, November 1908.
*Atlanta Constitution*, November 1904, November 1906, December 1907, July and November 1908.
*Baltimore News*, November 1904, November 1906, December 1907, July 1908, November 1908, September 1909.
*Baltimore Sun*, November 1904, July and November 1908, September 1909.
*Bemidji Pioneer*, 1904.
*Bemidji Sentinel*, 1904.
*Birmingham Age-Herald*, May 1908.
*Boston Evening Transcript*, November 1904.
*Boston Globe*, July and November 1908.
*Boston Herald*, December 1907, January and November 1908, September 1909.
*Brainerd Dispatch*, 1904.
*Brainerd Tribune*, 1904.
*Brown County Journal* (New Ulm), 1908–1909.
*Charleston News and Courier*, November 1904, December 1907, July and November 1908, September 1909.
*Chicago Record-Herald*, November 1904, November 1906, July and November 1908, September 1909.
*Crookston Times*, 1904.
*Duluth Evening Herald*, 1904, 1906, 1908.
*Duluth Labor World*, 1904, 1906–1909.
*Duluth News Tribune*, 1904.
*Eveleth Mining News*, 1904.
*Faribault Pilot*, 1904.
*Jordan Independent*, 1905–1909.
*Kansas City Star*, November 1904, November 1906, December 1907, September 1909.
*Louisville Courier-Journal*, November 1904, November 1906, May to August 1907, July and November 1908, September 1909.
*Mankato Free Press*, 1904, 1906, 1908.
*Martin County Sentinel* (Fairmont), 1904–1909.
*Midway News*, 1904–1906.
*Minneapolis Journal*, January to April 1899, January to April 1901, 1904–1909, and December 22, 1929, to January 28, 1930.
*Minneapolis Tribune*, 1904.
*Minnesota Stats Tidning* (St. Paul), October to November 1904, October to November 1906, October to November 1908.
*New Orleans Picayune*, July 1908, November 1908.
*New York Herald*, November 1904, November 1906, December 1907, July and November 1908.
*New York Times*, November 1904, November 1906, December 1907, July and November 1908, September 1909.
*New York Tribune*, November 1904, November 1906, June and December 1907, July and November 1908.
*New York World*, December 1907, November 1908.
*Northfield News*, 1904–1909.
*Preston Times*, 1904, 1906, 1908.
*Princeton Union*, 1903–1909.
*Rochester Post and Record*, 1904, 1909.
*St. Cloud Journal-Press*, 1904.
*St. Cloud Times*, 1904.
*St. Paul Dispatch*, 1904–1909.
*St. Paul Globe*, 1904–1905.
*St. Paul Pioneer Press*, 1900, 1904–1909.
*St. Peter Courier*, April 26, 1855, and January 1, 1858.

# BIBLIOGRAPHY 311

*St. Peter Free Press*, November 1857, November 1858, 1896–1900, 1903–1909.
*St. Peter Herald*, 1885–1909, and October 1, 1930.
*St. Peter Journal*, 1897.
*St. Peter Tribune*, 1888, 1894, 1898, 1904.
*San Francisco Chronicle*, July 1908.
*Svenska Amerikanska Posten* (Minneapolis), October to November 1904, October to November 1906, October to November 1908.
*Svenska Folkets Tidning* (Minneapolis), October to November 1904, October to November 1906, October to November 1908.
*Vicksburg Daily Herald*, May 1907.
*Washington Post*, December 1907, July and November 1908, September 1909.

## Memoirs, Letters, Speeches, Editorials

ABBOTT, LAWRENCE F., ed. *The Letters of Archie Butt*. New York, 1924.
BRYAN, WILLIAM JENNINGS, ed. *The Speeches of William Jennings Bryan*, 2 vols. New York, 1909.
———, and BRYAN, MARY BAIRD. *The Memoirs of Williams Jennings Bryan*, 2 vols. Chicago, 1925.
COLLINS, LOREN WARREN. *The Story of a Minnesotan*. [N.p., 1913.]
EDDY, FRANK M. *Way Back Yonder Personal Reminiscences of Frank Eddy*. [N.p., 1924.]
JOHNSON, JOHN A. "Commercial and Political Integrity." 1905.
———. "Minnesota and the Railroads." January 10, 1906.
KROCK, ARTHUR, ed. *The Editorials of Henry Watterson*. Louisville, 1923.
MANAHAN, JAMES. *Trials of a Lawyer: an Autobiograhpy*. Minneapolis, 1933.
MATTSON, HANS. *Reminiscences, The Story of an Emigrant*. St. Paul, 1892.
NEVINS, ALLAN, ed. *Letters of Grover Cleveland, 1850–1908*. New York, 1933.
O'BRIEN, THOMAS DILLON. *There Were Four of Us, or Was It Five*. [N.p., 1936.]
WATTERSON, HENRY. *"Marse Henry," An Autobiography*, 2 vols. New York, 1919.
———. *The Compromises of Life and Other Lectures and Addresses*. New York, 1903.

## Books and Pamphlets

BARNHART, THOMAS F. "The History of the Minnesota Editorial Association, 1867–1897." Unpublished master's thesis, dated 1937, in the library of the University of Minnesota.
BOWERS, CLAUDE G. *Beveridge and the Progressive Era*. Boston, 1932.
BREMER, FREDRIKA. *The Homes of the New World; Impressions of America*, vol. 2. New York, 1853.
BRYAN, WILLIAM JENNINGS. *The First Battle: A Story of the Campaign of 1896*. Chicago, 1896.
BYARS, WILLIAM VINCENT. *An American Commoner, The Life and Times of Richard Parks Bland*. Columbia, Missouri, 1900.
CASTLE, HENRY A. *Minnesota, Its Story and Biography*. Chicago, 1915.
CHENEY, CHARLES B. *The Story of Minnesota Politics*. Minneapolis, 1947.
CLAPESATTLE, HELEN. *The Doctors Mayo*. University of Minnesota Press, 1941.
DAY, FRANK A., and KNAPPEN, THEODORE M. *The Life of John Albert Johnson*. Chicago, 1910.
FILLER, LOUIS. *Crusaders for American Liberalism*. New York, 1939.
FLANDRAU, CHARLES E. *Encyclopedia of Biography of Minnesota*. Chicago, 1900.
———. *The History of Minnesota and Tales of the Frontier*. St. Paul, 1900.
FOLWELL, WILLIAM WATTS. *A History of Minnesota*, 4 vols. Minnesota Historical Society, 1921–1930.
GRESHAM, WILLIAM G. *History of Nicollet and Le Sueur Counties, Minnesota — Their People, Industries and Institutions*, 2 vols. Indianapolis, 1916.
HAINES, LYNN. *The Minnesota Legislature of 1909*. Minneapolis, 1910.
HALL, HARLAN PAGE. *History of the Minnesota Editors' and Publishers' Association, 1867–1896, with Sketches of Its Presidents*, in *Proceedings of the Minnesota Editors' and Publishers' Association*, 1896.
———. *Observations*. St. Paul, 1904.
HANSEN, MARCUS LEE. *The Atlantic Migration, 1607–1860*. Harvard University Press, 1940.

————. *The Immigrant in American History.* Harvard University Press, 1940.

HERBERT, B. B. *The First Decennium of the National Editorial Association of the United States,* vol. 1. Chicago, 1896.

HIBBEN, PAXTON. *The Peerless Leader, William Jennings Bryan.* New York, 1929.

HICKS, JOHN D. *The Populist Revolt.* University of Minnesota Press, 1931.

HOTALING, H. C. *History of the Past Presidents of the Minnesota Editorial Association, 1867–1934.* Printed by the *Mountain Lake Observer,* 1934.

JOSEPHSON, MATTHEW. *The Politicos, 1865–1896.* New York, 1938.

————. *The President Makers.* New York, 1940.

————. *The Robber Barons.* New York, 1934.

MCELROY, ROBERT. *Grover Cleveland, The Man and the Statesman,* 2 vols. New York, 1923.

*Minnesota in Three Centuries,* 4 vols. The Publishing Society of Minnesota, 1908. The authors are: vol. 1, Warren Upham; vol. 2, R. I. Holcombe; vol. 3, L. F. Hubbard and R. I. Holcombe; vol. 4, Frank R. Holmes.

NEVINS, ALLAN. *Grover Cleveland; A Study in Courage.* New York, 1933.

*Nicollet County, Minnesota, as an Agricultural and Dairying Section and St. Peter as a Manufacturing Center.* St. Peter, 1884.

ODLAND, MARTIN W. *The Life of Knute Nelson.* Minneapolis, 1926.

OPPEGARD, ROY W. "Governor John Albert Johnson and the Reform Era in Minnesota State Government." Master of Philosophy thesis, University of Wisconsin, dated 1937, on microfilm in Minnesota Historical Society.

PETERSON, CONRAD. *Gustavus Adolphus College, A History of Eighty Years, 1862–1942.* Rock Island, Illinois, 1942.

PRINGLE, HENRY F. *The Life and Times of William Howard Taft,* vol. 1. New York, 1939.

PYLE, JOSEPH GILPIN. *The Life of James J. Hill,* 2 vols. New York, 1917.

SHORTRIDGE, WILSON P. *The Transition of a Typical Frontier.* Menasha, Wisconsin, 1922.

STANTON, C. W. *Memorial Address on the Death of Governor John A. Johnson.* February 1910.

STANWOOD, EDWARD. *A History of the Presidency from 1897 to 1916.* New York, 1928.

STEPHENSON, GEORGE M. *A History of American Immigration, 1820–1924.* New York, 1926.

————. *American History to 1865.* New York, 1940.

————. *John Lind of Minnesota.* Minneapolis, 1935.

STRAND, A. E. *A History of the Swedish Americans of Minnesota,* 3 vols. Chicago, 1910.

SULLIVAN, MARK. *Our Times,* vol. 2. New York, 1929.

*The Republican Party in Minnesota: Its Achievements and Its Leaders.* 1910.

UPHAM, WARREN, and DUNLAP, ROSE. *Minnesota Biographies, 1655–1912. Minnesota Historical Society Collections,* vol. 14, 1912.

WITTKE, CARL. *We Who Built America.* New York, 1939.

## Articles

ADAMS, MOSES N. "The Sioux Outbreak in the Year 1862 with Notes of Missionary Work among the Sioux," *Minnesota Historical Society Collections,* vol. 9, 1898–1900.

"Another Man of Destiny," *Current Literature,* vol. 45, December 1908.

BAKER, JAMES H. "History of Transportation in Minnesota," *Minnesota Historical Society Collections,* vol. 9, 1898–1900.

————. "Lives of the Governors of Minnesota," *Minnesota Historical Society Collections,* vol. 13, 1908.

CASTLE, HENRY A. "Reminiscences of Minnesota Politics," *Minnesota Historical Society Collections,* vol. 15, 1915.

CHAMBERLAIN, WINTHROP B. "A Great Democratic Governor," *World's Work,* vol. 15, April 1908.

CHENEY, CHARLES B. "A Labor Crisis and a Governor," *The Outlook,* vol. 89, May 2, 1908.

————. "Johnson of Minnesota," *The Outlook,* vol. 88, January 25, 1908.

————. "Political Movements in the Northwest," *The American Review of Reviews,* vol. 31, March 1905.

DANIELS, DR. ASA W. "Reminiscences of the Little Crow Uprising," *Minnesota Historical Society Collections*, vol. 15, 1915.

"Dark Horses and Others," *The American Review of Reviews*, vol. 36, August 1907.

GIFFIN, DON E. "Governor Johnson, A Character Sketch," *The Independent*, vol. 64, pt. 2, May 14, 1908.

"Governor Johnson," *The Outlook*, vol. 93, October 2, 1909.

"Governor Johnson's Birmingham Speech," *The Outlook*, vol. 89, June 13, 1908.

"Governor Johnson's Last Tribute to Minnesota and the Nation," *Leslie's Illustrated Weekly*, November 18, 1909.

HARD, WILLIAM. "John Johnson of Minnesota," *The American Magazine*, vol. 64, October 1907.

HUMPHREY, JOHN AMES. "Boyhood Remembrances of Life among the Dakotas and the Massacre of 1862," *Minnesota Historical Society Collections*, vol. 15, 1915.

INGLIS, WILLIAM. "A Democratic Presidential Possibility, Governor John A. Johnson of Minnesota," *Harper's Weekly*, July 20, 1907.

JOHNSON, JOHN A. "The Political Situation," *The Independent*, vol. 64, pt. 2, May 14, 1908.

——, and CHAMBERLAIN, W. B. "Fifty Years of an American Commonwealth," *World's Work*, vol. 15, October 1908.

"John A. Johnson," *The Independent*, vol. 58, pt. 1, January 5, 1905.

"John A. Johnson, the 'Dark Horse,'" *Current Literature*, vol. 44, January 1908.

"John Johnson of Minnesota," *The American Review of Reviews*, vol. 36, October 1907.

LARPENTEUR, AUGUST L. "Recollections of the City and the People of St. Paul, 1843–1898," *Minnesota Historical Society Collections*, vol. 9, 1901.

MEYER, BALTHASAR H. "A History of the Northern Securities Case," *Bulletin of the University of Wisconsin*, no. 142, July 1906 (Economics and Political Science Series, vol. 1, no. 3, 1904–1906).

"Minnesota's Favorite Son," *The Independent*, vol. 67, pt. 1, September 30, 1909.

MOSS, HENRY L. "Biographic Notes of Old Settlers," *Minnesota Historical Society Collections*, vol. 9, 1901.

O'BRIEN, THOMAS DILLON. "John A. Johnson," *North American Review*, vol. 187, June 1908.

——. "Memorial Address in Honor of Governor Johnson," *Minnesota Historical Society Collections*, vol. 15, 1915.

PYLE, JOSEPH GILPIN. "John A. Johnson, the Democratic Governor of a Republican State," *Putnam's Monthly*, vol. 4, May 1908.

RUSSELL, CHARLES EDWARD. "Governor Johnson — New Style Politician," *Everybody's Magazine*, vol. 18, April 1908.

SATTERLEE, MARION P. "Narratives of the Sioux War," *Minnesota Historical Society Collections*, vol. 15, 1915.

STEFFENS, LINCOLN. "Bryan–Johnson on What the Matter Is in America and What to Do About It," *Everybody's Magazine*, vol. 19, July 1908.

STEPHENSON, GEORGE M. "Letters Relating to Gustaf Unonius and the Early Swedish Settlers in Wisconsin," *Augustana Historical Society Collections*, vol. 7, 1937.

——. "When America Was the Land of Canaan," *Minnesota History*, vol. 10, no. 3, September 1929.

"The Legislatures and the Railroads," *The American Review of Reviews*, vol. 36, July–December 1907.

# Index